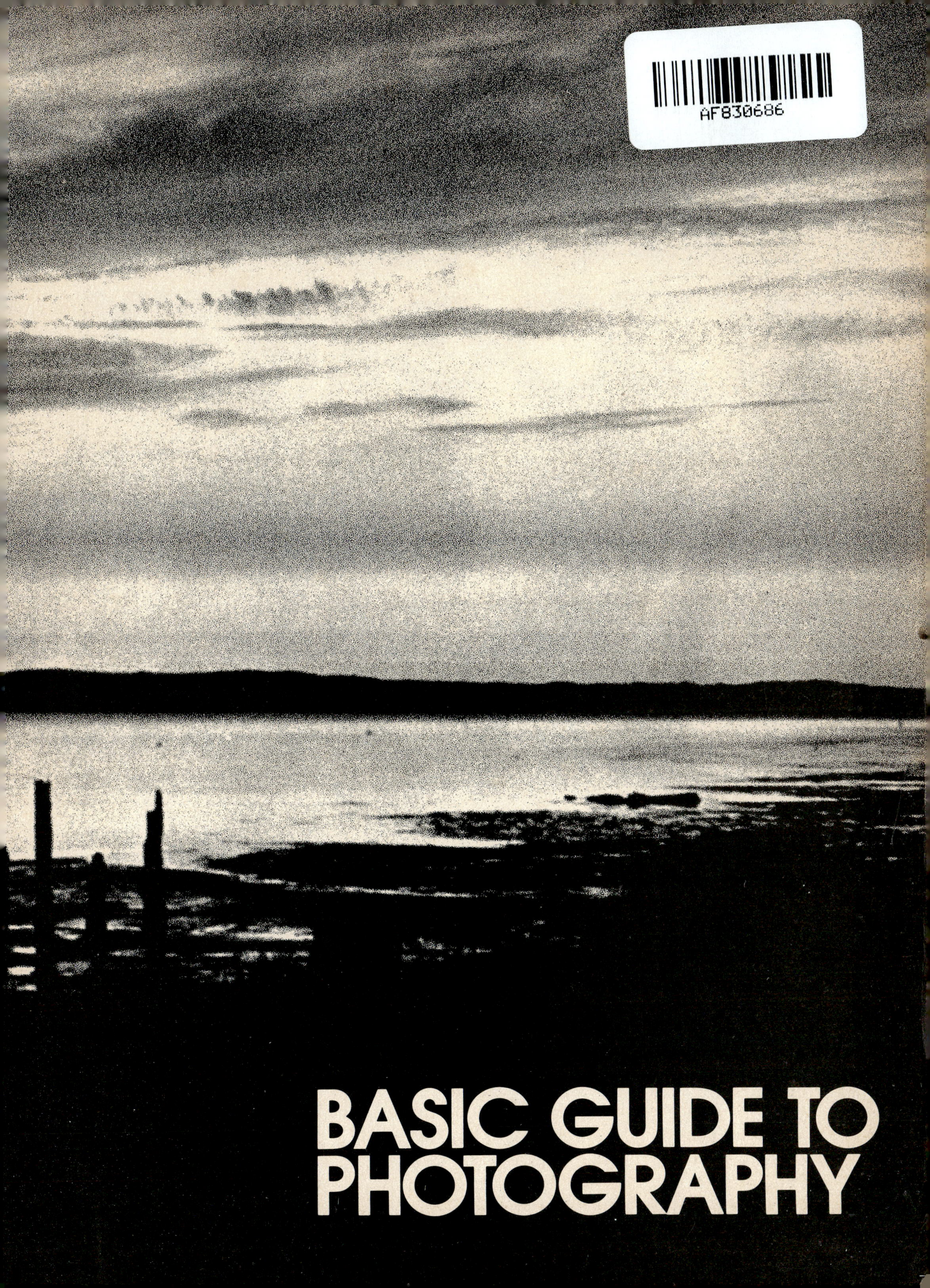

BASIC GUIDE TO PHOTOGRAPHY

BASIC GUIDE TO PHOTOGRAPHY

INTRODUCTION

Photography is a science, an art, a hobby, a career. It can be your way of life, or it can be merely a means of recording the growth of your loved ones. Whatever photography is to you, it will be far more satisfying if your photographs are what you want them to be—if you can record on the film just what you want to record, the way you want to record it. And that's what this book is all about—giving you what you need to know to make your pictures turn out the way you want them to.

Petersen's *Basic Guide to Photography* will not try to tell you which camera is best, which lenses or light meters are best; instead, it will give you guidelines to follow in deciding which equipment is best suited to your specific needs.

Just as there is no single answer to the question, "Which camera is best?" there is no single answer to "How do I do it?" There are many methods, techniques and theories in photography. Those explained here are simple, and they work. Many of the others work, too. Start with what you read here, and you'll have a sound working knowledge of photographic technique. Then try other methods and theories as you hear of them, and use the ones that best suit your needs, the ones that give you the best results.

The secret of photography is to shoot pictures. Sound too simple? Not really. You can read and learn theories, methods and techniques, but they won't mean a lot to you until you have tried them. Only by actually shooting night scenes will you learn how to produce the results you want in your night photographs. Only by shooting action shots, trying to stop the action at its peak, experimenting with shutter speeds, will you learn how to produce the results you want in your action photographs. Only by shooting close-ups will you learn how to deal with extremely shallow depth of field and produce the results you want in your close-ups. You see the point.

Basic Guide to Photography provides a lot of information and familiarizes you with the terms and the techniques, but only by going out and shooting photographs will you learn how to produce the results you want on the film. And that is photography.

Paul R. Farber/Editor
PhotoGraphic Magazine

BASIC GUIDE TO PHOTOGRAPHY

By Lou Jacobs, Jr. and the Editors of PhotoGraphic Magazine.

ISBN 0-8227-0006-9

Library of Congress Catalog Card Number 73-79969

Contents

CHAPTER 1 Photography

This book is dedicated to photographers everywhere who take pictures because they are inspired by beautiful scenes, interesting faces, poignant or exciting events. They are driven to capture on film the commonplace and the unusual, the fleeting moment and the stirring of the world around them, in reality or fantasy.

Using a camera for personal satisfaction is akin to learning to play a musical instrument. You have to keep at it, improving your technique through mistakes as well as through the satisfaction you feel from prints and slides that delight you. Skill in photography doesn't just come naturally to most people, any more than does playing a cello or piano. But taking pictures can be more fun than slaving over a musical instrument, and even if you never become an expert, you will have a lot to show for your efforts.

This book is a rather quick survey of basic photographic information, some of which may be familiar to you, and some of which is new. Photographers are all related, because at one time or another we all struggle with lighting, exposure, composition, close-ups, printing, etc. There's a ledgendary story that famed photographer Edward Steichen once photographed a cup and saucer every day for a month, until he could arrest on film all their subtleties of light and shade. Unfortunately, most of us don't have that kind of persistence, but perhaps many readers will have the patience to experiment and re-shoot those pictures they like best, until they come closer to their photographic goals.

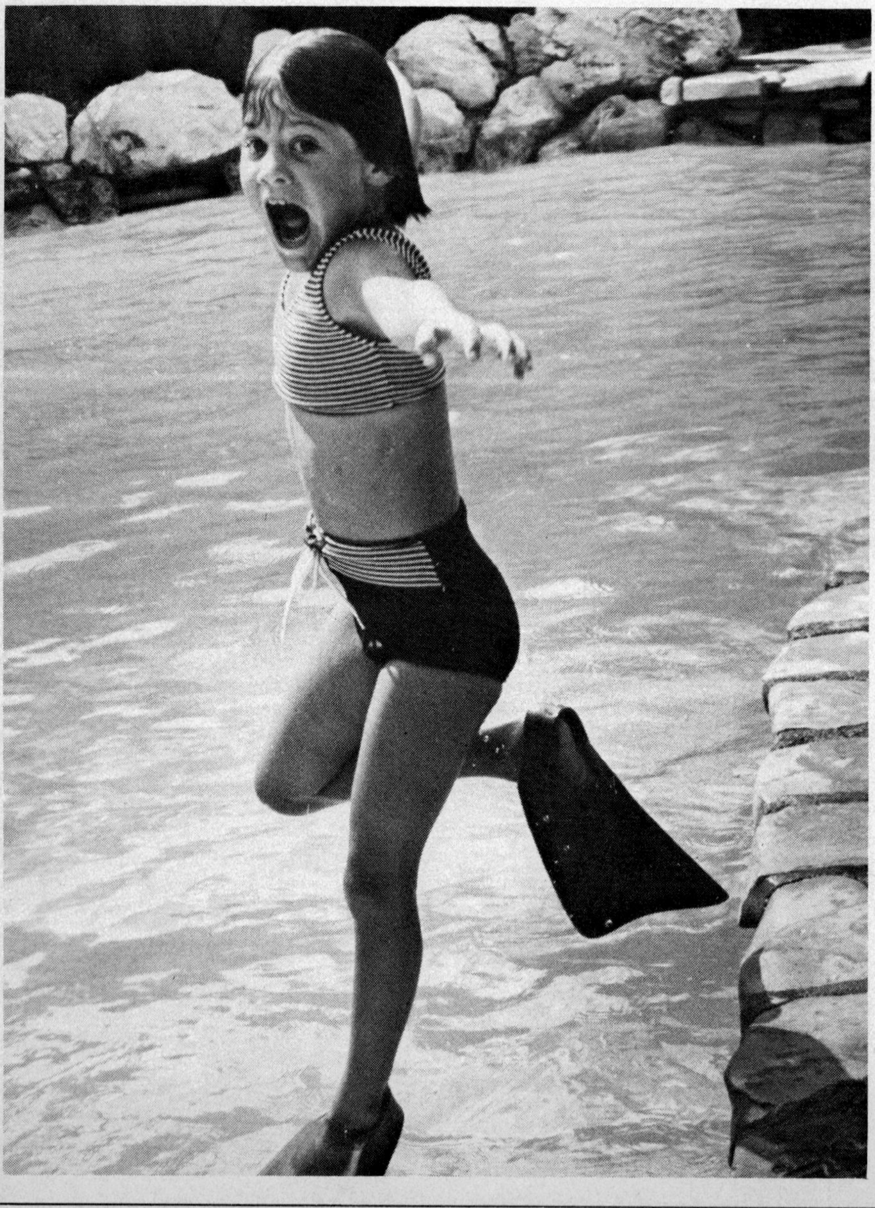

Not having to take pictures for a living is a real asset to the photographer. I've heard many professionals say they had more fun with their cameras before they went into business, and had to please editors, art directors and other clients, rather than merely indulging in subjective photographic fun and games. You have only yourself to please, plus any special audience to whom you show your pictures. Your own demands on yourself will stimulate you to grow, to get the most from lenses, film and picture opportunities. That's a challenge—and I hope this book will give you new motivation to meet it.

In this book, I approach photography with still cameras, since making movies requires its own techniques. Essentially, lighting, composition and the use of color are interchangeable for still or motion pictures, because they depend on certain principles—not rules—that apply to any graphic medium, including painting or drawing. Therefore, the topics covered in this book are specifically for taking one picture at a time with a still camera, and the particular techniques of movie photography will be covered in another book in the GUIDE series.

You may have heard it before, but I'll say it again: The quality of your pictures depends on how well *you see,* not on the price of your camera, or the number of lenses you can afford. We all know somebody who is loaded with equipment, has a fantastic darkroom and all the latest labor-saving gadgets. Some of these lucky people don't know what they're doing, and their treasuries of glass and machinery are somewhat wasted.

In contrast, I believe in basic photographic simplicity. One or two cameras that feel good to use, a few lenses, some accessories, combined with an unlimited supply of energy, curiosity, imagination and courage to take chances—these are the ingredients you really need. Guide your cameras and abilities with *discipline,* and photography can be a most rewarding pastime, a joy of fulfillment.

Keep shooting as you read. Continue to wonder why things happen on film, and how to get images that involve and excite the viewer. Everything we see or experience is new to us as we capture it with a camera, sometimes over and over again, until we can use our optical instrument with the grace and certainty of a Horowitz at the piano.

CHAPTER 2 Choosing a Camera

Whether you already own a camera and are thinking about another one, or you're using an obsolete model (10 years is ancient these days), the variety of types, models and brands available today may seem slightly staggering. However, we all dream about equipment that is newer, fancier, or more automated, and it is no longer an excuse that more expensive cameras may also be more complicated. Anyone can master a good quality camera in the 1970s, and our photographic opportunities offer meaningful incentives to make the effort.

Let's make a survey of the camera world as seen on a well-stocked dealer's shelves. In order to make sense out of this wealth of equipment, think carefully about the kind of pictures you take now, and the kind you would like to be able to shoot in the future. This introspection will help guide you to an appropriate camera at a price you can (sometimes) afford. Even if you have to pay for equipment on the installment plan, a quality camera will outlast most cars, and you don't have the expense of a motor overhaul at 60,000 miles!

You will note that more money usually buys increased camera versatility in terms of larger lenses, precision focusing, image sharpness, interchangeable lenses, a wide range of shutter speeds, and other useful features. Inexpensive cameras might be compared to small pocket radios from which you can hear words and music with limited sound quality. More expensive cameras are similar to high fidelity stereo combinations: the sound is lush and you can make all sorts of adjustments to suit your taste. Thus camera and lens controls are what you pay extra money for, in order to get creative potential. But you can legitimately limit the feeling that you must pay many hundreds of dollars for a camera and lenses. There is such an array of equipment at so many prices, that it is not necessary to buy a whole "system" including motor drives, unlimited accessories, or one-of-a-kind lenses unless you intend to compete with professionals. You can buy a fine camera for $150, and for between $200 and $300 you'll get even more controls to fill your needs for years to come. The possibilities will unfold as we go along.

SIMPLE CAMERAS

"Box camera" days are gone, and in their place has come the electric eye era. Even simple cameras with few adjustments offer automatic exposure that provides better prints or slides than grandpa ever imagined. Simple cameras, roughly those between $10 and $50, may be just right for people who merely want to make a record of places they've been and things they do. Birthday parties, visiting relatives, trips to Disneyland, and new babies (if you can forego close-ups) are all targets for snapshot photographers. In this sense I don't use the word *snapshot* in a derogatory way. (Later I shall.) You load a simple camera with color film, view through the finder, press the shutter release, and advance the film. "They" do the rest. If this satisfies your needs, you could be well off. In fact, you may not need to read any further.

Even simple cameras come in various shapes and sizes. There are the 110 film cartridge Pocket Instamatic cameras described below, as well as a number of models that use 126-size drop-in film cartridges which make negatives or slides about 29mm square. Brand names include the familiar Instamatic-X series by Kodak, plus cameras made by Argus, Minolta

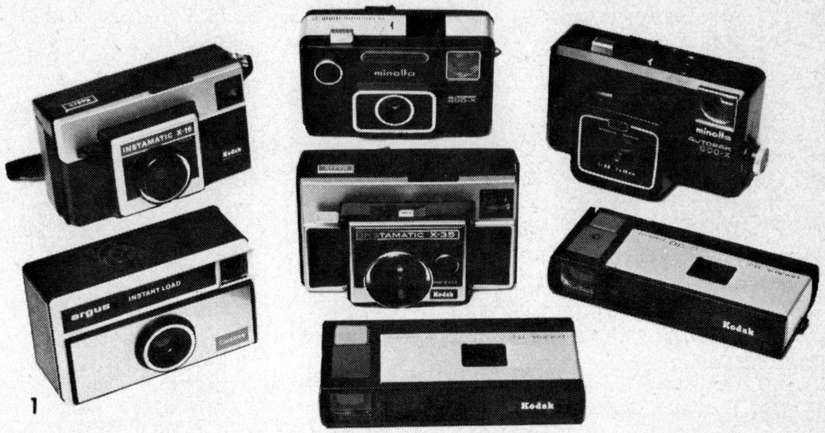

1

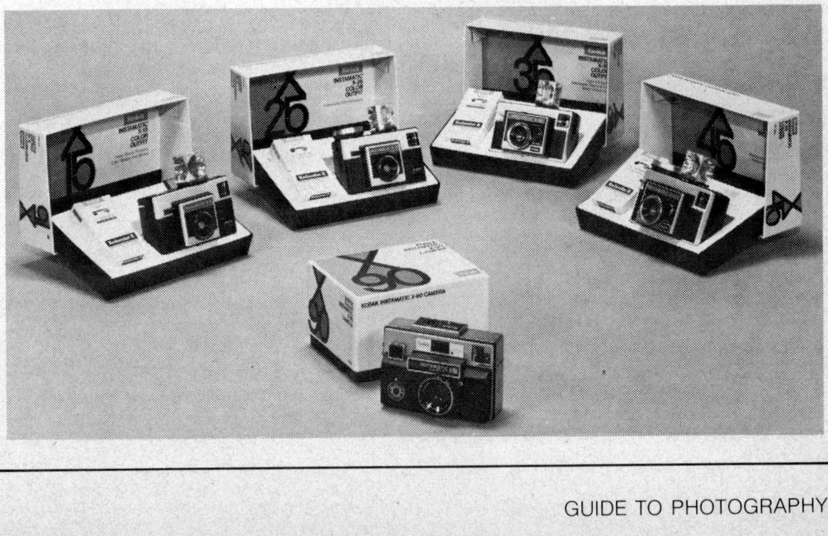

2

1. Inexpensive cameras, between $10 and $50, are made in various shapes and sizes, some available with electric-eye shutter control.

2. These cameras use drop-in 126 film cartridges, and range widely in price and sophistication from X-15 to X-90 model Instamatic Kodaks.

and others, all in the under-$50 class with a minimum of focus and exposure controls. There may also be a few 127-size film cameras around, making pictures 40mm square, but these seem to be phasing out in favor of cameras that use the easy-loading 126 and 110 film cartridges.

110 FILM CARTRIDGE CAMERAS

If 110-size film sounds unfamiliar, it was only introduced by Eastman Kodak in mid-1972, for their new line of Pocket Instamatic cameras, though cameras made by other companies using 110 film cartridges are coming along. Kodacolor II film and Verichrome film were both improved with better color fidelity and sharpness to make the tinier negatives and slides more practical.

At present there are five Pocket Instamatic camera models numbered 20, 30, 40, 50 and 60. These cameras, all only an inch thick, have been designed around the 110-size cartridge-loaded film that makes images approximately 13x17mm. Kodak has ingeniously appealed to people who want to take pictures for fun, since the cameras fit neatly into coat pocket or purse.

The Model 20 (listing at $27.95) is a simple camera with fixed focus, similar to the Model 30 ($47.95), which includes additional shutter speeds and electronic exposure, but the same relatively small f/9 lens. Model 40 ($62.95) has an f/8 lens and two-position focusing. In model 50 ($107.95) you get an f/2.7 lens, varying shutter speeds, and full manual focus. At the top of the line Model 60 ($127.95) has a coupled rangefinder and the same f/2.7 lens. All models take Magicubes (no batteries required) for flash, and because they are likely to be rather popular, I've described them in brief detail. However, for readers who want more versatility, more and larger lenses, bigger negatives to enlarge and a wider scope to photography as a hobby, 35mm cameras are preferable.

SUBMINIATURE CAMERAS

Even easier to carry than the Pocket Instamatic cameras are cameras that use 16mm film, and are popular with spies because they can be easily hidden. The best known brand is Minox, which is precision made, expensive, and capable of producing negatives from which good enlargements can be made—with proper handling techniques. The Rollei 16 and Minolta 16 are two others in this category that include automatic exposure or built-in meters. These small cameras are fine for travel, or as a second camera, but would not be first choice for the serious photographer.

35MM CAMERAS

When just making "clear" pictures isn't enough, and you are ready to spend a little more money to get a lot more pleasure from photography, 35mm cameras offer the widest choice of makes and models, and the best possibility of confusion. You must research the market in several ways before you buy. Begin by reading brochures offered by camera manufacturers, plus their current advertisements. When you know enough to make comparisons, discuss the brands and models you like best with a dealer you trust. If a camera shop is new to you, the more you learn before you shop, the more likely you'll get honest help. If you come in waving your checkbook, asking for the "best" camera around, you may get the most expensive, which may be overweight, nonautomated, overly systematized, and hardly appropriate if you knew the field better.

35MM RANGEFINDER (RF) CAMERAS

You view through a finder beside the lens, and focus with a pleasantly precise set of mirrors in the rangefinder. The only such camera made today with interchangeable lenses is the Leica M5. Leica was the pioneer 35mm camera first marketed in Germany back in 1925. Other brands followed, but have been discontinued (such as the excellent Nikon SP and Canon 7S) due to the popularity of the single-lens reflex. The Leica M5 has a through-the-lens metering system to make it even more versatile, costs over $500 and is generally more suitable for professionals than for most serious amateurs. Used Nikons and Canons may be good buys if you are hooked on RF focusing.

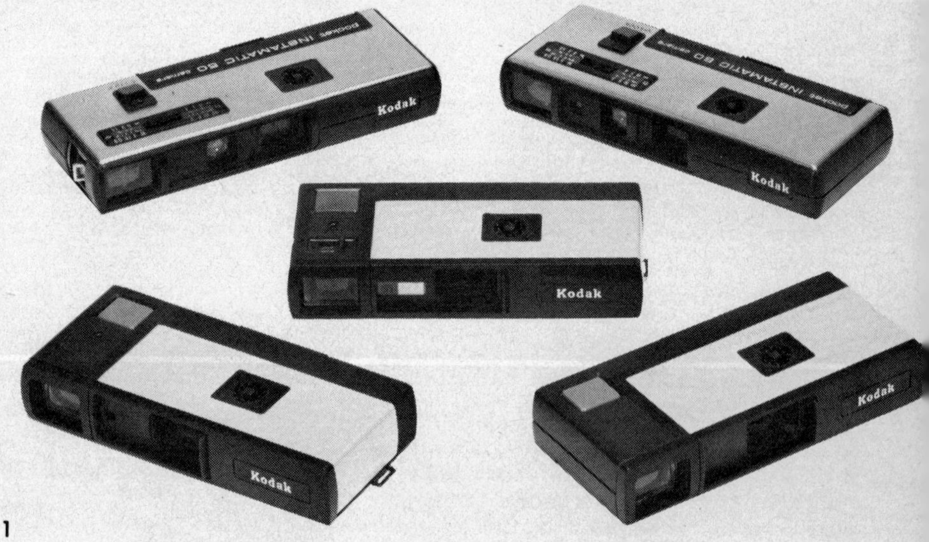

1

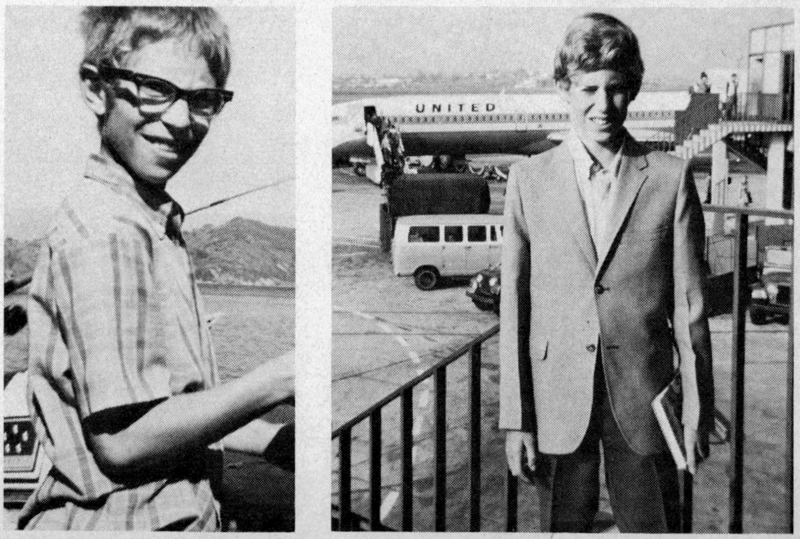

2

Also in this line, without interchangeable lenses, is a variety of lightweight, automatic exposure cameras such as the Konica Auto S3 and C35, the Olympus 35RC, the Ricoh 35, Yashica 35MC, Petri 35, and the Minolta Hi-matic 7S. Relatively inexpensive (between $75 and $150), portable, with good optics, easy focusing and exposure, these 35s are top rated for travel and fun. They are not as versatile as the SLRs described next, but their full 35mm negative or slide is preferable in my estimation to the 110 size. Some are as easy to carry as a Pocket Instamatic camera, with added advantages worth considering when you shop.

35MM SINGLE-LENS REFLEX (SLR) CAMERAS

You view *through* the lens via a mirror, prism and ground glass with an SLR camera, and see exactly the image the lens "sees." A majority of serious photographers prefer the reflex method of shooting for a number of valid reasons. You can mount any focal length lens, from wide-angle to telephoto, on most SLR bodies; many normal SLR lenses focus to 18 inches and making extreme close-ups is routine with special lenses. In addition, you can preview depth of field through the SLR finder to see approximately what's in focus from foreground to background. Most SLR cameras today include built-in exposure meters coupled to the aperture and shutter speed controls, or fully automatic exposure by which the camera selects its own lens opening (or shutter speed) according to the light and other settings you have made.

Since the instant-return mirror was introduced for the SLR around 1958, amateurs and professionals alike have spurred manufacturers to make amazing mechanical, electronic and optical improvements in this number one-type camera. You can *do more* with an SLR because of its through-the-lens viewing concept, because it is more intimate, more precise, and an excellent way of composing, be it portrait or landscape. Years ago I wrote a magazine article on the SLR in which I called it "a view camera on a neck strap," which is still a nice way to think of this 35mm system.

Doing more with the SLR is directly related to creativity and being imaginative, which is the real challenge in photography. Some readers may prefer a small RF camera for portability, and some a larger size (such as 2¼x2¼) for other reasons, but a majority of us find the 35mm SLR convenient, automatic, available in a wide range of prices, and continually being improved by manufacturers who profit by their ingenuity.

There are many quality SLR brands, and I'll name most of them alphabetically: Alpa, Argus, Canon, Edixa, Exakta, Fujica, Leicaflex, Konica, Mamiya, Minolta, Miranda, Nikkormat, Nikon, Olympus, Pentax, Petri, Practica, Ricoh, Rolleiflex, Topcon, Tower and Yashica. You almost have to take a course in camera shopping to become familiar with the similarities and differences between brands,

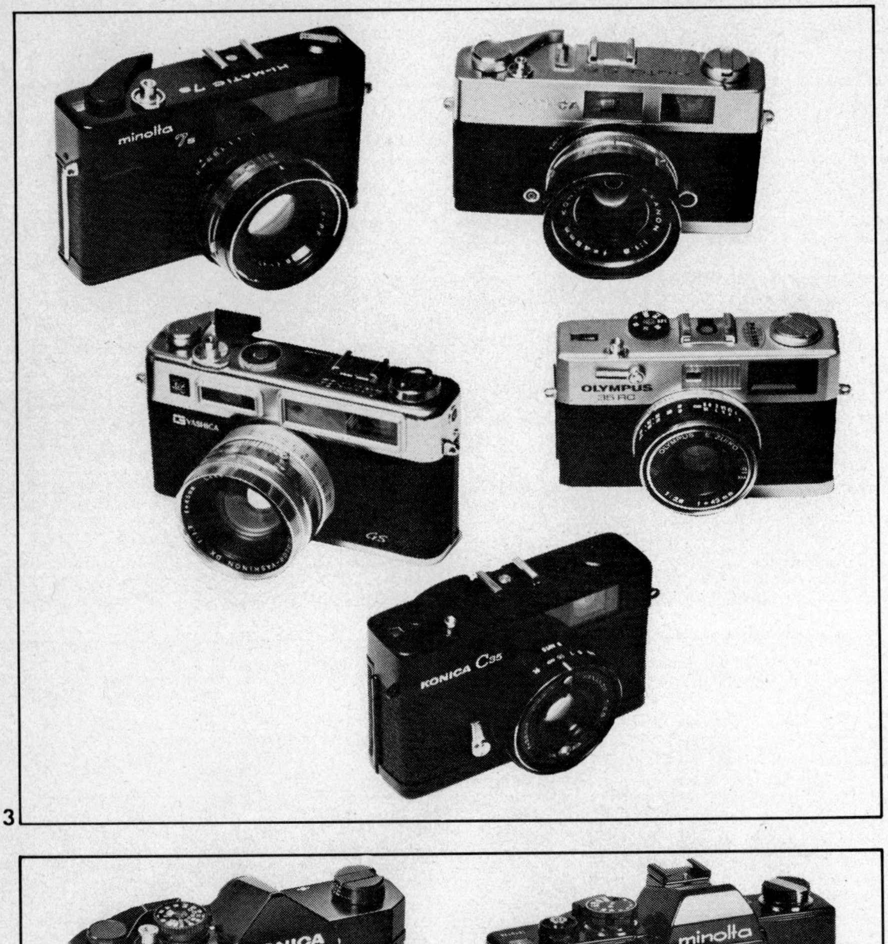

3

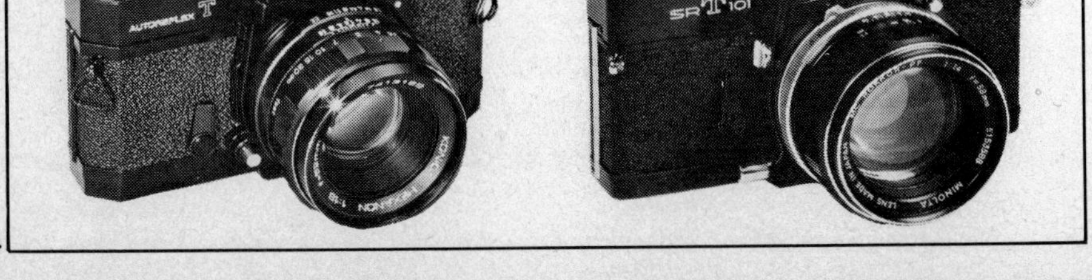

4

1. The lastest flat Instamatics (called Pocket Instamatics) use 110-size film; the least expensive Model 20 is at bottom right, with the most expensive Model 60 at top right.

2. These photographs were both made with simple cameras costing less than $20. Boy fisherman was slightly close to lens, and is not completely sharp; youngster at airport is very sharp in relation to the simple lens on the camera used for the shots.

3. Selection of 35mm rangefinder cameras all costing less than $150 and all with electric-eye exposure feature.

4. These two 35mm single-lens reflex cameras are typical of the great variety on the market. Konica Autoreflex T has automatic exposure system; Minolta SR-T 101 uses match-needle meter behind the lens for readings.

Choosing a Camera

but here are some particular features to consider in terms of utility and price when choosing one:

1. Does the camera use screw-mount or bayonet-mount lenses? Of the former there are literally hundreds made by many manufacturers, which means you have a wide choice of prices and focal lengths. Bayonet-mount lenses are not interchangeable between brands, though many types of adapters are available. However, be sure that the adapter does not prevent the use of certain automatic features built into the SLR camera body. Actually, with the proliferation of lenses on the market today, the most popular single-lens reflexes are made for *both* types of lens mounts.

2. Does the camera offer interchangeable finders? This is important if you need the ability to switch from eye-level viewing to waist-level, or to add split-image rangefinder focusing if it's not built in. Removable finders may not be necessary to many photographers, but you should be aware of the options.

3. What special accessories and equipment are available within the camera system which may have meaning for you? Such items include microscope adapters, angle finders, special multiexposure backs and camera motors. Professional photographers love motorized cameras, but only serious amateurs who want to concentrate on sports or action will spend the hundreds of extra dollars to have one.

4. How much automation is built into the camera? Almost every SLR includes a through-the-lens exposure meter system. You center a needle seen at the edge of the finder by adjusting either the aperture ring or the shutter speed dial, and thereby set correct exposure for the speed of film in use. A few cameras use colored lights as signals instead of a needle, and some have electronic shutter systems that provide minute changes in speed, but in general match-needle SLRs work accurately and conveniently. You don't need a separate meter, and you can set exposure through any lens you choose.

A step beyond matching needles is more complete automation offered by Konica, Mamiya, Miranda, Nikkormat, Pentax and Petri. With all but the Pentax you set the shutter speed, and the camera meter *automatically* adjusts the lens opening according to light intensity. With the Pentax you set the lens opening, and the camera sets an appropriate shutter speed. This automation saves time and leaves you free to concentrate on picture-taking. You can also override the automatic electric eye (EE) to make exposures manually in high contrast light. Don't buy a single-lens reflex 35mm camera until you have at least investigated the possibilities of an automatic-exposure model.

5. How heavy and bulky is the camera? There's a weight difference of many ounces between the lightest and smallest SLRs and the heavier, larger models. Biggest isn't necessarily best, so choose one that feels comfortable around your neck and in your hands.

6. How does the finder fit your photovision? Some SLR finders may seem brighter than others, and some may seem easier to focus. Be sure to try a camera in fairly dim light to determine image brilliance for *your* eyes. This is one reason why a split-image rangefinder is included in some SLRs, especially for use with wide-angle lenses and older eyes. Personally, I find it a handicap to composition, but plenty of photographers welcome split-image precision.

7. Does the camera have a good repair record? It may be difficult to discover if a particular brand has frequent shutter, film transport or aperture problems, but ask your dealer or

1. Bob D'Olivo was able to "do more" with his SLR because of its fast shutter speeds, adaptability to many lenses and motorized film drive back.

2. Typical of accessory equipment in 35mm SLR camera system is assortment for the Minolta camera, including lenses, bellows, finders, filters and eyepieces.

3. Years ago, photographers discovered it is not difficult to carry two SLR cameras around your neck if they are not the heavier models when wandering about to shoot scenes such as this college classroom. Try it today.

4. There are many considerations, including price, in the purchase of a single-lens reflex; some are shutter speeds, finders, selection of lenses available and reliability.

5. Larger format cameras, such as this 2¼x2¼ Bronica, are also designed in systems of lenses and accessories.

6. The definition possible from a 2¼x2¼ negative or transparency is superior to that of a 35mm because the degree of enlargement is less for a given size print. Yosemite waterfall was shot with 2¼x2¼ camera on Tri-X.

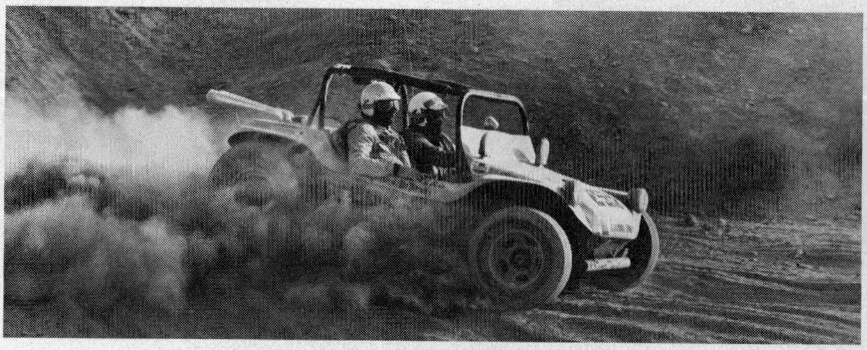
1

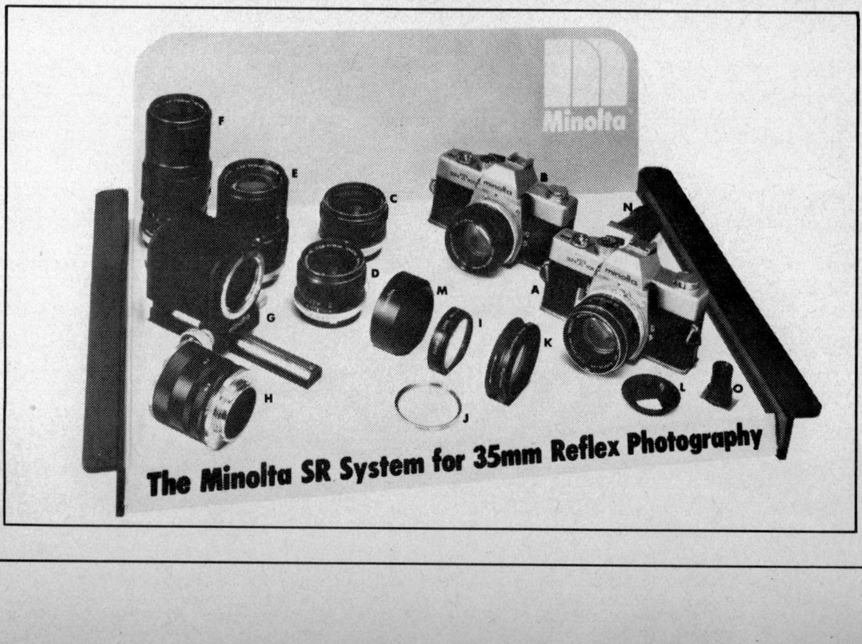

2

an independent repair man. Hopefully, a camera shop will not steer you toward an SLR that is known to be not reasonably durable.

8. How much do the camera and its lenses cost? You can buy an SLR without meter for about $100 (but I wouldn't advise it). The average SLR with meter, or with automatic exposure, ranges between $200 and $600. Less expensive models may offer fewer features such as a high shutter speed of only 1/500 second, no self-timer, smaller aperture lenses (though f/1.8 or f/2 is quite adequate), and other refinements available for more money. There is not always a corollary between price and camera versatility; some very expensive brands that offer a vast array of accessories won't enable the average photographer to do more than brands costing $100 or $200 less, with a less complete system, and perhaps less elaborate advertising. Check with friends who have SLRs, handle their cameras and ask their opinions. At the camera shop, get the feel of each camera that interests you by going through the motions of shooting. Try to balance the most desirable features of any brand against your budget. Keep two things in mind: If you buy a quality SLR that seems to have everything you want, it will last for a decade or longer; and discounts vary from store to store, so shop and compare before you buy.

I'm not going to recommend one brand over the others, even if I have my favorites. If a camera has been on the market for five years, it is worthy of consideration, and you can find partisans for almost every brand. Be careful and you'll be satisfied.

LARGER FORMAT CAMERAS

In this category are twin-lens reflex, single-lens reflex, eye-level reflex, view and press cameras. You only need investigate these when you want a larger negative or slide to make huge enlargements, or you find a larger finder image more suitable to your eyes. There is something beautifully satisfying in shooting 2¼x2¼ negatives or color transparencies, but unless you get into professional advertising photography, or specialize in portraiture, you don't need the added weight, size and expense.

Pioneer of the twin-lens reflexes is the Rolleiflex, made in several models with add-on lenses available. Other manufacturers make semicopies of the Rollei at lower prices, and they are worth comparing. There is also the Mamiya C series with interchangeable lenses. All of these, plus the SLRs and eye-level models mentioned next, make 2¼x2¼ negatives and slides (also known as 6x6cm), which means you can crop a square horizontally or vertically and still have more image area than you get with the 35mm size.

In the larger SLR class are the Hasselblad, Bronica, Rollei 66, Mamiya, Kowa and Kalimar. The first four are somewhat heavier and more expensive than the others, but offer a wider assortment of lenses and accessories. There's a motorized Hasselblad (EL) made famous by astronauts visiting the moon, and a Bronica with electronic shutter. In fact, several 2¼x2¼ systems are very elaborate, easily paralleling those available in 35mm.

The third type of hand-held larger-format camera is the eye-level SLR, such as the Pentax 6x7, the Norita and Fujica, which are shaped like oversize 35mm cameras and make 6x6cm or 6x7cm images. Interchangeable lenses are available for these, and if you don't mind hefting twice or three times the weight of a 35mm camera, you get a considerably larger negative or slide.

VIEW AND PRESS CAMERAS

These make pictures 3¼x4¼, 4x5, 5x7 or 8x10 (all inches), and are for very specialized use by students,

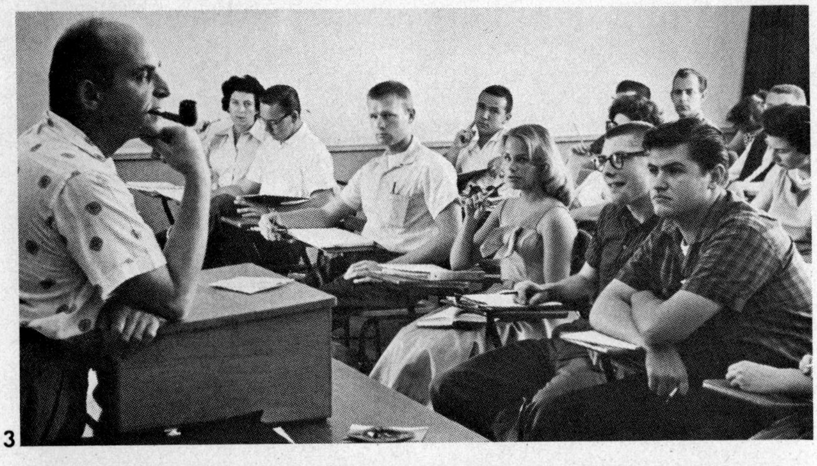
3

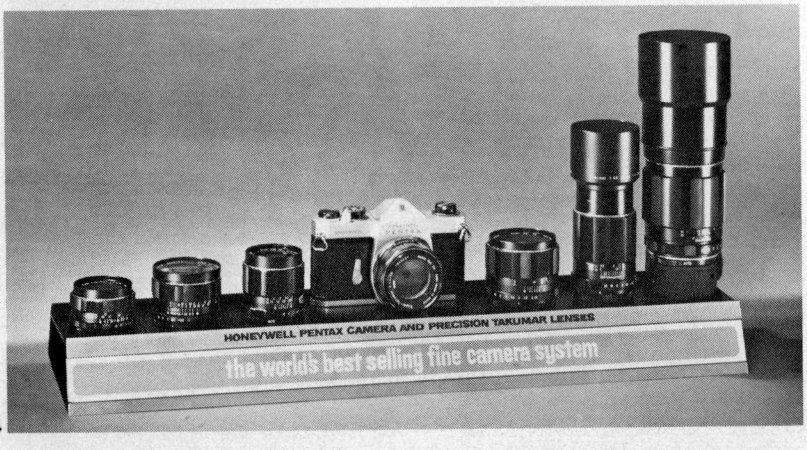

4

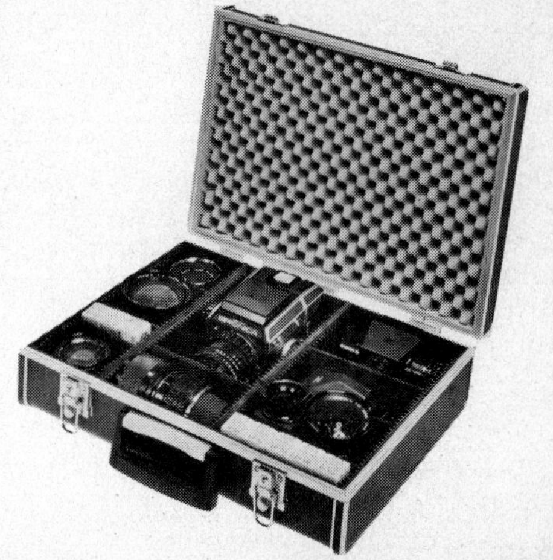
5

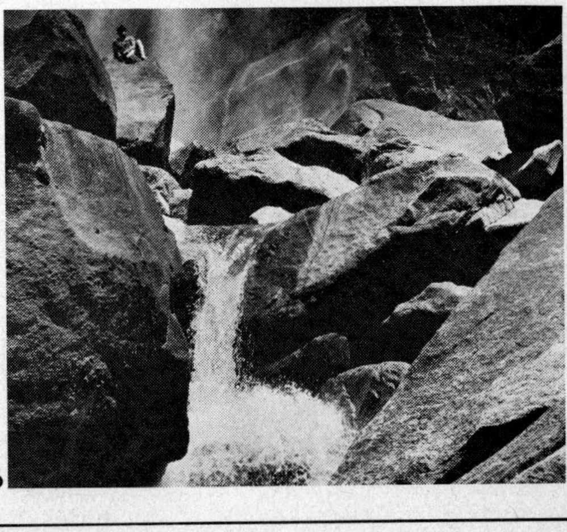
6

commercial, advertising and architectural photographers. While you are learning photographic techniques thoroughly, there is a distinct advantage to using a view camera on a tripod, composing a relatively large image on a ground glass (upside down), and processing one sheet of film at a time. But though picture quality is unexcelled, there's little or no mobility with a view camera, and even press photographers use 35mm and 2¼x2¼ cameras today because the old faithful Speed Graphic's unwieldiness (4x5) has become an unnecessary handicap. However, swings and tilts on a view camera (and some hand-held cameras such as the Linhof) allow an architectural photographer to control perspective of buildings handily, and really serious students find these adjustments important to know as well. (There's a Nikkor PC [perspective control] lens for the 35mm Nikon camera in case you're interested.)

On top of everything else, 35mm and 120-size films (for 2¼x2¼ and 6x7cm cameras) have such excellent grain and sharpness qualities today, that larger format cameras are necessary only for specialized work. A Kodachrome slide reproduces in *National Geographic Magazine* with such fidelity that it equals the quality of a 4x5 transparency of two decades ago.

INSTANT-PICTURE CAMERAS

At the moment only Polaroid Land cameras make prints in seconds, but eventually, other manufacturers are likely to introduce equipment using Polaroid films. There is a series of Polaroid models—numbered 420, 430, 440 and 450—offering more and more features for more money. Known as Color Pack cameras, they include focused flash, which is part of Polaroid's unique automatic exposure system.

Two other modestly priced Polaroid cameras are the Big Shot, which makes only head-and-shoulders close-ups, and the Square Shooter, which features square pictures at less film cost. These cameras are lightweight but bulky, and not as versatile as the 400 series.

The latest Polaroid model, SX-70, is flat and portable, but unfolds to a larger size. It features SLR focusing, automatic exposure and an electric motor that propels the film out of the camera, where you watch it develop in broad daylight. Handling prints is more convenient than with the other Polaroid models, but the SX-70 retails for approximately $180, making it cost almost as much as a good 35mm SLR with interchangeable lenses.

There is no substitute for a Polaroid camera if you want to give grandma prints today, rather than send them to her next week; or if you're traveling and use the camera as an ice-breaker to gain the friendship or assistance of strangers. Besides this convenience, instant-pictures give you the opportunity to correct composition on the spot, which makes the Polaroid an excellent tool while learning photography. There are limitations, of course, since you must have negatives made in order to do your own darkroom work later, and you don't have the creative versatility of conventional interchangeable lens cameras. For the serious photographer, a Polaroid camera is an extra which has its own unique value for many occasions.

In the realm of 35mm RF and SLR, or 2¼x2¼ cameras, there are often good used bargains on dealer's shelves. You can buy with confidence from a reputable shop that gives at least a 30-day guarantee. How much can you save? As an example, if you select a new camera that lists for $300, it would cost about $240 at a 20 percent discount. As a used camera, the same model should sell for between $140 and $180 depending on its condition and age. Older used cameras cost less because newer models are taking their place.

Buying a used camera from a private party can be risky because you usually take it "as is." If possible, pay half the price and sign a note for the other half, contingent on perhaps a week's testing. If something goes wrong, arrange to have the seller pay for repairs to a certain limit, or share

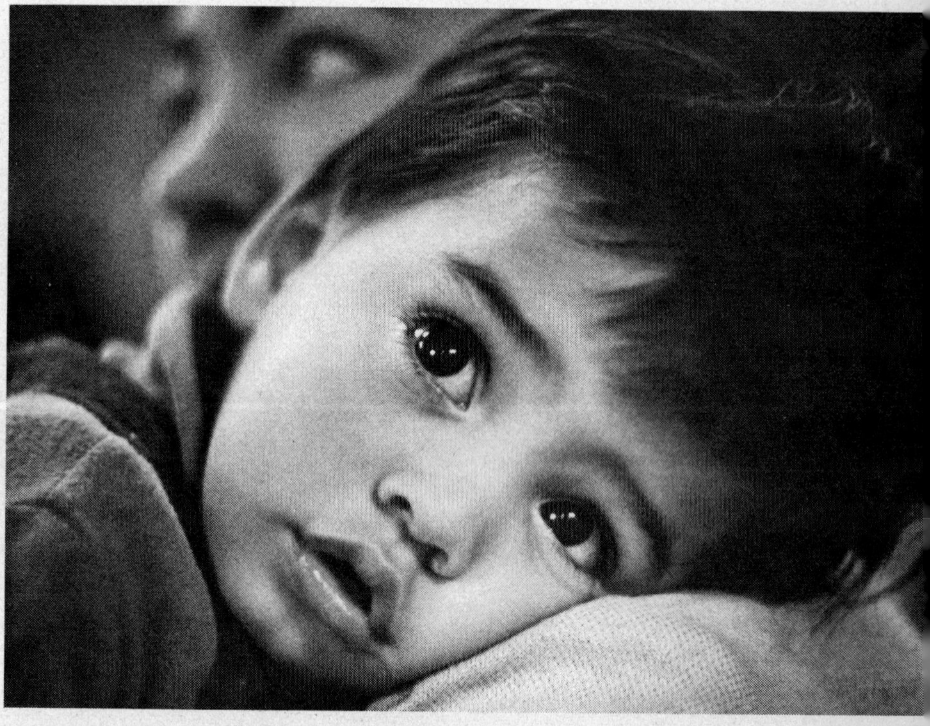

1

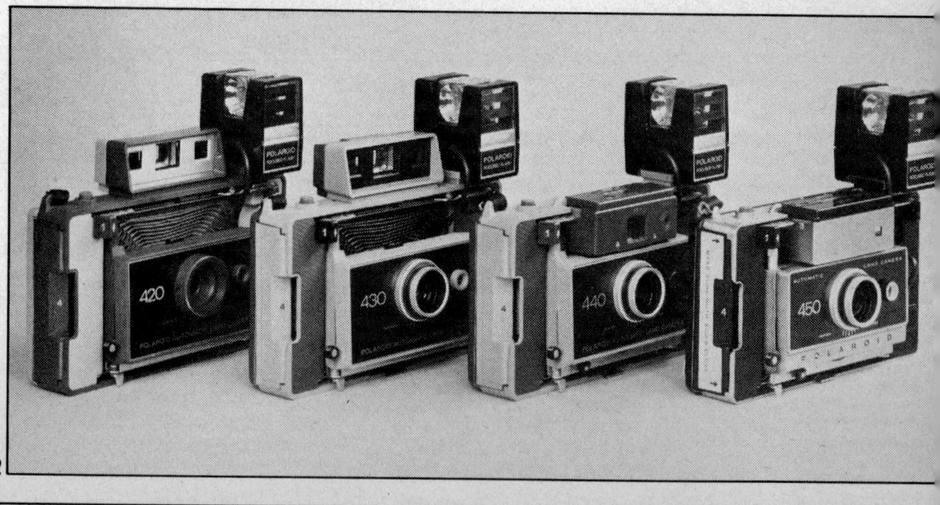

2

the cost equally. In this way you have some assurance that the camera shutter and film transport are reliable, that film is not being scratched, and that lenses focus accurately with normal sharpness.

TAKING CARE OF A CAMERA

It should be apparent that a fairly expensive camera must be handled with care to assure faithful and consistent service. Here are a few things to remember:

1. Store the camera with shutter uncocked; springs last longer when not in tension for long periods.

2. Guard the camera and lenses from dust, sand and water. Keep the camera in a case or gadget bag when not in use, especially at the beach or in dusty circumstances.

3. After each time you shoot, dust the camera interior with a soft brush, and wipe or dust the exterior as well. Clean lenses delicately with lens cleaning solution and tissue. Inspect the camera interior carefully for bits of broken film that can jam the mechanism so easily.

4. Keep lens caps on all lenses; front and back for those not mounted on a camera body.

5. If the shutter-cocking lever won't turn freely to wind film, don't force it. Something inside is probably malfunctioning, and you can compound the problem by excessive force. See a camera repair man.

6. Unless you have taken a course in camera repair, and understand what you're doing, don't attempt to take apart or repair a camera that costs more than $15. Do-it-yourself camera repair is akin to do-it-yourself brain surgery.

7. Check battery condition according to directions in the instruction manual that comes with the camera. Small mercury batteries are inexpensive and easy to replace, so there is no excuse for disappointing exposures due to low battery voltage.

8. Naturally, don't drop or jar a camera unless you enjoy paying $20 and $30 repair bills.

At the moment I own five 35mm cameras (two RF and three SLR), and I use them more often than the average reader would. By following the same advice I'm giving you, I rarely have to endure camera malfunction on a job. Cameras are somewhat delicate, but so is my treatment of them.

FINAL NOTES

Select a camera according to the kind of pictures you will shoot most often, and then learn to use it in the dark with your eyes closed! Don't stint on film—expressions, places, or events may never be such ready subjects again. Cameras are fascinating—to some people even more so than actually taking pictures. Cameras are only tools, of course, and it's how you use them to *see* imaginatively that really counts.

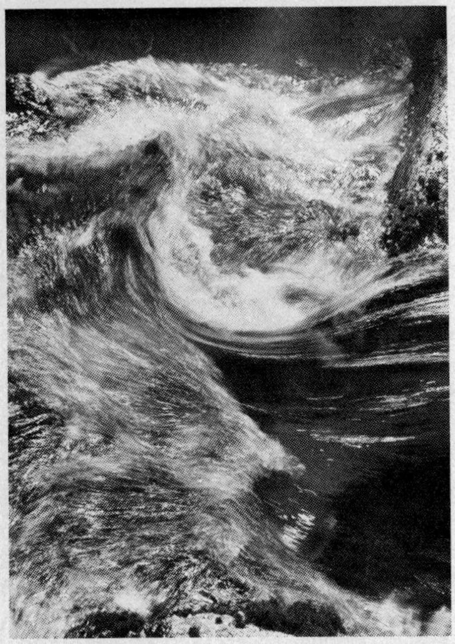
3

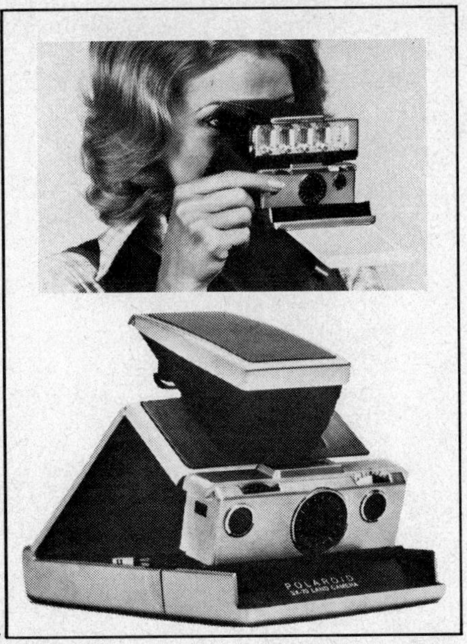

4

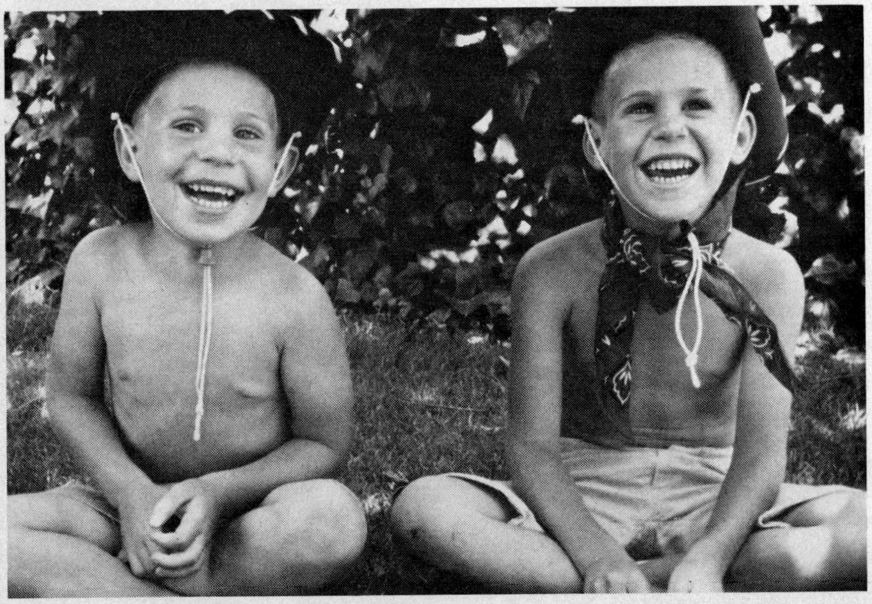
5

1. Ron Contarsy kept his single-lens reflex camera clean and in good condition, so he was ready for this candid photograph in existing light, shot at f/2.8, 1/60 second on Tri-X. It won a Scholastic/Kodak Award.

2. These Polaroid Land cameras in 400 series increase in price from left to right; all have automatic exposure as well as flash.

3. The tone quality and sharpness with a 4x5 negative or transparency is gratifying; this view-camera shot of swirling water was exposed for ½ second at f/32, tripod-mounted. However, a view camera has no finder to use at the moment of exposure.

4. Latest marvel in Polaroid line is SX-70, which propels a color print forward immediately after exposure. SX-70 is a reflex camera that will focus as close as 10 inches.

5. Polaroid prints lend themselves to very acceptable enlargements if the original picture is sharp enough and properly exposed. This was made with a Model 180, no longer manufactured.

CHAPTER 3 Lenses, Equipment and Accessories

Photography probably offers more opportunities to invest in new equipment, expand your horizons and impoverish yourself than any other hobby. If you collect stamps, sew, or even make furniture at home, there's a reasonable limit to the number of magnifying glasses, superstitching needles and multiple-duty machine saws you can collect. But photography has a way of making the acquisition of new accessories and gadgets seem desirable, but an endless goal. There are hundreds of optical, mechanical and labor-saving devices to assist and tempt you, with new ones pouring from factories and shops at an amazing rate.

However, I mentioned being in favor of simplicity, and the equipment covered in this chapter is both functional and optional. One can limit financial outlay to a few of the items described, and still be ready to shoot in a great variety of situations. Here, then, is a guide to spending wisely once you have a good camera that inspires you to be skillful, artful and resourceful.

HOW LENSES WORK

Ordinarily, we can see only the front and back *elements* of a lens in its barrel. Elements are the individual pieces of glass (or plastic) designed (by computer nowadays) to collect light rays reflected from a subject and focus them into a sharp image on a segment of film. A lens element has two surfaces, both curved, or one curved and the other flat. Rays of light passing through a lens are bent according to the shape and thickness of the lens elements which work in unison to produce an image where light rays meet at the picture plane.

Because a simple camera uses only one or two pieces of molded plastic to form an image, sharpness is not as well defined as if the lens were assembled from a series of elements. A more complex lens has anywhere from three to 18 elements, cast in special glass, ground and polished, and arranged very precisely with carefully calculated air spaces

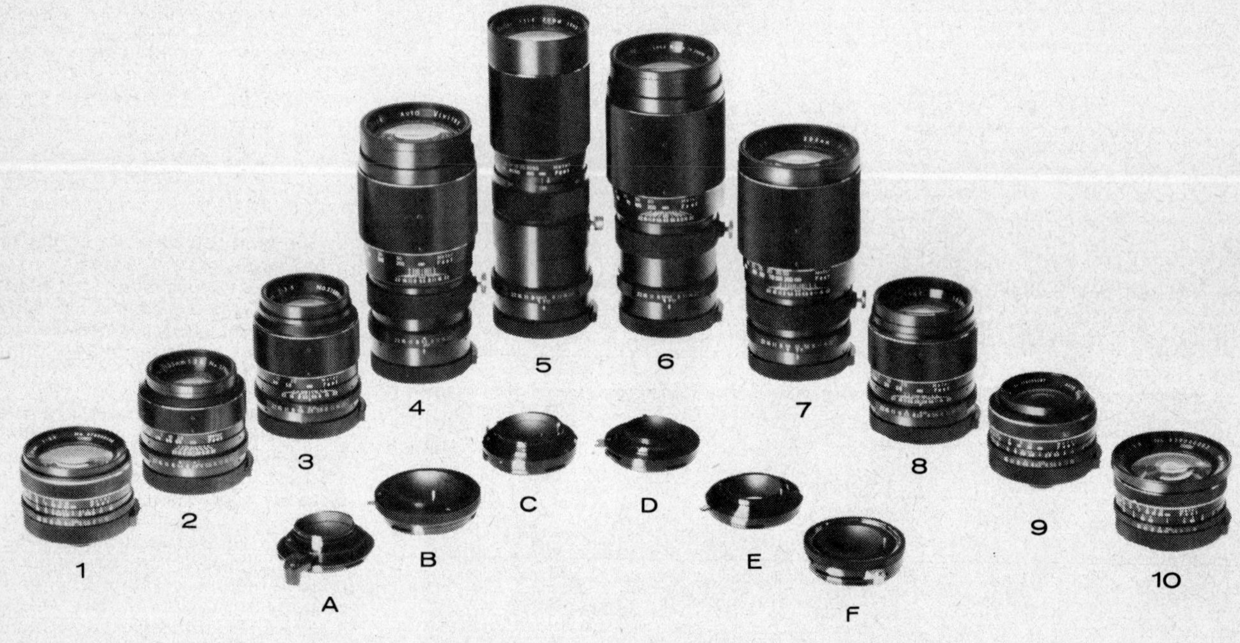

Vivitar Auto T-4 Lenses with Interchangeable Auto T-4 Adapter System

1. 28mm f2.8
2. 105mm f2.8
3. 135mm f3.5
4. 300mm f5.5
5. 90mm to 230mm f4.5 Zoom
6. 250mm f4.5
7. 200mm f3.5
8. 135mm f2.8
9. 35mm f2.8
10. 21mm f3.8

A. Auto T-4 Adapter for Exakta
B. Auto T-4 Adapter for Canon
C. Auto T-4 Adapter for Minolta
D. Auto T-4 Adapter for Nikon
E. Auto T-4 Adapter for Pentax
F. Auto T-4 Adapter for Miranda

1

between them to achieve fine definition. A series of elements is necessary to:

1. Correct for color fidelity and aberrations, which refers to rendering lines accurately and so they are distinctly separated.

2. Retain sharpness from edge to edge even at wide apertures.

3. Allow for extra light-gathering power in wide-aperture lenses such as f/2 or f/1.4.

4. Adapt to close-ups in some cases.

5. Provide for varying focal length in a zoom lens, which has the largest number of elements, some of which shift to change focal length.

A number of basic lens formulas have been devised over many years, which are frequently varied by manufacturers to make lenses sharper, lighter, more compact or faster. If you compare the cross-section diagram of one focal length lens with another brand of the same focal length, you will usually see differences in shape, number and placement of the elements. However, to determine if one brand or design is superior to another, you must take pictures with the lens (on a tripod) to make a fair comparison.

There is a scientific means of measuring lens sharpness and performance called bench testing. Years ago, many professional photographers routinely had their new lenses optically tested by specialists to be sure of top-notch quality. Today bench testing is unnecessary for the average amateur or pro. Uniformity of excellence in lens design and manufacture is well established in the photographic industry. If you should buy a lens which does not perform satisfactorily, simply take it back to the dealer along with some test photographs, and ask for a replacement.

(Some advice if you buy a lens by mail: Write your own contract. Along with your check, send a letter stating that you are purchasing the lens with the understanding that you may return or exchange it if it does not perform properly. Keep a copy of the letter. If the mail-order company cashes your check, they've agreed to your letter contract.)

THE LENS OPENING OR APERTURE

A lens opening, or aperture, is provided by an adjustable diaphragm that widens or closes to control the amount of light that exposes the film. Lens openings are expressed in the familiar f/numbers (or f/stops) which are determined by dividing the focal length of the lens by the diameter of the aperture. Unless you are making your own lens (a real rarity), there is no need to remember this formula that is explained like this: when you have a lens opening of f/4, you know the aperture is only ¼ of the focal length, or at f/8 your opening is ⅛ of the focal length. Realizing that f/numbers are fractions of the focal length makes it easier to understand that the smaller the f/number, the larger the lens opening.

Calculating f/stops and shutter speeds is one of the first things to learn in the language of photography.

1. Series of interchangeable lenses made by Vivitar includes adapters for many single-lens reflex cameras.

2. Diagrams show location of elements in wide-angle Minolta lenses.

3. Portraits are usually shot with lenses of twice normal focal length.

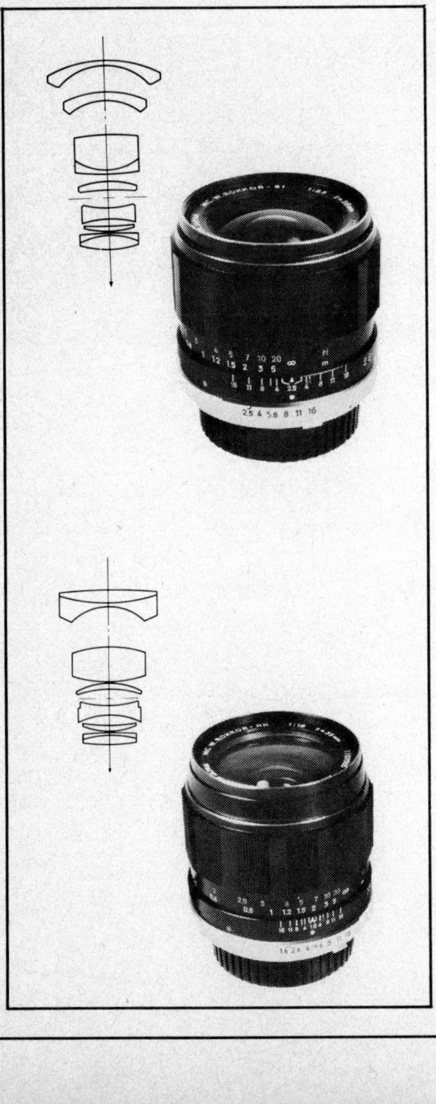

2

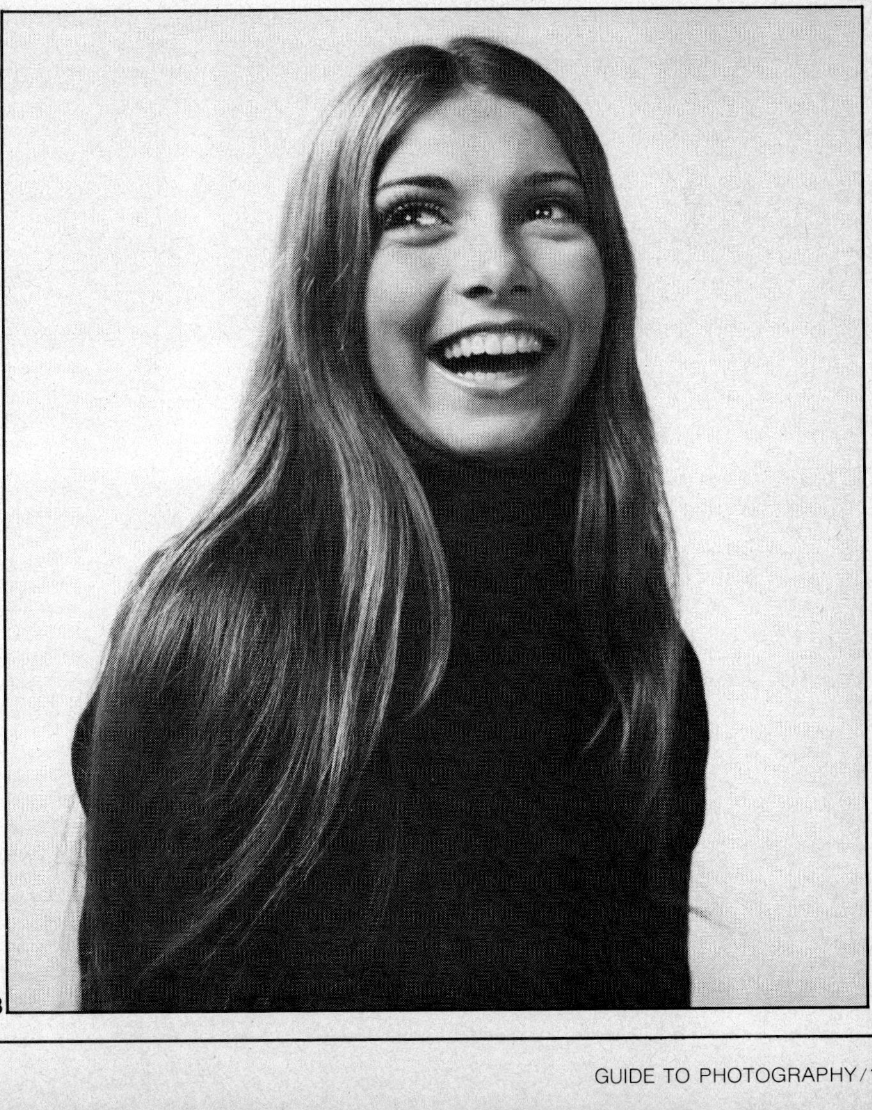

3

These numbers on the camera aperture ring represent full stops or lens openings: f/1.4, f/2, f/2.8, f/4, f/5.6, f/8, f/11, f/16 and f/22. (A few lenses for view cameras, etc. continue on to f/32, f/64, f/128 and f/256.) Half stops, usually indicated by clicks on a camera aperture ring, are f/1.8, f/2.5, f/3.5, f/4.5, f/6.3, f/9, f/12.5 and f/18.

The relationship of shutter speeds is probably easier to understand immediately because each is half as much, or twice as much, as the one following or the one preceding. Thus 1/250 second is half the exposure of 1/125 second, or 1/125 second is twice the exposure of 1/250 second. But how much more exposure is f/5.6 than f/11? Since each full stop lets in half as much light as the one before it, f/5.6 is obviously four times more exposure than f/11. Mastering this numerical language becomes easy with practice, and you may wonder why it ever seemed a mystery—if it did.

The term *relative* aperture indicates that f/8 (or any opening) on a 35mm lens provides the same exposure as f/8 on a 135mm lens, or any other focal length. Though a longer focal-length lens must have a physically larger opening at a given stop than a shorter focal-length lens, it is consistent to their comparative sizes, or relative in terms of light transmission.

However, there seem to be certain exceptions that may be disputed by optical experts. I have found that wide-angle lenses shorter than 35mm tend to be slower than normal focal-length lenses at the same apertures. I've used 28mm, 25mm and 21mm lenses of different brands on both SLR and RF cameras, and have discovered that by increasing exposure about one-half stop (with normal development), I get the same negative density or color saturation as I would with a normal lens. This seems to be true whether I'm using a built-in meter or a separate hand-held meter. I'm not sure why this is so, but I have discussed it with a few other professionals, and they agree. If you want to test this heretical theory for yourself, shoot the same scene in the same light at the same exposure with a normal or longer lens, and again with a 28mm or wider-angle lens on the same roll of film, and compare the results. They may be surprising.

COLOR CORRECTION AND COATING OF LENSES

From the time photography was invented (about 1839), pictures were made on metal or glass plates; after that only black-and-white film was available until primitive color arrived in the 1920s. At first, black-and-white materials were sensitive only to blue light, but later they were improved to be orthochromatic, which means sensitive to both blue and green light. Many early lenses did not focus light rays of different colors at the same point behind the lens. But as long as film could only register blue and green light, it didn't make too much difference when red light rays were not in focus at the same point as the others.

However, orthochromatic films (which can be developed under red safelights without fogging) left a lot to be desired. Red subjects, such as lips, were rendered almost black in prints. Photographers made allowances for such limitations, but the world began looking more realistic when panchromatic films were intro-

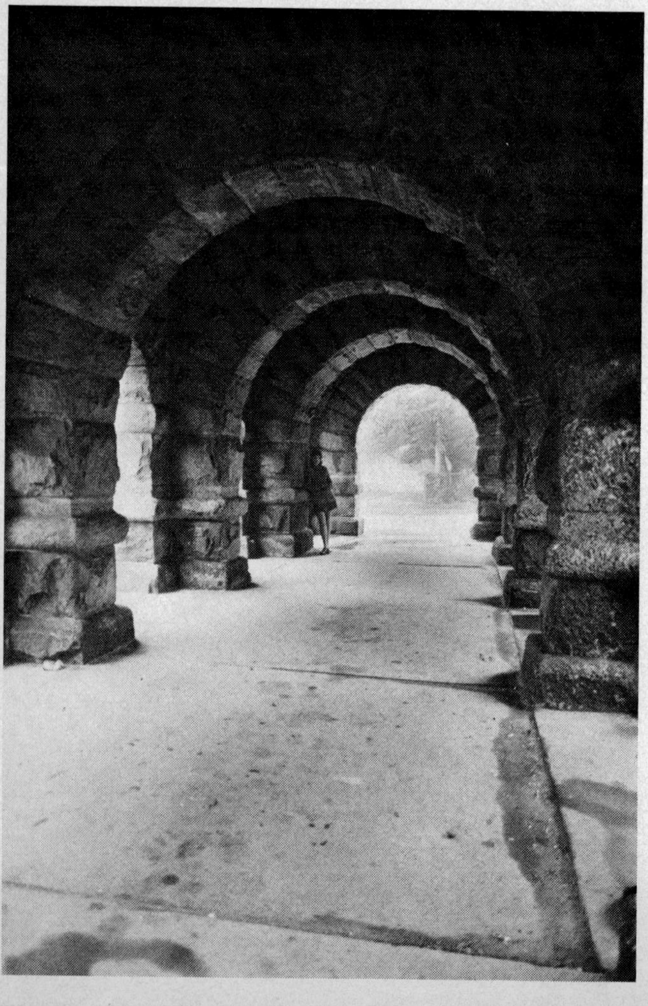

1

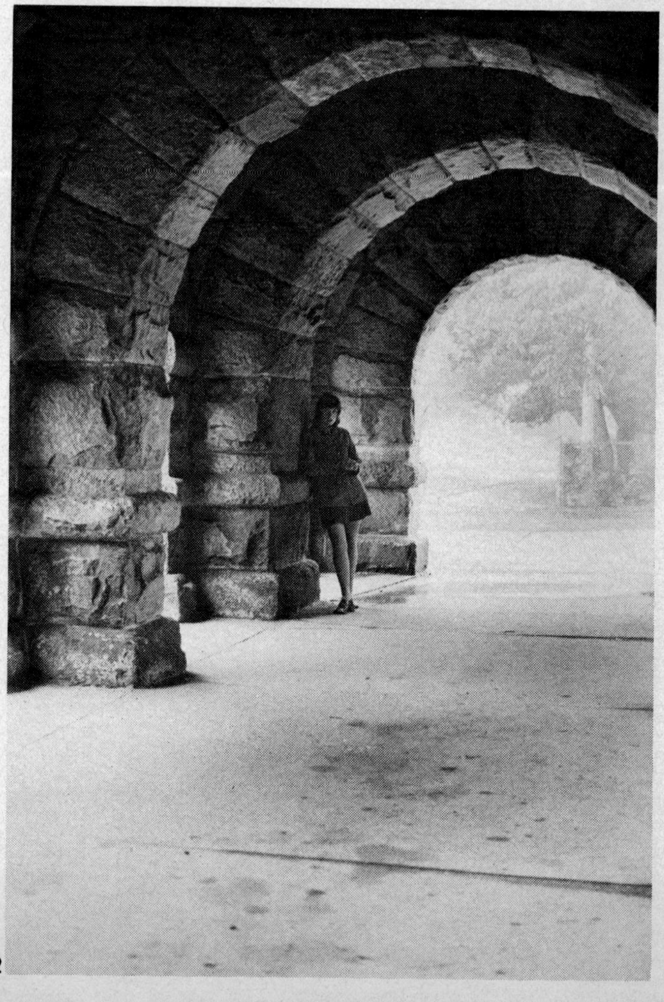

2

duced. These are the ones we use today, sensitive to all colors, which are rendered in their proper relative degrees of black and gray. At this time it was necessary to make lenses that would bring all the spectrum (with the exception of infrared) into focus at the same point. New lens formulas and different types of glass were developed to provide fully color-corrected lenses, which were essential long before color film was available for use.

When Kodachrome and Agfacolor were introduced in 1938, lenses that rendered color accurately were even more important. Years ago, chromatic aberration, or irregularities in producing accurate color images, was an affliction suffered by some lenses. Today it is expected that all modern lenses are adequately corrected for color by design and manufacturing techniques.

Lens coating/ If you examine an ancient lens (made before about 1938), you may notice it does not have a tint of blue or amber that is noticeable on the surface of more modern coated lenses. An uncoated lens allows light rays to "bounce around" between the elements, which degrades the image formed. In other words, a small percentage of light is reflected *back* from a lens surface, as the major amount of light rays pass through it. In a multiple-element lens this light bounce is increased considerably between glass surfaces and air spaces, and image definition is softened.

To greatly reduce the amount of light reflected back from glass surfaces and between elements of a lens, each element is coated with a microscopically thin chemical film. This contributes to a clearer, crisper image, and makes a lens more efficient by increasing the amount of light that passes through it. Some camera and lens manufacturers claim to have devised superior coating techniques which almost eliminate the flare produced when shooting into the light. (A lens hood is still necessary to shield against bright-light flare.)

Incidentally, the color of lens coating does not affect the color in pictures taken with the lens. And coated enlarging lenses are equally important to image quality. I found this out to my chagrin many years ago when I switched from an uncoated to a coated lens and discovered definite improvement in image sharpness and gradation.

THE FUNCTION OF FOCAL LENGTH

In simple terms, focal length is the distance between the optical center of a lens and the film—when the lens is focused at infinity. Focal length is usually expressed in millimeters, and descriptions of various "families" of focal length lenses for 35mm cameras are listed below.

There is a direct relationship between the focal length of a lens and the image size of a subject that it records on film: the longer the focal length, the larger the image produced. For example, a 35mm lens records a smaller image than a 135mm lens from the same camera position. In fact, the 135mm image is about a three times enlargement compared to the 35mm image (2 x 35 = 70 and 2 x 70 = 140).

1. Full-frame scene with 24mm lens.

2. Same full-frame scene, 50mm lens.

3. Same full-frame scene, 100mm lens.

4. Same full-frame scene, 200mm lens.

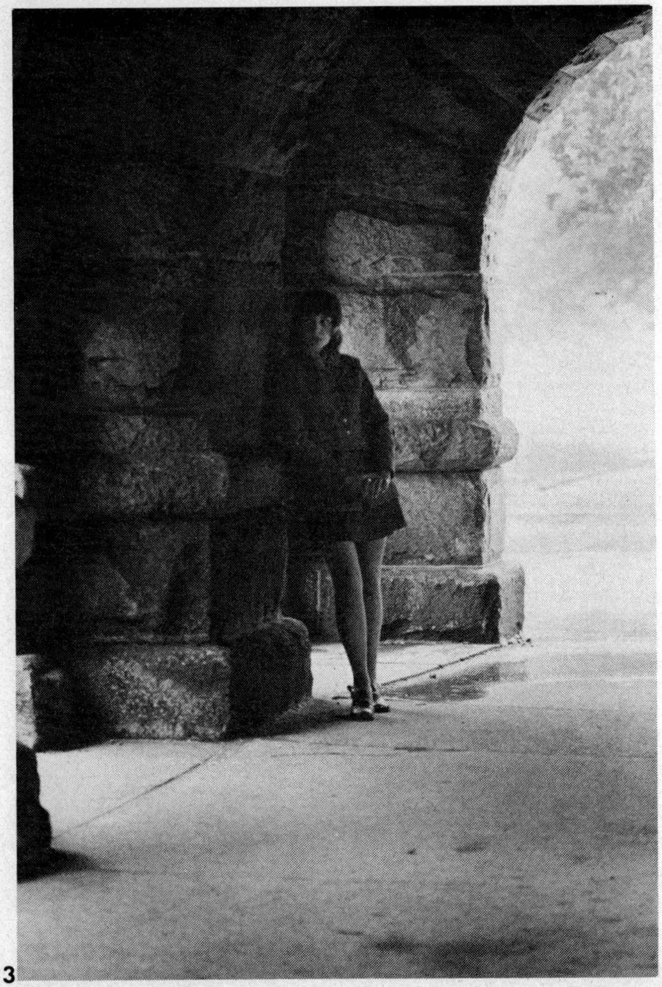

3

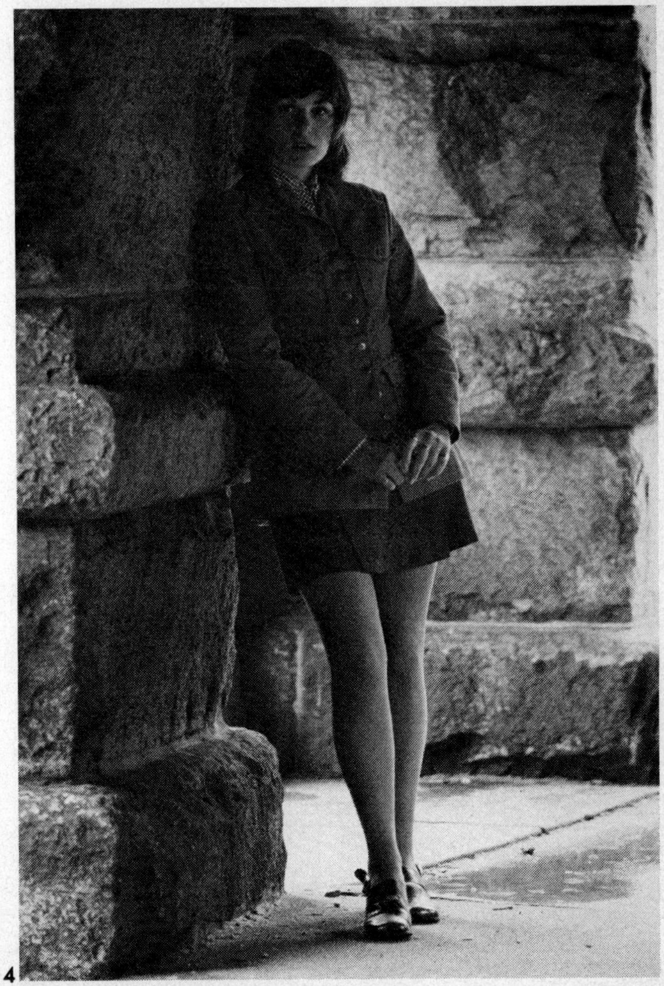

4

Lenses and Accessories

Focal length is related to enlargement in two ways: either the area included by the lens is larger or wider (characteristic of short focal-length or wide-angle lenses) or the image size itself is larger (in a long focal-length or telephoto lens compared to a normal lens). This bit of theory is behind an important reason for owning more than one focal-length lens. You cannot always move away from or closer to a subject (standing at the edge of the Grand Canyon is my favorite example), but you can vary the image by "seeing" the view through a different focal-length lens.

FOCAL LENGTH RELATED TO PERSPECTIVE

Perspective is the "drawing" of three-dimensional shapes in space on a two-dimensional surface, such as film or paper. Photographers often harbor a misconception that goes like this: Different focal-length lenses change perspective of a subject. The truth, however, is this: Perspective doesn't change with focal length; wide-angle lenses do not give expanded perspective, nor do telephoto lenses compress perspective—from a given viewpoint.

This misconception comes from confusing perspective with two other pictorial characteristics: *separation* and *relationships.* The word perspective does not denote the separation of the fore-and-aft parts of a photographic image. But relationships of foreground and background subjects *do* change as focal length is changed or not, *if* the camera point of view moves forward or backward to alter the image.

To illustrate this thesis, *PhotoGraphic's* technical editor, Mike Laurance, made a series of pictures of the same scene with four different lenses (24mm, 50mm, 100mm and 200mm). I have borrowed his pictures along with his theme condensed here from the December, 1972 issue of *Photographic Magazine.* Full-frame shots of the girl in the archway show the image size is doubled as the focal length doubles. However, perspective does *not* change because the camera position remains the same.

To demonstrate this, Mike enlarged the negatives made with each of the four lenses so the girl was the same size as she appears in the 200mm shot. Definition and grain size do change, since the 24mm negative required an eight-times enlargement to equal the image size of the 200mm lens, but all the pictures show exactly the same subject-to-background relationship.

However, when you shoot the same portion of a scene with different focal-length lenses, and you change camera position each time to accomplish this, there is a very noticeable change in perspective. This is demonstrated by Mike's third group of photos, shot from 12 feet with the 200mm lens, 6 feet with the 100mm lens, 3 feet with the 50mm lens and 1½ feet with the 24mm lens. Quoting Mike, "My problem with these pictures was that the perspective changed to the point that I found it difficult to maintain the same camera angle and the same subject size. If I had been able to move in closer on exactly the same axis as the center of the subject, the results would have been perfect. Though the results here are not perfect, you can easily see that while the subject size is almost constant, the perspective is completely different."

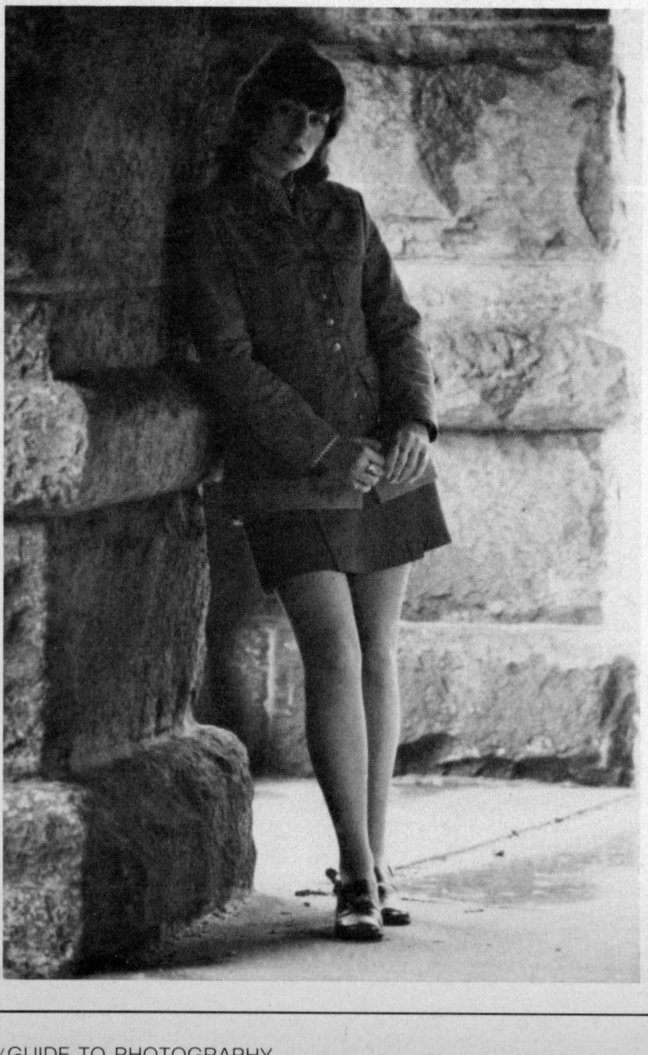

1

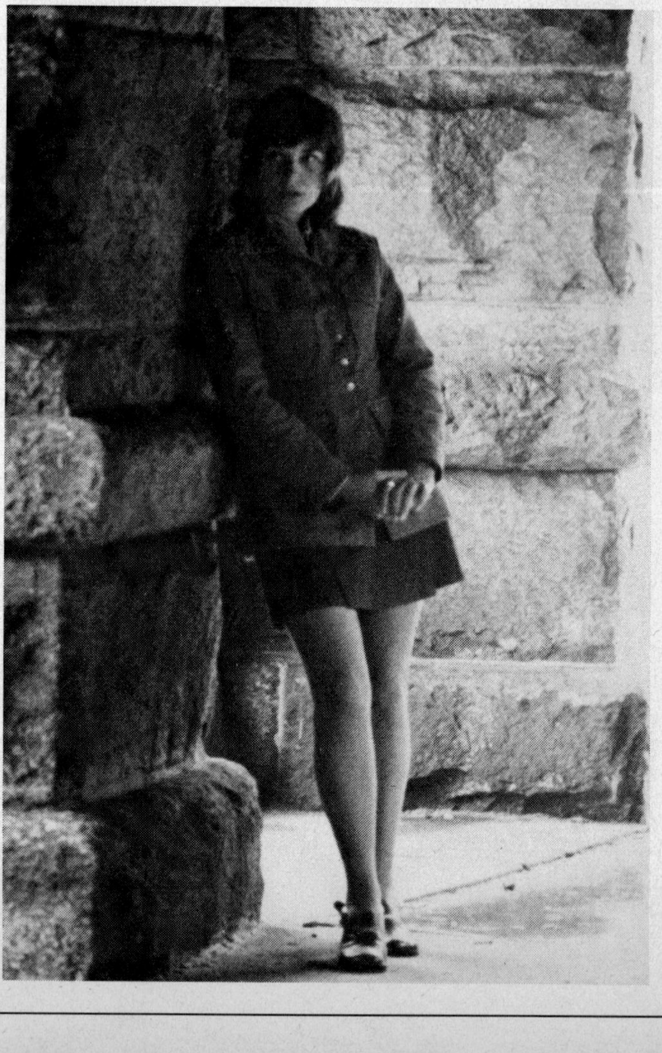

2

This establishes the distinction that perspective changes with point-of-view, creating different relationships between foreground and background objects. A three-story building recedes in perspective at a moderate rate with a 135mm lens, but the same building looms high and recedes steeply when photographed from a closer point with a 28mm or 21mm lens. There is a parallel between changing focal length of camera lenses and changing relationships of objects and the space around them as we see them with the naked eye, when our viewpoint shifts.

If you have a zoom lens, stand in one spot with it and adjust it forward and backward; image size changes, but perspective remains the same. Duplicate a single scene with a zoom or a variety of lenses by moving the camera's position, and watch perspective and spacial relationships change. Wide-angle lenses do "draw" with a kind of distortion that can add drama to a photo, or look very strange, depending on your subject and how close you are to it. Long telephoto lenses do compress perspective when compared to seeing the same scene with a normal lens, for instance, but you often need a telephoto to get a larger image when a shorter lens is inadequate. It's all a matter of optical illusions made possible by your involvement in the photographic process.

DEPTH OF FIELD

This is one photographic term you hear frequently in regard to lens performance and picture quality. Knowing how to increase or decrease depth of field is another means of making photography more than a casual hobby.

Depth of field is the distance range between the nearest and farthest objects or people in a scene *that will appear in acceptably sharp focus* in the finished print or slide. Three things govern depth of field: lens opening, lens focal length and the distance at which the lens is focused.

Aperture/ The larger the lens opening, the less depth of field you get at a given focal distance. The area in focus increases as a lens is stopped down. To check this, note the depth of field scale on the lens barrel of your SLR. There is a series of aperture numbers repeated on both sides of the center index mark. As you focus, depth of field for any lens opening is indicated between the f/ number on the left and its corresponding number on the right. Focus the lens and watch the depth of field range increase or decrease according to the distance you set.

Keep in mind that the indications on the camera depth of field scale are only approximate, but adequate to guide you while shooting. Depth of field tables are available for each lens focal length, should you want to study them.

1. Changing focal length does not change perspective, as this series demonstrates. This is full-frame view with a 200mm lens.

2. View with 100mm lens enlarged to give same image size as in 200mm shot shows identical perspective.

3. View with 50mm lens enlarged to give same image size as in 200mm shot shows no perspective change.

4. View with 24mm lens enlarged to give same image size as in 200mm shot shows a lot of grain because of great degree of enlargement, but the perspective is same as in 200mm shot.

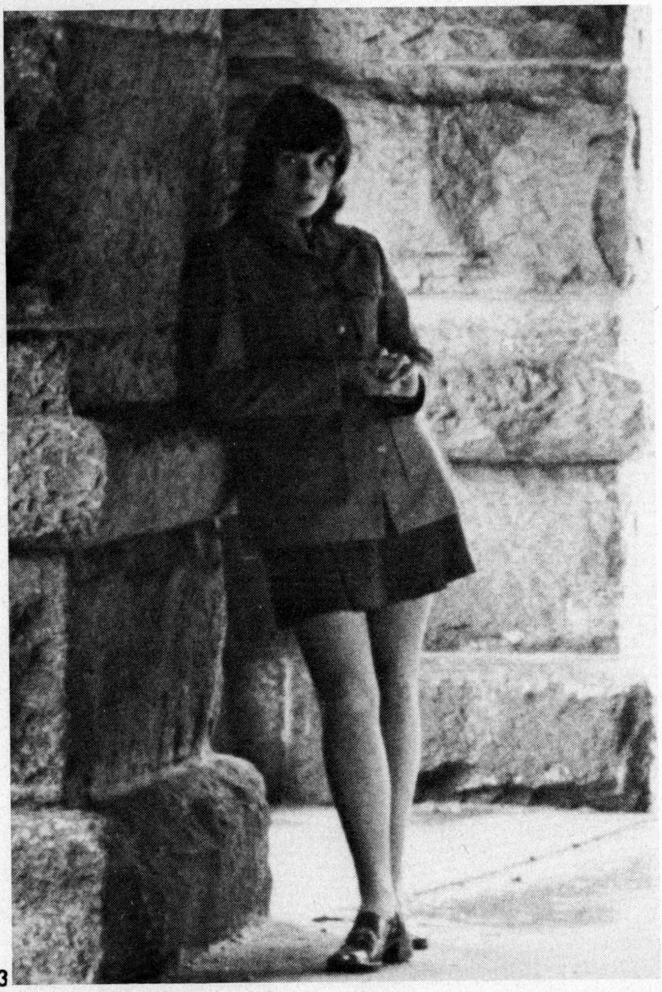

3

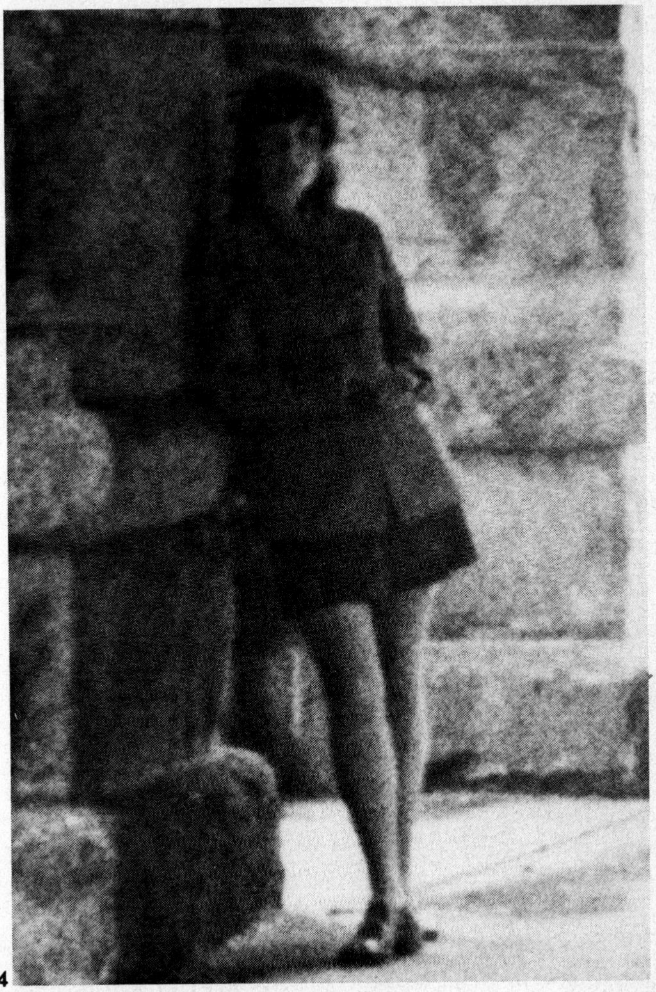

4

Lens focal length/ The diameter of the lens aperture plus the focal length of the lens are both used to determine depth of field via a formula you don't need here. What you should remember is this: The shorter the focal length of a lens, the greater the depth of field it produces at any given aperture. Here is a comparison to illustrate this for two lenses, each set at f/8 and focused at seven feet:

35mm lens—Depth of field runs between 5 feet and 12 feet

135mm lens—Depth of field runs between 6.3 feet and 7.8 feet

Purists may point out that those two lenses produce quite different size images of a given subject from seven feet. It is true that if you move back far enough with the 135mm lens to get the same image the 35mm lens encompasses at seven feet, you will also have equal depth of field. However in practical terms, choosing a lens for its depth of field characteristics is a lot more sensible than technical nitpicking!

Focusing distance/ This element of the depth of field story has been explained and applied. In summary, with any lens the closer you focus to an object the less its inherent depth of field. In reverse, the farther you focus from lens to subject, the greater the depth of field span.

Note/ Depth of field increases faster *behind* the plane of focus than in front of it. With a 35mm lens at f/16, focused at seven feet, compared to results mentioned previously at f/8, you will see the closest distance increases from 5 feet to 4 feet, but the farthest distance increases from 12 feet to about 80 feet. When you focus, and have depth of field in mind, choose a point or plane a little closer to the camera, knowing sharpness increases so much faster behind that focal distance.

It is also worth noting that sharpness falls off gradually before the eye can distinguish an area out of focus. This is apparent in prints and slides, and very noticeable when previewing depth of field through the finder of a single-lens reflex camera.

PARTING SHOT

I've discovered that many people operate a camera well enough, and *talk* a good line of photography, but don't really understand why some of their equipment and materials work they way they do. Depth of field, for instance, is often mistakenly called depth of focus, which refers to the distance range over which film might be shifted inside a camera, and still maintain sharp focus.

INTERCHANGEABLE LENSES

This is directed primarily to photographers using 35mm single-lens reflex cameras, though many lenses are also available for 35mm rangefinder models and 2¼x2¼ equipment as well. Since one of the chief assets of these versatile cameras is being able to choose from a variety of lenses made for them, this question soon faces the average photo hobbyist: What lens should I buy first, and after that one, what next?

As in the case of other photographic dilemmas, the answer lies in analyzing what sort of pictures you take, or will be taking, most often. Sports and action enthusiasts, as well as those turned on to portraits or landscapes, will choose a longer-than-normal lens such as the 85mm, 100mm, 135mm, or a zoom. If you

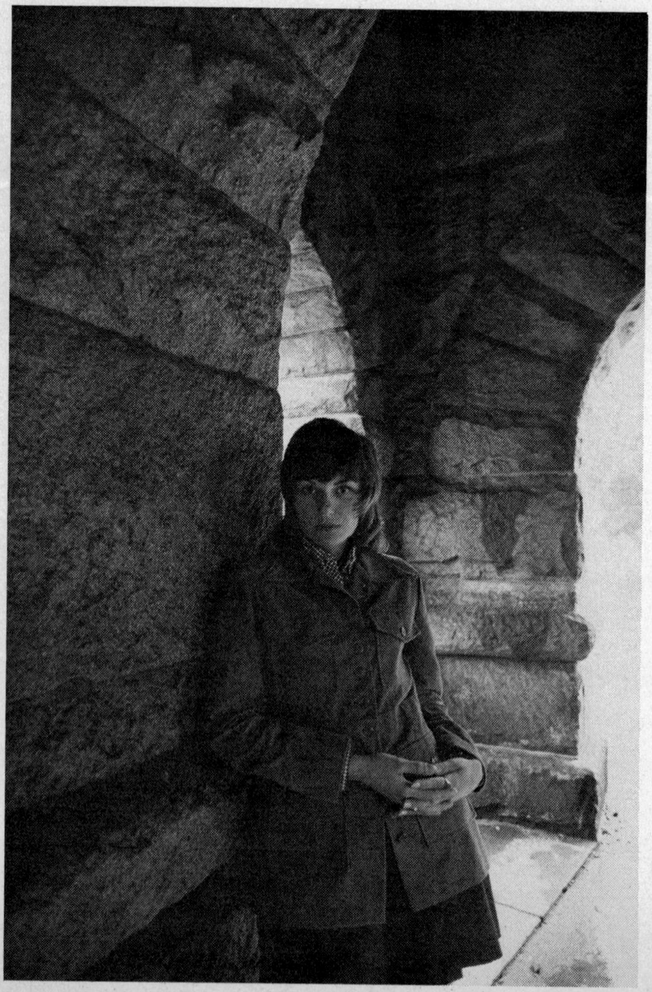

1

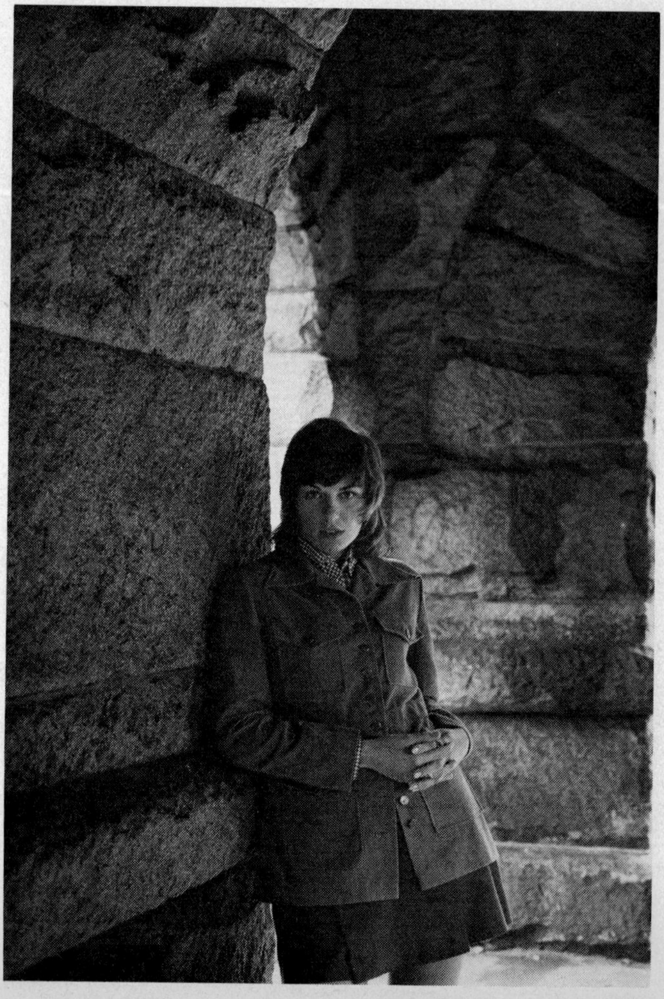

2

plan to shoot groups, nearby action, or in crowds, wide-angle lenses have priority. Let's examine each category of lens briefly.

WIDE-ANGLE LENSES

These focal lengths run generally from 20mm to 35mm, with apertures from f/1.5 to f/3.5. The most popular focal length is 35mm which falls midway between the short 20mm and the normal 50mm range. A leading feature of a wide-angle lens is its relatively great depth of field (discussed in detail in the next chapter) at a given aperture, compared to a normal or longer focal length lens. To illustrate this, note these figures for four lenses focused at seven feet and set at f/8:

52mm lens: Sharp focus extends from 5′11″ to 8′11″

35mm lens: From 5′ to 11′11″

28mm lens: From 4′3″ to 21′1″

21mm lens: From 3′4″ to infinity

In other words, in good light, or when light levels are low and you want to shoot without flash, you'll get better depth of field, or include more area in focus at larger apertures with a wide-angle lens. Or, if you are shooting fairly close to a mobile subject, such as kids playing football, you can set your nearest distance on the depth of field scale opposite the aperture mark you are using and get a relatively wide range of focus with a short focal length lens. This is called zone focusing (more in Chapter 4). With a 28mm lens at f/8, focused at 7 feet, you can move around freely and get sharp images from about 4 feet to 21 feet.

A wide-angle lens is not recommended for portraits, however, because it tends to distort things close-up. You've seen caricature-like faces taken with a 21mm lens, for instance, with huge noses and tiny ears. When distortion makes an image more striking or interesting, of course, a wide-angle lens can't be beat.

Focusing with a wide-angle lens on a single-lens reflex camera may present difficulty because differences of sharpness are less distinguishable on the small ground glass. Some people like a split-image rangefinder in the SLR finder to prevent this problem. Zone focusing is another alternative to seeing wide-angle sharpness with an SLR.

A well-equipped photographer has at least one wide-angle lens, but which focal length you choose, and in what sequence of time, is a personal matter. Try a number of them on your camera at the place you shop, and discuss their pros and cons with knowledgeable sales people. There is a great divergence of price from least to most expensive, but I've found some inexpensive models quite sharp. Don't buy a preset lens in any focal length (except 300mm or longer, which may not be made with automatic diaphragms) to save money. The slightly higher price of an automatic diaphragm—which stops itself down to the setting you select, and opens wide again after each exposure—is worth paying for in

1. Perspective does change when the position of the camera relative to the subject changes. This is a full-frame view with 24mm lens at 4½ feet.

2. Full-frame view with 50mm lens at 9 feet gives same subject size, but different perspective.

3. Full-frame view with 100mm lens at 18 feet gives same subject size but perspective changes again.

4. Full-frame view with 200mm lens at 36 feet gives same subject size and changed perspective once again. This series shot by Mike Laurance.

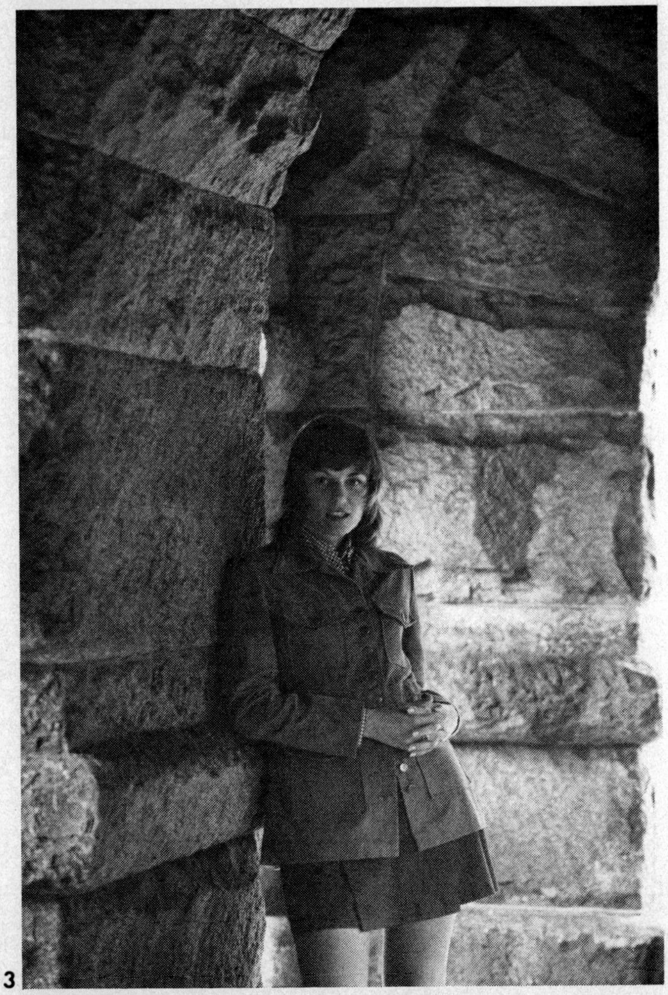

3

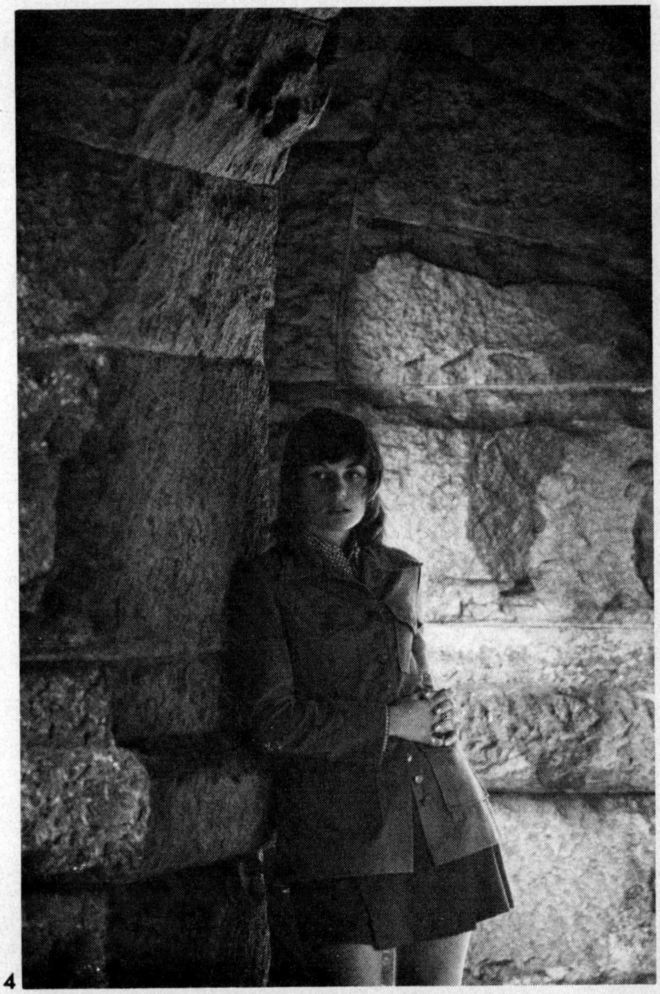

4

terms of convenience, saving time, and more consistently exposed film.

NORMAL LENSES

You are pretty much confined to the lenses that are supplied with your camera, usually 50mm, 52mm, 55mm or 57mm. Normal focal lengths are useful for many types of shooting, from portraits to seascapes, and an f/1.8 or f/2 lens is adequate. Larger apertures such as f/1.4 or f/1.2, mean more weight and cost, and I am convinced the average amateur doesn't need so much heavy glass to achieve very limited advantages to shooting in low light levels without flash or flood. Faster films compensate very nicely for making "candid" pictures that were once so novel.

SEMITELEPHOTO LENSES

This category ranges from 85mm to 135mm and has intermediate focal lengths of 100mm and 105mm. One of these is first choice for portraits, "reaching out" at landscape details or getting larger images of distant players at sports events. Again, you'll have to try several focal lengths on your camera, and choose the one

1
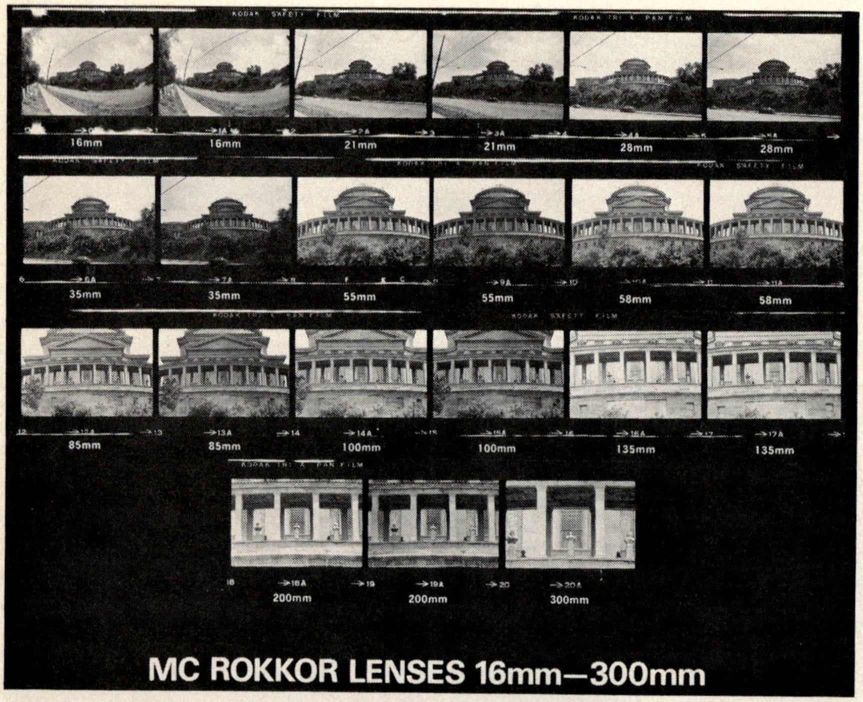

2
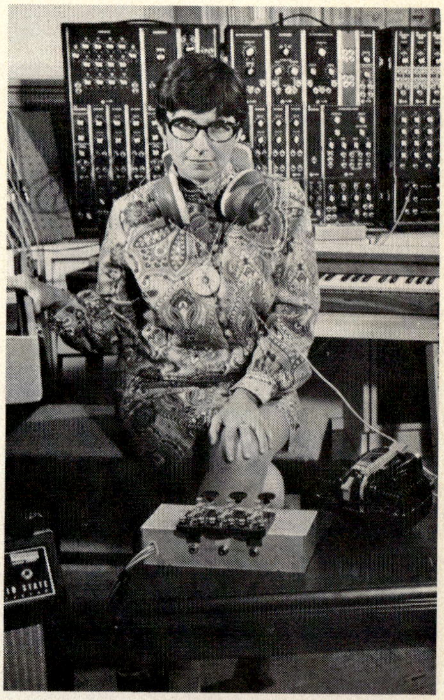

3
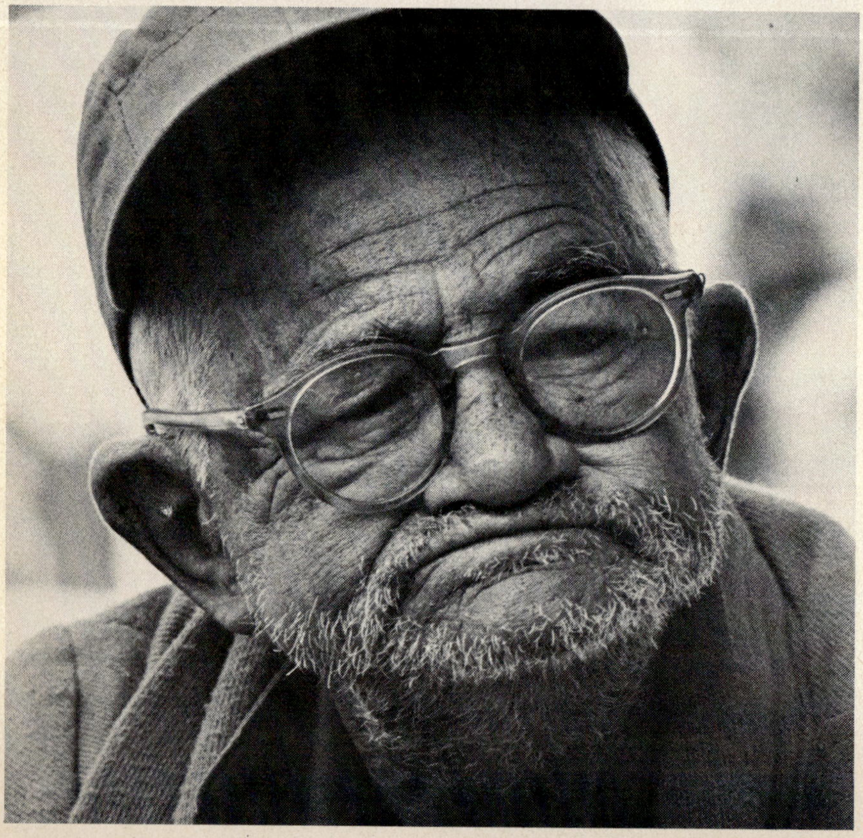

4
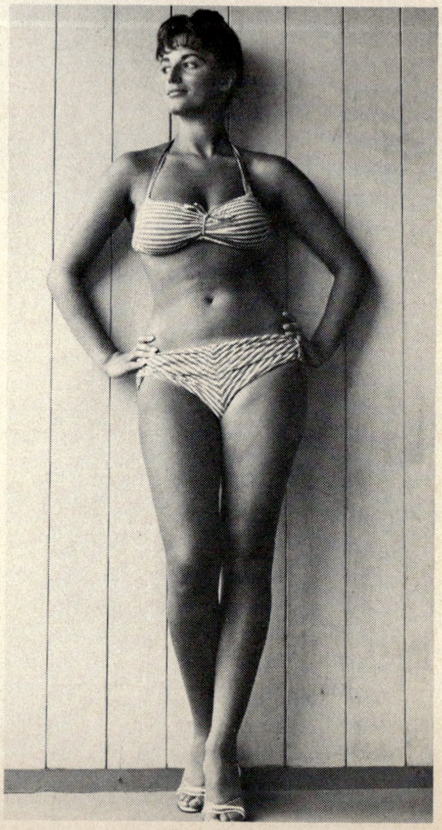

that seems to best fit your particular needs. Prices vary widely, according to manufacturer and store, but modern semitelephoto lenses are lightweight with retractable lens hoods, making them a delight to use.

TELEPHOTO LENSES

Along with very wide-angle optics, these seem to be the "glamour" lenses, perhaps because they are the least conventional lenses today. Focal lengths start around 200mm and include 300mm, 400mm, 500mm and up. Only a minority of serious photo hobbyists will benefit enough to warrant purchase of a telephoto lens longer than 300mm. Their weight and price are also deterrents, because a telephoto lens can feel like a miniature canon hanging from your neck. Consider a zoom lens ranging up to 200mm before you decide on one of these three- or four-pound whoppers.

ZOOM LENSES

In the longer-than-normal class, zooms are probably favored more today than ever, and new models seem to be introduced every month. Focal lengths range from 43mm to 86mm (one Nikkor lens only), 55mm to 135mm, 80mm to 200mm, 85mm to 205mm, etc. Modern zoom lenses are more carefully made than when they were introduced around 20 years ago, which means they produce sharper images (almost equal to most individual focal length lenses) and operate more smoothly. Though a zoom lens may cost twice as much as one semitelephoto lens, and more than a telephoto lens, if you don't mind carrying a little extra weight, a zoom lens can be a very practical investment. It precludes your having to buy a series of other lenses, so shop the field carefully, even when you're looking for a lens that's your first other-than-normal optic.

NOTE

No lens is as sharp at its widest aperture as it is stopped down to the f/4 to f/11 range. Today's lenses are designed with many glass elements, either cemented together or separated by carefully calculated air spaces. No matter how deftly these elements are shaped and polished, a lens has slight aberrations (distortions in definition) wide open. Only the center portions of a lens are in use when it is stopped down, and hence the improved sharpness often noted in camera magazine tests. However, almost all lenses are made and inspected with such technical attention today that you can be confident when you

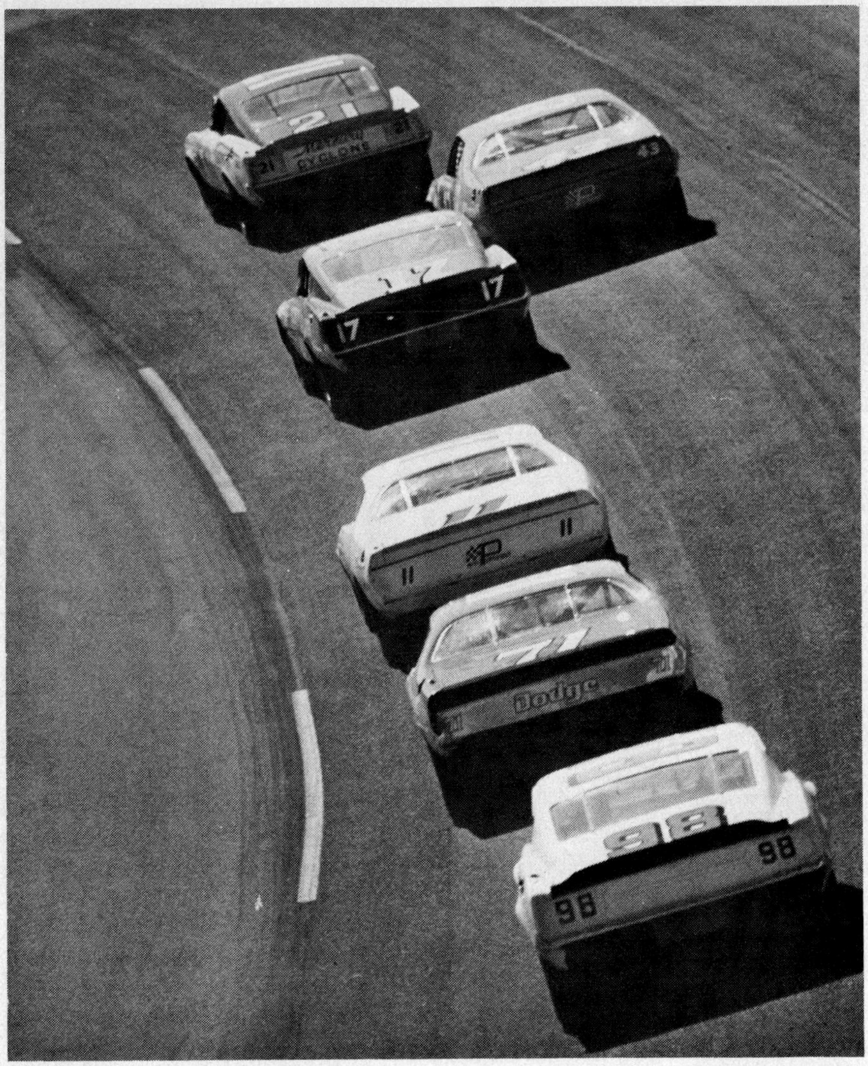

5

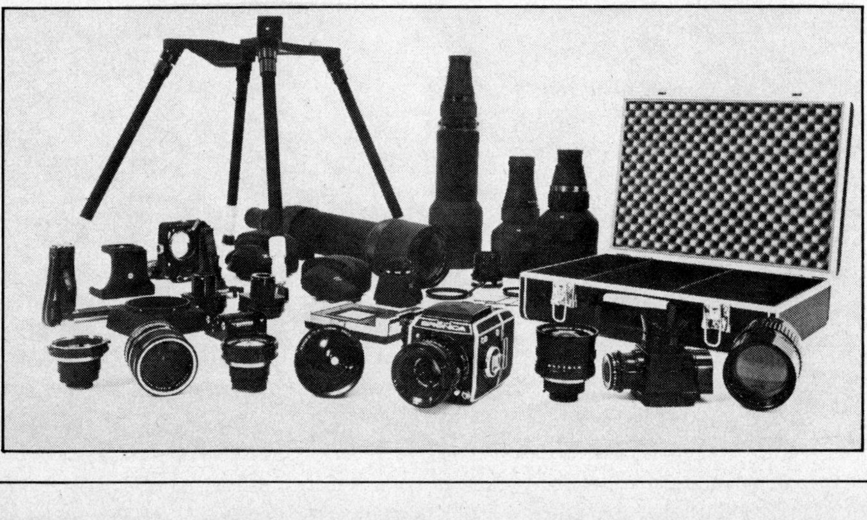
6

1. Two frames each were shot with a series of MC Rokkor lenses, beginning with wide-angle 16mm. All were made from same camera position for dramatic comparison of focal lengths. Note characteristic curvature with 16mm lens, absent in modern 21mm lens.

2. Sharp lens can make sharp photos.

3. Ron Contarsy used a 105mm lens to keep a distance from this old man for a candid portrait that won a Scholastic/Kodak Award for him.

4. Though wide-angle lens is not recommended for portraits (too much distortion), a 35mm lens worked well for this figure shot on balcony where the author could move back only a limited distance from shapely subject.

5. Photographer Bob D'Olivo produced "telephoto look" with his 300mm lens that compacted the race cars, making them appear closer together.

6. Many cameras come in "systems" with complete line of lenses.

buy one from a dealer's stock to take it home and start shooting. In your first prints or slides you'll be able to judge its sharpness. If you get a very rare lemon, take it back and exchange it for another.

SPECIAL LENSES

These include superwide angle lenses such as the fisheye, which practically includes your feet in every frame, and macro lenses designed especially for close-up photography. Superwide photographic effects are fun, but the lenses for them may be a luxury. There are also fisheye add-on attachment lenses at lower prices. On the other hand, a macro lens might be a necessity, since it will focus as close as one inch from a subject. The usual macro lens focal length is 55mm.

LENS EXTENDERS

Made for specific magnification, such as 2X and 3X, extenders are auxiliary lenses that fit between the camera body and another lens. With a 2X extender, for instance, a 50mm lens becomes 100mm (and at the same time f/2 becomes f/4). Optically, using an extender slightly reduces image sharpness, but not enough to prevent your investigating these relatively inexpensive (under $30) additions to your equipment. Be sure the extender you buy for an SLR allows continued use of the normal lens automatic diaphragm.

CLOSE-UP ATTACHMENT LENSES

For under $20 you can buy a set of three lenses that alone or in combination will permit you to shoot with a normal camera lens from its closest focusing distance up to about six inches from a subject. Attachment lenses are not as versatile nor as sharp as a macro lens, but are more than adequate for average use. Also available are variable focus or zoom-type close-up lenses that also screw into the front of the camera lens, taking the place of multiple close-up lens attachments. Chapter 10 covers photography of small objects and copying in more detail.

FILTERS

These circles and squares of glass or gelatin are made in a variety of colors to alter the way light affects film, either for correction to make a scene seem more "natural," or for pictorial purposes. The number and type of filters you need depends on the kinds of film you shoot, the light sources, and often, your imagination.

Filters for black-and-white films/ Filters change the color of the light that strikes the film by absorbing (subtracting) all colors but their own from the light. (Colored filters may be used with color films to tint slides or prints proportionate to the filter's color saturation for pictorial effects.)

White, or "colorless" light is actually composed of every color in the spectrum; these are broken down, in physics to the primary colors: red, blue and green. (Note: These are primary colors of *light,* not to be confused with the artist's primary colors of *pigments* which are red, blue and

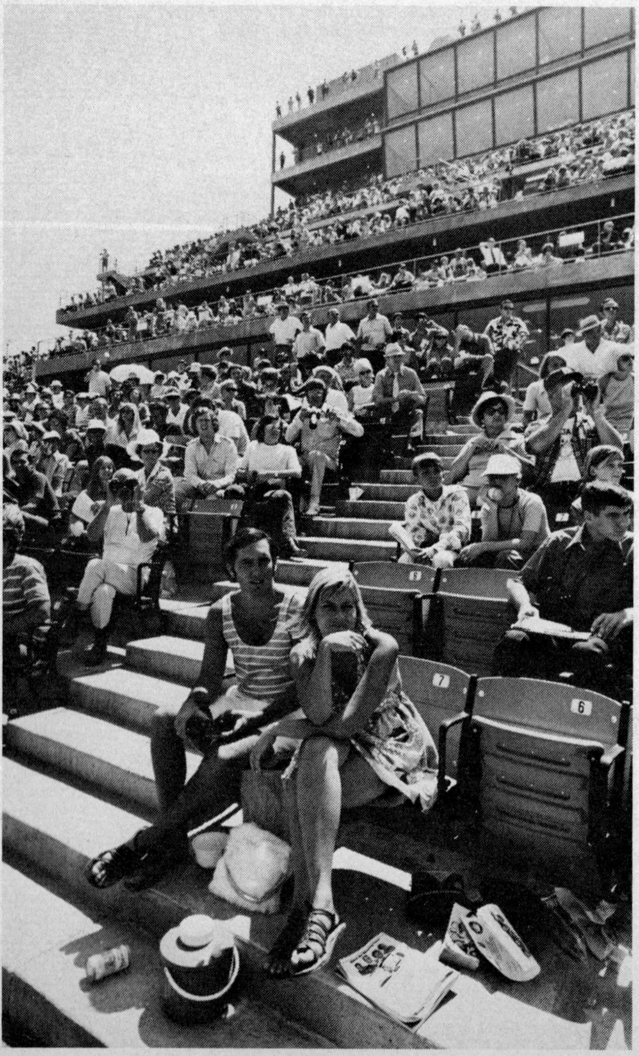
1

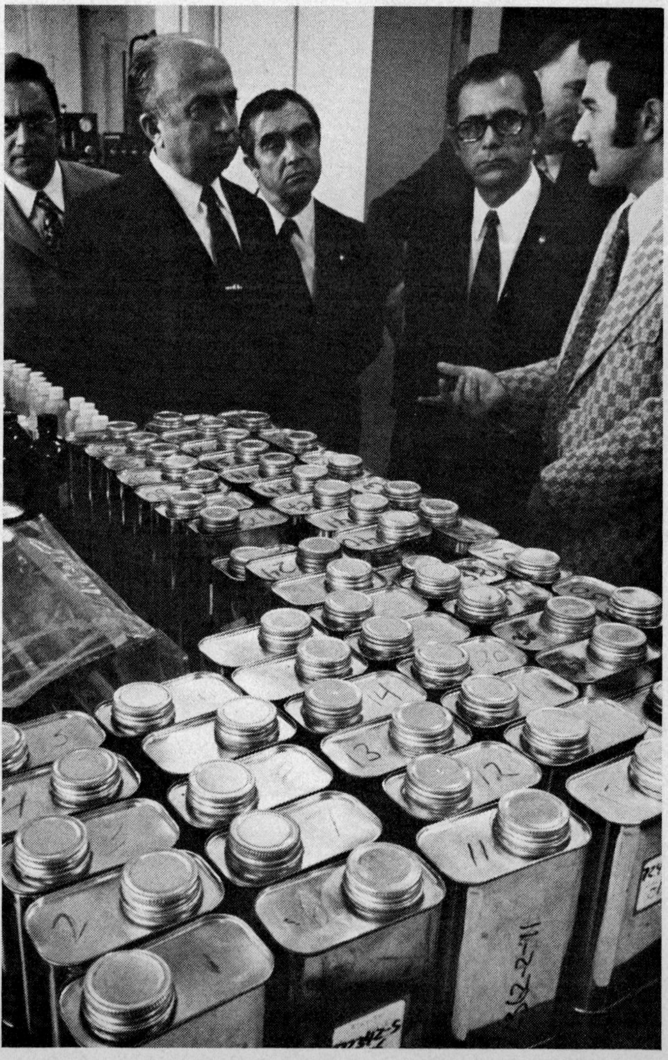
2

yellow.) Practically every other color can be produced by combinations of the primary colors. Red plus blue equal magenta (or purple in some vocabularies), blue plus green equal cyan, and red plus green equal yellow. The last combination sounds strange, but it is a law of physics.

Each colored filter serves to subtract its complementary color, or those that are opposite. Thus a red filter subtracts blue and green (or cyan) light, letting only red light pass. A magenta filter absorbs green light, and lets red and blue (magenta) light pass. A cyan filter absorbs red light, and lets only blue and green (cyan) light pass.

When you photograph an outdoor scene on black-and-white film, there are usually two main colors: blue sky and green foliage. Blue tends to come out lighter in a print than we expect because daylight contains a lot of blue and ultraviolet (UV) to which most black-and-white films are more sensitive than our eyes are. Therefore, the sky produces more density on a negative than it should, and so prints lighter than it should. To correct this, or better emphasize the blue, you choose a yellow filter, which is blue's complement. The yellow filter, such as a K2 (old Kodak designation), absorbs just enough of the blue and violet to reproduce them naturally on film and later in a print. Should you wish to lighten green foliage, a green filter will do this by absorbing variations of red, giving added contrast to greens, which appear lighter in a print. A green filter also provides more pleasing flesh tones in portraits while giving blue sky a slightly darker value in prints.

So much for filters to emphasize the "normal" look of things. What about accentuating colors to dramatize a scene? The answer lies in using a darker filter to absorb the color, such as a red or orange filter instead of yellow to snap up the contrast between white clouds and a blue sky. Without a filter, unless you are photographing where the air is very clear and the sky is fairly dark blue, sky and clouds may tend to blend together in tonality. The orange (G) or red (A) filter, by absorbing more blue, makes the sky register lighter-than-normal on a negative and darker-than-normal on a print. You have seen dramatic red-filter shots of clouds and sky when the latter is almost black. (The last word for such an effect is a red filter with infrared film, which is insensitive to green,

1. By using a 21mm lens at f/16 and 1/500 second on Tri-X, author was able to guarantee depth of field from foreground to distant background. Extreme wide-angle lenses are very useful in tight situations.

2. Depth of field is graphically illustrated by overall sharpness from foreground cans to background figures. Taken with 28mm lens at f/11, 1/30 second on Tri-X, reference was made to camera's depth-of-field scale.

3. This pair of pictures by photographer-editor Mike Laurance shows the relationship between aperture and depth of field. Wide aperture (in this case f/2.8) decreased depth of field to frame model Jan Carpenter in out-of-focus leaves in foreground and background. In second shot, with lens set to f/16, the leaves are sharp.

3

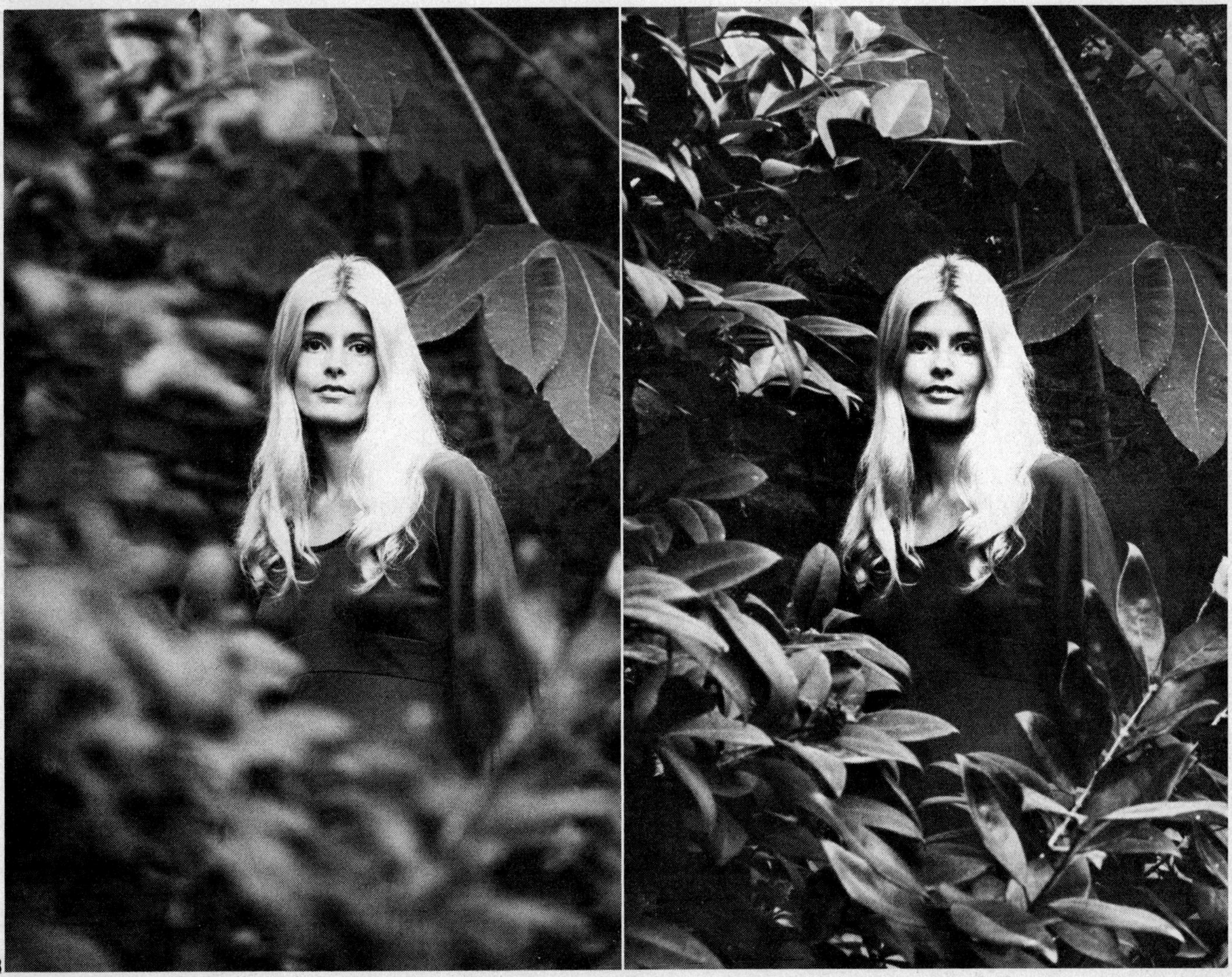

and causes foliage to come out looking white or pale gray in a print. The contrast can be weird and striking.)

Filter factors/ These are simply numbers which tell you how much to increase exposure when using a given filter. A filter factor of two means the exposure time must be doubled or increased by one stop, etc. You may also alter exposure by changing the shutter speed, but shifting f/stops may be more convenient to get intermediate steps for factors that call for one-half a stop. If you use a hand-held light meter, divide the filter factor into the normal ASA rating of the film and reset your meter accordingly. As an example, with an ASA 125 film, a filter factor of two would mean resetting the film speed to ASA 64. Be sure to go back to normal ASA speed when you're not using a filter.

Filter factors are influenced by the light source and the filters involved, and should be thought of as approximate until you make your own tests. What is more, if you use a filter on a camera with a built-in through-the-lens meter system, filter factors usually need not be considered because the meter compensates automatically. However, light meters don't necessarily respond to colors the same way film does, so experiment at first to understand the response of your own equipment.

Haze filters/ True atmospheric haze scatters a lot of blue and ultraviolet light, and black-and-white film's excess sensitivity to these bands of the spectrum will give you a photograph with more haze in it than was in the original scene. A yellow filter will absorb enough blue and UV to make things look at least as natural as the original scene. Deep yellow and red filters that absorb more blue and UV give even more haze reduction.

Keep in mind that colored filters are effective only when there is color present. You can't darken an overcast gray sky or cut through white mist, because there's no color there to absorb.

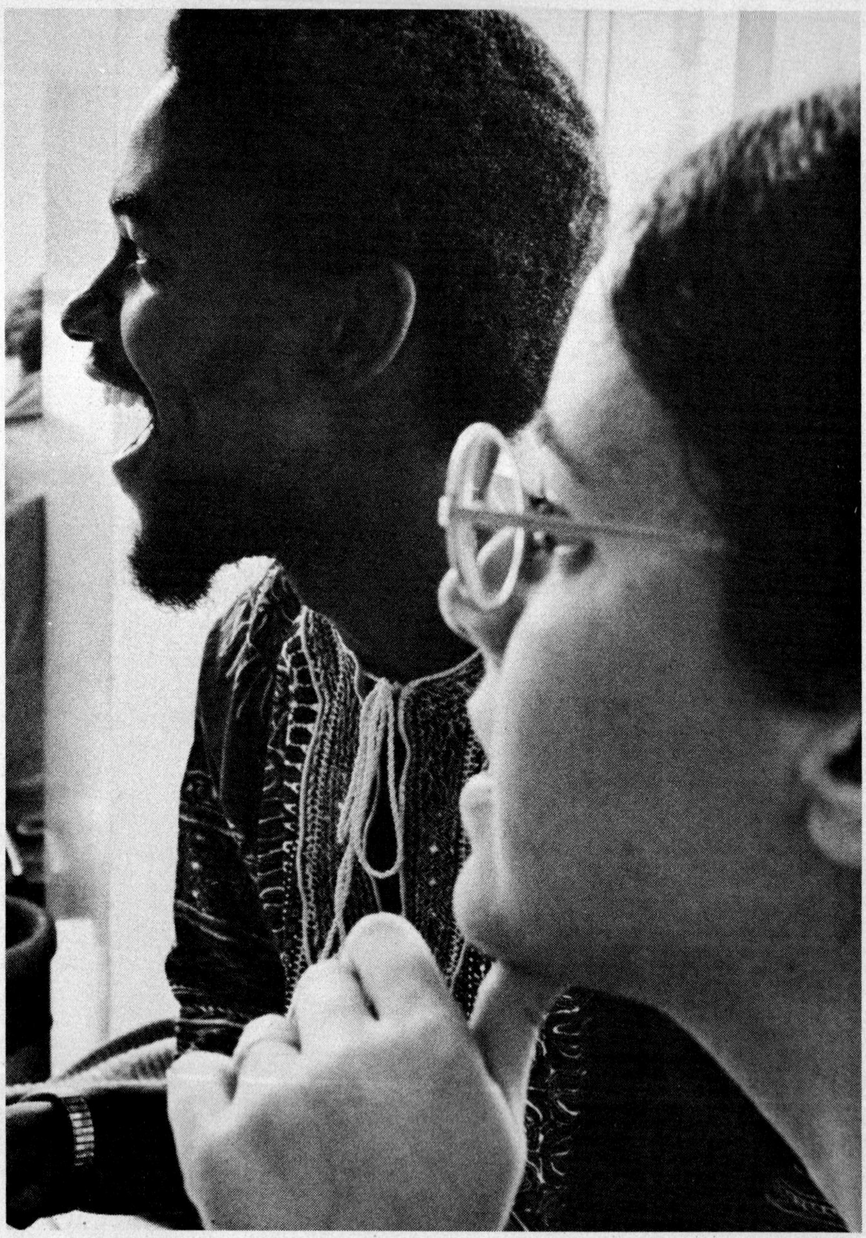

1

Filters for color films/ Most often used is the skylight (1A) filter which is pale pink, has no filter factor, and absorbs some blue light along with some UV. The skylight filter is used with daylight color slide films to remove the bluish cast and warm up color in general when pictures are taken in the shade or on overcast days. Color negative films don't need a skylight filter because they can be corrected, if necessary, during printing. And when one of the 85 series of conversion filters is used to convert indoor color film for outdoor photography, the skylight's correction is included.

An ultraviolet (UV) filter, sometimes called a haze filter, does not penetrate haze, but reduces the bluish cast in distant scenes caused by scattering of UV rays in the atmosphere. If there's no UV there, the filter does nothing, but it has no filter factor, looks like clear glass, and some photographers leave the haze filter on the lens all the time to protect it from finger marks and scratches.

Unless a colored filter is used with color film for effect, e.g., to tint or exaggerate existing colors, the principal use of other filters is to convert or balance a particular color emulsion to a specific light source. The color quality of light is measured, as you may know, in degrees Kelvin (K). Daylight is between 5500 and 6500°K, an overcast cast sky may be 10,000, photoflood bulbs are 3400°K (for Type A film) or 3200°K (for Type B film), and the average living room lamp light is about 2900°K The higher the Kelvin temperature, the colder (bluer) the light, while lower Kelvin temperature light is warmer (more red). Though the eye does not make these color distinctions ordinarily, film is manufactured with specific response to render color accurately in a fairly narrow range of degrees Kelvin. Daylight film exposed by photoflood illumination will have an overall red cast, maybe objectionably warm toned. Tungsten films exposed in daylight will have an overall blue appearance, which is usually annoying, but may be useful if you want a cold-toned picture.

Fortunately, films balanced for daylight can be exposed by tungsten

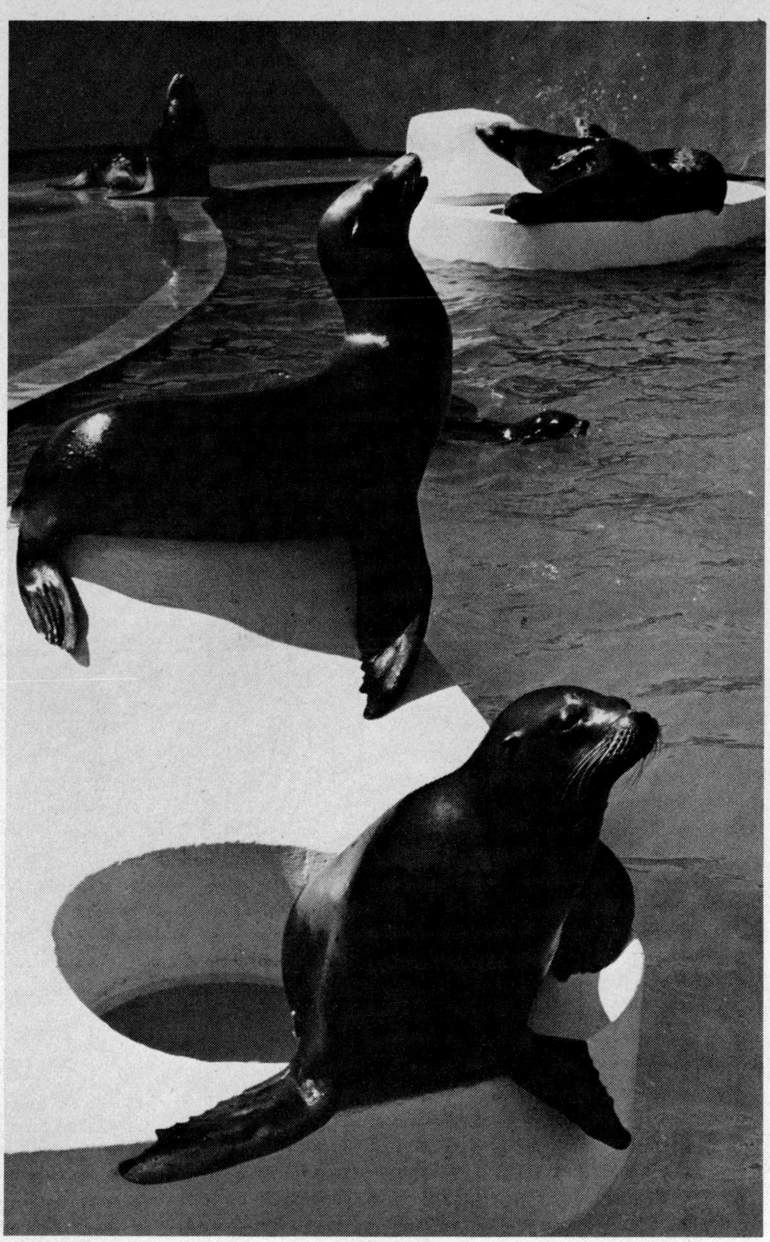

2

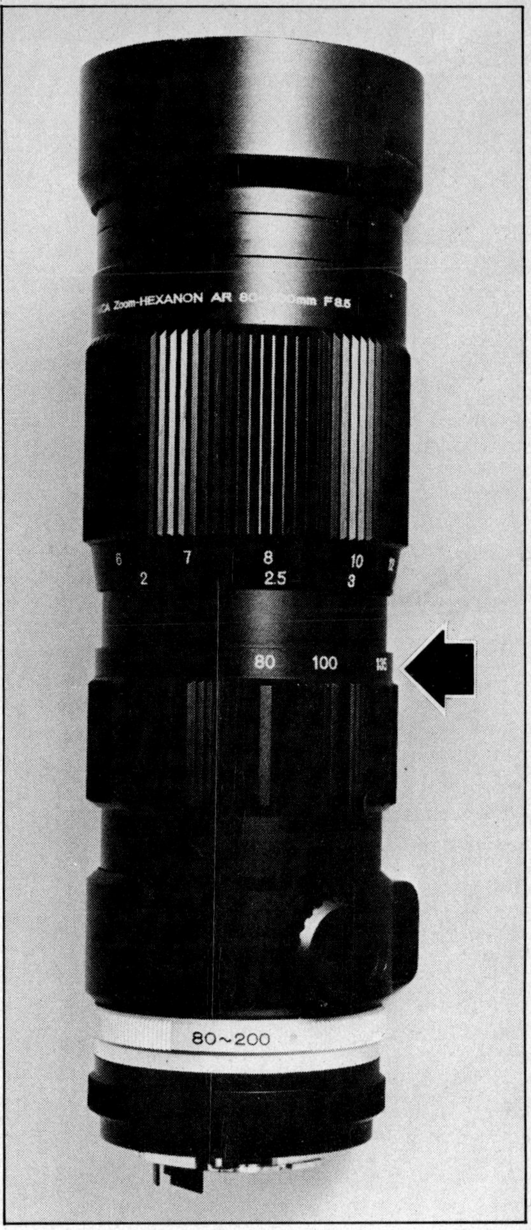

3

light, and vice versa, with normal results, if the proper filter is used to convert the color temperature of the light source to match the film in use. Conversion filters come in two series: the 85 series warms daylight sufficiently to balance it for tungsten type color films (85 with Type A film and 85B with Type B film). The 80 series cools the light by absorbing enough yellow to convert daylight films for use in tungsten (photoflood) illumination (80A for 3200°K bulbs and 80B for 3400°K photofloods). Other conversion filters are used to correct the color of light from flashbulbs for daylight films. The chart shows the most important filters to use for color film correction.

Color compensating filters/ This group (known as CC filters) is made in six colors—red, blue, green, magenta, cyan and yellow—and in various densities. They allow the amount of color absorbed, or the correction to be made, to be closely controlled. CC filters may be designated by film manufacturers to precisely correct a specific emulsion for deficiencies due to manufacturing tolerances. A CC2OY filter, for instance, is yellow with a density of .20 to absorb blue light, while allowing red and green light to pass. CC filters make small changes and are necessary for only a limited number of uses by the average photo hobbyist.

Filters for Polacolor/ Polaroid Land color films are balanced exclusively for daylight, blue flashbulbs or electronic flash, which can be a handicap when you want to shoot indoors by photofloods. In such a case, Tiffen makes an 82OB filter for use with 3200 and 3400°K floodlights, and an 84OB filter for use in ordinary room light using 75W to 150W lamps. Correction may not be perfect, but the objectionable warm tones you would get without a filter are eliminated.

Fluorescent light filters/ One of the trickiest light sources in which to shoot color films is fluorescent light

1. Because camera was very close to foreground face, at f/8 there was not enough depth of field to capture the girl sharply, though the man further from the lens is in sharp focus. Lens was 35mm; 1/125 second.

2. Taken with normal 52mm lens, this picture is sharp from foreground to background because author carefully set camera focus within the depth-of-field distance marks for f/16.

3. Zoom lens has focal-length scale (arrow) as well as usual scales.

that affects color film in a variety of ways (all of them annoying), depending on the color of the fluorescent tubes. The tubes are made in tints such as warm white, cool white, white and daylight. Their spectrum is unlike tungsten bulbs, and without a filter, color slides come out with a blue-green cast that makes people look like Martians. As Kodak says in its Data Book E-76 *(Applied Color Photography Indoors),* "The best color photograph made by fluorescent lighting involves some compromise."

If you know exactly what type of fluorescent tubes are in use at a specific location, in Data Book E-76 is a chart of color compensating filters for Type A and B films as well as Kodacolor-X. Combinations of magenta, cyan and yellow CC filters are recommended, and I refer you to that chart for precise work in fluorescent illumination.

However, there's an easier way, because it is usually impractical to hoist yourself up to the ceiling to learn the exact color of fluorescent lamps. Besides, it isn't necessary to take time experimenting, or spend money on a stock of CC filters, if you need not be too critical about your photographs. The simple answer is fluorescent light filters that correct for blue-green flesh tones and give rooms a more natural appearance. These compromise filters, each with a factor of two, are the Tiffen FLB (for Type B films) and FLD (for daylight films). They are the expedient way to shoot, and though color correction may not be perfect, skin tones look more naturally warm and pleasing enough under most circumstances.

Filters for either color or black-and-white films/ The first of these are neutral density filters, made in various shades of gray with no effect on colors being photographed. Neutral density filters are valuable to decrease the intensity of light, especially when you are shooting with fast films in bright sun, and can't stop the lens down far enough for proper exposures. For instance, when I rate my Tri-X at EI 1000 for indoor pictures, and have to shoot outdoors on the same roll, I use an ND filter. A 2X ND filter cuts the light in half (open one stop), a 4X ND filter cuts the light two stops and an 8X ND filter cuts it three stops. They are very handy to prevent overexposure.

Neutral density filters are also helpful when you want to use a larger lens opening to decrease depth of field and throw a confusing background out of focus. If the meter reads f/16 at 1/250 second, an ND 4X filter will alter exposure to f/8 where you will have better control of depth of field.

Harrison & Harrison market a special ND filter called a graduate-clear-to-neutral filter which is half clear, blending to half neutral density. It is

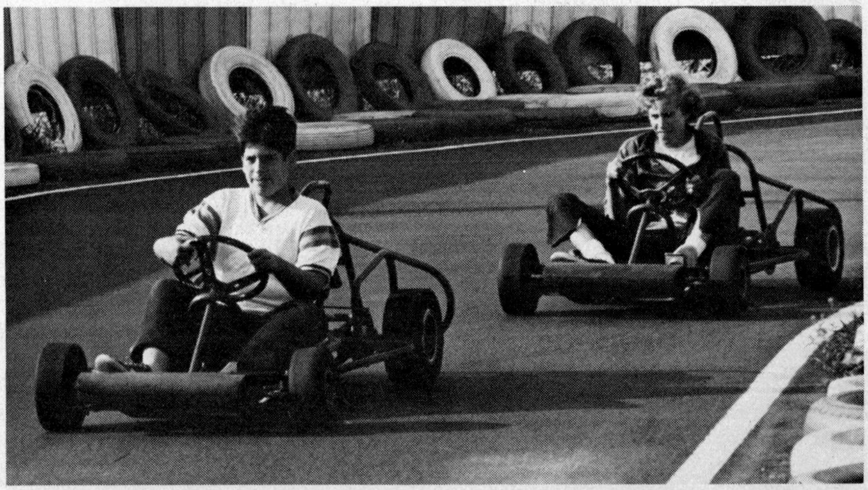

1

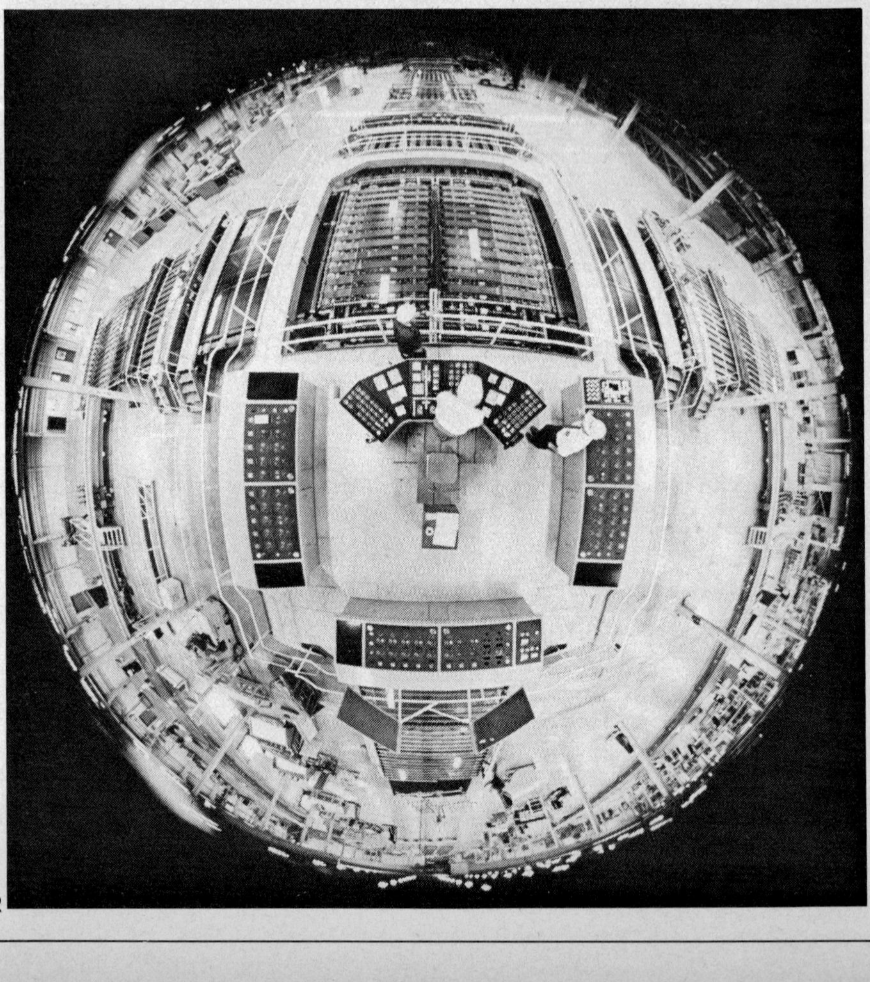

2

1. Following kids with 80-200mm zoom lens made keeping them within useful image size, close or distant, easy for author, who exposed Tri-X for 1/1000 second at f/11 to make shot.

2. Special fish-eye lens produced eye-catching view of plate-glass production line at PPG Industries. Other ultra-wide-angle lenses such as 16 or 18mm do not cut corners, but fish-eye produces a circular image.

3. Photographer-editor Jim Cornfield shot series of six pictures showing zoom lens as composition tool. Pictures in top sequence were shot with 55mm lens at progressively shorter distances from model. In pictures in bottom sequence, image size was increased by altering focal length of 55-135mm zoom lens from a constant distance. Pictures at left, both taken with 55mm focal lengths are similar, but pictures at center and right of bottom row (at 90 and 135mm settings on zoom) show striking differences in perspective. Zoom allows easy selective cropping without concern for camera-to-subject distance.

useful on scenes where the foreground is rather dark, for instance, and the background is very bright, such as a partly cloudy sky. There could be four or five stops difference between foreground and sky, and the graduate-clear-to-neutral filter can reduce that difference to a ratio the film's latitude can handle. It cuts down the sky's brightness without affecting the foreground when placed correctly.

The second filter for either color or black-and-white films is the Polarizer. It eliminates annoying reflections from nonmetallic surfaces, makes colors richer, and is the only filter that will darken a blue sky without affecting the other colors in a scene. The Polarizer works by reducing light rays that are vibrating in only one direction such as light from a blue sky or from surface reflections (except from metal). It is easy to use a Polarizer by simply holding it up to the scene and rotating it. When you see reflections reduced, you simply place the filter over the lens in the same position. You can do this right on a single-lens reflex camera, and what you see in the finder is what you will get on film. The Polarizer has a factor of 2.5, but a built-in camera meter compensates for this automatically. This filter is somewhat expensive, but what it does and the control it gives you are worth the investment.

Buying filters/ With so many filters available, which ones will be most useful to you? It is extravagant to own more filters than you need, and they take up too much room in a gadget bag as well. However, there is a basic set to consider, depending on the type of films and subjects you usually shoot.

For black-and-white photography, a

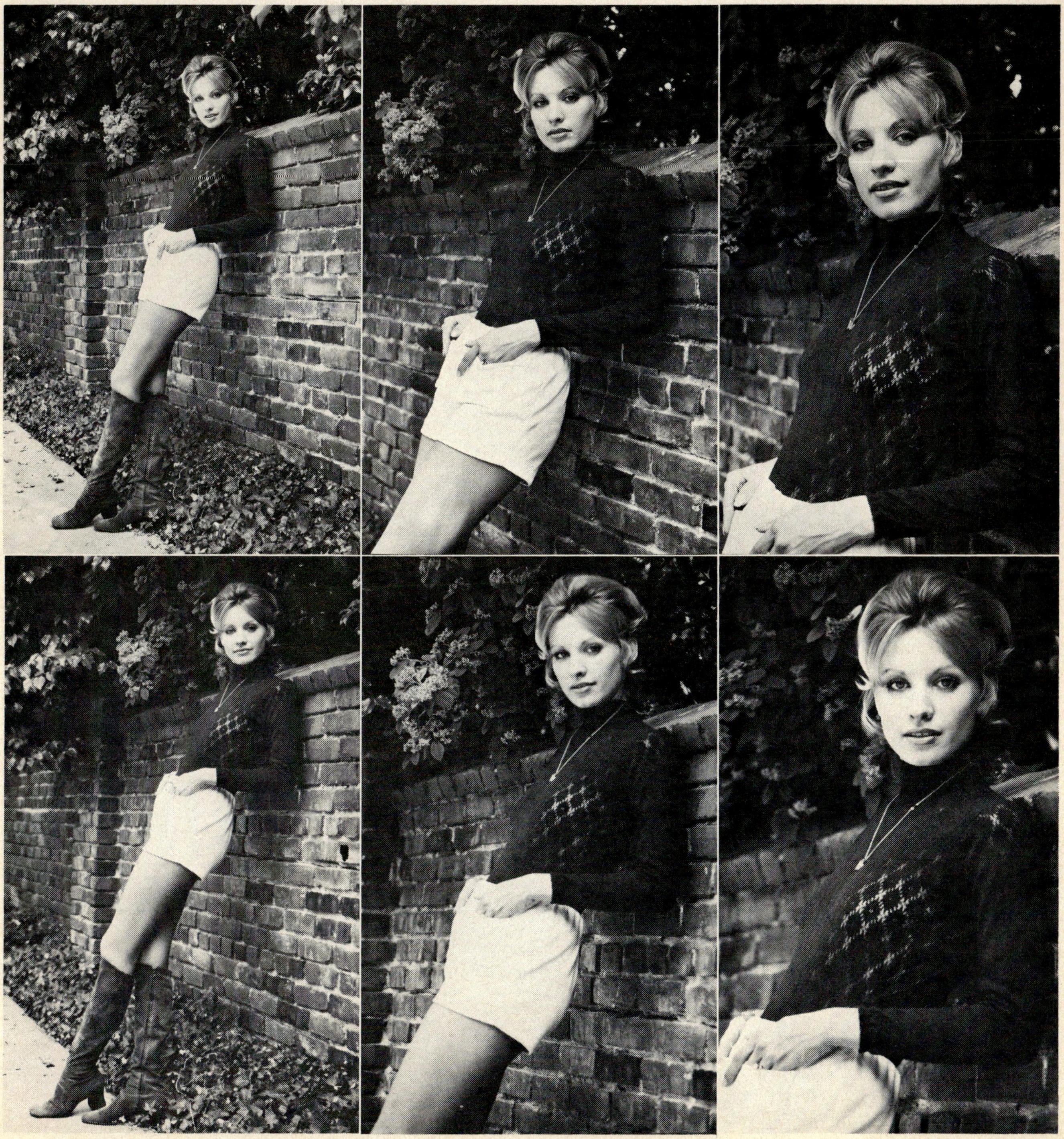

3

medium yellow such as the K2, a deeper yellow or orange, a red such as the 25A and a green are all helpful for outdoor scenes, flesh tones, dramatic clouds and other effects. Add the Polarizer to the list for black-and-white or color films.

For color work, conversion filters are necessary if you intend to switch from shooting tungsten film indoors to outdoor scenes, or vice versa. A skylight filter is a must for warming colors in the shade and on overcast days, and a UV filter cuts some haze in distant scenes and doubles as a lens protector.

Filters are made in three forms: gelatin, solid glass and laminated glass. Not all filters are available in all the types, but the most commonly used ones are.

Gelatin filters come in 2-, 3-, 4- and 5-inch squares, are the least expensive, the most precisely colored, scratch easily, and are the hardest to handle. Glass filters are more durable (though they should be treated as delicately as lenses), and probably most practical. Laminated filters (gelatin between two pieces of glass) require more care than glass alone, but are often more precisely colored than the glass ones.

Store filters in a cool, dry, dark place because they may fade in time, especially the gelatin and laminated types. If a filter has been stored for several years, you might test it before doing any critical work.

Filters come in various sizes to screw into the front of a lens or drop into a ring between lens and lens hood. You can buy step-up or step-down adapter rings to fit one size of filter to another size of lens diameter, so there is no need to buy duplicate filters for different cameras or lenses in most cases.

EXPOSURE METERS

Facts about exposure meters are covered here, while theory and use of meters follows in Chapter 5 under "Outdoor Exposure."

Actually, many 35mm SLR owners may feel that learning more about meters is superfluous, since their cameras have built-in meters that work quite reliably—except in certain circumstances. Those circumstances are either atypical lighting conditions or photographic subjects, both analyzed in Chapter 5. In truth, until you are familiar with how an exposure meter functions, and how to translate its measurements into proper camera adjustments, you may be having difficulty trying to evaluate your own negatives and slides. When you end up with over- or underexpo-

CONVERSION FILTERS

If your film is balanced for:	And you want to expose it by:	Use this filter or its equivalent:	Or your picture will look too:
Daylight	3200°K light	80A	Orange
Daylight	3400°K light	80B	Orange
Daylight	Aluminum-filled flashbulbs	80C	Orange
Daylight	Zirconium-filled flashbulbs	80D	Orange
3200°K light	Daylight	85B	Blue
3400°K light	Daylight	85	Blue

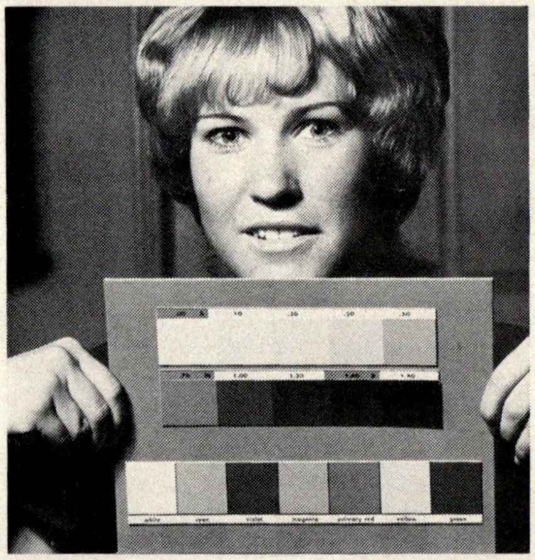
1

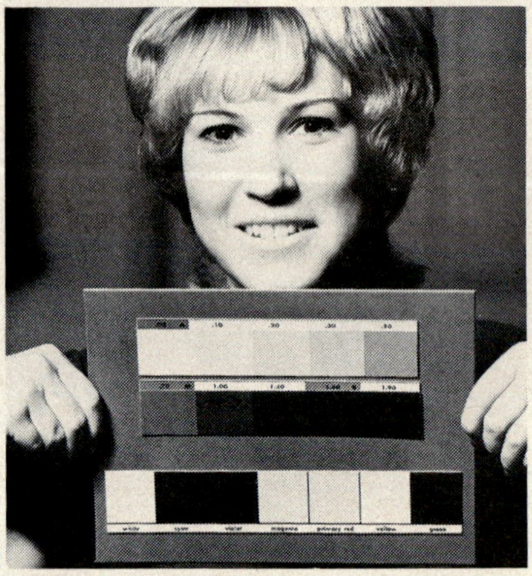
2

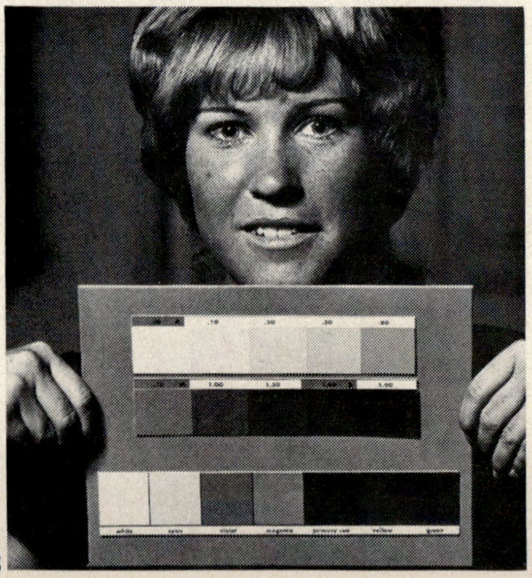
3

FILTER FACTOR-F/STOP INCREASE TABLE

If the filter factor is:	Open the lens this many stops:
1	0
1.25	1/3
1.5	2/3
2	1
2.5	1 1/3
3	1 2/3
4	2
5	2 1/3
6	2 2/3
8	3
10	3 1/3
12	3 2/3
16	4
20	4 1/3
24	4 2/3
32	5
40	5 1/3
48	5 2/3
64	6
80	6 1/3
100	6 2/3

For filter factors between the numbers shown, use the f/stop increase for the filter factor closest to the factor of your filter.

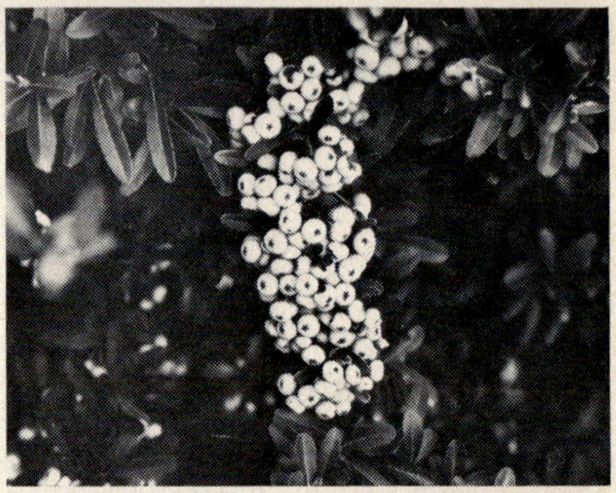
4

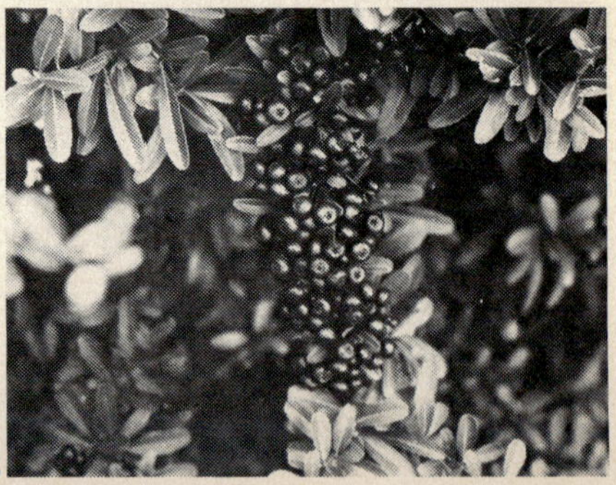
5

FILTERS FOR FLASH

If you use this type of flash:	And your film is balanced for daylight; use this filter:	And your film is balanced for 3200°K light, use this filter:	And your film is balanced for 3400°K light, use this filter:
Electronic	None, or 81A or 81B	85B*	85B*
Blue flashbulbs	None	85B*	85B*
Zirconium-filled flashbulbs (AG-1, M3, M5)	80D	81C	81C
Aluminum-filled flashbulbs	80C	81C	81C

***These film/flash combinations are not recommended.**

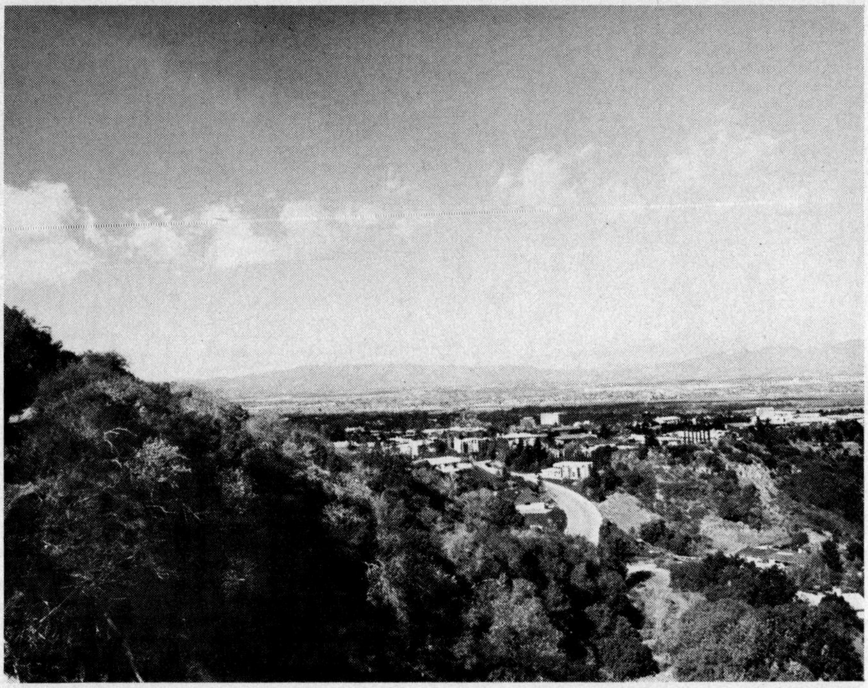
6

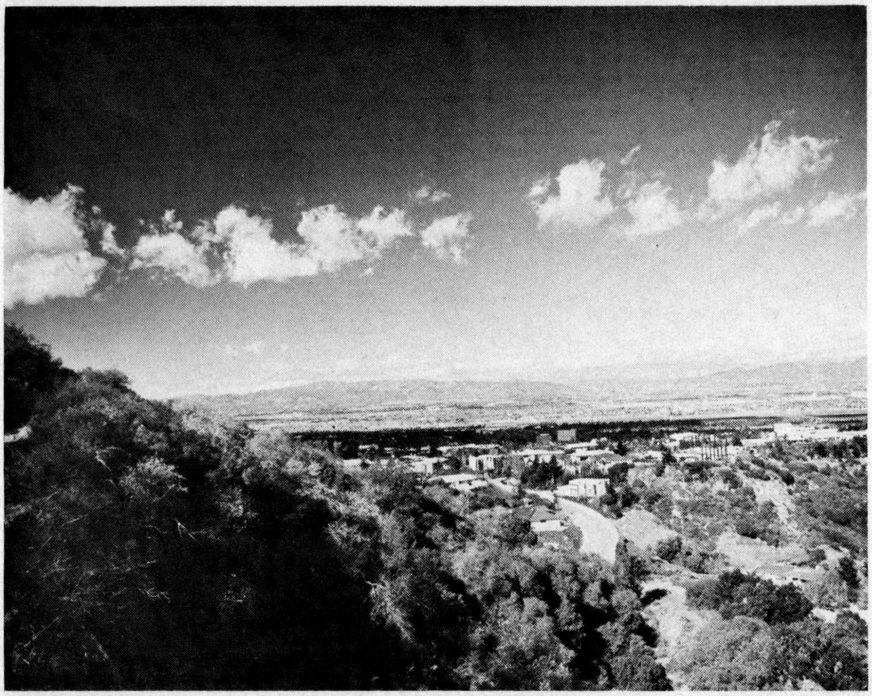
7

sure, you may ask yourself, "What happened?" Familiarity with exposure meter systems and how they work will help you answer that question, and perhaps avoid having to ask it.

Meter cells/ Both types of exposure meter cells are popular with photographers. The older type is the selenium cell, which is sensitive to light via chemical composition, and may be best known in the Weston meter. The newer type is the cadmium sulfide (CdS) cell, which is battery operated, and more sensitive than the selenium cell to very dim light, often less intense light than we can see detail in with the naked eye. Both types of cells work very well, but the CdS cell can go "blind" temporarily if held up to a strong light, such as the sun, for a short period. Its sensitivity returns after a short interval.

Reflected-light meters/ The average photographer uses this type of meter, either because it is built into his camera, or because it is somewhat easier to take a reading from camera position and shoot. However, a survey of photo processing labs seems to indicate that the reflected-light meter is as misused as the incident-light meter is ignored. Much of the problem is caused because photographers take meter readings as gospel—they don't really understand what information the meter is supplying and how best to apply that data.

A reflected-light meter measures the light that is *reflected from* a scene or subject. The meter is held at camera position and pointed at the subject. The average hand-held meter reads an area of about 30 degrees. As it measures light intensity, it is interpreting everything it sees as a middle gray, the same middle gray repre-

1. Filters lighten colors similar to their own and darken their complementary colors in black-and-white photography. Note appearance of colors in color strip across bottom of card in this unfiltered shot (colors are white, cyan, violet, magenta, primary red, yellow and green, from left to right), as well as skin tone of model.

2. Note what red filter does to colors and model's skin.

3. Note what blue filter does to colors and model's skin.

4. Red filter turns red beebleberries white against a dark green bush.

5. Green filter turns red berries black against a light bush.

6. Film's excess sensitivity to blue light and ultraviolet causes sky to appear too light in photographs.

7. Yellow or red filter will absorb blue and ultraviolet, thereby darkening sky in photographs, and providing contrast between sky and clouds.

sented by a Kodak Gray Card. In other words, a reflected-light reading averages all tones into a gray tone of 18-percent reflectance.

If you meter the light reflected from a black card, a gray card and a white card, each reading will indicate an exposure that will reproduce the card as a tone value equivalent to an 18-percent gray surface. You can check this out for yourself by setting up three cards—black, gray and white—and shooting three pictures based on separate readings from each card. If you read the middle gray card and shoot all three cards based on that reading, the black card will photograph as black, the gray card as gray and the white card as white. But if you read from the black card, the meter will give you an exposure that will reproduce *that* card as gray; the same camera setting will overexpose the gray and white cards. A reading off the white card will give you an exposure that is too short, in order to reproduce the white card as gray, and will reproduce the gray and black cards entirely too dark. This demonstrates that there are times when you have to "think" for your meter by making several readings at a given scene and averaging them mentally or on the meter dial, for correct exposure. Or you can buy a Kodak Gray Card and take reflected-light readings from it to standardize exposures. (More on learning to make value judgments about light and on the importance of subject matter follows in Chapter 5.)

Many reflected-light meters include a translucent white plastic "hemisphere" which you can slide over the meter's light-sensitive cell in order to use the meter to measure incident light. You may have such a meter, but its incident-light mode is virtually unused, misunderstood or forgotten.

Incident-light meters/ This type is usually the choice of professional movie cameramen, which does not mean that it is too complicated for the average photographer, nor that it is better for movies only. An incident light meter, via its white hemisphere that is the equivalent of the subject, measures the light *falling on* the subject. It is held at subject position and pointed at the camera. If you have not used a meter in the incident-light mode, hold it next to the subject (or opposite the camera in the case of a scenic), and note that highlights and shadows fall on the hemisphere in the same pattern that they fall on whatever you are photographing. In a front-lighted situation, all of the hemisphere is lighted; in sidelighting only half of the hemisphere is fully il-

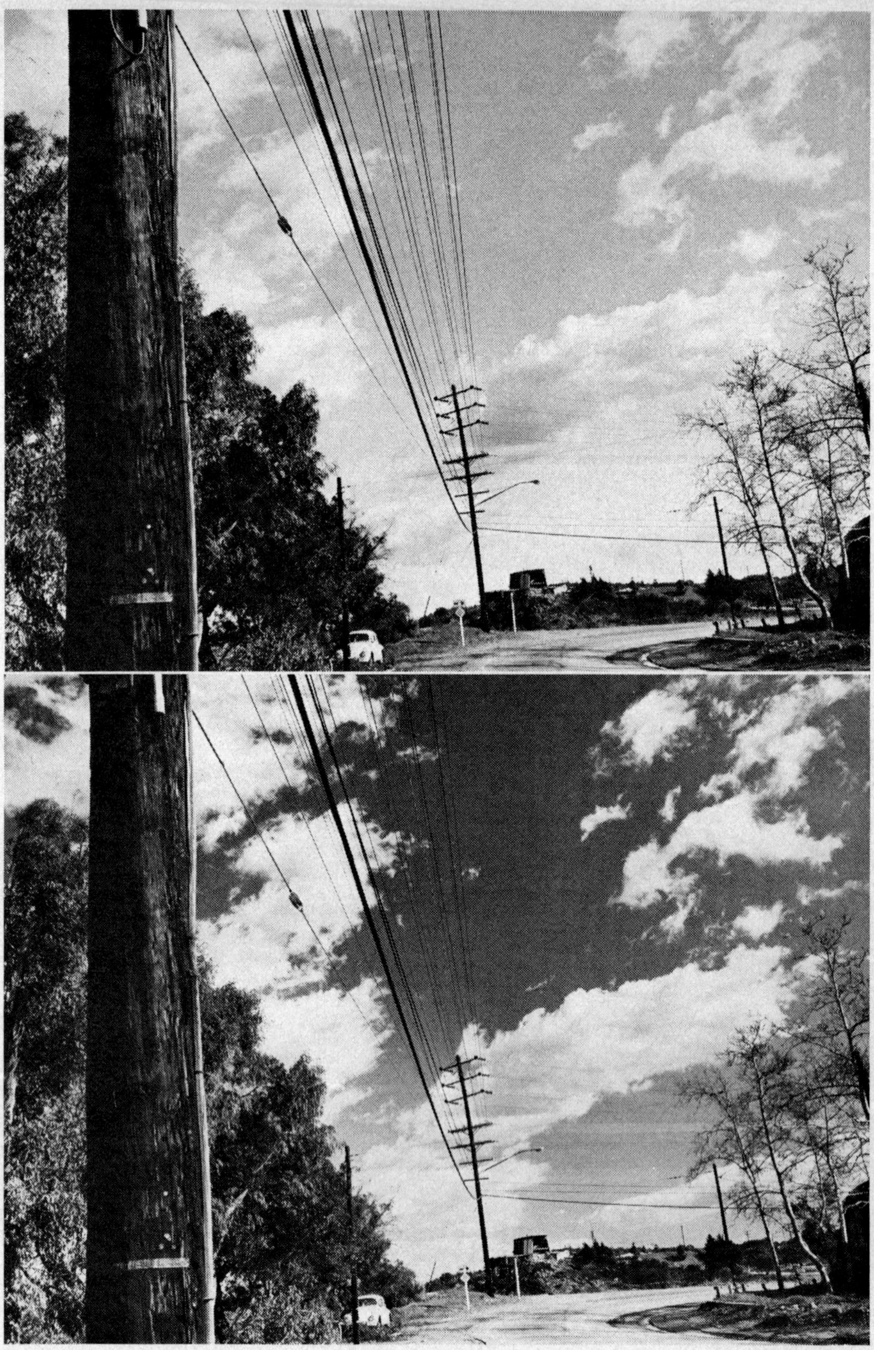

1

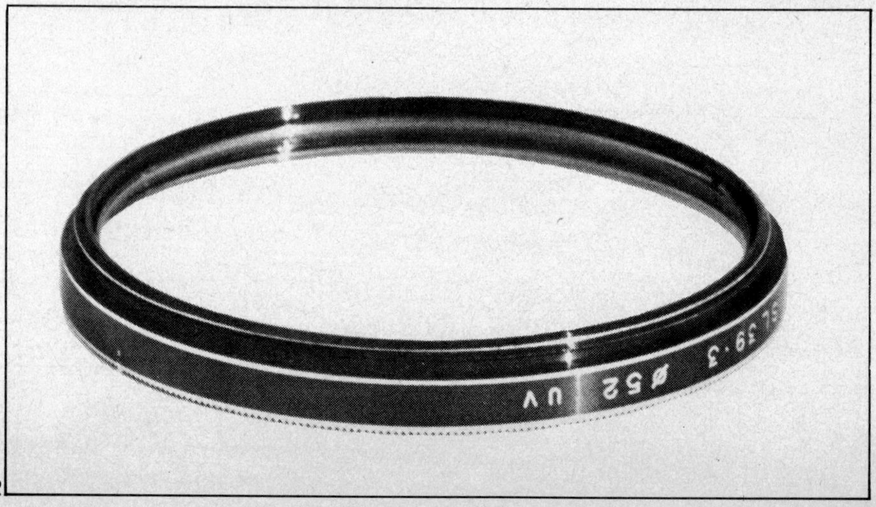

2

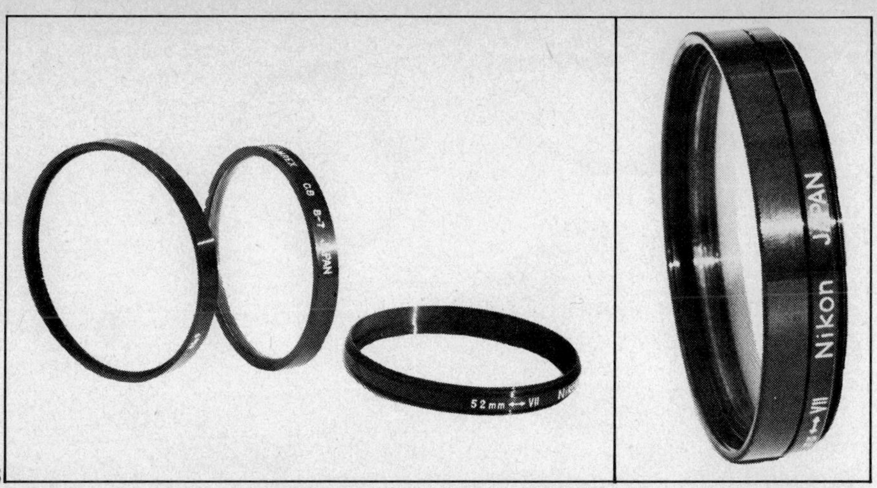

3

FILTERS FOR BLACK-AND-WHITE FILMS

Filter No.	Color	Suggested Uses	Daylight Factor	Tungsten Factor
6 (K1)	Yellow	Absorbs excess blue, darkens sky slightly	1.5	1.5
8 (K2)	Yellow	Produces greater contrast in clouds against blue skies	2	1.5
9 (K3)	Yellow	Deep yellow for stronger cloud contrast	2	1.5
11 (X1)	Green	More pleasing flesh tones in portraits against the sky; good for landscapes	4	4
12	Yellow	Cuts haze in aerial pictures; for use with Kodak Aero Ektachrome Infrared	2	1.5
13 (X2)	Green	Lightens foliage; good for portraits in tungsten light, especially men	5	4
15 (G)	Deep yellow	Renders dramatic dark skies, good for marine scenes	2.5	1.5
23A	Light red	Darkens sky and water; not recommended for flesh tones	6	3
25 (A)	Red	Dramatic sky effects; simulated "moonlight" scenes with slight underexposure	8	5
47 (C5)	Blue	Accentuates haze and fog	6	12
ND	Neutral Density	Uniform reduction of light intensity with no change in color values	Factors of 2,4,8	
Polarizer	Neutral	Eliminates surface reflections, darkens blue sky	2.5	2.5

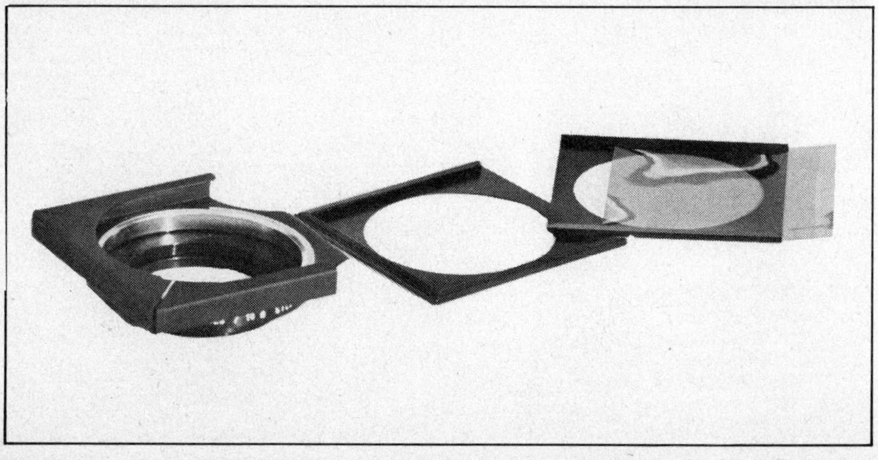

4

luminated; and in backlighting, direct light glances off the hemisphere, most of which is in shadow.

Almost all reflected-light meters are convertible for incident-light readings. Two of the best known are the Weston and the Gossen Luna-Pro. Somewhat more expensive, but cherished by professional cinematographers, is the Spectra Combi-500 which is essentially an incident-light meter, but makes reflected-light readings as well. In addition, there are many other brands and models of meters at economy prices and higher. Their reliability and versatility can be discovered by by inquiry and by personally testing them.

Spot meters/ These are fairly expensive and precise pieces of equipment with a small finder through which you aim the meter at tiny segments of a subject. Since a spot meter measures along a thin one-degree path, from a distance you can read light reflected from a model's forehead or the side of a small building many yards away.

A spot meter can be of most value to meticulous photographers who wish to take the time to measure light intensity on various sectors of a subject and average the readings for a proper exposure. This type of meter is also valuable for distant subjects, such as actors on a stage, which cannot be read accurately or easily by the other two types of meters. Some professionals carry spot meters as well as combination reflected/incident-light meters to backstop and reassure themselves in special situations. Both Honeywell and Minolta make excellent spot meters in the over-$100 category.

Black-and-white vs. color/ There are several theories about whether reflected- or incident-light meters are best suited to black-and-white or color. Obviously, either type can be used successfully. When you read the "Outdoor Exposure" section in Chapter 5, you will note Guy Draughon's test scoring which showed his incident-light readings to be 92 percent "right-on" vs. 82 percent "right-on" results with reflected-light meters. His tests were made with color film and substantiate my own theories

1. Polarizing filter will darken sky as red filter does, but without affecting other colors in scene, important in color photography.

2. Screw-in glass filter is easiest kind to handle, screws into lens.

3. Series-size filters, attached by means of retaining rings, are more versatile than screw-in filters.

4. Gelatin filters utilize the most complex mounting method, but are the least expensive filters

based on many years experience with both types of meters:

Incident-light meters are more consistently accurate, reading the light falling on a subject, when you shoot with color films. They are likely to indicate shorter exposures compared to a reflected-light reading, which provides richer, more saturated color.

Reflected-light meters are more consistently accurate, averaging the light values of subject matter before the camera, when you shoot with black-and-white films. They are likely to indicate longer exposures than incident-light meters under the same circumstances, which provides more shadow detail in a negative, and I prefer a little "more" rather than a little "less" negative density. I use quotes on those words because they are relative to individual judgment.

If you choose a meter that reads both modes, you can—and should—switch from one to another to make comparisons, and to match the method to the film in use. In this way, as the man said, you will have the best of all possible worlds.

TRIPODS

There are many times in every photographer's life when time exposures, slow shutter speeds, close-ups or use of heavy telephoto lenses call for a steady camera support, unless you like strange blurred prints or slides that may be called "art," but are often rubbish. Emergency camera supports, such as rocks, tables or light clamps, may be available, but the most versatile answer is a tripod. This essential piece of photo equipment is the best way to secure a camera in precisely the position you want it, and yet you can move the camera fractions of an inch with excellent control. Tripods are made in various shapes and sizes, but before describing some of them, let me suggest an experiment to test your nerves—and camera steadiness.

Hand-held camera tests/ Even well-trained photographers whose pictures rarely show real camera movement are subject to *camera shake. PhotoGraphic's* editor, Paul Farber, devised a neat test for shake about which he says, "Camera shake? Sure, you've heard of it, but it doesn't happen to you, it only happens to the other guy. Why, you can remember taking hand-held exposures at 1/15 or 1/30 that produce 'pin-point sharp negatives.' Or were they? Beginning to have some self-doubts? Well, try this simple experiment.

"Take a large coffee can, or a small cardboard box, and place a 60-watt frosted lamp inside. Punch a

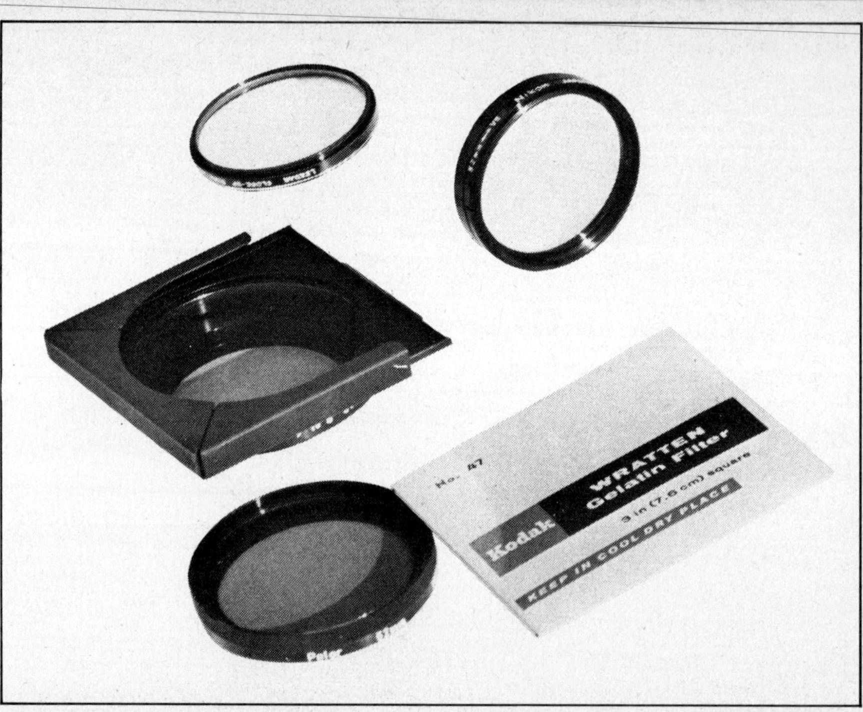

1

FILTERS FOR COLOR FILM

Filter No.	Film Type	Lighting	Suggested Uses
Skylight (1A)	Daylight	Daylight	Reduced blue cast in shade and on overcast days
UV15	Agfachrome Anscochrome Daylight	Daylight	Haze filter, reduces UV light
Haze 1	Daylight	Daylight	Reduces excess blue caused by haze and UV rays
80A	Daylight	3200°K floods	Converts daylight film for use with 3200°K floodlights
80B	Daylight	3400°K floods	Converts daylight film for use with 3400°K floodlights
80C	Daylight	Clear flash	For use with clear flashbulbs
81	Daylight	M2 flash	Yellowish warming filter
81A	Type B	Electronic flash 3400°K floods	Balances daylight films to electronic flash if necessary; corrects Type B films for use with 3400°K photofloods
81C	Type A, B	Clear flash	Corrects for clear flashbulbs
82A	Type A	3200°K floods	Corrects for 3200°K photofloods
85	Type A	Daylight	Converts Type A film to daylight
85B	Type B	Daylight	Converts Type B film to daylight
FLB	Type B	Fluorescent	Eliminates blue-green cast from fluorescent lamps
FLD	Daylight	Fluorescent	Eliminates blue-green cast from fluorescent lamps
ND	Any type	Any light	Reduces light intensity without changing color values
Polarizer	Any type	Any light	Eliminates surface reflections, darkens blue sky
820B	Polacolor	3200°K or 3400°K	Converts daylight film to floodlights
840B	Polacolor	75-150W house bulbs	Converts daylight film to indoor use

clean round hole in the box or can using an ice pick or similar tool. Then, glue a piece of plain white paper in back of the hole. In the dark, at a distance of several feet, make a series of exposures of the glowing dot of light on a distant white wall. Load your camera with fast film, set the aperture at f/5.6, and run through the entire range of shutter speeds—hand-held. Accurate exposure is not important. The idea is to record the dot of light—nothing more.

"If you have difficulty trying to hold the spot of light, *at a precise point,* without movement of any kind, you may suspect that you're on the verge of a nervous breakdown. Let me assure you that most of us are in the same fix.

"Process the roll of film. When it is dry, examine the negatives under a magnifier or a low-power microscope. In each frame, providing that you held the camera rock-steady, the dot of light should be recorded as a perfect circle. If it shows elongation of any kind, you can be certain of camera shake. Also, by studying any dots of light that appear elongated, you can quickly determine at which speeds you suffer most from camera shake, and which direction the movement takes! Once determined, you can take remedial steps in the future by adjusting your grip-and-release tactics. This experiment is well worth the little effort as it gives you an immediate set of guidelines to follow."

Once you are more aware of camera shake, Farber says you may overreact for a while by gripping your camera self-consciously, and possibly increase tiny personal vibrations. You will get over this, and your shooting technique should improve thereafter. However, the convenience—and necessity—of a tripod are amply established.

Paul Farber made another demonstration to show we even have difficulty with camera shake at 1/500 second. Notice the pictures of the two resolution charts. Details are in the caption, and you are likely to be amazed, as I was, that we humans can't match a solid tripod in supporting a camera—even at high shutter speeds.

Tripod features/ Tripods vary in

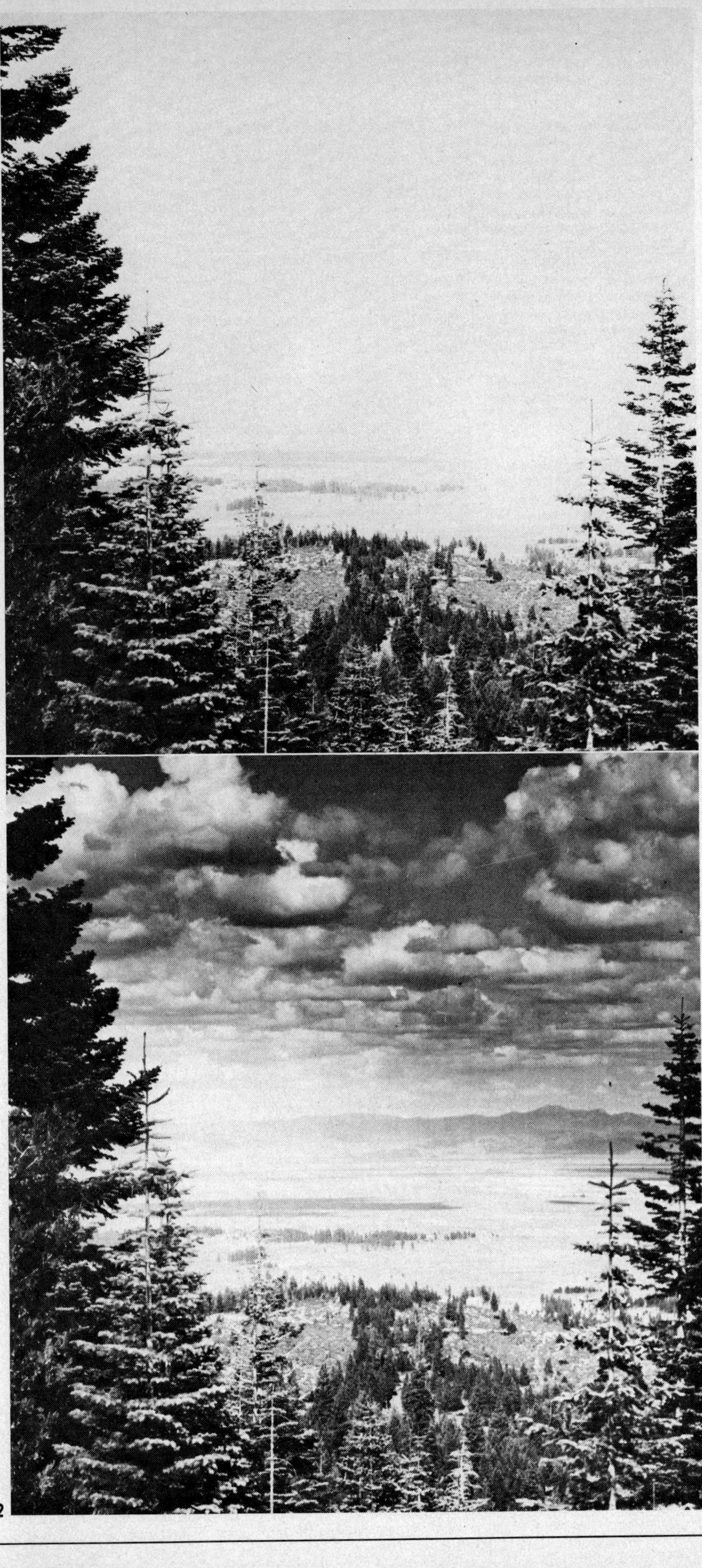
2

1. Various filter types include, clockwise from top, screw-in, series-size with retaining ring, gelatin in package, rotating polarizer, gelatin filter with filter frame and filter frame holder for attachment to lens.

2. Harrison & Harrison graduate clear-to-neutral filter's neutral-density top half cut down brightness of sky to bring scene's brightness range to something the film's latitude could handle, producing good picture.

many ways according to weight, length, leg-locking design, type of elevator, maximum extension, head mobility, etc. For years I used a neat, fairly compact elevator model that telescoped to about 20 inches and was easy to carry in a suitcase or by hand. At the time I was shooting almost entirely with 35mm cameras, but when I needed a 2¼x2¼ camera for certain jobs, this otherwise adequate tripod became a marginal support. It was just too flimsy for my Bronica, and I eventually got rid of it in favor of another model that weighs twice as much and is 31 inches long. It is not as portable, but it offers a lot more peace of mind.

Not only does my new tripod extend 7½ feet high (the older one was limited to 5 feet), but it has a completely adjustable head that will hold a 35mm camera vertically, plus other versatile features. It looks somewhat bulky with a 35mm camera mounted on it, but its choice of movements and the rock-steady feeling I get when I'm using a telephoto or zoom lens are pleasantly rewarding.

Many tripods, lighter and shorter than the one I've described, would be adequate for 35mm and larger cameras. However, there are some good-looking pieces of equipment that are too skinny and "under-powered" for confidence. One type closes to about 12 inches, but also collapses in use, and is not recommended except for space travel when your baggage is severely limited.

Paul Farber has made a check list for tripods which I quote here. It covers everything you need to research when shopping for a tripod that may range in price from $20 to over $100. On today's market you should find a model that fits these specifications for between $30 and $50. Here are Farber's recommendations:

"When buying a tripod, there are some features that should be investigated beyond the cosmetic appearance of the unit. First, take the tripod and extend the legs to their maximum length. Do they extend easily? Are the legs easily locked and unlocked? Then, place the tripod on the floor, and with the flat of your hand, press down on top of the tripod—hard—and watch the legs. Do they warp? Do they flex and give? If so, then the tripod may not be suitable from the standpoint that weight or camera pressure can easily give rise to movement or vibration.

"Next, check to see if it is possible to remove and reverse the center post of the tripod. That is, with the pan head facing the floor instead of the ceiling. Many photographers like to take low-angle shots, and having the option of mounting the camera *underneath* the tripod cannot be emphasized too strongly. Then, speaking of pan heads, see if the camera can be easily mounted. Does the camera locking bolt have easy access, or do

1

2

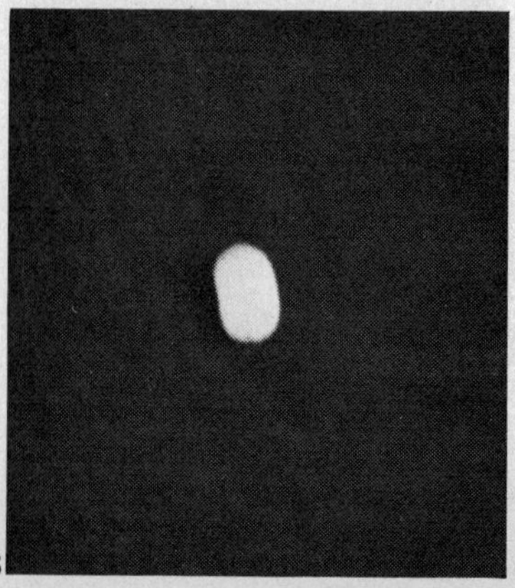
3

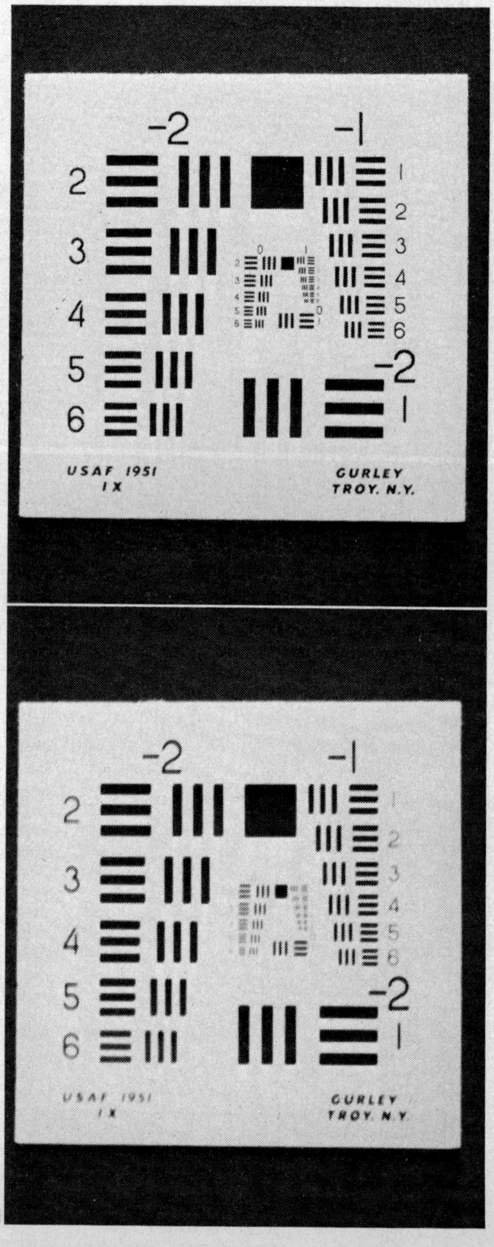

4

1. This 50X enlargement made from negative exposed at 1/125 second with camera mounted on tripod shows perfectly circular dot of light.

2. Exposure of 1/125 second with hand-held camera produced elongated dot of light, indicating camera movement occurred.

3. Hand-held exposure at 1/60 second shows even more camera movement. All enlargements in this series were 50X blow-ups of image.

4. Loss of resolving power due to camera shake is illustrated in these two photos. Standard Air Force resolution target was photographed with tripod-mounted camera and hand-held camera, both at 1/500 second, on ultra-high-resolution H & W Control Film. Difference is evident.

5. Pan head of good tripod will offer option of both horizontal and vertical mounting while retaining panning ability in both modes. Pan heads that do not offer this feature can cause aggravating problems for photographer when he desires to make vertical shot.

6. Good pan head will permit mounted camera to be rotated 360 degrees in horizontal position. Check motion for binding, etc. before making purchase.

7. Vertical panning ability should be checked before making purchase. Pan head that does not permit reasonable usable degree of upward tilt (or full downward tilt) can also cause problems in use. Also, lock pan head at various positions and test for holding ability, preferably with a camera mounted on head. Check ease of mounting and unmounting during this test.

you have to jam your fingers to get to the bolt? Is the camera being tightly held, or does it exhibit evidence of easy movement after the locking bolt has been tightened? Does the pan head move easily? How far up, and down, can you tilt the head? Can the camera be mounted vertically? And if so, can it also be panned as it can when the camera is mounted horizontally upon it?

"Check the rising center post. If it is crank operated, does the crank handle move easily, or does it bind? If the center post is raised manually, does the locking bolt or collar *securely* tighten the post? Press down with the flat of your hand to verify. Check the bottom of the tripod. See if you have the option of metal tips to prevent movement on soft surfaces, or hard rubber or plastic tips to prevent movement on smooth surfaces. Check the weight of the tripod. Can you handle it comfortably? Check the collapsed length of the tripod. Can it be easily transported?"

If you also use a movie camera, be certain that the tripod you choose has a smoothly panning head which does not tip up or down as you swing it laterally. If you keep all these points in mind *before* you make your final purchase, you should choose wisely. Remember, a good tripod will last a lifetime.

All 35mm cameras are sold with snug-fitting cases that help protect the camera when carried or stored. I've never liked using such cases, no matter how cleverly they come apart. Camera cases are always in the way, and must be removed to change film, which for a professional is fairly often. Therefore, I attach a good adjustable neck strap to my cameras, and keep them, along with film, filters and other gear, in a shoulder gadget bag. Soft leather cases are put away in a closet, or I avoid buying them if they are extra options.

Choose a gadget bag just large enough to hold the equipment you want to carry. I have several with zip-open upper compartments for extra lenses, and room in the main section for two SLRs with lenses mounted. Cameras are protected in the bag while I'm on the move or stored at home, and everything I need is within easy reach. Most camera shops have a selection of bags, so take your camera(s) and other equipment to the shop, and find one that carries everything snugly. You can abandon your individual soft camera cases, and use

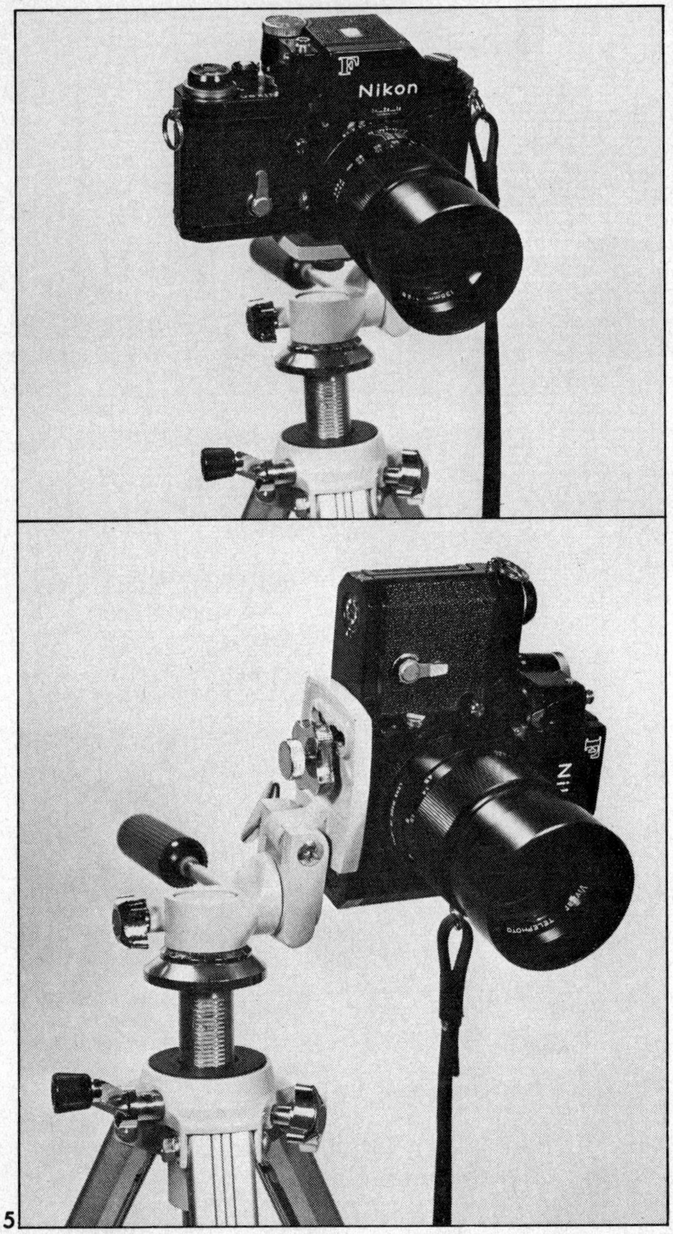

5

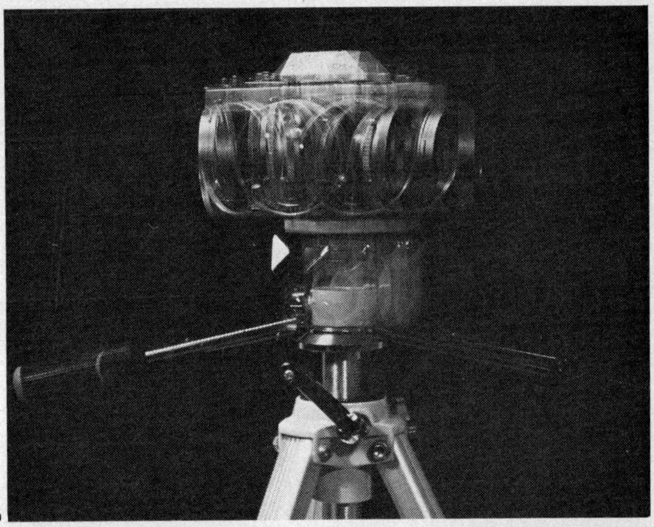

6

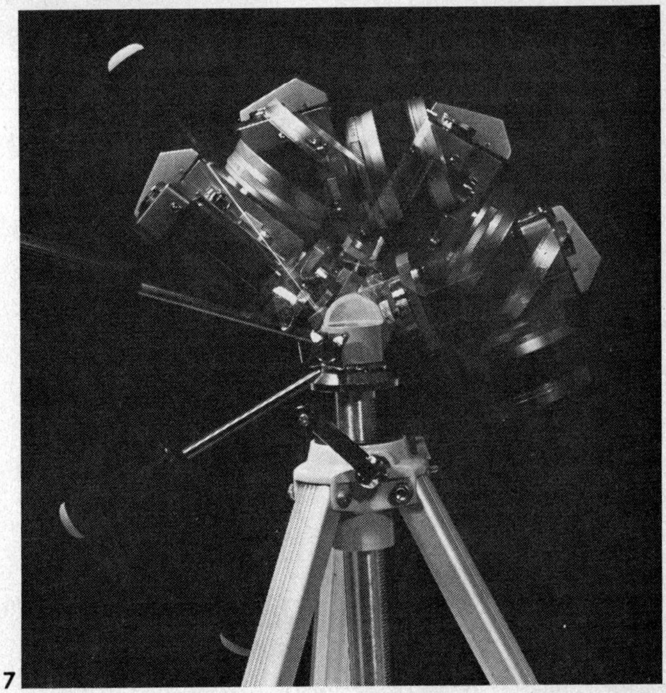

7

ordinary care while your camera is around your neck.

Some people prefer suitcase-type carrying cases with thick foam rubber inside that is hollowed out to the shape of cameras and lenses. Such cases are undoubtedly superior for shipping cameras, but I much prefer a gadget bag I can feel and have at my fingertips at all times. The suitcase-type of carrier is too remote for my taste.

SLIDE PROJECTORS

Most modern projectors use circular trays that hold slides from several rolls of film. Prices range from about $65 to $150 and up. You'll have to decide whether you want remote controls, automatic self-focusing, zoom lenses, and other conveniences that affect prices. A good projector, along with a screen at least 40x40 inches, should last many years. Until you need or can afford a projector, however, you can do nicely with a small battery-powered hand-held viewer that magnifies slightly. More elaborate viewers even have provision for feeding slides into them from a stack.

MISCELLANEOUS EQUIPMENT

Browsing in the average camera shop, you'll find many other gadgets that seem useful or appealing. A few are even necessary, depending on

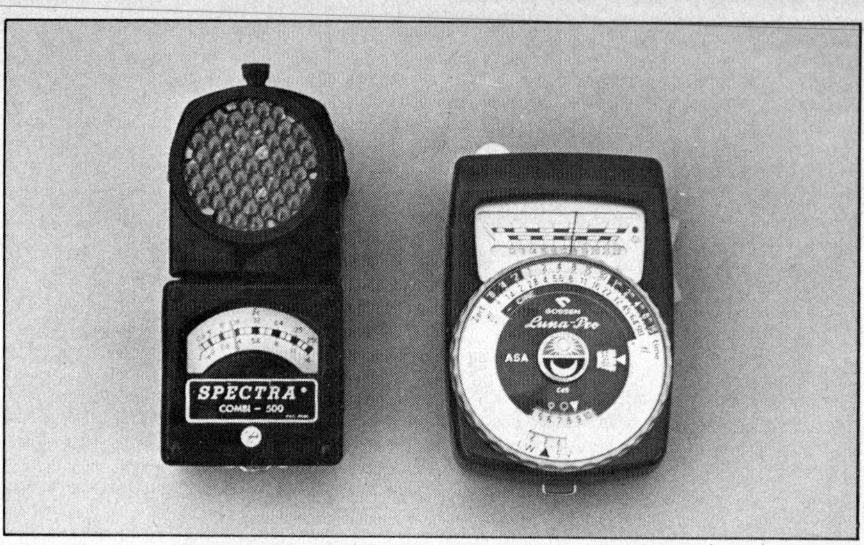

1

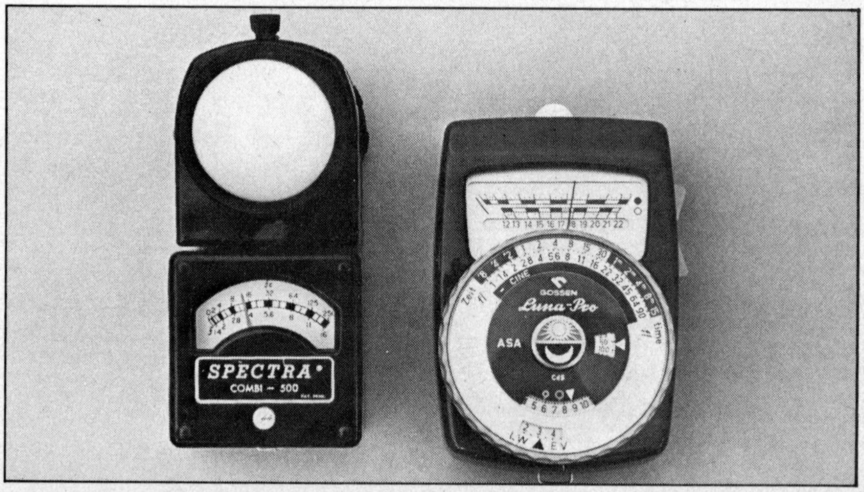

2

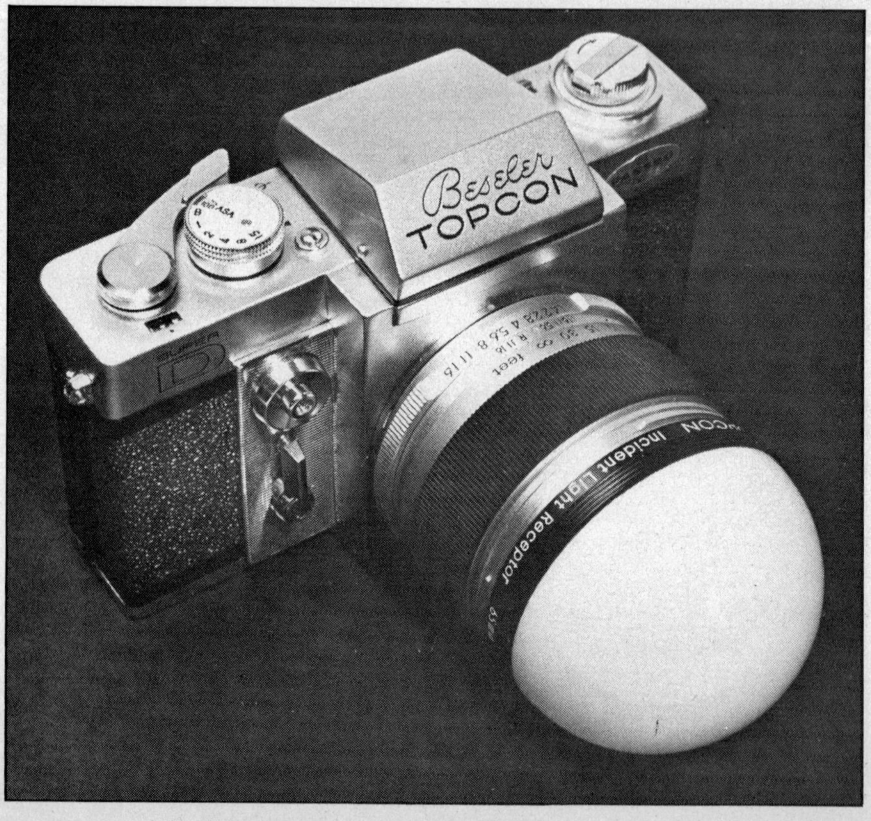

3

1. Spectra Combi-500, primarily an incident-light meter, and Gossen Luna-Pro, primarily a reflected-light meter, are shown in reflected-light mode.

2. Combi-500 and Luna-Pro are shown in incident-light mode.

3. Built-in through-the-lens light meters are reflected-light meters, but Beseler Topcon Super D camera has accessory incident-light attachment.

4. Rising center columns should be checked carefully. Some are crank operated, others require column to be raised or lowered manually. Both types should have more than adequate locking features, and should be checked carefully for slippage. Crank-operated columns should have teeth checked to see that they mesh without binding. Check all moving parts for burrs.

5. Typical of circular-tray (Carousel type) slide projectors on the market are these by Kodak and Minolta.

6. To test either locking method, partially extend all three legs and slightly raise center column. Make certain all locking devices on legs and column are secure. Then, place palm of your hand on top of tripod and press down firmly. Check legs to see if they bend or warp. Some tripods have leg braces, others do not. A small pencil line on legs, examined after testing, will determine if any slippage is present. A tripod that bows, warps or slips should be avoided.

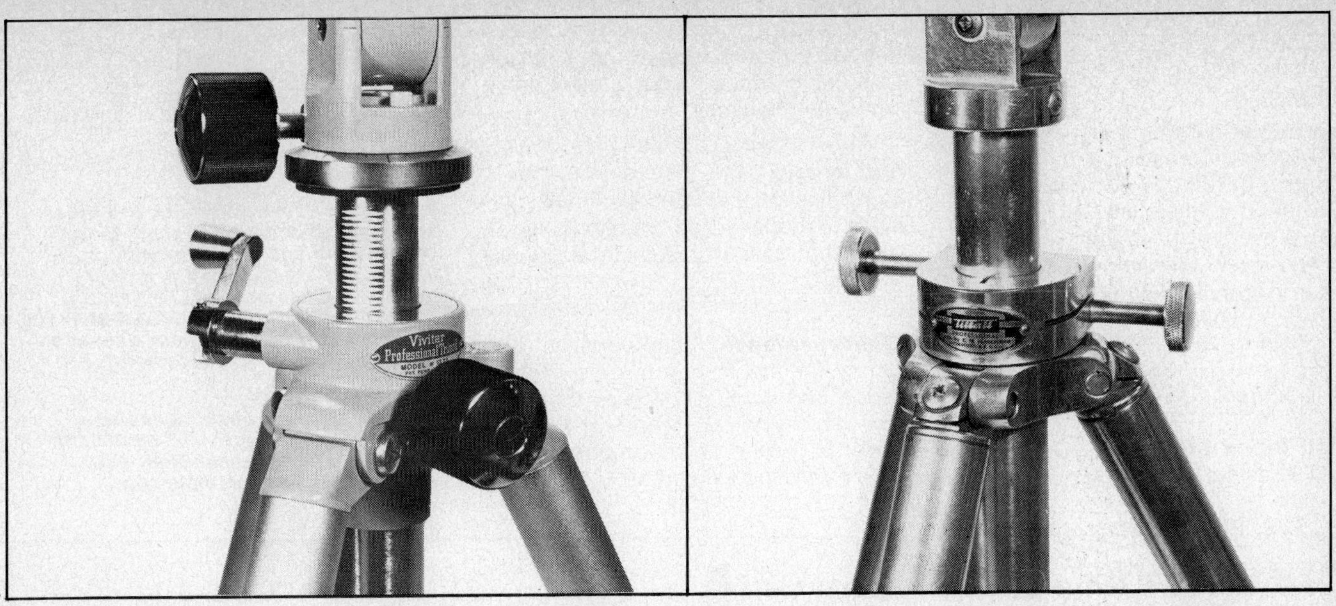

4

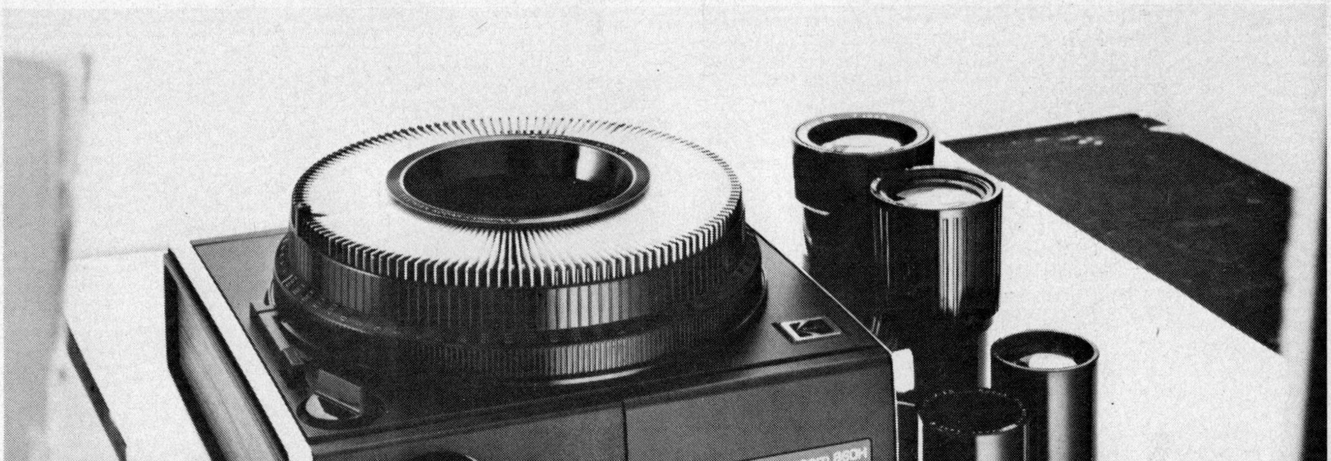

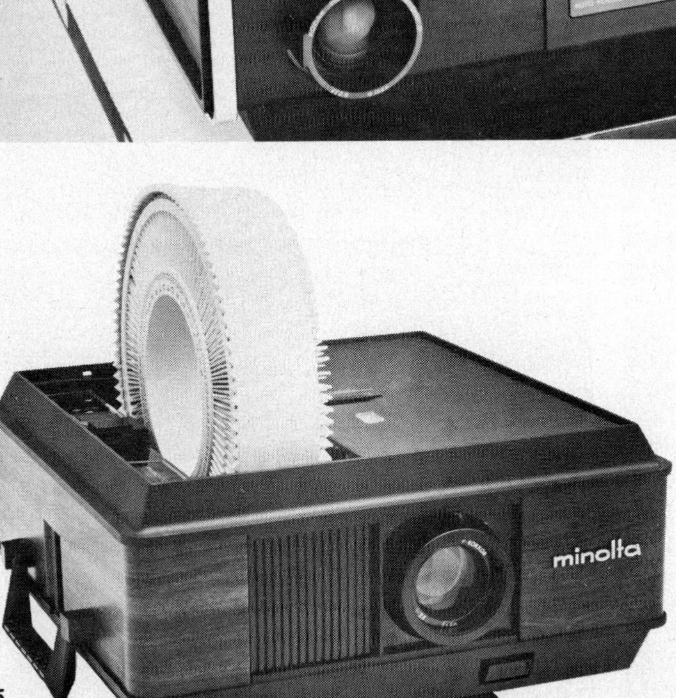

5

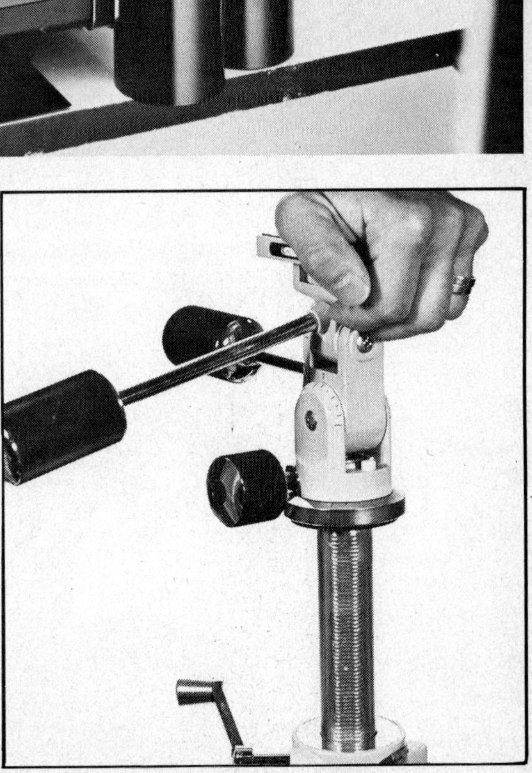

6

your taste and style. Here are a few such items:

Lens hood/ If one doesn't come with each of your lenses (and the lens isn't inset to form its own hood), supply a hood to fit each lens. A lens hood prevents stray light rays from partly diffusing an image, and protects the lens from scratches and fingermarks while you are shooting. Some types have a rubber front section that can be rolled back when the lens is stored.

Small tripod head/ This is made on a universal-joint principle. When attached to a tripod, it allows free movement of a camera in any direction. Especially nice for copying if your main tripod head doesn't have complete movement.

Soft brush/ One that retracts into a small plastic case can be carried easily in a gadget bag, ready to whisk dust from inside or outside a camera or lens.

Cable release/ Inexpensive and handy for the time you shoot from a tripod and want to be sure the camera isn't jiggled. Made in various lengths, some with locking mechanism for time exposures.

A grease pencil/ This is the last item on my list, but a useful one to mark notes on film canisters or cartridges, helping you keep order, and identify people, places and things at a later time.

1. Carrying cameras, lenses and other equipment in a shoulder-slung gadget bag enabled author to stay with crowd at Hoover Dam and have necessary films, etc. close at hand. This photo was shot with Bronica, on Tri-X at 1/500 second and f/16 with 50mm wide-angle lens (Bronica is 2¼x2¼ camera).

2. San Francisco street scene was shot with 2X tele-extender on 200mm Nikon lens, giving equivalent of a 400mm lens for hand-held shot.

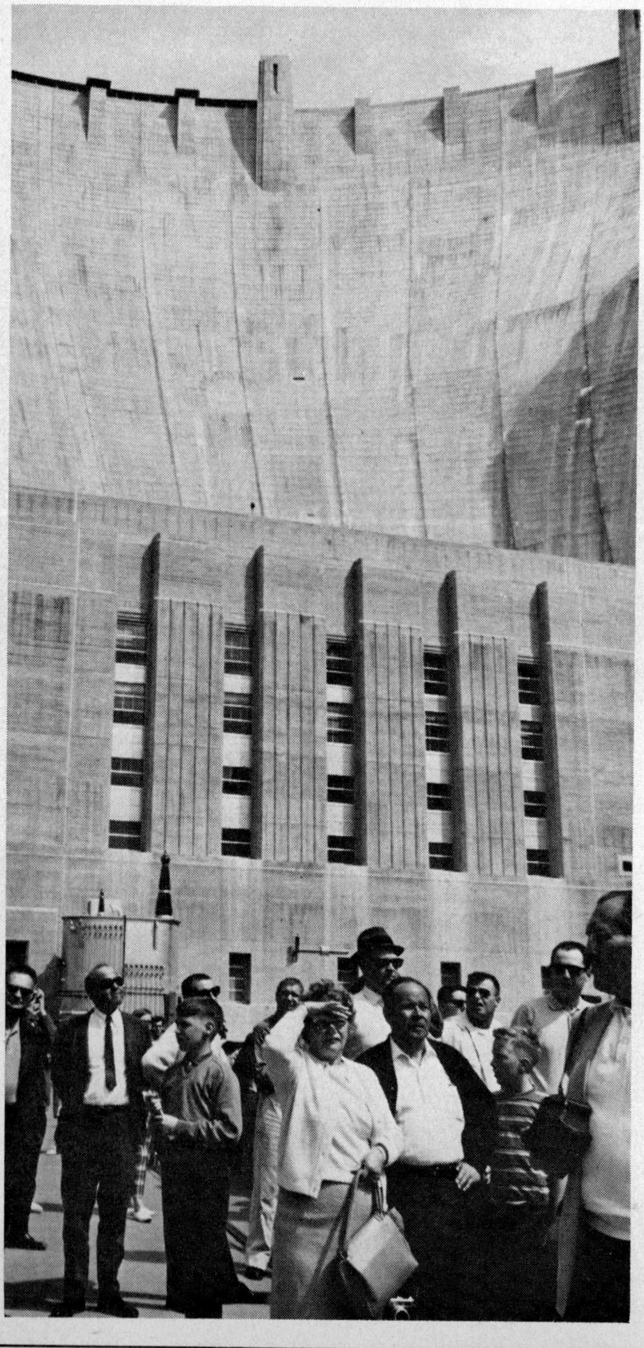

1

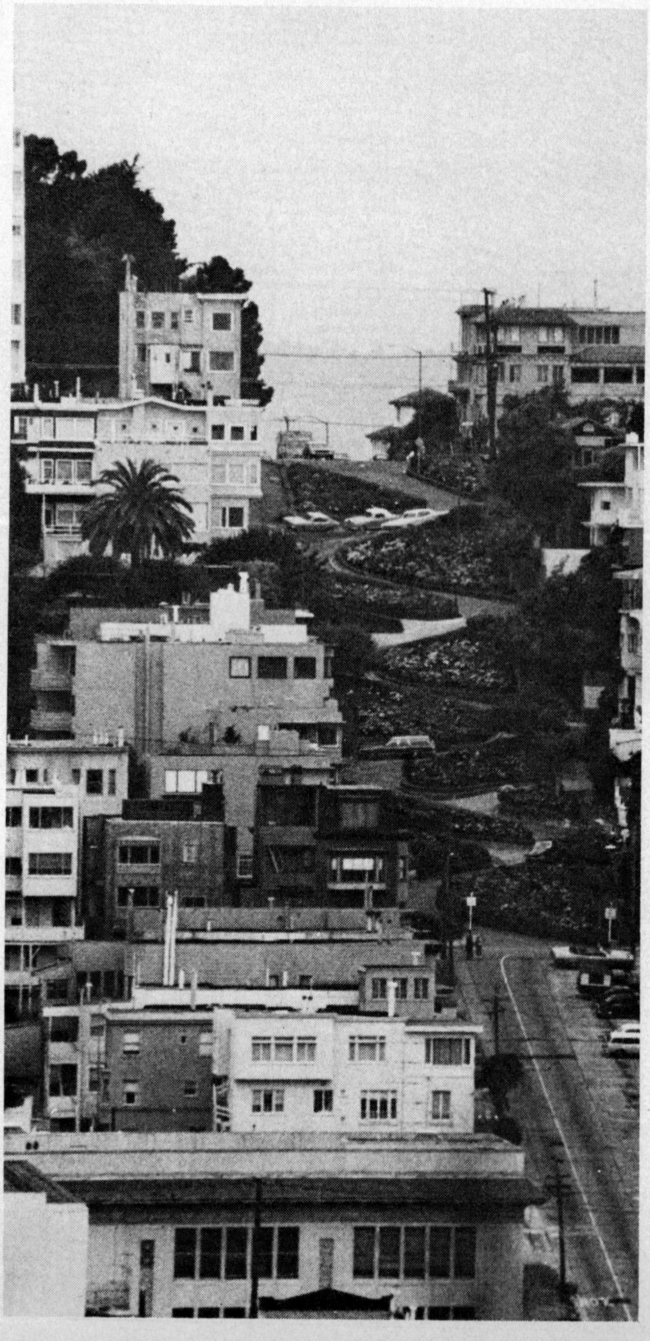

2

CHAPTER 4

Camera Handling and Film

Taking a picture is actually very simple, though achieving worthwhile pictures requires more than mere mechanical involvement. Your mind needs to be programmed like a computer; before you press the shutter release, data from both accumulated knowledge about photographic principles and experience in shooting is instantly (often unconsciously) available to guide your vision. This data includes ways of holding a camera, the nuances of exposure, facts about film, sensitivity to different kinds of light and awareness of composition. All these, and more, add up to a thorough understanding of what happens when you photograph a subject you hope will become a meaningful image on film.

Also within your mental computer are picture *ideas,* which may be as literal as catching your child blowing out candles on a birthday cake, as aesthetic as the mood of a summer evening, or as symbolic as poverty, speed and beauty. Ideas are discussed in later chapters; here I'll try to link photographic theory with visual perception to better prepare or program you to make the most of pictures you shoot.

HANDLING A CAMERA

Most people are right-eyed, so it is natural to hold an SLR horizontally with both hands, and close the left eye. The right index finger rests on the shutter release, and you focus with either hand that seems comfortable. In the vertical position, you can either grip the camera from the top with the right hand, and focus with the left, or support it from the bottom with the right hand, leaving the left hand to focus and grip the camera at the top for stability.

You need move the average SLR only an inch or two from your face to advance the film and cock the shutter. Some models indicate the shutter speed you've selected at the bottom of the finder, so you hardly have to lower the camera at all while you're shooting.

Keep the camera strap around your neck at all times, for dropping a camera can be fatal. When you use two cameras at the same time, hang one on a shortened neck strap and the other beneath it on a longer strap. Be sure to read the instruction booklet with your camera, and you'll soon be operating it quickly and easily.

A neck strap is also essential with a 2¼x2¼ camera, which is usually held firmly with the left hand beneath it, leaving the right hand free to depress the shutter release and focus. Most 2¼-square or 2¼x2¾ cameras include a built-in magnifier above the viewer against which you place your viewing eye. If you use an eye-level prism on a larger format camera, it is still held with the left hand and operated with the right. A prism is handy to correct the reversed mirror image seen in the look-down viewing mode, but a prism offers a slightly dimmer view than the ground glass alone.

Other eye-level 35mm rangefinder cameras are held and operated in a manner similar to that described for the SLR. Polaroid Land cameras are also easy to hold and shoot with, except the new SX-70, which must be gripped far enough back so that your

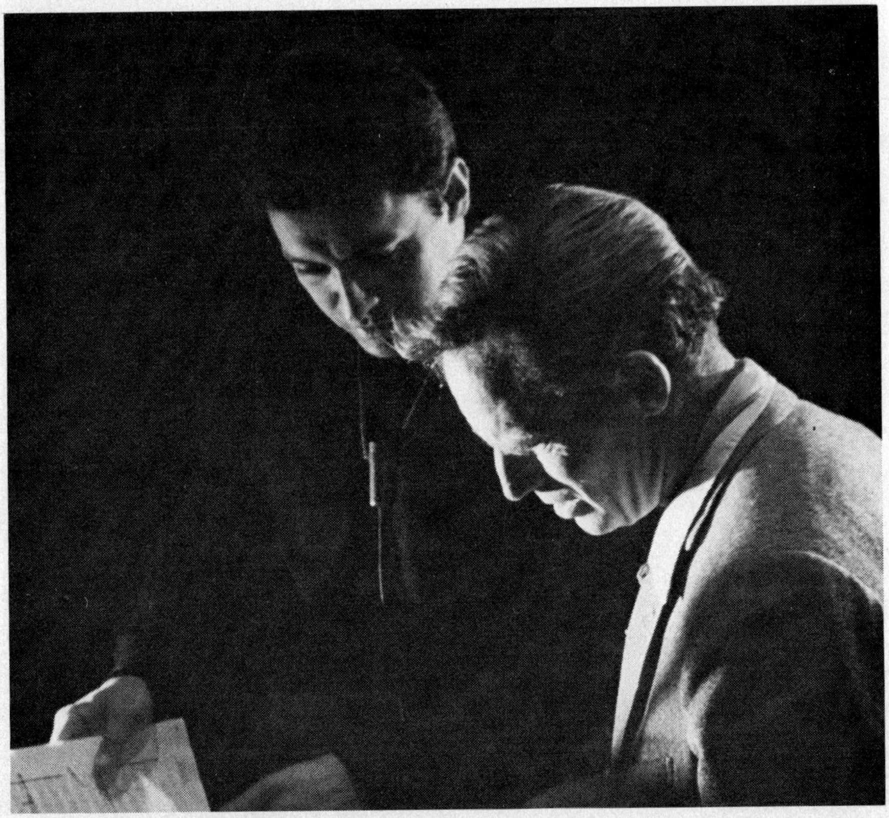

1

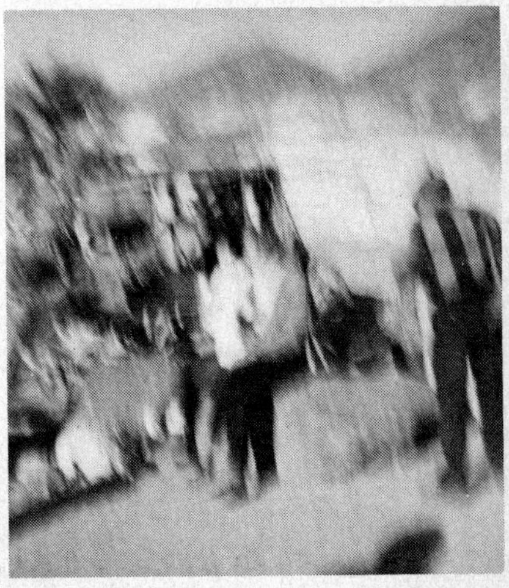

2

1. The unusual mood of this picture by Barbara Jacobs came from awareness of film and lighting as she observed Charlton Heston conferring with conductor Zubin Mehta. Photo was taken with a Pentax, 105mm lens, on Tri-X, exposure of 1/60 second at f/6.3.

2. Extreme example of camera movement with camera in the hands of a youngster who jerked the camera as he depressed the shutter release button. Less obvious blur from movement can also be annoying in photos.

hand does not block the print as it is ejected from the camera.

CAMERA MOVEMENT

If you are using a fairly simple camera with a single shutter speed (around 1/100 second) or a limited selection, you may have found a number of your prints or slides are slightly blurred, though the subject was still. This annoying lack of sharpness is the curse of photography, usually caused by camera movement. Even users of more expensive cameras suffer from it unless they are careful as they shoot.

A camera will only produce a sharp image (relative to lens quality) if:

1. The shutter release is pressed smoothly rather than abruptly.

2. The photographer is breathing softly or holds his breath at the instant of exposure.

3. The camera is gripped firmly, but not desperately.

4. The camera is anchored to a tripod or other stationary spot for exposures longer than 1/30 second.

5. A fast enough shutter speed is selected to freeze fast action.

You learn through experience to hold a camera properly and to depress the shutter release button quickly without jarring the camera. When you have the option, it is wise to shoot at 1/125 second or faster to help negate even minimum camera movement and arrest subject action as well. Of course, very fast action demands 1/500 second or 1/1000 second for reasonable sharpness. More of this in Chapter 9, where you will also find that with practice many people can shoot a hand-held 35mm camera at 1/60 and 1/30 second by steady nerves and disciplined breathing. Slower speeds, such as 1/15 or 1/8 second are often attempted in emergencies, but acceptable sharpness is a matter of unpredictable luck.

CHANGING LENSES

When attaching a screw-mount lens, be careful to seat it properly so you don't strip the thread. On bayonet-mount lenses there is usually a red dot or mark on the lens that must be placed opposite a corresponding dot on the camera body, after which you can set the lens, twist it and hear it click into place. If a lens doesn't seem to go on smoothly, never force it, but check the fit.

While a camera body is without a lens, you may softly brush the mirror surface inside, but *don't touch it* with bare fingers. If lens cleaning fluid and tissue are necessary, use them delicately. When you carry or store a camera without a lens, buy a body cap that covers the opening and pro-

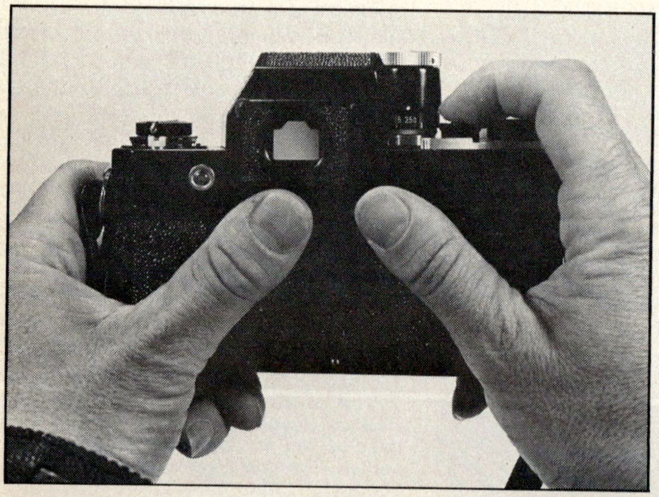
1

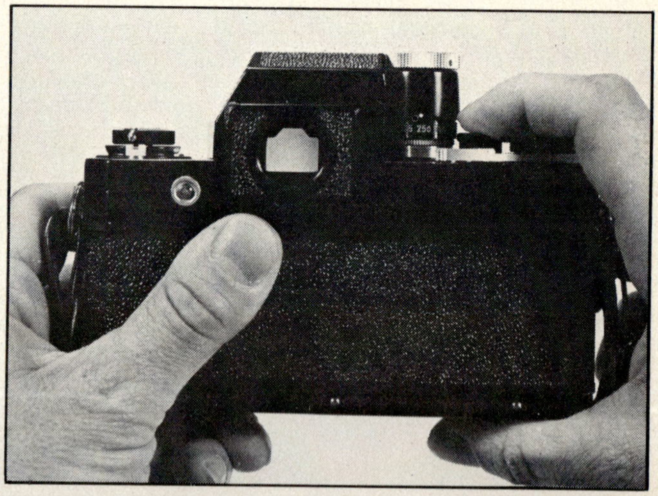
2

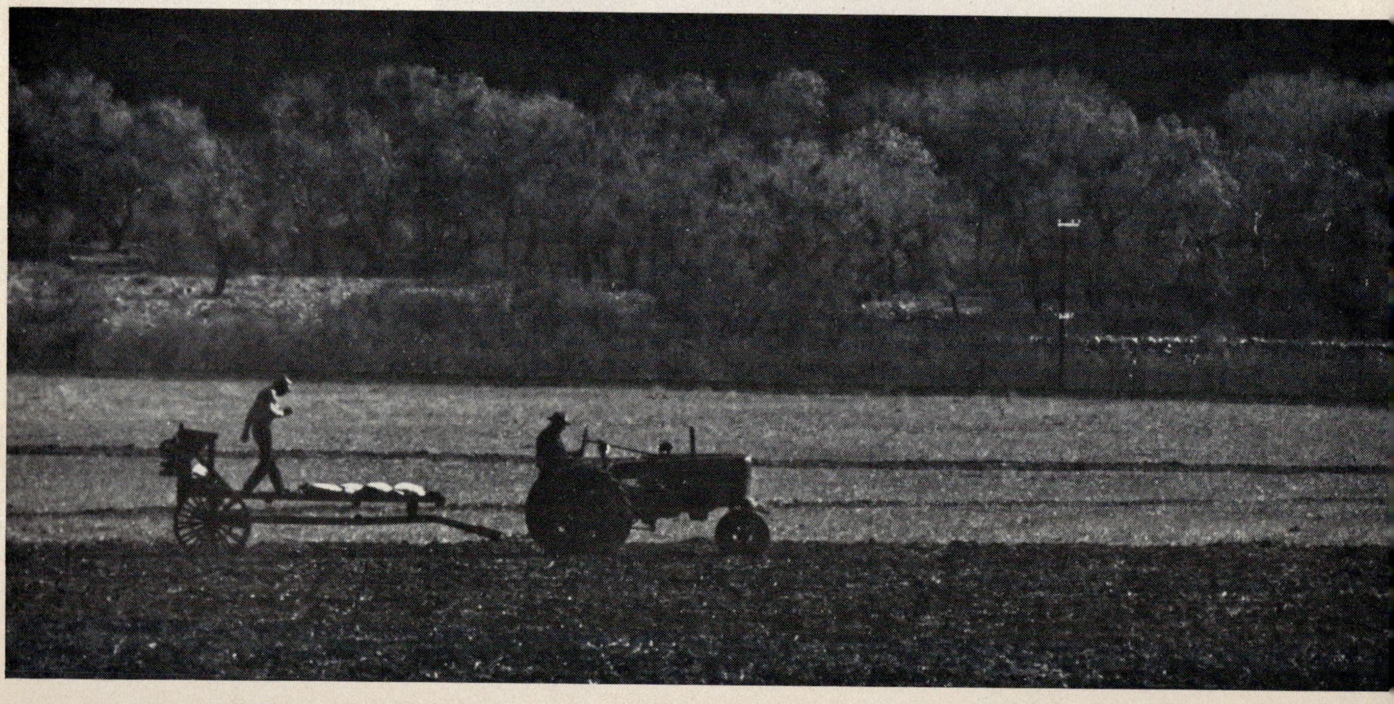
3

tects the interior from dust, dirt and inadvertent damage.

FACTS ABOUT FILM

Film (or emulsion) speeds are rated in ASA numbers by the American National Standards Institute (ANSI), and these ratings are usually printed on the outside of the film box. In addition, the EI (exposure index) rating is sometimes used to designate a deviation from the film's official ASA speed. An EI rating is a kind of personal film speed you or a chemical manufacturer chooses to use rather than the ASA number.

Exposure meters and the film-speed dial on cameras with built-in meters (often in an opening atop the shutter-speed dial) are marked with a series of film-speed numbers that guide the meter to make proper exposures. When you switch from one type of film to another, don't forget to reset the film speed on the camera or separate meter. I've had some disappointing experiences because of such negligence.

COLOR FILMS

Negative color films/ These are especially popular with users of cameras under $150, and records show that about four times as many rolls of negative color are sold in the U.S. compared to transparency or slide films. Brands include Kodacolor-X, Ektacolor and Agfacolor. Prints made from negatives are generally more satisfactory than prints from transparencies, though the latter are usually acceptable and often excellent. You can also have black-and-white prints or slides made from color negatives, which is another reason for their wide popularity.

Kodacolor-X is balanced primarily for daylight, blue flash bulbs and electronic flash, with an outdoor ASA of 80. It has fairly wide exposure latitude, which means pleasing results even though your exposure settings may be somewhat inaccurate. Discrepancies can often be compensated for during the printing process. Indoors with photofloods, Kodacolor-X has an ASA 25 rating with 3400°K bulbs and 80B filter; with 3200°K bulbs, the speed is ASA 20 with an 80A filter. However, when you must shoot in mixed light, partly daylight and partly tungsten, printing labs have a knack of balancing the color prints through filters for usually satisfactory results.

Ektacolor Professional Film, Type S is for "professional" use according to Kodak, but that does not mean *you* won't enjoy shooting with it. The ASA speed is 100 in daylight, blue flash or electronic flash, and exposures must be 1/10 second or shorter, or filters are called for. Color properties are slightly superior to Kodacolor-X, and the film (like most color films) should be stored under refrigeration until it is used. After exposure, because the latent image of this film changes more rapidly than that of Kodacolor-X, Ek-

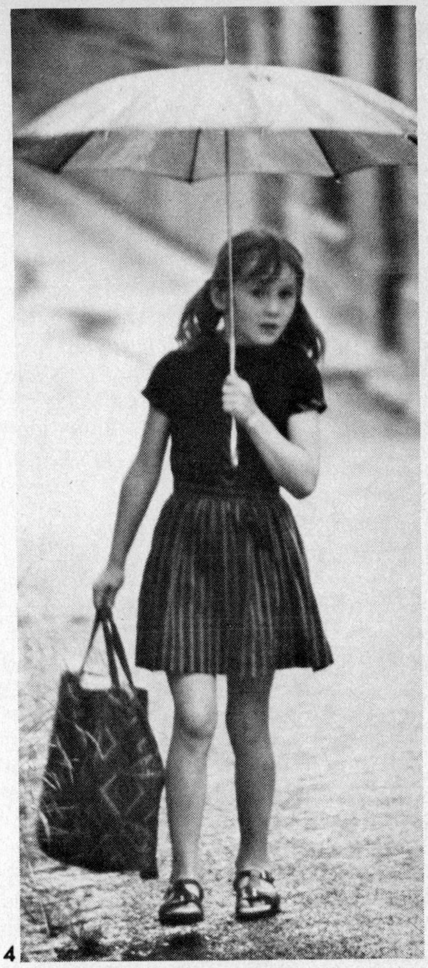

4

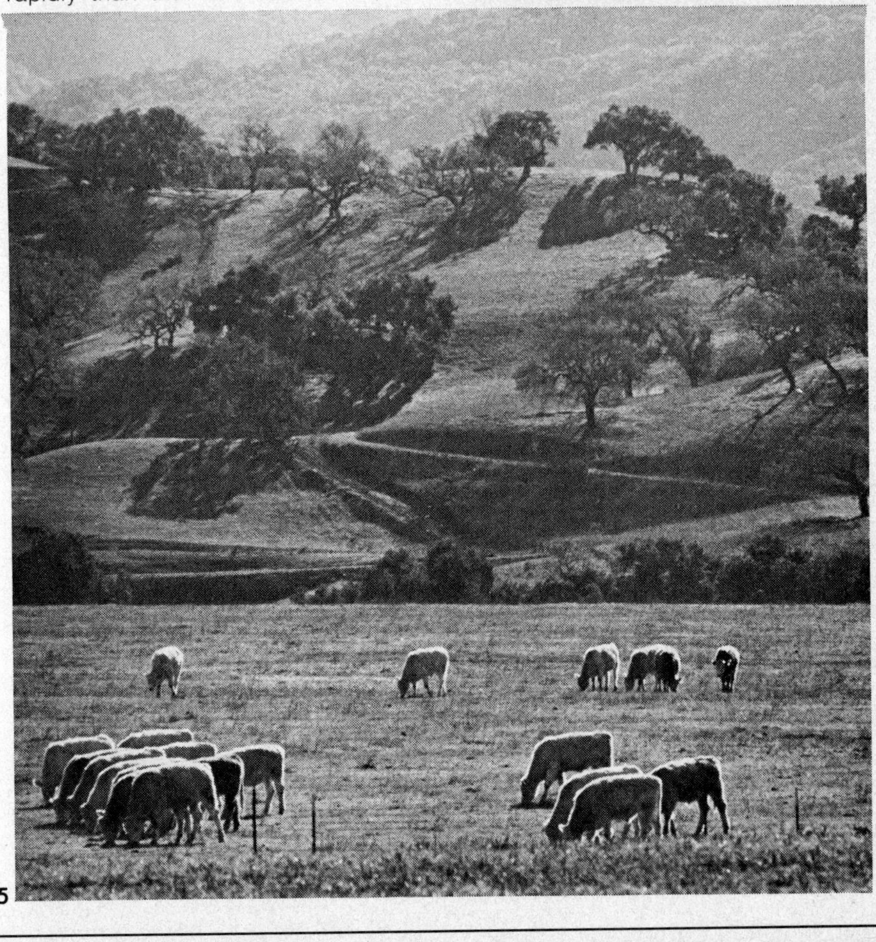

5

1. Most people hold a camera like this. Note finger on shutter release. The pressure is all exerted downward.

2. To counter the downward pressure of finger on shutter release, and possible movement of camera, it is advisable to apply counter-pressure with thumb. Downward pressure of release finger is balanced by upward pressure of thumb.

3. One of Ron Contarsy's award-winners, farm scene was shot on Kodacolor-X film in late afternoon with normal lens, 1/125 second at f/8.

4. Gil Smith held his SLR firmly and shot at 1/30 second at f/5.6 on Plus-X for this rainy-day picture, a Scholastic/Kodak Award winner. The little girl is not critically sharp, but she was moving.

5. Ron Contarsy was able to change lenses quickly on his SLR camera to capture this pastoral scene which he stopped for on an impulse. He switched from a normal lens to a 135mm, and shot Tri-X, 1/250 second at f/16. It was a Scholastic/Kodak Award winner.

tacolor Professional should be processed as soon as possible.

Agfacolor negatives are similar to those from Kodacolor, though greens may have slightly more fidelity. Agfacolor is also balanced for daylight, and has an ASA 80 rating.

Other good color negative films include Kodacolor 11 (for 110 cameras), Fujicolor and Dynacolor.

Color transparency (slide) films/ Along with increased photographic sophistication seems to come the desire to shoot color slides rather than negatives. There are a number of brands and types, some of which have an advantage of high speed, and some are balanced for tungsten light. Color qualities vary from one film to another, and each has its boosters. You can have negatives, and then color prints, made from color slides which may also be copied or contact printed.

As a *general* rule-of-thumb, slower speed slide films offer more brilliant color and finer grain, while faster films allow you to shoot in difficult lighting conditions at reasonable apertures and shutter speeds. Differences in film speeds affect the way you shoot and the type of pictures you may take. If you are trying to capture football action on a semi-sunny day, Kodachrome II will provide the ultimate in grain-free sharpness—but you will be shooting at 1/500 second at f/3.5. High Speed Ektachrome pushed to ASA 400 will reduce the quality of enlargement, but will allow 1/1000 second between f/8 and f/11. On a dull day or at night, you must choose a high-speed film, of which GAF 500 is the fastest.

Kodachrome II (daylight ASA 25) has long been the standard of comparison for color and sharpness, since it is uniquely made to be grainless. Its colors are brilliant and saturated, its contrast is greater than most other color films and its slow speed can be somewhat frustrating in low light situations. Kodachrome II Type A is the tungsten-light version, balanced for 3400°K floods, with a speed of ASA 40. You can also use Type A in daylight at ASA 25 with an 85 filter.

Kodachrome-X (ASA 64) is a higher-speed version of the old favorite, and its colors are slightly subdued compared to Kodachrome II. Kodak says most viewers can't see any difference in sharpness or graininess compared to Kodachrome II when projected, but my own observations indicate that Kodachrome-X has perceptible grain.

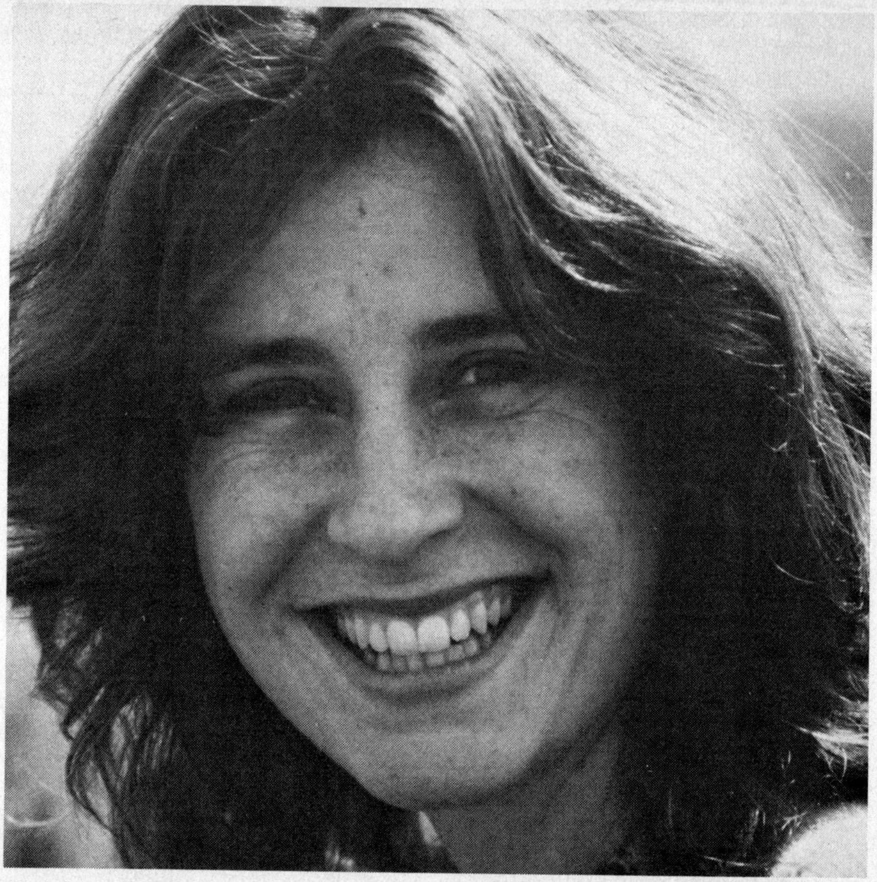

1

Ektachrome-X (ASA 64) is "not as sharp as Kodachrome-X," says Kodak, but "it's difficult to see the difference on the screen." Since I prefer this film to either of the Kodachromes (for speed, contrast and color characteristics), it is appropriate to say right here that the best way to decide on the color film(s) *you* prefer is to shoot a roll or two of those most likely to please you, and make your own comparisons. Each transparency film has its pros and cons; none has a monopoly on excellence.

Ektachrome Professional (ASA 50) is made only in 120 rolls, and according to Roger Davidson (who operates a quality color lab in Santa Monica, California), "The big thing about EP is its rendering of skin tones." People of different complexions and coloring will come out with distinctly different flesh tones, he reports, but on Ektachrome-X by comparison, everyone will "look the same." Mr. Davidson continues, "EP is very sensitive to anything you do to it that is not normal—filter changes, exposure, or a change in the reflectivity of surrounding surfaces. This is not true with Ektachrome-X. Hardly anything you can do will change it—and yet, for outdoor scenes and general purpose photography, it probably renders those scenes better than *any* film. Ektachrome-X gives a brilliant

1. This and the next four photographs offer comparison of films and of film terms defined in text. All are equivalent of 8x10 enlargements. This is how model Kris Mufich looks on Panatomic-X, a slow (ASA 32) film with extremely fine grain, extremely high resolving power, very high sharpness.

2. Medium-speed (ASA 125) Plus-X has very fine grain, high resolving power, and very high sharpness.

3. High-speed (ASA 400) Tri-X film has fine grain, medium resolving power, and very high sharpness.

4. Extremely high-speed (ASA 1250) Royal-X Pan film has moderately coarse grain, moderately low resolving power, and very high sharpness. Royal-X comes in 120 film size only; other photos in series are from 35mm.

5. Extremely high-speed 2475 Recording film can be exposed at Els of 1000-4000, has coarse grain, low resolving power, very high sharpness.

'Kodachrome-type color' and has a teriffic latitude in relation to accessories like filters and other modifications. The fact that it gives you one kind of color only can be lived with because most of the time the scenes and the color it renders are quite compatible."

Very interesting and contrasting comment, I feel, and I have included it to show how genuine—and different—opinions can be about color films. If you shoot 35mm slides, Ekta-

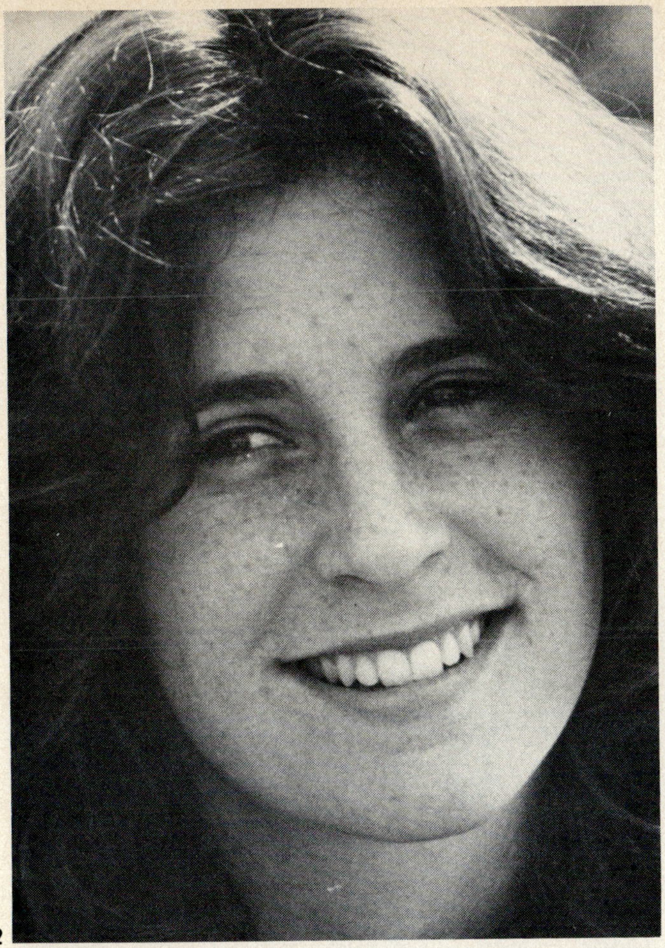

2

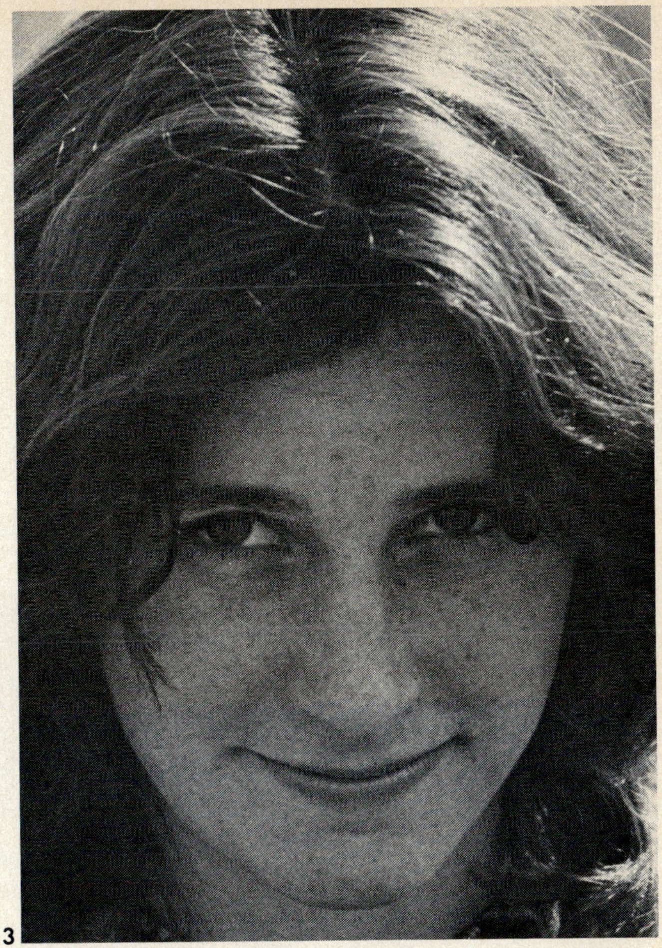

3

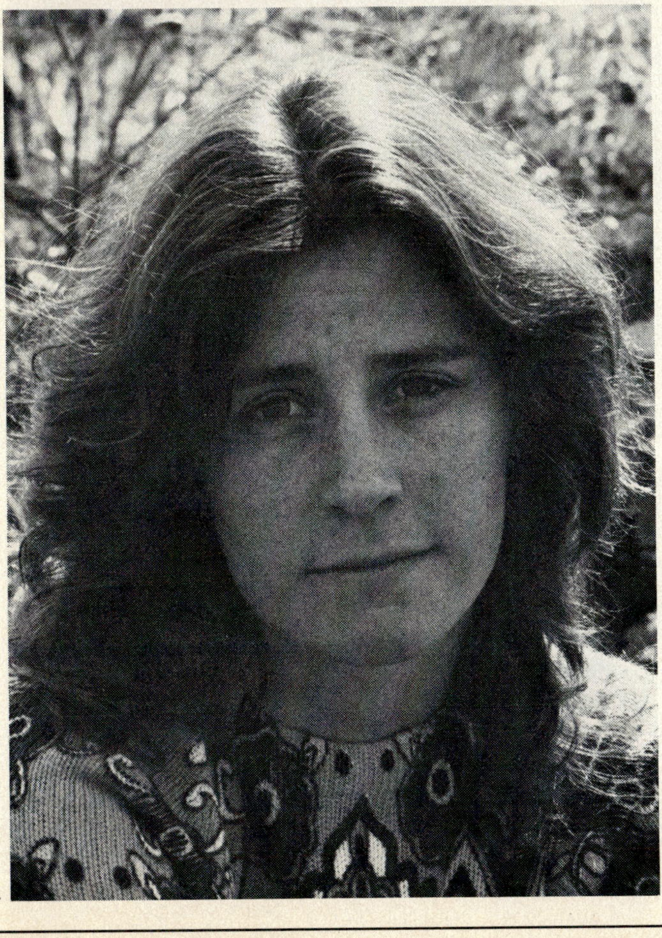

4

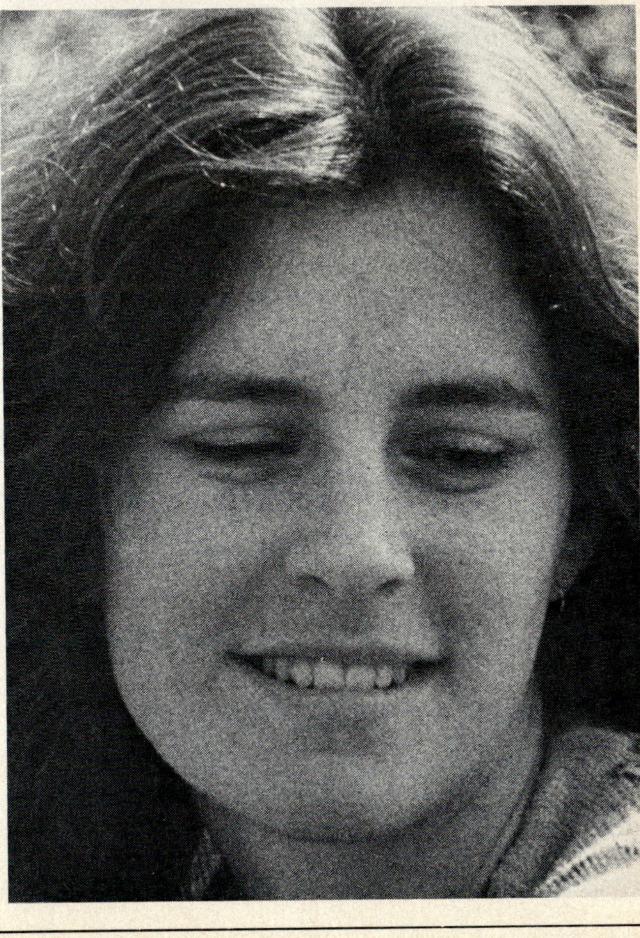

5

chrome Professional is not available, anyway, and if you discover, as I have, that Ektachrome-X is the best *compromise* color film around for speed and fidelity, you may also find it is capable of subtleties despite Davidson's professional attitude about it.

High Speed Ektachrome (Daylight ASA 160) can be a lifesaver in existing light indoors, or outdoors when depth of field and/or higher shutter speeds are important. It is slightly grainier than the other Kodak films and offers slightly less color saturation and contrast. Kodak offers special processing, allowing you to shoot HSE at ASA 400, and ASA 320 for the Type B emulsion. High Speed Ektachrome Type B (ASA 125) is designed for use with 3200°K photofloods. You may also use it in daylight with an 85B conversion filter, reducing the speed to ASA 80.

Roger Davidson points out, "The latitude of high-speed films is quite large. Anything on the basis of overexposure should be avoided, but underexposure adds to the inherent speed of the film." He suggests doubling the film speed rating, and have the lab develop accordingly. "This brings up contrast and gives you good clean whites that look like Ektachrome-X." I feel this technique can be worthwhile *if* you need the extra speed, but High Speed Ektachrome at ASA 160 works quite suitably.

There are a number of other good transparency films that are listed with comments where they apply:

Agfachrome CT-18 (ASA 50) yields beautifully rich, warm images that are lovely for nature or portraits.

Fujichrome RK (ASA 64) and Fujichrome R-100 (ASA 100) combine subtlety with richness.

GAF 64 (ASA 64), GAF T/100 (ASA 100), GAF 200 (ASA 200) and GAF 500 (ASA 500) run the gamut of film speeds for all-around use. GAF 500 is best shot in low-light conditions for which it is designed.

Dynachrome 64 (ASA 64) reproduces colors accurately, but not harshly.

The speed and balance of color slide films can change very quickly (four weeks in a warm room) and they should be kept refrigerated before using them, and not left in hot, moist places for more than a few hours. When removing film from the refrigerator, allow an hour or so for warm-up. If high humidity can't be avoided, carry film in a can or jar with a top and a packet or two of silica gel to dry the air. All film should be used before the expiration date stamped on the package, but if you keep color rolls refrigerated, you can extend their time a few months. I have used Ektachrome-X four or five months outdated (and refrigerated, not frozen) with no critical shift in color quality—but the practice is not recommended.

BLACK-AND-WHITE FILMS

Ilford, Inc. is a British manufacturer trying to make a comeback in distribution of its black-and-white films (plus printing papers and chemicals) in the U.S. In past years the Ilford line of films was popular with a num-

1

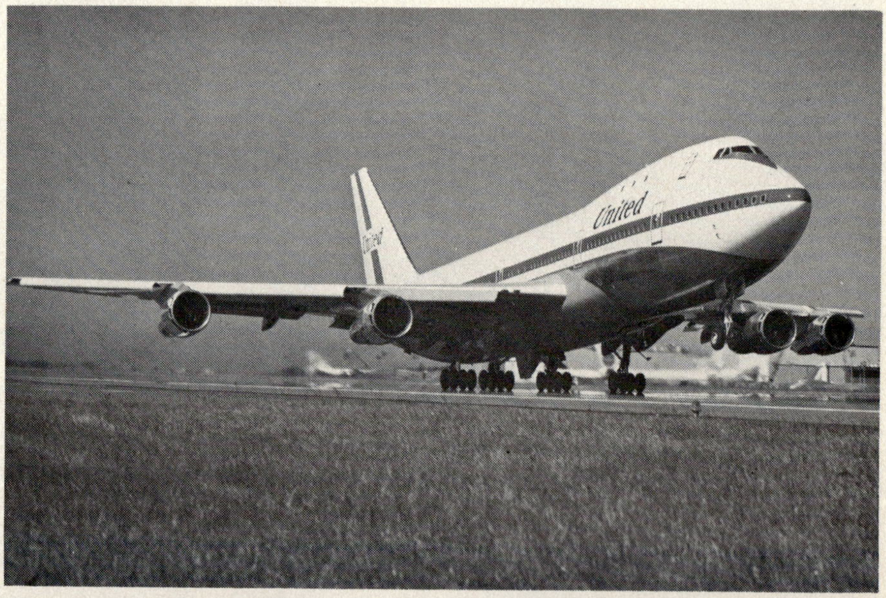

2

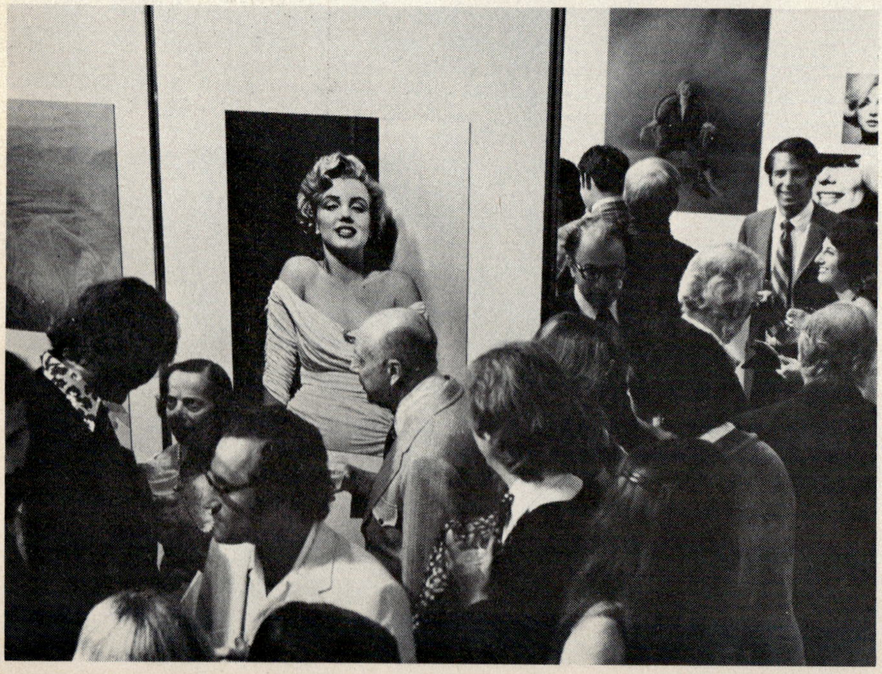

3

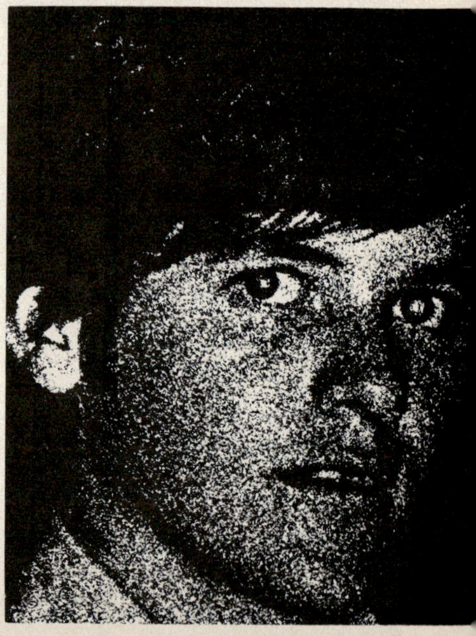

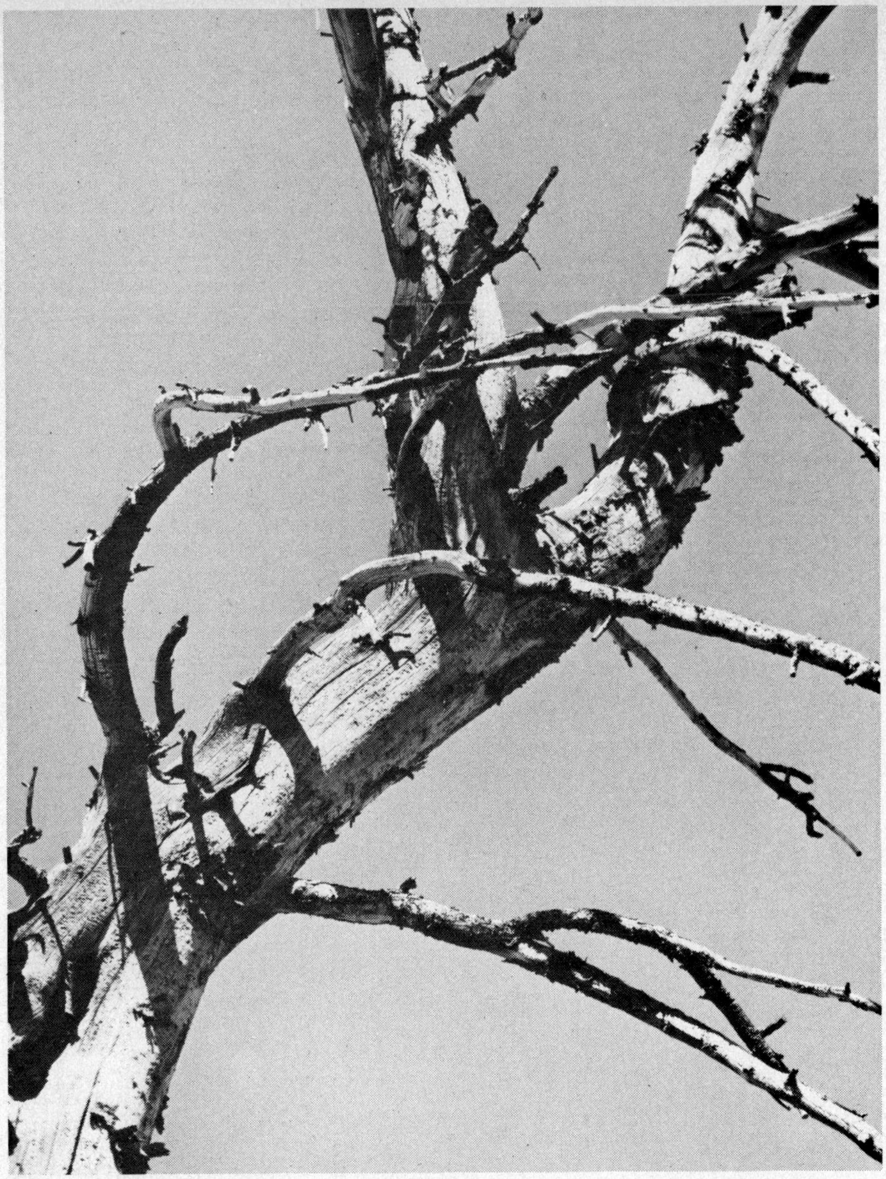

4

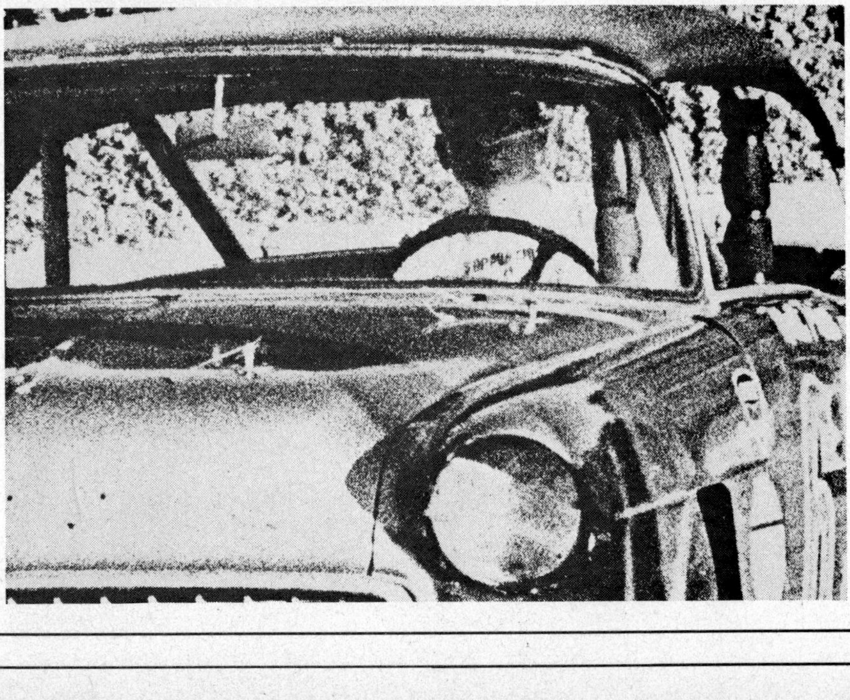

ber of photographers for tonal characteristics and good grain structure. Their three films are: Pan F (ASA 50), FP4 (ASA 125) and HP4 (ASA 400), which almost match Kodak's films in speed, and may be worth trying in order to discover Ilford qualities for yourself.

Kodak also makes two very fast black-and-white films which are both grainy, but quite useful in very low light levels. Recording Film 2475 (35mm only) has an ASA rating of 1000, but can easily be boosted well beyond that. Royal-X Pan Film (120-size only) is rated ASA 1250, but it, too, can be used at higher Els and developed in Acufine, Ethol UFG or other high energy developers. Both films are also adaptable to special grain effects when printed on high-contrast paper, and 2475 Recording Film may be rated at El 4000 and developed for nine minutes at 68°F in Kodak DK-50 developer.

Keep in mind that developers and developing techniques have enormous influence on film speeds and negative quality, according to need and personal taste. There is an unbelieveable amount of room for experimentation in regard to films and developers, because of the large number of film-and-developer combinations. For instance, there are seven possible Kodak developers for Panatomic-X: HC-110 in Dilution A, HC-110 in Dilution B, Polydol, Microdol-X, Microdol-X diluted 1:3, D-76 and D-76 diluted 1:1. In addition, Pan-X (and many other films as well) may also be developed in Ethol UFG, Acufine, Autofine, Diafine, and others. Ilford allows you a choice between Microphen (for which you increase the film speed by 50 percent), ID-11, ID-48 and D-76. GAF suggests its own line of developers for its films (GAF 125 and GAF 500)—Isodol, Isodol 1:1, Permadol and Hyfinol, though

1. A United Air Lines photographer chose fine-grained Panatomic-X for 747 take-off shot which had to be enlarged mural size to hang on wall. Shot with 150mm lens on Hasselblad.

2. Tri-X is the old dependable of many professionals who must work in existing light as author did at opening of a Marilyn Monroe photo show. Exposure was 1/60 second at f/5.6 with a 35mm wide-angle lens.

3. When exposed at an El of 4000 and developed 50 percent longer than normal, then printed on No. 6 high-contrast paper, 2475 Recording film produces interesting grainy effects.

4. Medium-speed film such as Plus-X is often ideal for outdoor pictures when sharp detail and contrast are desirable. Author shot this with Bronica at 1/125 second, f/11, no filter.

they add that "any standard developer" may be used.

This need not be a source of confusion, however, because if you zero in on one or two developers and like the results, stay with them.

A FEW TECHNICAL EVALUATIONS

Photographers are apt to do a lot of talking, comparing and even bragging about the quality of their pictures, using terms that may or may not be accurate. A few of these terms related to film, lenses, prints and slides are worthwile defining:

Film characteristics/ These can be plotted objectively by means of sensitometry, which means testing that shows how film responds to exposure and development. The density of the film is measured and plotted on a graph as a *characteristic curve.* This curve demonstrates the range of a film from absolute underexposure to absolute overexposure. At the underexposed end of the curve is the "toe," followed by a "straight line" for middle areas of the exposure and a "shoulder" for the overexposed area. Shadow detail and some lower middle tones are represented by toe-area exposure. A negative that is overexposed or overdeveloped moves up to the shoulder area of the curve, and the result is highlights that block up and lose detail. If you are eager to learn more technicalities about film curve characteristics, *Kodak Professional Black-andWhite Films* is a good buy for $1.50.

Sharpness or definition/ Most photographers claim to be seeking "sharp" pictures, though it is more proper to say good *definition,* since sharpness is only one of several factors which decides the overall appearance of detail in a photograph. Definition = sharpness + resolving power + fine grain + acutance. Let's take those terms one by one.

Grain/ As a general rule, low-speed films have finer grain than high-speed films—and sharpness and resolving power are better in fine-grain films. Graininess in black-and-white films is caused when grains of silver clump together during development. In color film, clumped up dye particles are to blame. Excessive grain, that is, greater than is inherent in a film, can be caused by overdevelopment or overexposure in black-and-white and by underexposure or overdevelopment of color negatives. This makes time-and-temperature controls very important in the darkroom. Even rinse water temperature can influence grain size after it is developed but before the film is properly fixed. Therefore, expose and develop your negatives for *minimum* density that pleases you, for when a black-and-white negative becomes too dark, dense, opaque, etc., it inherits the disease of graininess.

Resolving power/ This refers to a film's ability to record fine detail. To

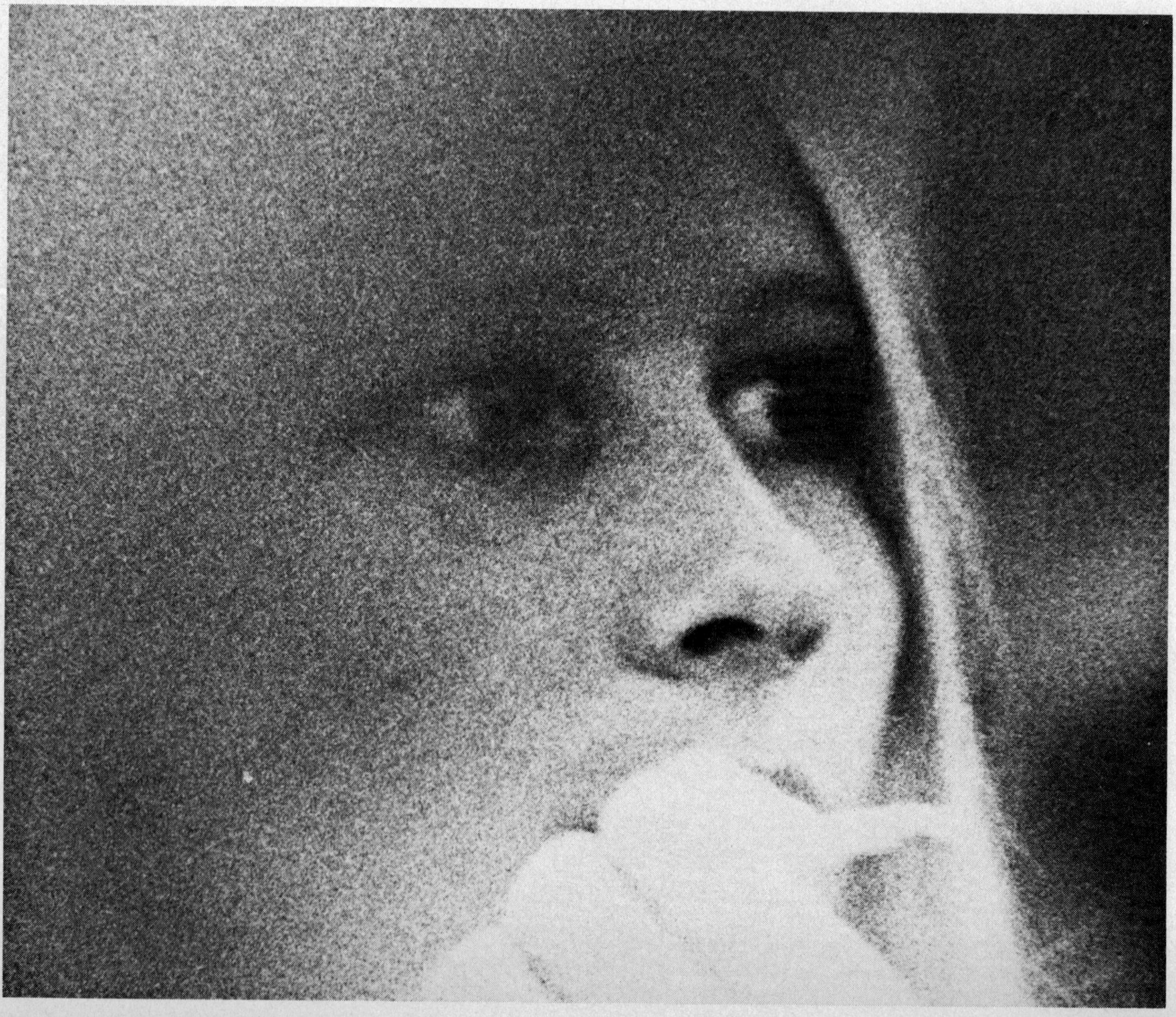

1

measure resolving power, a test chart is photographed. Lines on the chart (which is greatly reduced in size) are separated by spaces of the same width. The negative image is examined under a microscope and the number of lines per millimeter that can be recognized separately is determined. The resolving power of a camera lens must be at least three times greater than the resolving power of the film to realize the latter's potential resolution. As examples, Kodak describes Panatomic-X as having extremely fine grain, extremely high resolving power and very high sharpness with a very high degree of enlargement. Tri-X is rated as a fine grain film with medium resolving power, very high sharpness and with a moderate degree of enlargement.

Sharpness/ This often-misused word really refers to how well-defined the edges are between areas of varying contrast. A line between light and dark objects does not photograph as a perfectly sharp line because diffusion in the film emulsion causes the dark area of a negative to bleed over into a light area. This is not a disease, but a characteristic of emulsion. Sharpness depends upon the type of emulsion, its thickness, the film base and its backing. Improved film-making has produced thin emulsion and anti-halation (in the backing) properties, so Kodak says both Panatomic-X and Tri-X have "very high sharpness."

Acuity/ This is closely related to sharpness. If you put the edge of a razor blade against the emulsion surface of a film and expose the the emulsion to light, the sharpness of the etched line would determine the film's acuity. The line can be just as well-defined in grainy film as in fine-grain film, for acuity or acutance is a measure of the sharpness with which a film can reproduce the edge of an object.

What do all these terms mean to you as a photographer? They help guide your search for the right film and developer combinations in order to make "maximum" enlargements. Just what maximum means to you depends on many variables, but it might be said roughly that if you like to make 11x14 or 16x20 enlargements, the quality of your negatives, lenses and processing are all involved. Each must fit your needs, and knowing the terms for at least precise *semantic* evaluation of negatives, slides or prints will be of use when you make *visual* evaluations.

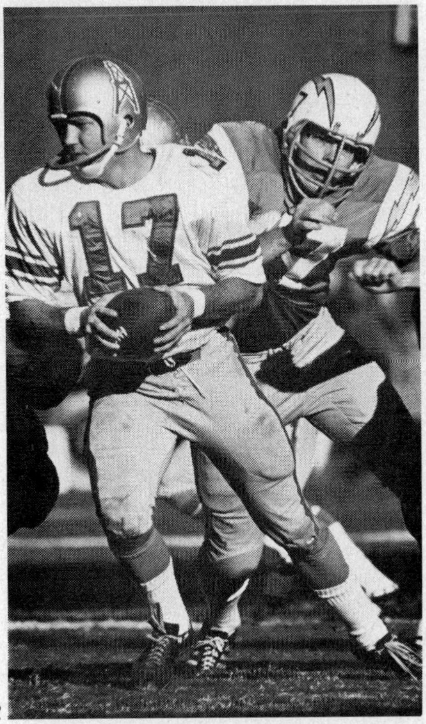

2

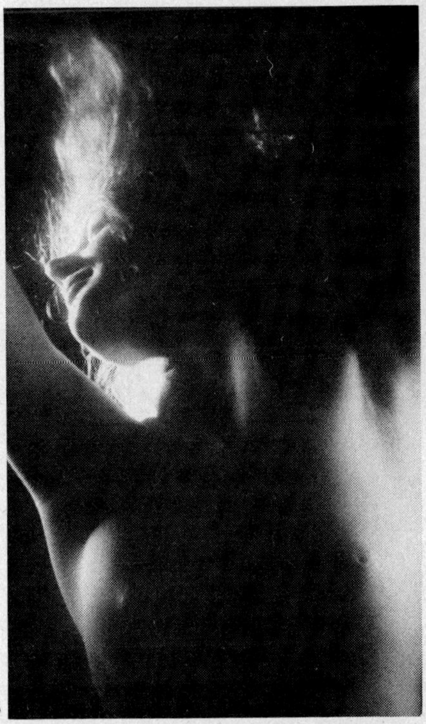

3

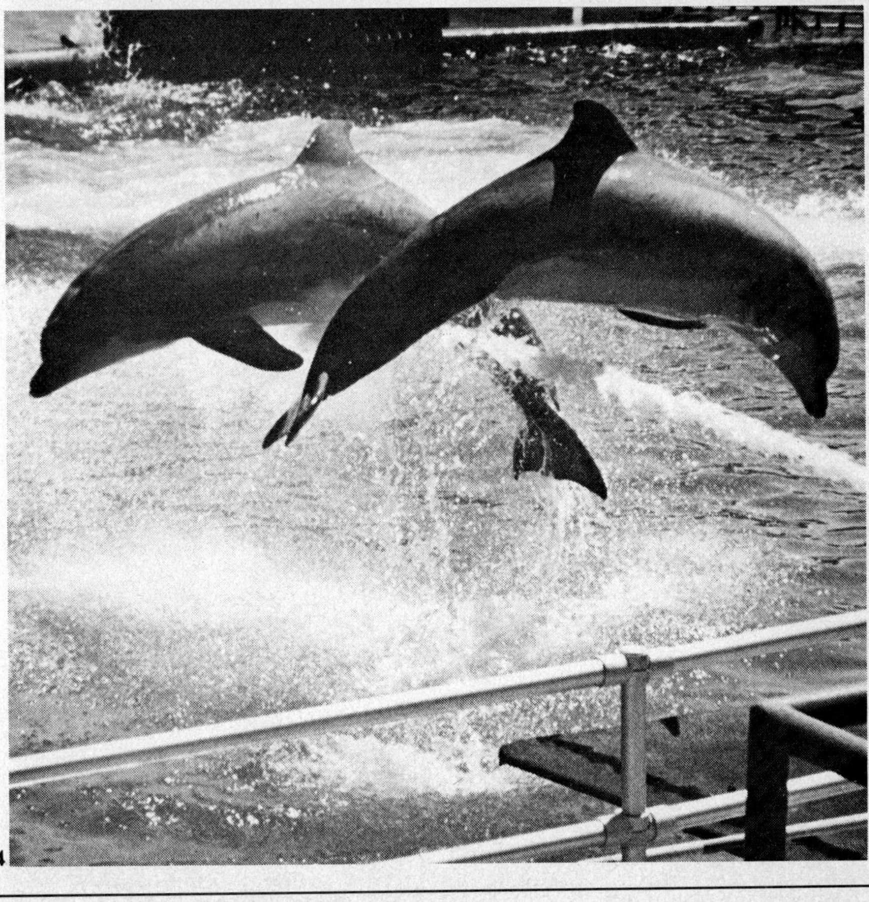

4

1. Larry Kostroski intentionally amplified grain pattern of Tri-X film in portrait by making huge enlargement of which this is only a section. It won Scholastic/Kodak Award.

2. Contrast created by sunlight gives punch to exciting action shot by Darryl Norenberg, who shot from sidelines with telephoto lens at 1/1000 second.

3. Both contrast and tonality add drama to Jim Cornfield's backlighted nude, which also illustrates the latitude of modern films.

4. Even at f/16, camera focused on leaping dolphins 12 feet away did not carry depth of field completely in foreground or background, but this is not a pictorial handicap here. Exposure on Tri-X was 1/1000 second with 52mm lens on Konica Autoreflex T.

CHAPTER 5

Outdoor Lighting

There are only two sources of light, natural and artificial. Within these categories, however, are dozens of variations to puzzle, challenge, and reward photographers. In this chapter natural outdoor light is examined according to its direction and intensity. Photographers discover that awareness of light, any light, is all one related subject. As you learn to recognize the qualities of light, you also gain a feeling for where to *put* it when shooting indoors, which is covered in the next chapter.

Outdoor lighting involves not only exposure, but influences the mood and impact of your pictures. Let's "see the light" photographically.

DIRECTIONAL LIGHT

Indoors or out, if light falls sharply enough to create distinct shadows, it has a primary direction. Generally, there are three main directions, each of which lends its own distinct character to pictures.

Front light/ You have probably heard the ancient advice, "Shoot with the sun coming over your shoulder," which aware photographers *ignore* because it is superficial. When the sun is behind you, your subject is largely front lighted, and while you need not avoid this direction when shooting, there's no proscribed reason to achieve it as a matter of course.

Front lighting, outdoors or with floodlights, can effectively *model* the form of people, places and things, depending on the angle of the light. Modeling means to delineate shape, texture and color. If the sun shines directly in front of a person, it may create pleasant shadows, it could accent details of a building, but the contours of a mountain would blend together and look flat. In other words, overhead front sunlight has its value depending on the shape and direction of your subject, but overhead sun at high noon in summer should be avoided. It causes eyes to be lost in dark pockets, and is rarely as useful as sunlight slanting toward a model from one side or the other.

Sidelight/ Many outdoor subjects are more interesting in light from the side, because form and texture stand out with more emphasis. Mountains, buildings, or faces are all more dramatic in sidelight, even if shadows turn somewhat dark. Take someone outdoors when the sun is no more than halfway above the horizon. Stand your model facing the sun, then with the sun at one side, and finally with it coming from behind. You'll see how much more visual excitement there is in sidelighting, and backlight has its own special advantages, too.

Backlight/ When the sun, or artificial light, is primarily behind a subject, the effect can be striking. The top of a head or the edge of a face is *rim lighted,* an effect often created by portrait photographers and theater lighting experts. A thin, bright rim of light outlines a form and separates it from the background. Backlight is exciting, and it's a favorite of photographers who know how to use it to achieve outstanding effects.

Exposure in backlight requires certain precautions. To obtain a suitable balance between highlights and shadows, professional motion picture and still photographers fill (illuminate) the front shadow area of a backlighted face or object by adding artificial light (flood or flash), or by using a portable reflector. This light from the front reduces the extreme contrast and allows for near-normal exposure, making shadow detail more explicit.

Incidentally, you can buy ready-made reflectors, or make your own by covering a piece of heavy cardboard with crinkled aluminum foil, or you can use white cardboard itself. Two sections of cardboard, perhaps

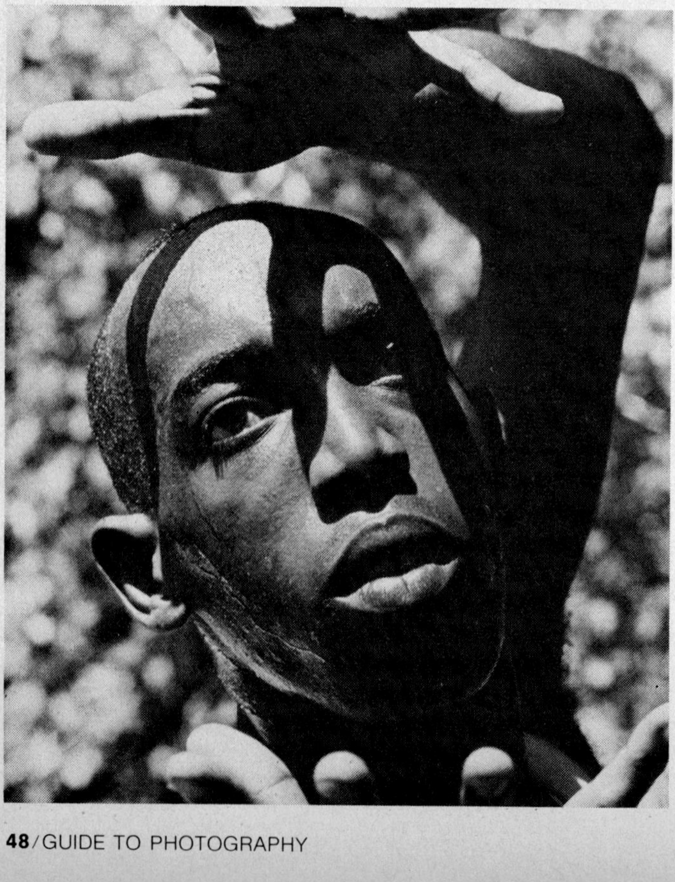

1

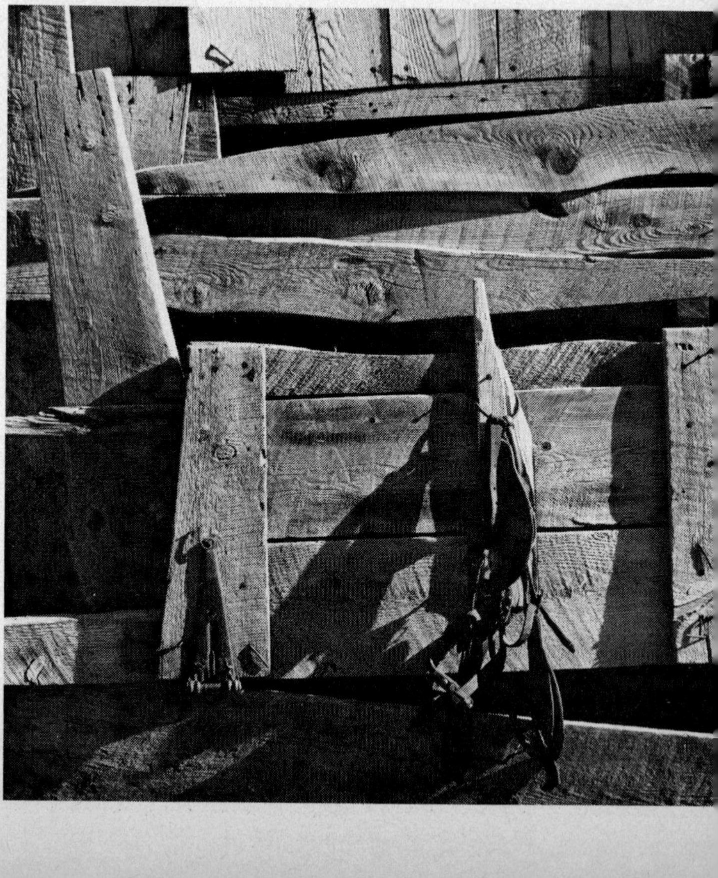

2

24x30 inches each, may be hinged with heavy tape, and folded together to carry. You may also use a white photographic umbrella as an outdoor reflector, or make a stationary substitute. Insert the ends of two sections of a telescoping light stand into holes at top and bottom of a bowed piece of white cardboard, maybe 30x40 inches. The reflector can be adjusted to a convenient height in the light stand, or held by a friend to gracefully illuminate a backlighted face.

If you do not fill backlighted shadows, you can compensate through exposure to lighten faces, etc. by opening your aperture about two stops more than highlights call for. For example, using a medium-speed color film, my camera meter might indicate that a model in backlight should have an exposure of 1/125 second at f/11. I'll open the lens to f/5.6 or f/6.3, maintaining the same shutter speed, and shadow detail will be fine. Of course, the brightest areas of the picture will "burn out" or be overexposed, but I don't mind since the face and figure on which I'm concentrating will be exposed in good detail on my negative or slide.

To check backlight exposure, read the total scene with your meter (hand-held or built into your camera), and then move close to take another reading of the model's face. You'll discover about a two-stop difference. If background detail is important and you can't use a reflector or a fill light, compromise at a one-stop increase.

3

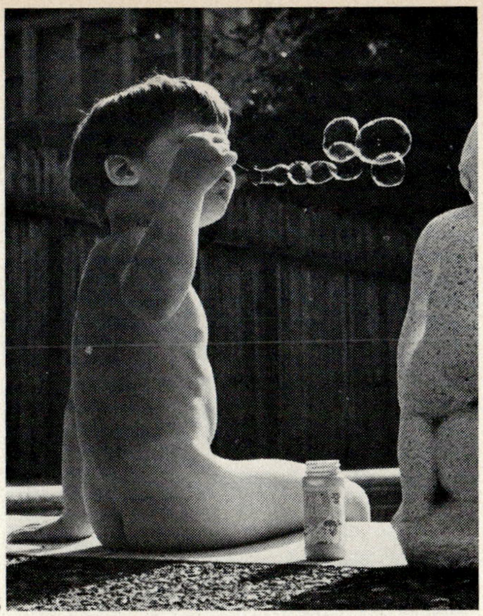

1. Strong, overhead front sunlight provided effect in this picture of dancer by Bruce Aronson, a Scholastic/Kodak Award winner. Fortunately, sun was not higher, or man's eyes would have been dark pockets.

2. Sidelighting gives this Utah barn its distinctive appearance. Author used view camera with 8-inch lens, and printed the full negative.

3. Backlighting accentuates form of child and bubbles in charming photograph by Scholastic/Kodak Award-winner Bill Kuniholm. Child's body was also rim lighted.

4. Sidelighting is ideal to show many kinds of natural form such as sand dunes in Death Valley. Camera was a Bronica, exposure was 1/250 second at f/16 on Tri-X film.

Backlighting also means that a subject does not have to squint, and it creates dramatic landscape effects that can turn an ordinary scene into one that has real pictorial impact. Once you've enjoyed the pleasures of backlight, you'll be more conscious of how to keep it under control for many purposes.

HAZY SUN AND OVERCAST SKIES

When the sky is partly cloudy, or the atmosphere is misty, sunlight is diffused or muted. Though bright sun is usually preferable to show form and accentuate color, a hazy sky is a blessing for portraits. Colors are bright-to-pastel, people are comfortable and facial features are pleasantly recognizable without harsh, unflattering shadows. Some amateur photographers who don't know the score are dismayed "when there's no sun," and they want to photograph outdoor activity or make portraits. But when they discover the welcome virtues of hazy sun, they begin looking for ways of avoiding bright days for people pictures.

Nearly the same can be said for an overcast day, short of rainfall, though when there's no sun at all, contrast is diminished and a certain dullness may set into some picture situations, especially when shooting color. Use a 1A Skylight filter to warm the color in outdoor pictures on an overcast day; it does wonders to produce brilliance not seen as vividly by the naked eye. The reason a Skylight filter works, in-

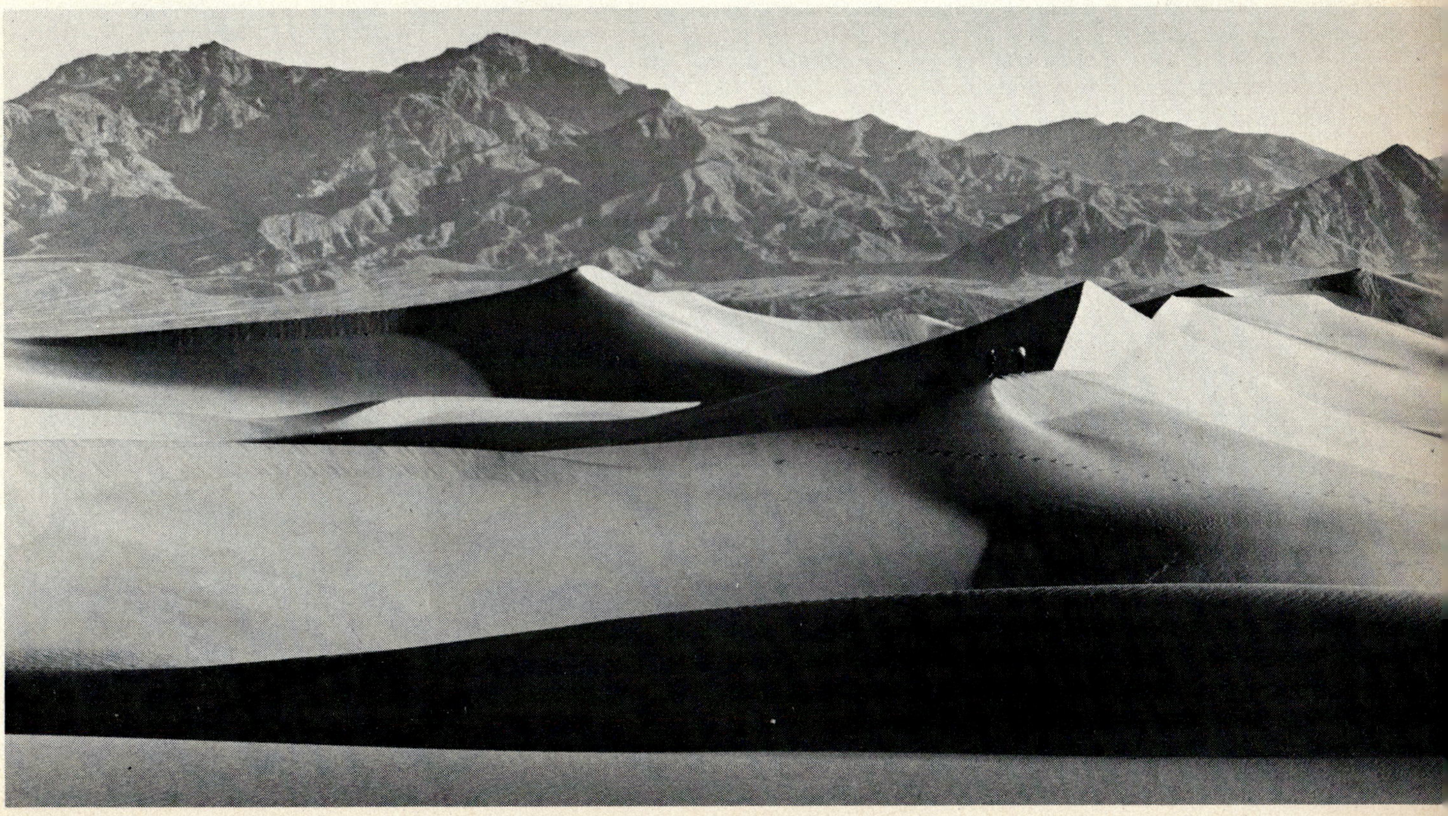

4

cidentally, is that overcast daylight is colder and bluer than sunlight, and the slight tint of a filter snaps color into your film.

In black-and-white, if you are faced with a dull day and feel like shooting, you can increase contrast by underexposure and increased development. Of course, you have to keep track of what you are doing so you know where to cut the underexposed film off for special development. If you decrease exposure by a full stop, add about 25 percent to your developing time. This technique perks up contrast quite nicely, so negatives will print on normal or slightly contrasty paper. Experiment for yourself.

REFLECTED DAYLIGHT

I mentioned using a reflector to illuminate shadows outdoors in strong sunlight, but there is another way to profit by reflected light, especially for portraits. You don't have to wait for a hazy-sun day to put your model at ease and enjoy soft light, if you choose an outdoor location in shadow, either opposite a reflecting surface or with your own reflector. A light-colored wall next to a shadow area acts as a natural reflector. I often use the patio of my home, which is partly shaded on one side; from a wall on the other side sunlight bounces neatly into the shade. Thus a limited, very convenient area becomes an outdoor studio with lovely, indirect illumination, similar to that which professional photographers create outdoors with expensive banks of diffused light or large reflectors. Facial features are distinct and glowing in reflected daylight, and models are comfortable. You'll find such locations under trees, at the sides of buildings, opposite walls, etc.

OUTDOOR EXPOSURE

This topic was introduced in Chapter 3 under "Exposure Meters," where it was noted that built-in through-the-lens camera meters measure reflected light. A majority of SLR and non-interchangeable-lens camera meters are called *center weighted,* which means the meter reads an approximate oval-shaped area in the center of the finder rectangle. In some cameras this area of sensitivity is fairly wide with wide-angle lenses and fairly narrow with telephoto lenses to assure a reading from a representative section of a scene.

In addition, some cameras have separate spot metering systems which measure light on a narrow path of several degrees. You can aim the lens at a shadow area alone and determine exposure without the influence of highlights. Using a camera with a dual-metering system, you can switch from averaging to spot metering, and conveniently suit your exposure reading to the type of lighting at hand. You may end up with an exposure between the two readings, but that is the essence of outdoor exposure (and indoors as well)—personal judgment. Be sure to read the instruction manual with your camera to become familiar with its metering system before using it.

Facts and figures about reflected-, incident-light and spot meters were included in Chapter 3, some of which were based on the findings of *PhotoGraphic* staffer Guy Draughon. Another excerpt is very pertinent here "You might argue that the incident-light meter measures only the light and does not take into consideration the brightness of the subject, therefore forcing the photographer to make his own value judgments. This is true only to the extent that *no* meter thinks for you; that is the photographer's domain. But advocates of incident-light meters argue that you have to think a whole lot less when measuring incident light rather than reflectivity. You will still have to consider a few basic rules—for example, if you want a rim-lighted picture with dark shadows across the face, you'll have to point the hemisphere at the main light source, not at the camera.

"But with a reflected-light meter you would have to take the reading off the rim-lighted area of the face and *also* compensate for the fact that

1. To shoot indoor portrait by daylight Jim Cornfield placed sheet of white cardboard beside model as reflector which effectively filled shadow side of model's face. Note soft, shadowless effect produced by reflector. The portrait has good modeling and very pleasant tonality.

2. Exposure for this backlighted shot was 1½ stops more than camera meter indicated for front lighting to give shadow detail. Pool was burned-in during printing, resulting in balanced tonality in the finished print.

3. Another means of using reflected daylight outdoors is to shoot opposite a white wall which bounces light brilliantly into model's face.

4. Overcast day did not discourage Ron Contarsy from shooting snowed-in shack. Originally in color, it translates well to black-and-white because the black accents prevent monotony. Shot is a Scholastic/Kodak winner.

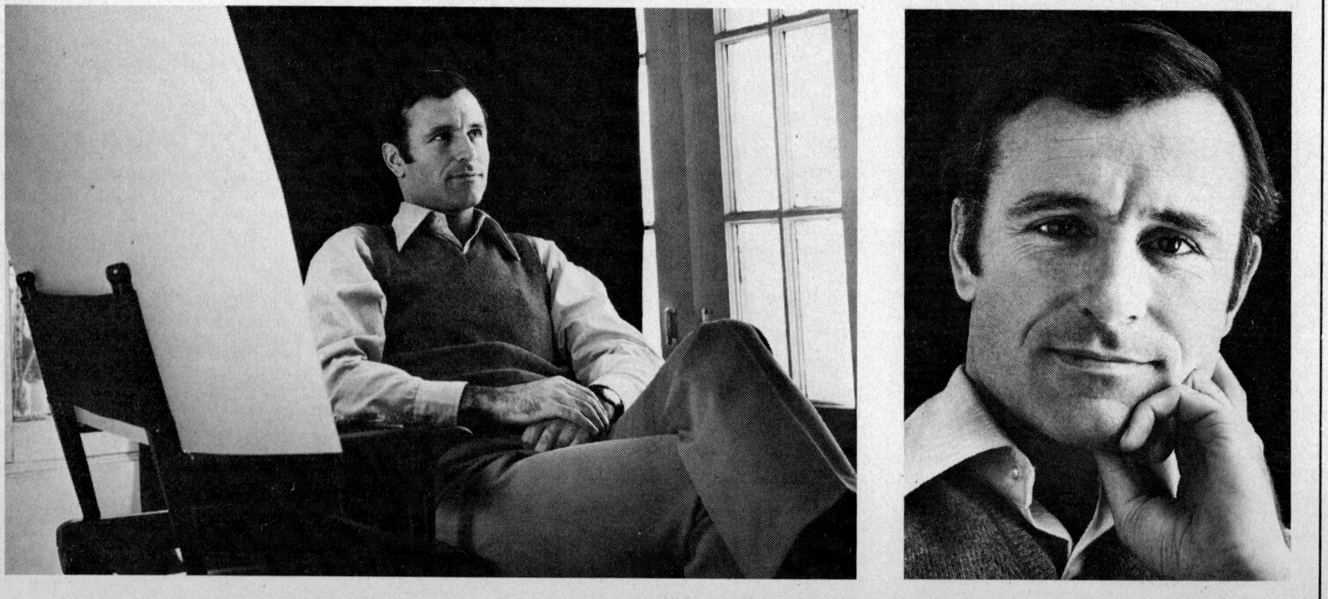

1

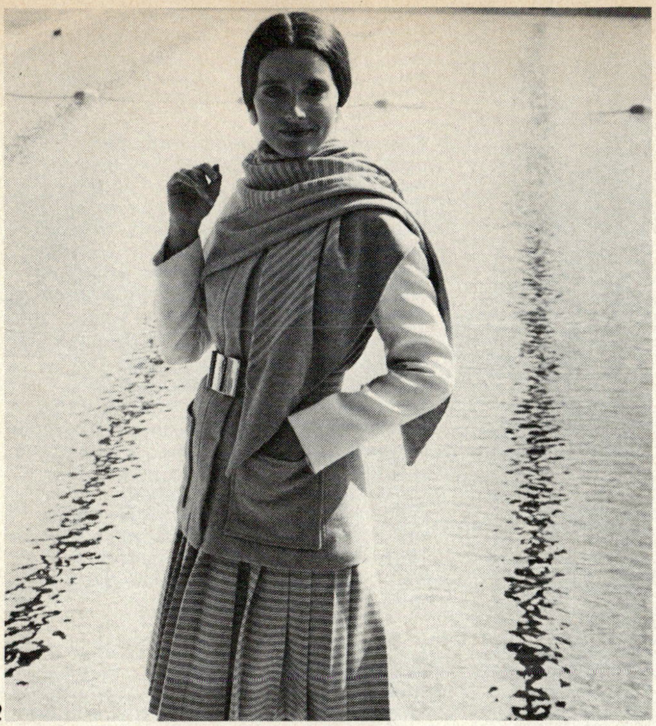
2

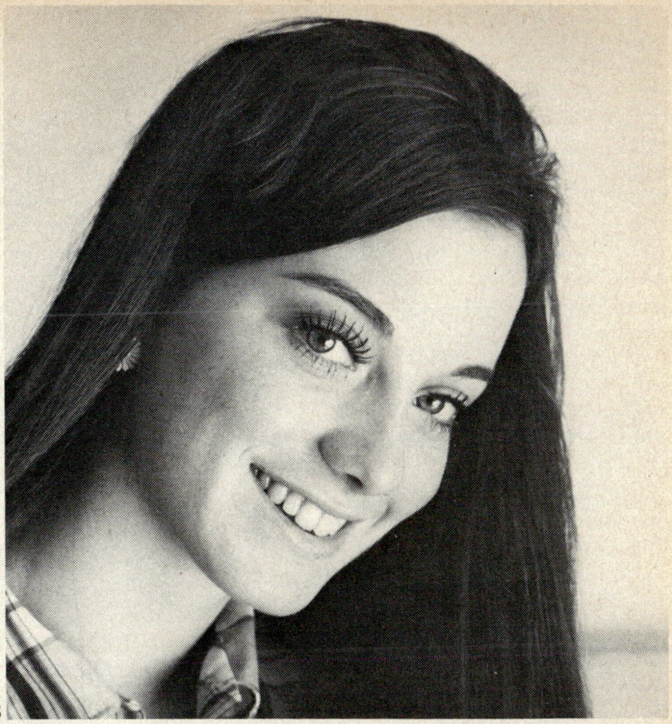
3

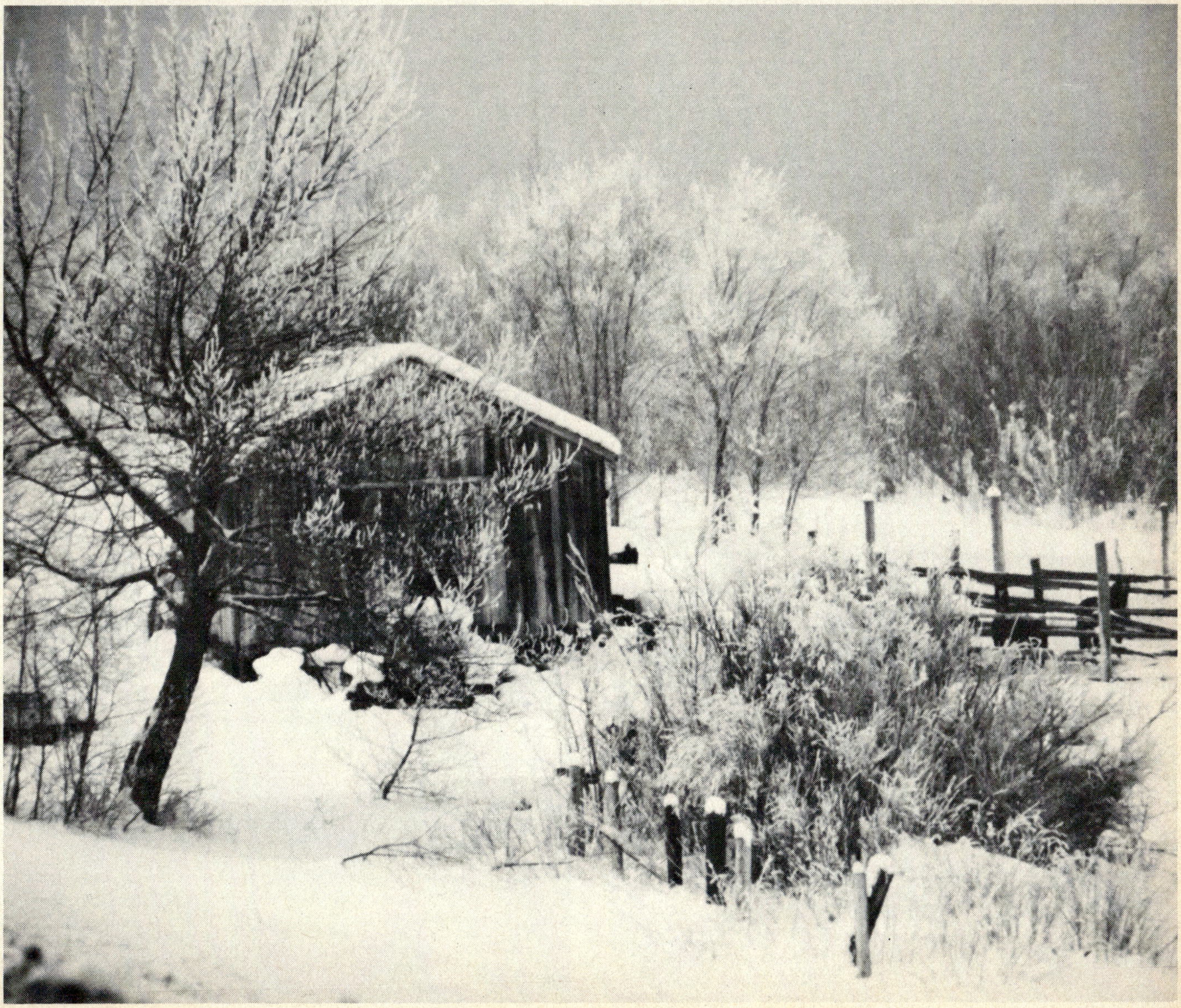
4

the average face reflects twice as much light as an 18-percent-reflectance gray card. You must consider another factor, too, when switching from color film to black-and-white film. In black-and-white photography we are concerned with the shadow areas in which we want detail. In color work we are more concerned with the highlights for rich color. Therefore, a slightly longer exposure may be required in black-and-white photography, while slightly shorter exposures are sometimes called for in color work."

Draughon's last few statements are an intentional repitition of material in Chapter 3—because the information is particularly important. As he continued, "We are attempting to determine which type of light readings will provide the most consistent exposures with the least interpretation."

Some observations/ For his article, Draughon made a series of exposure tests with both reflected-light and incident-light meters, some illustrations from which are included on these pages. In making such tests he suggests shooting several "average scenes" at the exposure indicated by your meter, and then bracket in half-stop increments. This means to give half a stop more and half a stop less exposure than the original aperture indicated by the meter. Transparencies or prints can then be judged accordingly, and you will store in your memory bank the circumstances of lighting, contrast, and which exposure gave the best results.

Here are some of Draughon's notes concerning the tests he made: "Flesh tones are critical, particularly in color photography, and tests proved the incident-light meter excelled here. Reflected-light readings produced consistently underexposed pictures...The reflected-light meter, used without allowing for the fact skin reflects twice as much light as a middle gray card, produced pictures that became progressively underexposed as the models became blonder and fairer. The reflected-light meter would

1. Author used hand-held Weston meter for candid shot of boy-meets-girl, taken with Nikon SP, 50mm lens. Nikon SP is a rangefinder camera, and SLRs with built-in meters simplify matters.

2. In strong backlighted situation, camera meter is likely to be "tricked," meaning that it will indicate setting that will result in underexposure of subject unless you open lens to accommodate shadow detail. Debra Schuster made manual compensation when she shot Scholastic/Kodak Award winner.

3. Photographer/editor Guy Draughon compared two exposure-meter systems. Reading by reflected-light meter was influenced by brightness of water, thereby underexposing foreground subjects and resulting in dark print. Incident-light meter reading called for a little more than a stop additional exposure, which lightened foreground and water as well. When there is contrasty light, aware photographers may take both types of meter readings, and split results as a compromise.

4. Incident-light meter excells when shooting brightly illuminated, backlighted subjects such as this stark white mission at Santa Ynez, Calif. as it was photographed by Guy Draughon. The exposure indicated by incident-light meter opened up shadow areas.

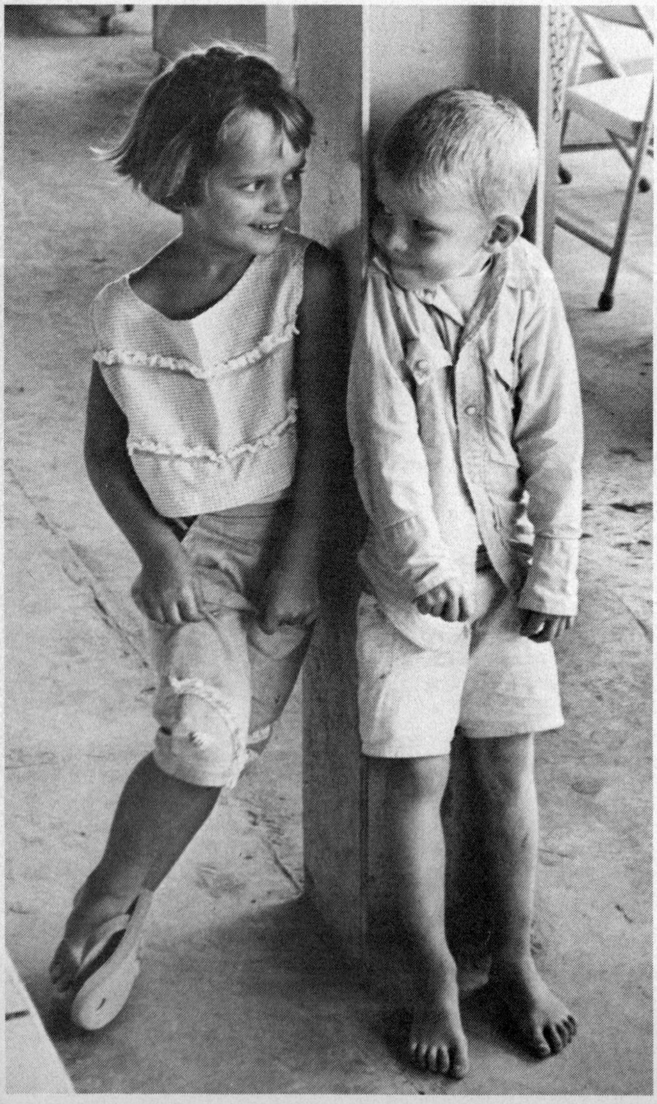

1

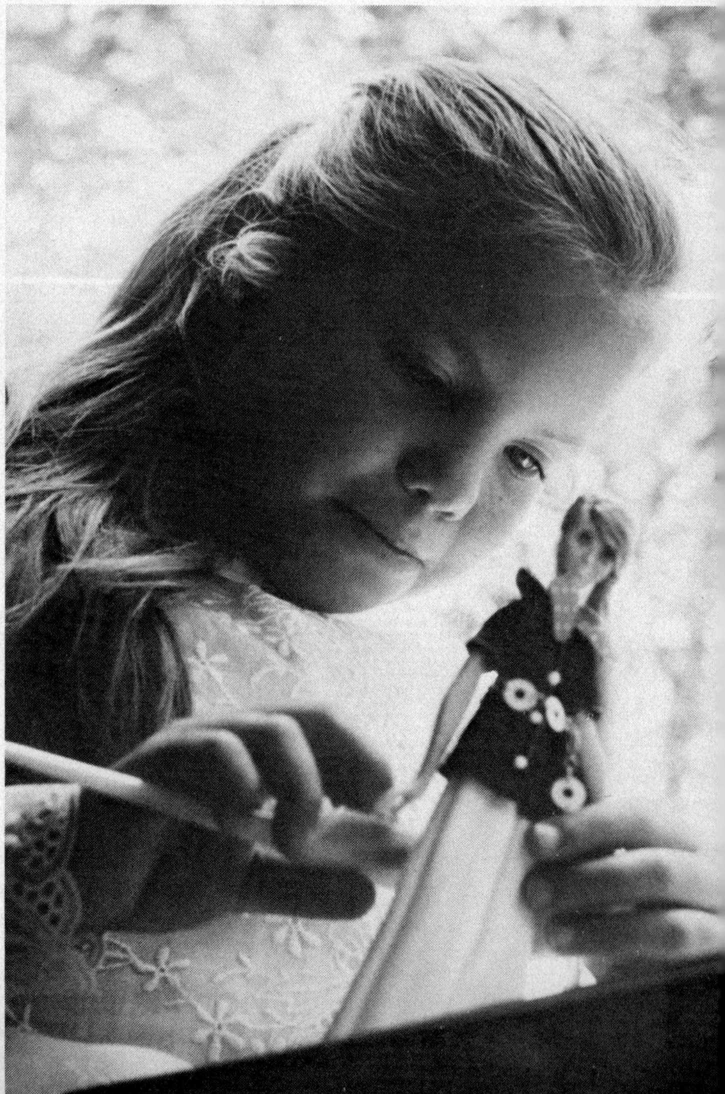

2

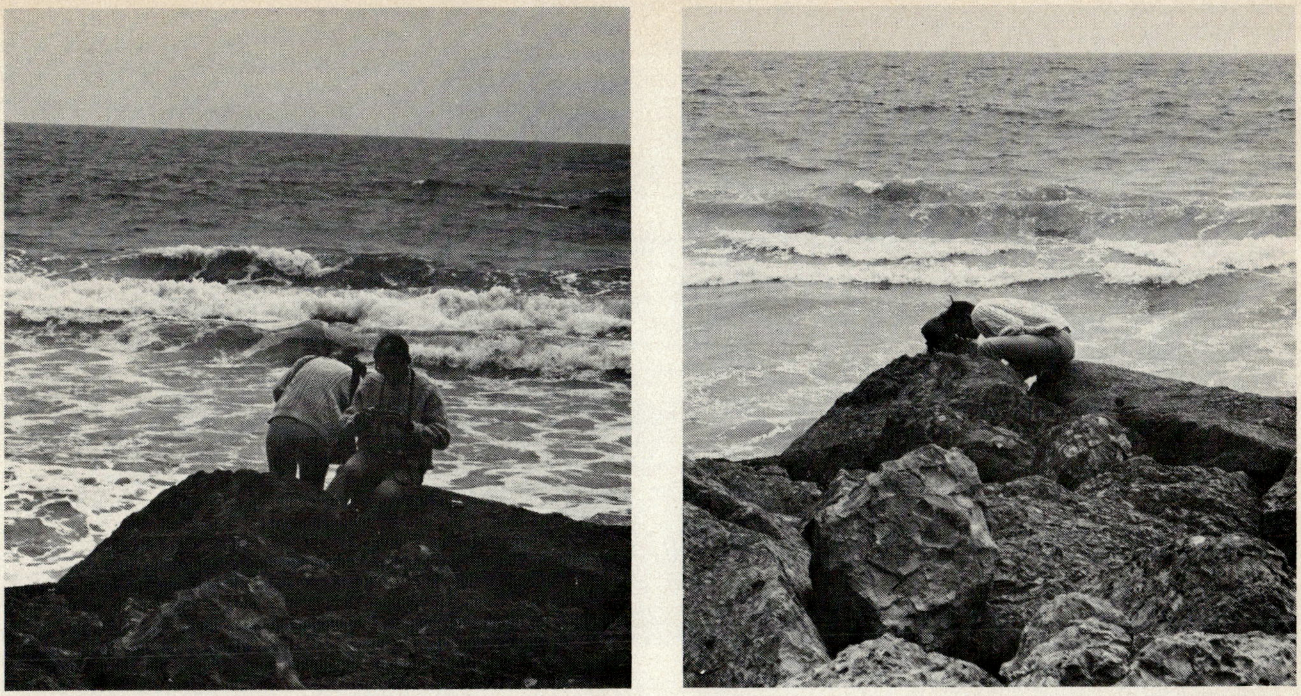

3

have worked fine if I'd taken a reading off a gray card or had opened up a stop after reading the skin tones—but even then, blondes reflect more light than brunettes and more value judgments have to be made.

"In taking comparative readings of 'average scenes'—which included white buildings, dark shadows, grass, streets, trees and a little sky—it became obvious that not many scenes were *totally* average. However, the differences between readings in the reflected-light and the incident-light modes were so small as to be negligible, generally in the range of f/11 as opposed to f/12. This department (effectiveness of the meters) was a toss-up between the two types.

"However, the moment you add a large white building or a large shadowy area to an otherwise 'average' scene, a photographer has three choices:

1. Mentally compensate for the non-average areas that affect your reading.

2. Take a reflected-light reading off a gray card.

3. Switch to incident-light mode.

"I shot backlighting, sidelighting, dark objects and light objects in studio setups and judged the incident-light meter as the clear winner for inside work." At this point Draughon described tests at the beach where the reflected-light meter was highly influenced by white clouds and sand, and indicated an exposure that resulted in too little detail in dark rocks. The incident-light meter reading was a stop more exposure, resulting in a sky a little too white and shadows somewhat too open. An exposure between the two readings would have been more accurate. He then reiterated the essence of photographic exposure, saying:

"In an actual shooting situation, you have to make value judgments on whether sunlit areas or shadow areas are *more important* (italics are mine), because the brightness range of many scenes exceeds the ability of the film to record it."

Where does all this leave photographers already accustomed to using a built-in camera meter or just getting used to one? The first answer is that *awareness* of all the ramifications of exposure will better prepare you to evaluate your negatives and slides more accurately and with more satisfaction. The second answer is that you can and will learn to trust your own meter, and with experience, shoot "right-on" pictures consistently. Like many professionals, I have been through the entire reflected-light/incident-light/built-in meter saga that is rife with disappointments and frustration, until I feel confident with a hand-held meter in either mode, and trust my SLR built-in meters as well. Through knowing what meters are likely to indicate in a variety of lighting situations and a multiplicity of subject matter, through a "feeling for" the response of several films and through analyzing thousands of pictures, I usually realize when and where to exercise my own judgment in relation to meter reading(s). Trial and error plus joyful experience will help build similar confidence

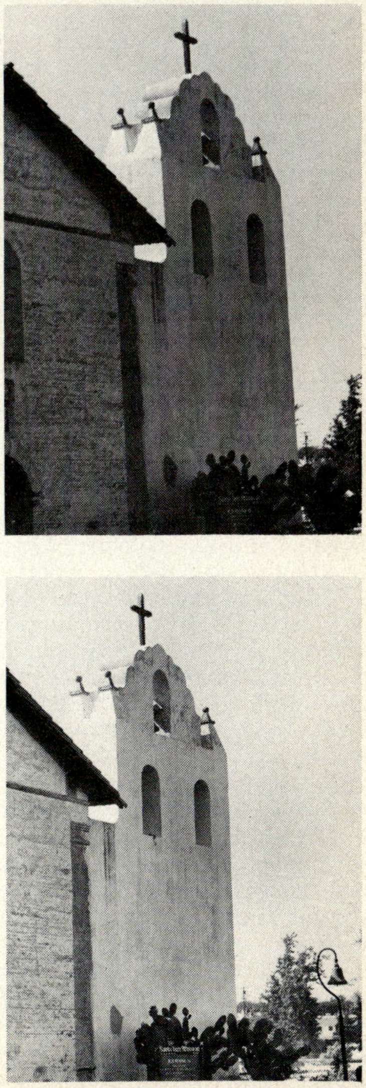

4

Outdoor Lighting

If you don't have a light meter, you can use this rule of thumb for your outdoor exposures: For front-lighted subjects in bright sunlight, your basic exposure is f/16 at a shutter speed of 1/ASA speed of your film. If you are using Plus-X (ASA 125), your basic exposure is f/16 at 1/125 second. With Ektachrome-X film (ASA 64), you'd use f/16 at 1/60 second.

Should it be partly cloudy or the subject sidelighted, you should open the lens up one f/stop from the basic exposure—you'd shoot Plus-X at f/11 and 1/125 second, or Ektachrome-X at f/11 and 1/60 second. (Or, if you still wanted to use f/16, you could shoot Plus-X at 1/60 second or Ektachrome-X at 1/30 second, since halving the shutter speed is the equivalent of opening the lens up one f/stop.)

If your subject is backlighted, or if it is overcast, open up two stops from the basic exposure—f/8 at 1/125 second for Plus-X, or f/8 at 1/60 second with Ektachrome-X.

This basic daylight exposure rule of thumb is just that—a rule of thumb. It's a starting point. Experiment with it; shoot a few rolls of film. After you gain some experience, you'll be able to determine the proper exposure for almost any kind of outdoor lighting condition without a meter.

LIGHT IS A TOOL

Indoors or out, it is enlightening to create your own lighting exercises. Photograph someone in sunlight or floodlight originating from various directions, until you are more aware of the advantages and disadvantages pictorially. At the same time, pay special attention to shadows wherever you shoot, and in pictures you see in print, on TV or in movies. Shadows tell a distinct lighting story, for they indicate where the light is coming from, even if you are not able to see the light source.

Look carefully at food pictures in magazines; they are almost always backlighted to separate shapes and colors, bring out delicate textures and add subtle brilliance to the food. Portraits for many purposes are often lighted from a front 45-degree angle. (Nose shadows are like sun dials when you are analyzing the position of lights in relation to a face or object.) Landscapes are usually shot in side light, by the low sun of early morning or late afternoon. Stop to think about the most successful pictures you've taken. It is likely that the type and direction of the light had an important bearing on their impact.

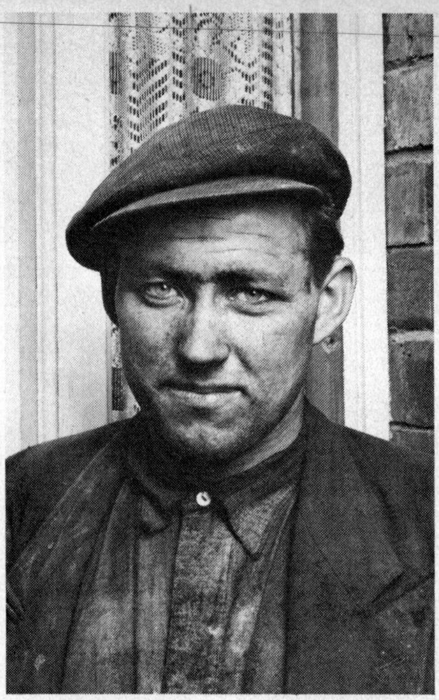

1

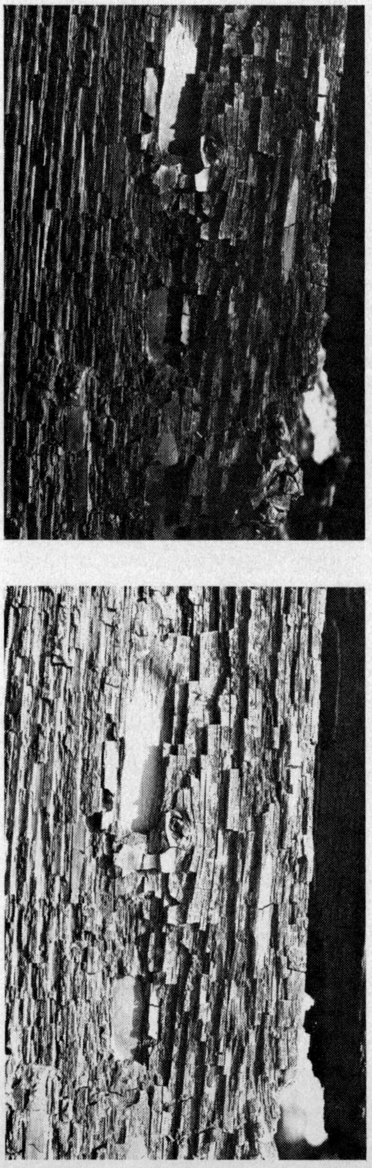

2

To coin an alliteration, the payoff is pictorial punch, and it comes from many things besides lighting, such as expression, emotion, action, differences in scale, color brilliance or subtlety, and various kinds of contrast. There are contrasts of age, size, tone value, psychological factors, etc. The familiar pictures of a baby's hand resting in an adult's hand, the rich woman passing the down-and-out bum, or the brilliant white church against brooding dark storm clouds, are all illustrations of contrast—and pictorial punch.

Thinking of light as a tool, I recall an instruction given me when I was studying photography: "Place light against dark, or dark against light." Applications of this are legion in everyday photography. We think and see light/dark contrasts all the time without being aware of them, but when there is a choice, through lighting and composition, tone and color contrasts pay off.

Light not only delineates form, it also separates one form from another. Shadows, highlights, rim light, color distinctions—all of these are techniques of separation. If you want forms or lines to blend or blur together, that's fine, but when you prefer things seen distinctly, light is one of your main tools.

Outdoor lighting is easy to analyze, challenging to master. As you realize how light can make or break a picture, through observation and experience you will have an increasing number of satisfying prints and slides in your personal portfolio.

1. Pictorial contrast between grimy coal miner and lace curtains attracted the author while photographing in England. View camera with 8-inch lens was used for careful composition.

2. Fire-blackened beam was reproduced far too light by exposure based on reflected-light meter reading, which gave correct exposure to produce beam as neutral gray tone. Incident-light reading gave exposure that produced beam as dark tone, which is as it appeared to the eye.

3. Quality and direction of light are responsible for drama in scene of Valley of Hell on Japan's Hokkaido Island. Sharp contrast resulted from backlighting that emphasized form. (Japan Air Lines photo.)

4. "Place light against dark or dark against light" is demonstrated in this tranquil picture of ducks on the move. Both light and subject tonality were responsible for the contrasts.

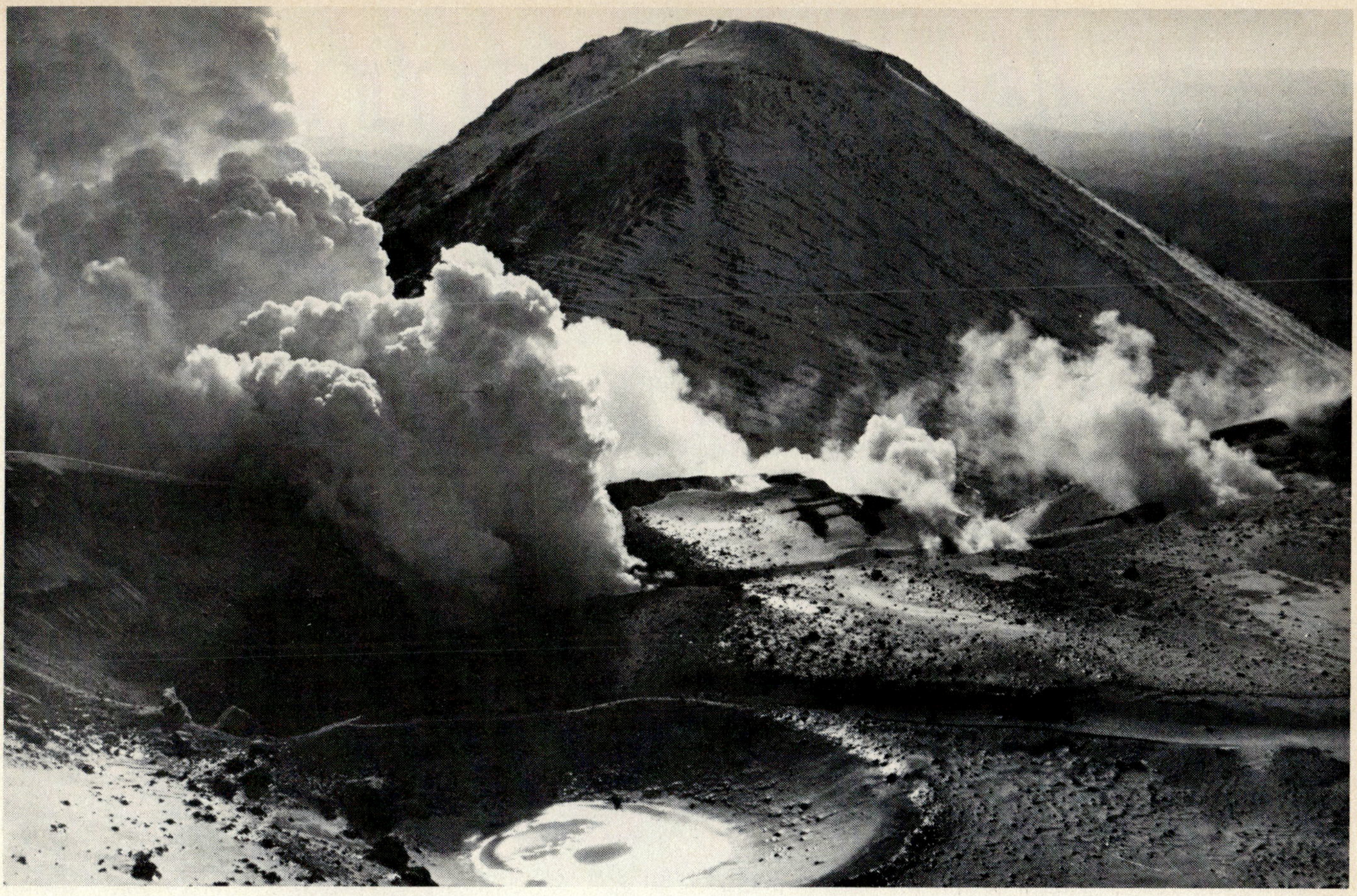

3

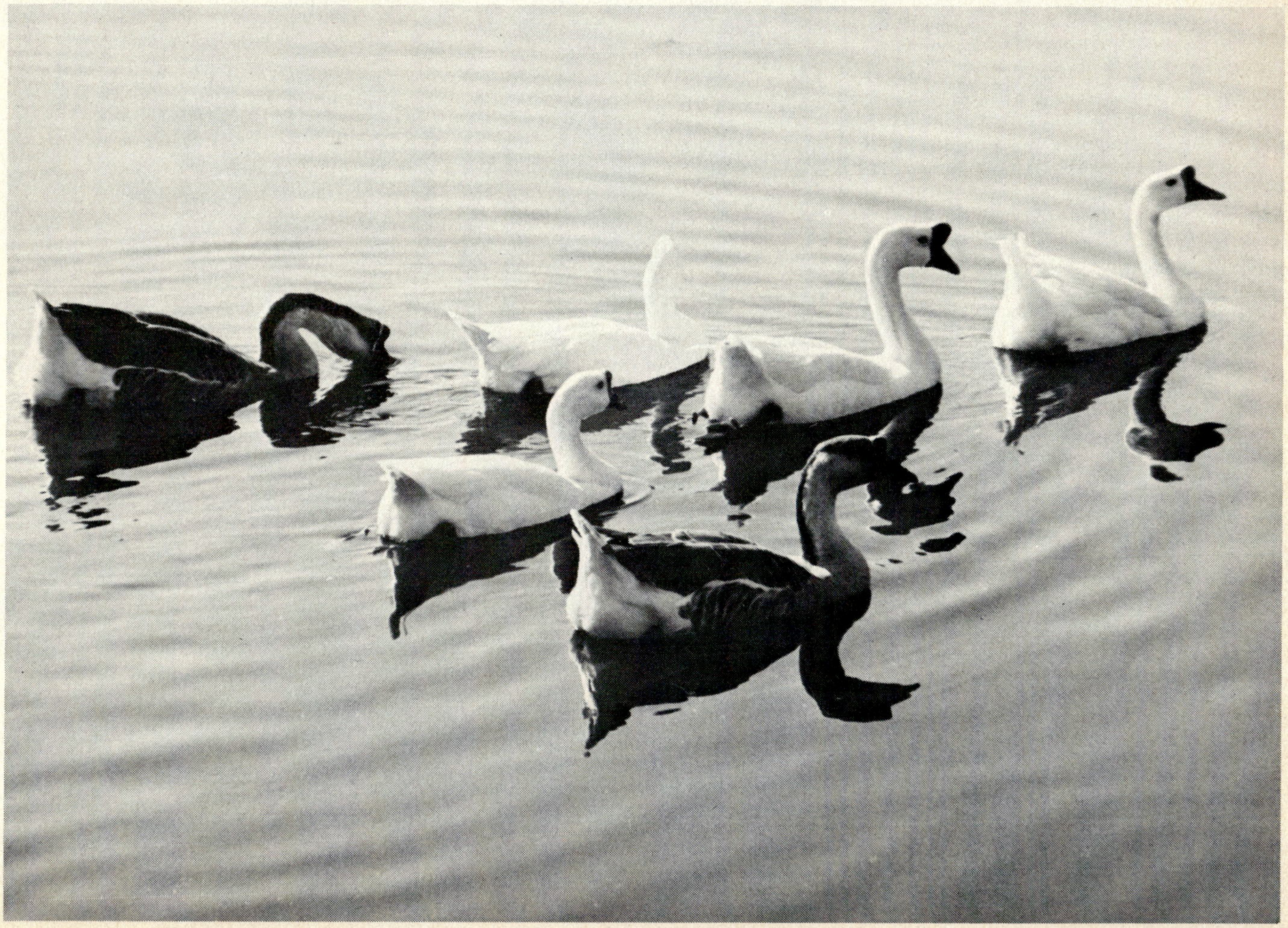

4

CHAPTER 6 Indoor Lighting

While researching this book, I talked to a friend who works for a company that makes a large assortment of equipment, including portable electronic flash units. "What gets me," he said, "is watching amateur photographers at a huge open place such as a football field. They'll stand up in broad daylight to shoot a picture of play 200 feet away, and pop their little strobe units. The same thing happens at night baseball games. I have the urge tm yell out, 'The flash is only good for 10 or 15 feet!'"

Whether through innocence or ignorance, knowledge about flash and the use of floodlights often seems diffused and deficient. Each of these methods of artificial lighting plays a valuable role in photography, and each has its place. However, many people seem to rely on their flashcubes or small electronic flash units everywhere, and there is definite reluctance to try floodlights.

If you fit the above description, I will outline some antidotes. First, let's look at indoor lighting with an eye to its versatility, as well as your confidence with basic lighting techniques.

AVAILABLE LIGHT

The terms *available, existing* and *ambient* light were a big deal in the 1930s and 1940s when lenses and films were becoming faster. If you recall the first few years of *Life* magazine (may it rest in peace), indoor pictures were usually made with multiple flash bulbs. Two, three and more bulbs were set carefully to cover groups and activities; images were sharp, action and expressions were vivid, but the feeling of reality was diminished. Gradually, photojournalists began shooting without flash, in existing light, because they could shoot at f/2.8 and 1/60 second or even faster with 35mm cameras and black-and-white film speeds as high as ASA 100!

Today Tri-X, for instance, can be boosted to EI 1200 (using a developer such as Acufine), and indoor exposures might average 1/125 second at f/5.6, depending on the illumination and reflectivity of rooms. High Speed Ektachrome Type B (for floodlights) can be shot at ASA 320. Available light photography has come a long way.

Using the ambient light, when it is suitable, not only precludes having to pop flashcubes or strobe, but it helps retain the natural mood and character of people, places and things. In authentic lighting, people are more comfortable because bulbs are not flashing. Modern lenses, films and exposure meters are usually quite adequate in medium and low light levels. Shutter speeds such as 1/30 and 1/60 second can save the day and stop action suitably—if you hold the camera steady. Even if you need a tripod in available light, it is often better to shoot slowly than to use flash. However, you may resort to bounced

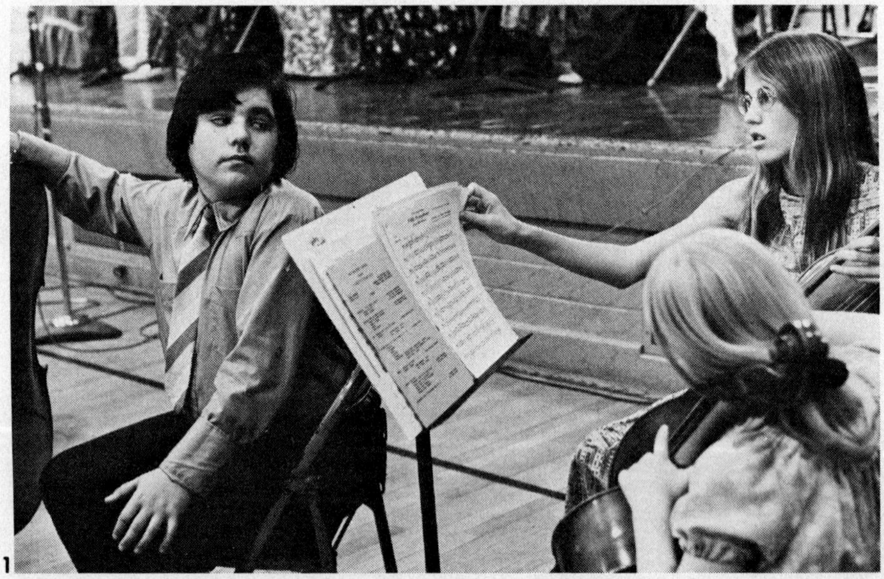

1

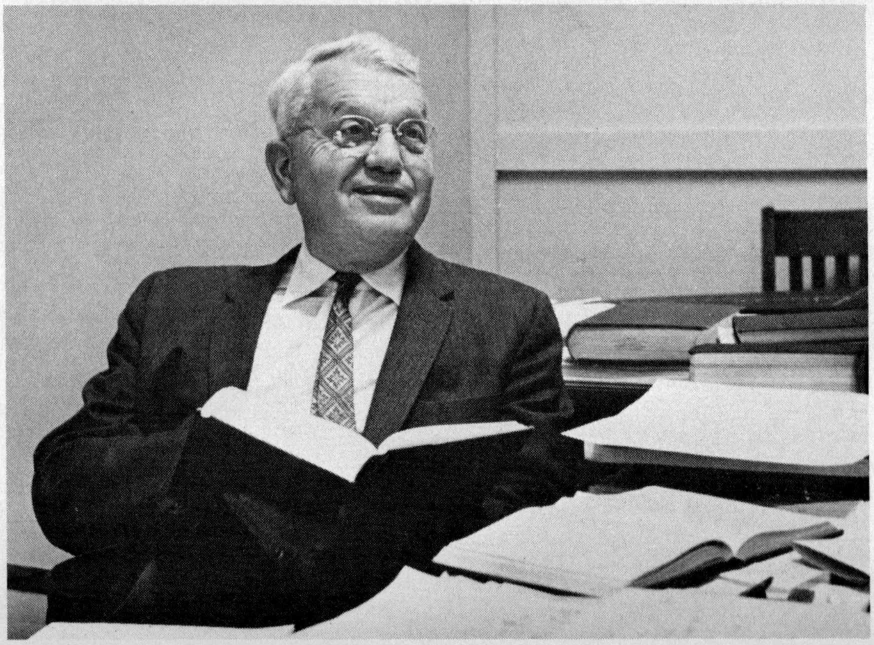

2

1. Available light served author's wife Barbara well in gymnasium where she observed youth orchestra practicing, with special attention to her son, the cellist. Barbara used 100mm lens, Tri-X at EI 1000, 1/60 second at f/5.6

2. People are more comfortable in their own surroundings when you use ambient light for pictures. Author had overhead fluorescent lights in this setting for Dr. Harold Urey, the world-famous physicist. Exposure on Tri-X was 1/60 second at f/6.3.

3. A feeling for light is one of the most valuable things any photographer can gain from experience. Ron Contarsy showed his sensitivity to the charm of his subject as well as the adaptability of daylight coming through a window with this shot, part of his Scholastic/Kodak Award-winning portfolio.

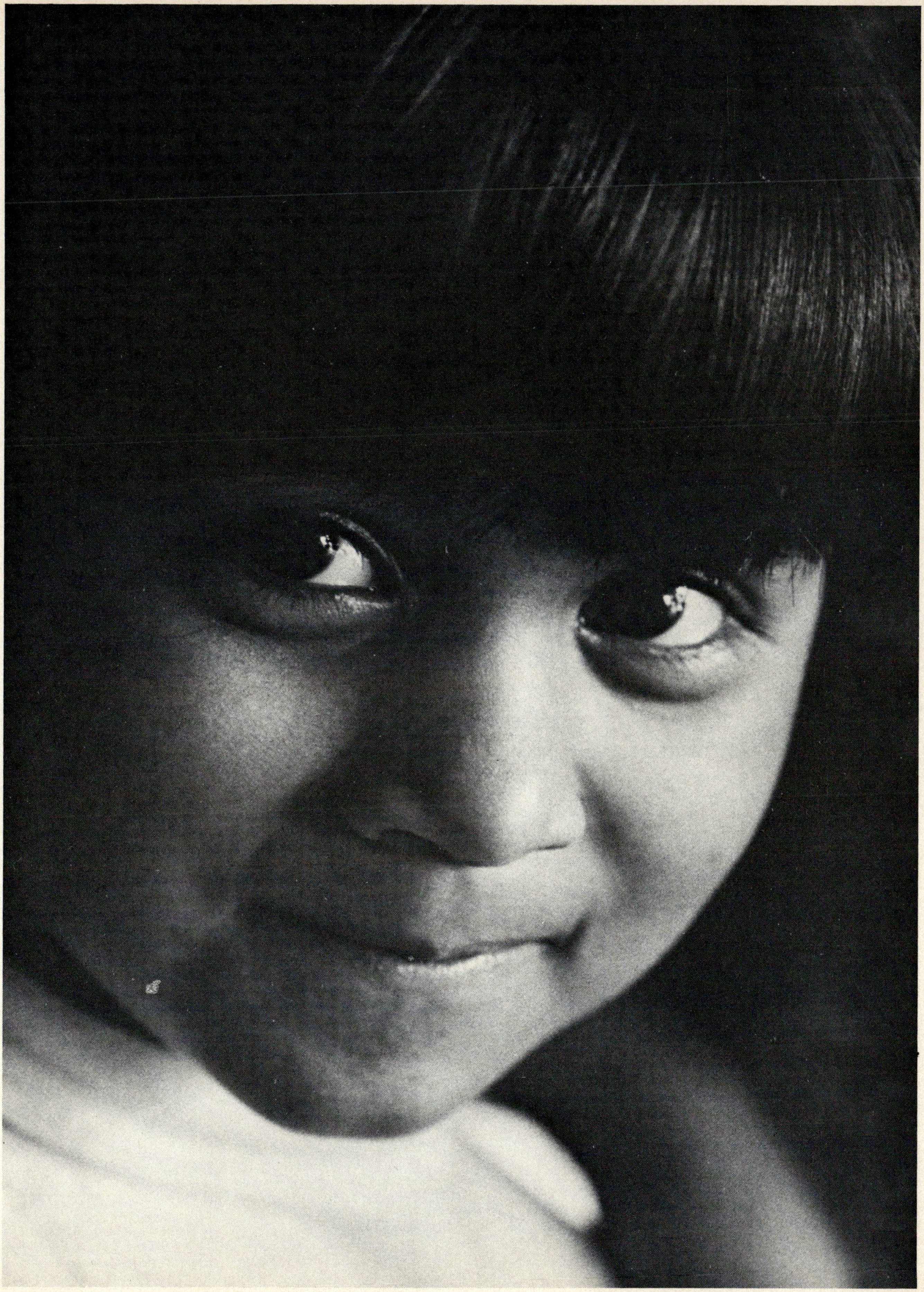

3

floodlight or flash to build up light levels with minimum distraction, and retention of a natural feeling. Details on bounce light are covered later.

Before you pop that flashcube or electronic flash (EF) unit, take a meter reading and decide if you'll have enough depth of field plus protection from subject and camera movement if you expose in the existing light from windows, doors, overhead fixtures, lamps, etc. If your lens opening and shutter speed feel comfortable, start shooting. If you need more light, consider bounce light first. Then, if direct flash or floodlight still seem the best answer, use one of them by all means. There are certainly times when available light is not strong enough or appropriate in character.

FLASHCUBES

With simple cameras or more expensive ones, it's easy to fire a flashcube for adequate lighting up to 10 or 12 feet away. New Magicubes need no battery power to activate them, and you get four shots from each cube for 8 to 10 cents per shot. Small reflectors that fold up like a fan are available for miniature flash bulbs (such as the AG-1).

In all, flash for the average photographer is the handy light, the expedient way to assure pictures when lenses are not large enough, film is slow and light levels are low. (Read on, for. electronic flash may be even *handier* and cost less per shot.) Too many people are restricted by their cameras to shooting with the flash on the camera, which is flat front light that makes dark shadows behind people, does little for form, and is far more functional than artistic. News photographers use flash-on-camera (usually electronic) when action is breaking quickly and they have little choice, but hobby photographers have other options: bounce the flash or EF, take it off the camera, or turn to floodlights for more creative control of the lighting.

1. Sue Harris shot picture series of little girl preparing for bed, using flashcubes as expedient light, and won Scholastic/Kodak Award for it.

2. News photographers often use an auxiliary power pack with their EF units to assure fast recycling time. Joel Goss was thinking quickly to catch player in mid-air, using SLR.

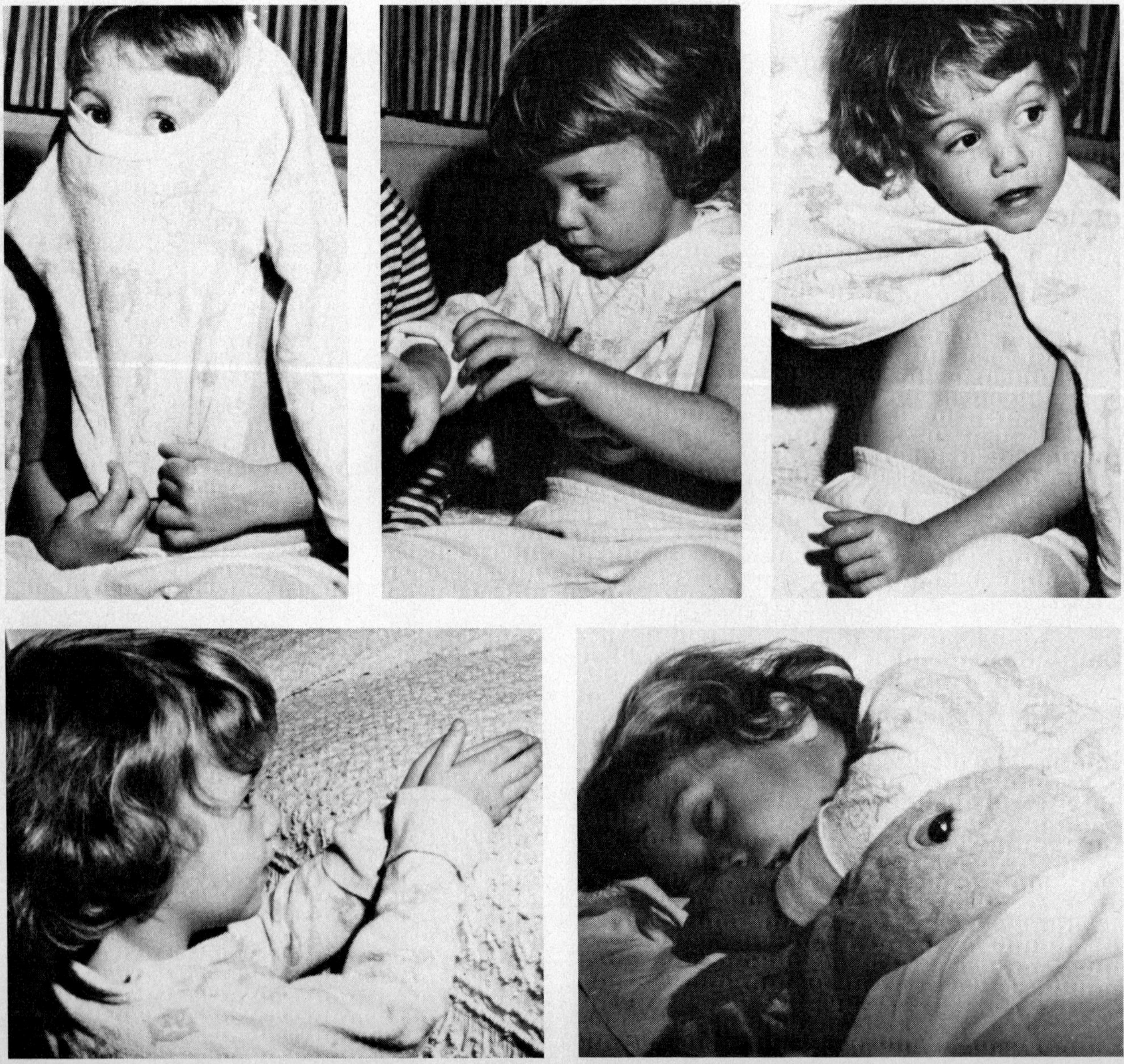

1

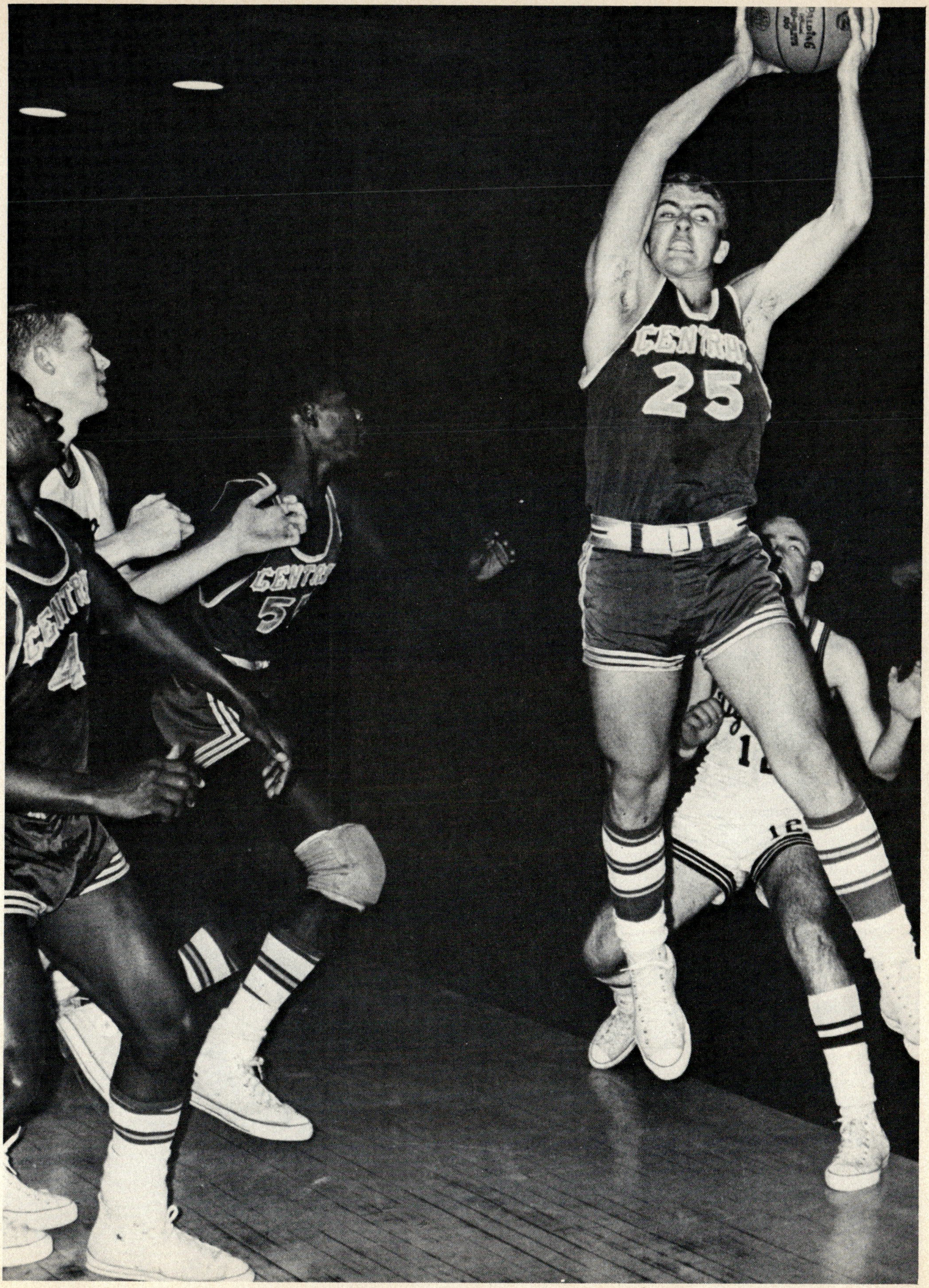

2

Indoor Lighting

ELECTRONIC FLASH

Having finished that miniature sermon, I'm going to extoll the virtues of electronic flash (also known as strobe). In the past few years EF units have been so redesigned, miniaturized and reduced in price, that anyone with an adjustable camera should seriously consider using one instead of flashcubes or bulbs. There are a number of good reasons for this statement, but in case you are not familiar with how electronic flash works, let's get into that first.

Inside EF/ Several components comprise an electronic flash unit, all molded into one small container, except for more powerful models which may be two-piece. There's the covered reflector fitted around a gas-filled tube that is ignited by an electrical charge to flash instantaneously. Electricity comes from either a battery or ordinary household AC current, and is stored in a capacitor. A triggering circuit sets off the flash when you depress the camera shutter release. Within the camera is another circuit that synchronizes firing the flash at the precise moment when the shutter is open at proscribed speeds such as 1/40 second, 1/60 second or 1/125 second, depending on the SLR camera.

Note: The maximum allowable shutter speed for EF with a focal-plane shutter (used in almost all SLR cameras) is usually marked in red on the shutter-speed dial. At this speed, and speeds slower than maximum, the result in only partially exposed film because the shutter is not yet wide open as the camera synchronizes the flash to fire. (With a leaf-type shutter found in small rangefinder cameras, and on several 2¼x2¼ models, EF can be synchronized at any shutter speed.)

Since EF fires at an average 1/1000 second, and the fastest maximum shutter speed setting for EF with focal-plane shutter on an SLR is 1/125 second, shutter speed is not a determinant of exposure. Adjustments according to distance of the light from camera to subject are made only by changing lens openings. Thus in a room where the ambient light is weaker than the electronic flash, shutter speeds slower than maximum do not result in overexposure because the aperture setting

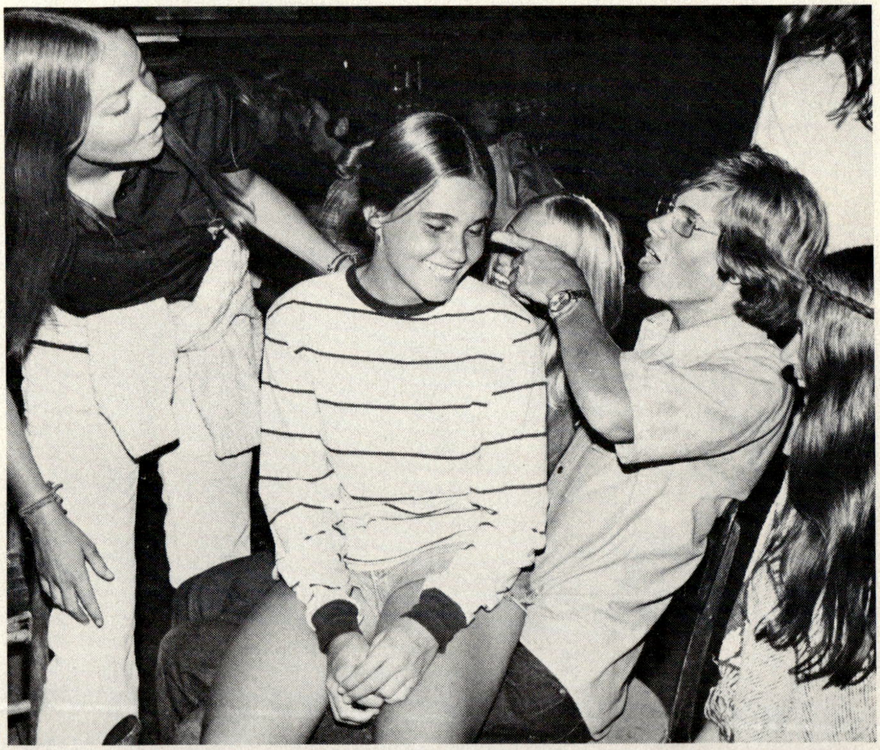

1

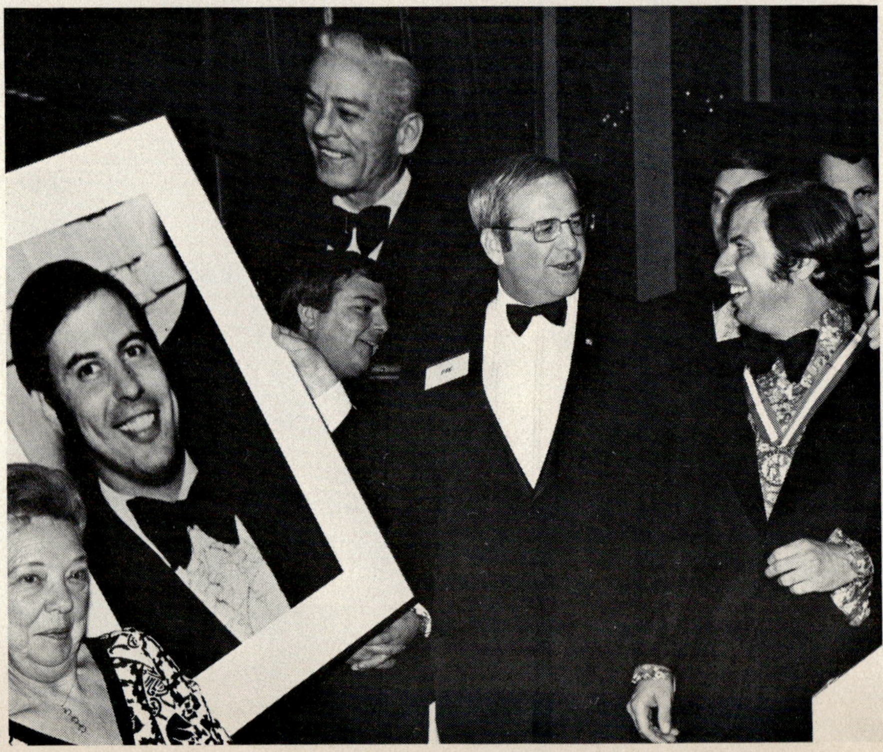

2

1. Electronic flash firing at average of 1/1000 second is ideal to freeze almost any sort of action. These teens were clowning around in large dining hall where bouncing light was not feasible. Small portable EF unit gave exposure of f/11 with 35mm lens.

2. When photographing fast-happening event, news photographers and advanced hobbyists alike appreciate electronic flash unit that recycles quickly. Author was able to shoot a picture every three seconds at awards banquet, using Tri-X in Konica Autoreflex T, 1/125 second between f/11 and f/16.

3. Guide numbers or reference to an exposure calculator built into most portable electronic flash units give photographer approximate lens opening for specific flash-to-subject distances. Author's guide number for small EF unit was 110 and he was about 10 feet from happy Deb Stars being covered for magazine story, so f/11 was used.

4. Two EF units illuminated group of summer campers, one at camera and one at right activated by slave photoeye. Note that light is too strong in foreground, but falls off in background. Author used 35mm lens on 35mm camera, Tri-X, 1/125 second at f/8.

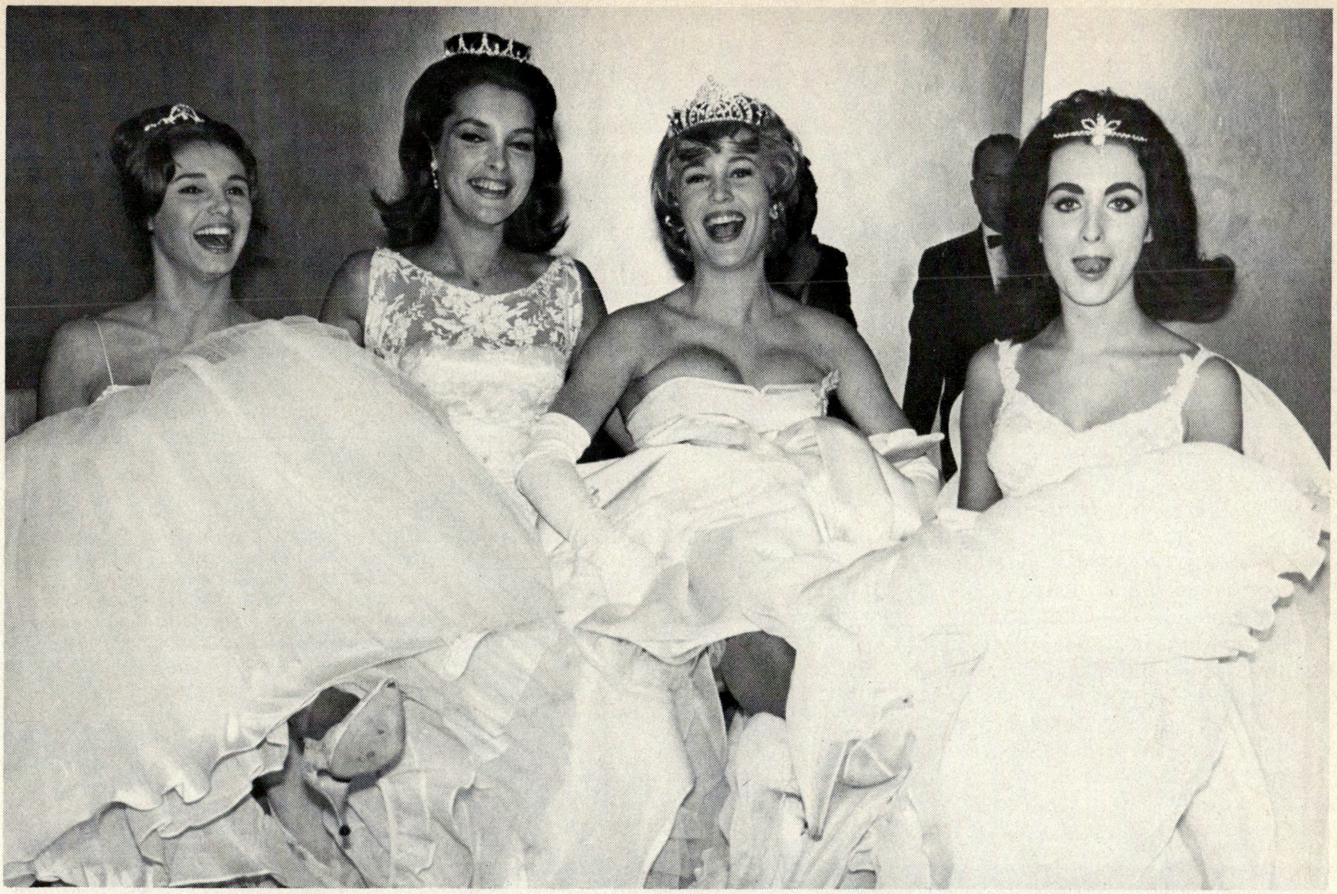
3

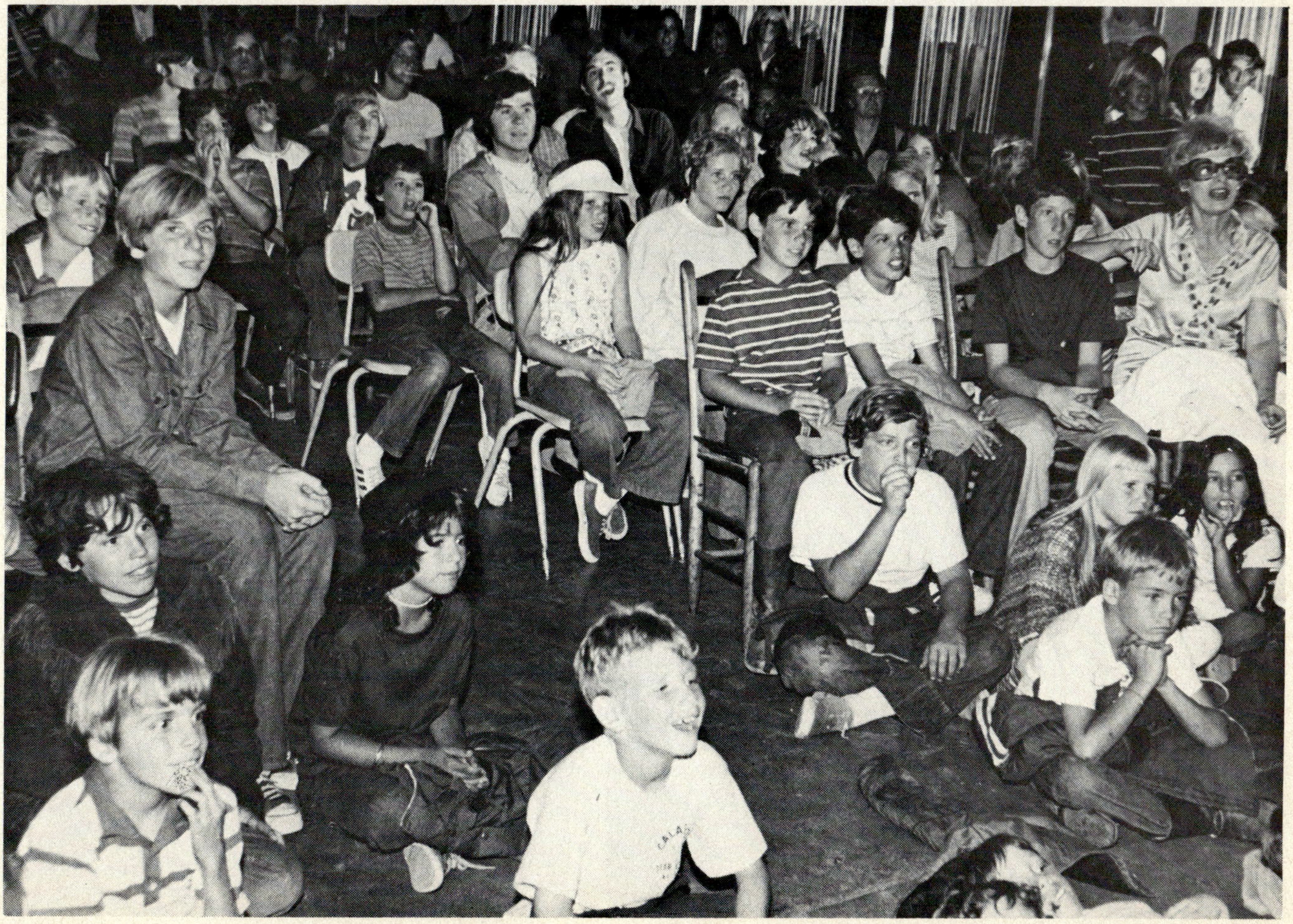
4

alone determines correct exposure. Existing light as strong as or stronger than the EF light will cause ghost images; therefore use of maximum allowable shutter speeds with EF is usually advisable.

After you flash an EF unit, the capacitor immediately builds up electrical energy again, a process called recycling. Small units with modern circuitry, and larger units powered by high-energy batteries (carried in a separate pack usually) may recycle in less than a second to eight or nine seconds, depending on the type of unit and power supply. Fast recycling time is important to professionals, but no big item to the average photographer, unless he's shooting an event that is happening in a hurry. Then a few seconds can seem an eternity.

Recycling time is also dependent on the design and efficiency of an EF unit, as well as the type and condition of batteries. As the latter become weaker, recycling time increases. Most EF units have a small ready light that glows when the capacitor is recharged and the unit can be fired again. It is good practice to wait a few seconds after the ready light goes on to be sure the unit is firing at full power. When it takes 15 or 20 seconds for a unit to recycle, it's time to replace (or recharge) the batteries.

Since an electronic flash tube lasts for approximately 10,000 flashes, the economy of an EF unit should be apparent, compared to discarding flashcubes or bulbs after each flash.

Advantages of EF/ Convenience, economy and high photographic speed are the three main reasons why electronic flash is widely popular. Rather than carry several packages of flashcubes in a pocket or gadget bag, you can store a small EF unit in the same or less space, you don't face the distraction of replacing bulbs (or finding a place to throw them), and you won't easily run out of ready portable light.

Economy has been mentioned, but in addition, once you purchase a unit, if you shoot indoors on AC current, there's no cost per flash. With a set of alkaline batteries, you get about 150 flashes at a cost of less than a penny each. The newest automatic units are designed for up to 500

1. Some of the latest EF units include automatic exposure components that make close-up pictures easier because unit measures proper amount of light for a given distance. Philip Lee was about two feet from cat with close-up attachment lens on his SLR for shot.

2. Outdoors in harsh sunlight, flash fill to brighten shadows can be effective when subjects are close enough and effect is appropriate. Exposure for these teens was 1/125 second at f/8 against the light, using slow Panatomic-X film. Same exposure was retained for flash fill because of camera-to-subject distance. A slow film or neutral density filter is necessary for EF fill with most SLRs because EF synchronizes at relatively slow shutter speeds.

3. On-camera flash cannot be avoided in some situations where ceilings are too high to bounce light, or surroundings too dark for adequate bounce exposure. Visiting officials from Middle East were enjoying lunch when author photographed them for USIA, using Tri-X, 1/125 second at f/11 and small portable EF unit.

4. Flash fill helped balance strong outdoor light in this situation exposed at 1/125 second, f/16, using Tri-X and 2X neutral density filter to reduce the speed of the film.

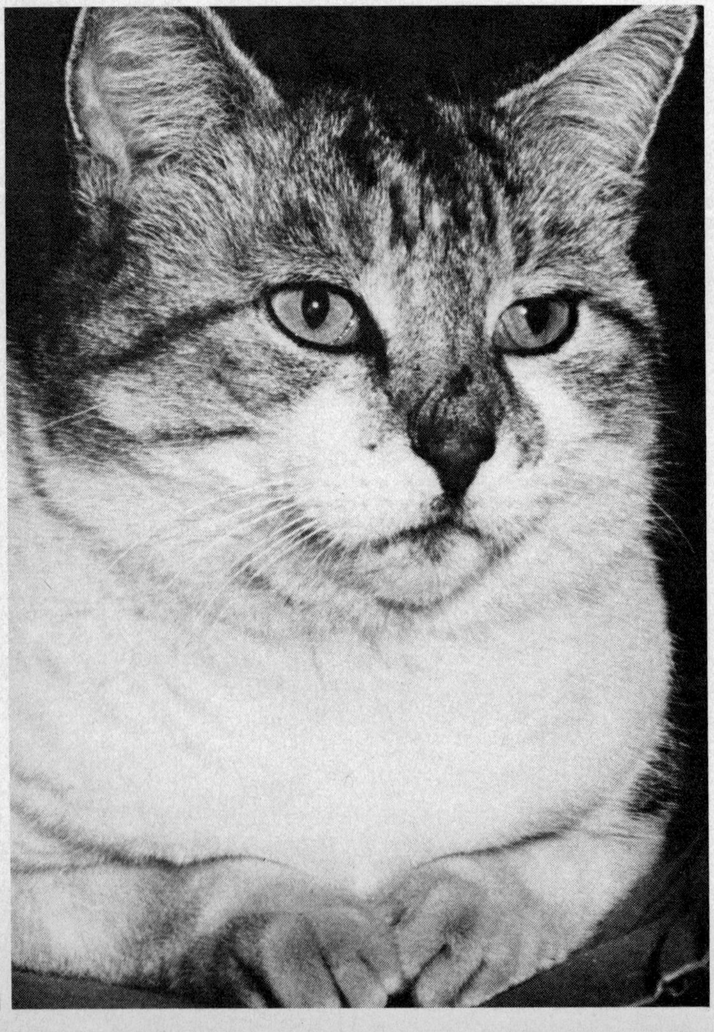

1

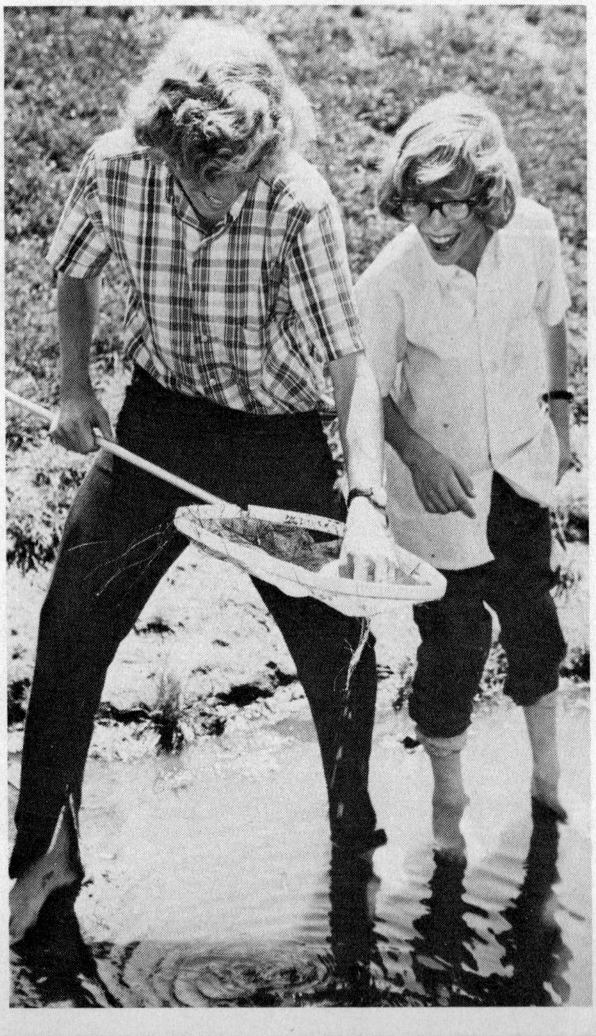

2

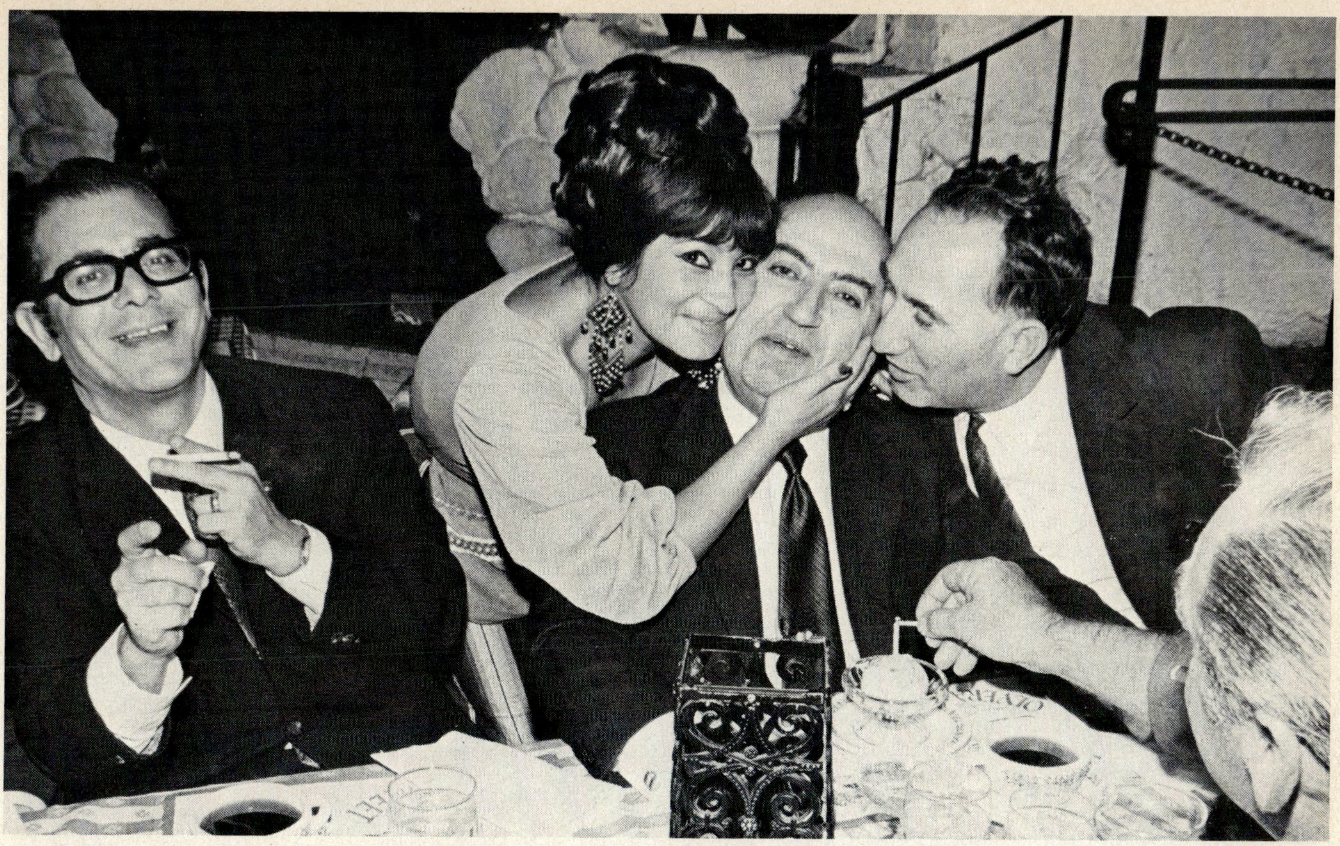

3

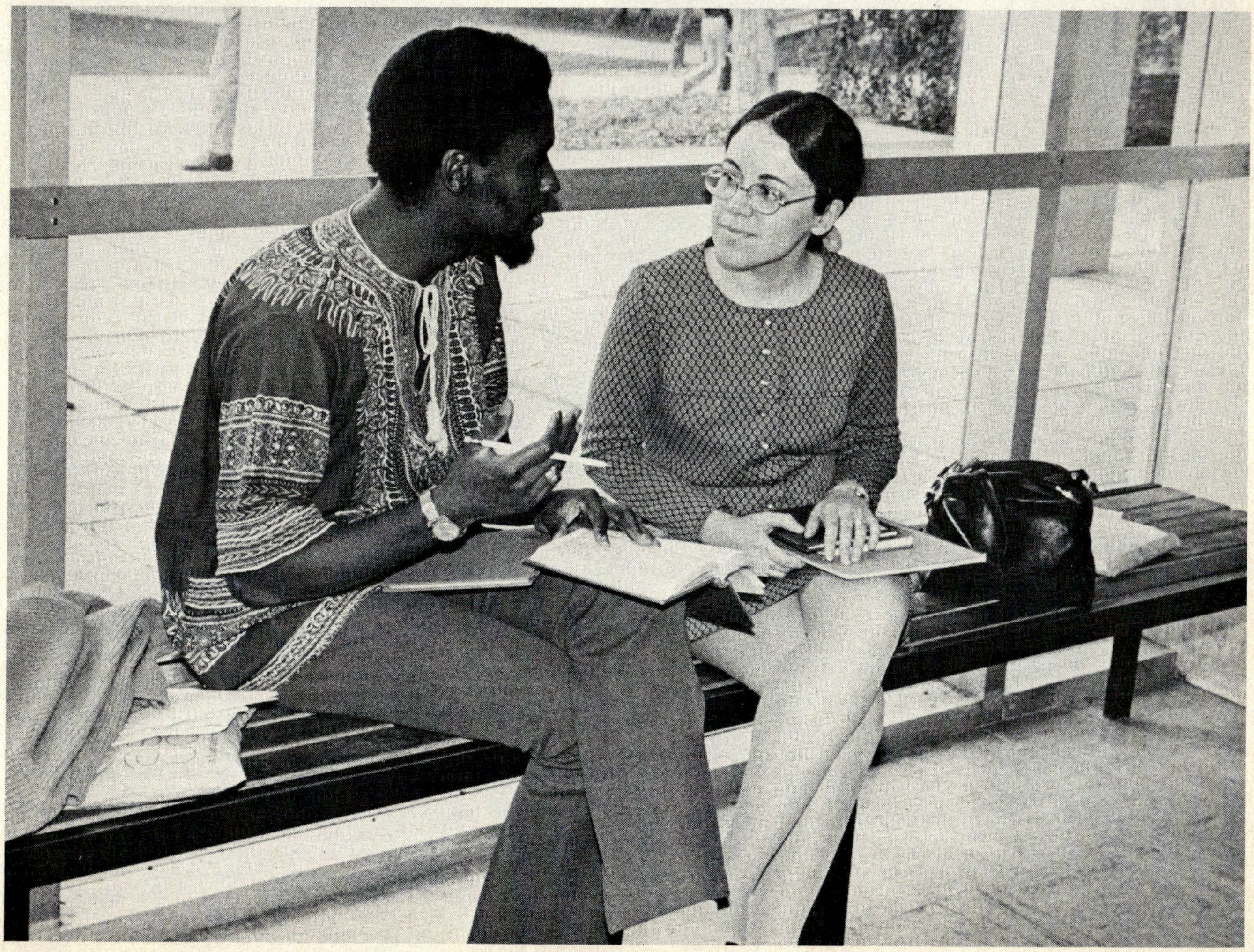

4

flashes with the same alkaline batteries. Rechargeable batteries cost more at the beginning, but they can reduce the cost per flash even more than with alkaline batteries if you use your unit often enough. Note: If you use one flash bulb or cube for each shot on a 36-exposure roll of film, the cost will be $2 to $3.

As for exposure speed, the high speed of the flash itself governs your action-freezing power, not the shutter. Thus pictures taken with EF are often sharper than those taken with flashcubes (which fire at about 1/50 second), because camera movement is negated. A dancer's movement can be frozen in midair.

EF power sources/ Here is a closer look at battery types already mentioned. There are two varieties of replaceable batteries: standard carbon cells (e.g., flashlight or photoflash types) and alkaline. The former cost less, have a relatively short life and increase recycling time. Alkaline cells, which are more expensive (about 60 cents for the penlight size), last much longer, provide faster recycling and are definitely worth the extra money, even if you shoot only one roll of film per month.

Rechargeable nickel-cadmium batteries are still higher priced, but can be recharged hundreds of times for a very long life. However, you must recharge them once a month, whether you use them or not, or they lose their efficiency.

High-energy batteries (240V or 510V) are comparatively expensive offer fast recycling and are preferred by professionals for more powerful EF units. Unless you need higher guide numbers (explained shortly) for slow color or broad areas, forget high-energy battery EF.

Using AC current with the connecting cord that comes with an EF unit usually provides reasonably fast recycling time and no battery drain. You can add an extension cord to range 25 or 30 feet from a wall outlet, which gives you plenty of mobility even in a large room.

Note: The number of flashes you get from one set of replaceable batteries depends on the type and design of an EF unit. If you shoot two or three rolls of film with EF in a few hours, batteries will have a shorter life than if you shoot a dozen pictures and don't use the unit again for a day or two. Energy in a dry cell builds up slightly during a rest interval, and battery power can be maintained for weeks by storage in a freezer (removed from the EF unit, please). I have read about battery chargers for ordinary carbon or alkaline cells, but from what I can gather, they aren't effective enough to make them worth using. Some EF units are designed with a "battery saving circuit" that reduces energy drain between flashes while the unit is on. It is simple conservation to switch an EF unit off for any reasonable period between flashes. Ordinary alkaline cells have a very extended life span with the latest automatic units described later.

EF light and exposure/ Though the flash of an EF unit *appears* extremely

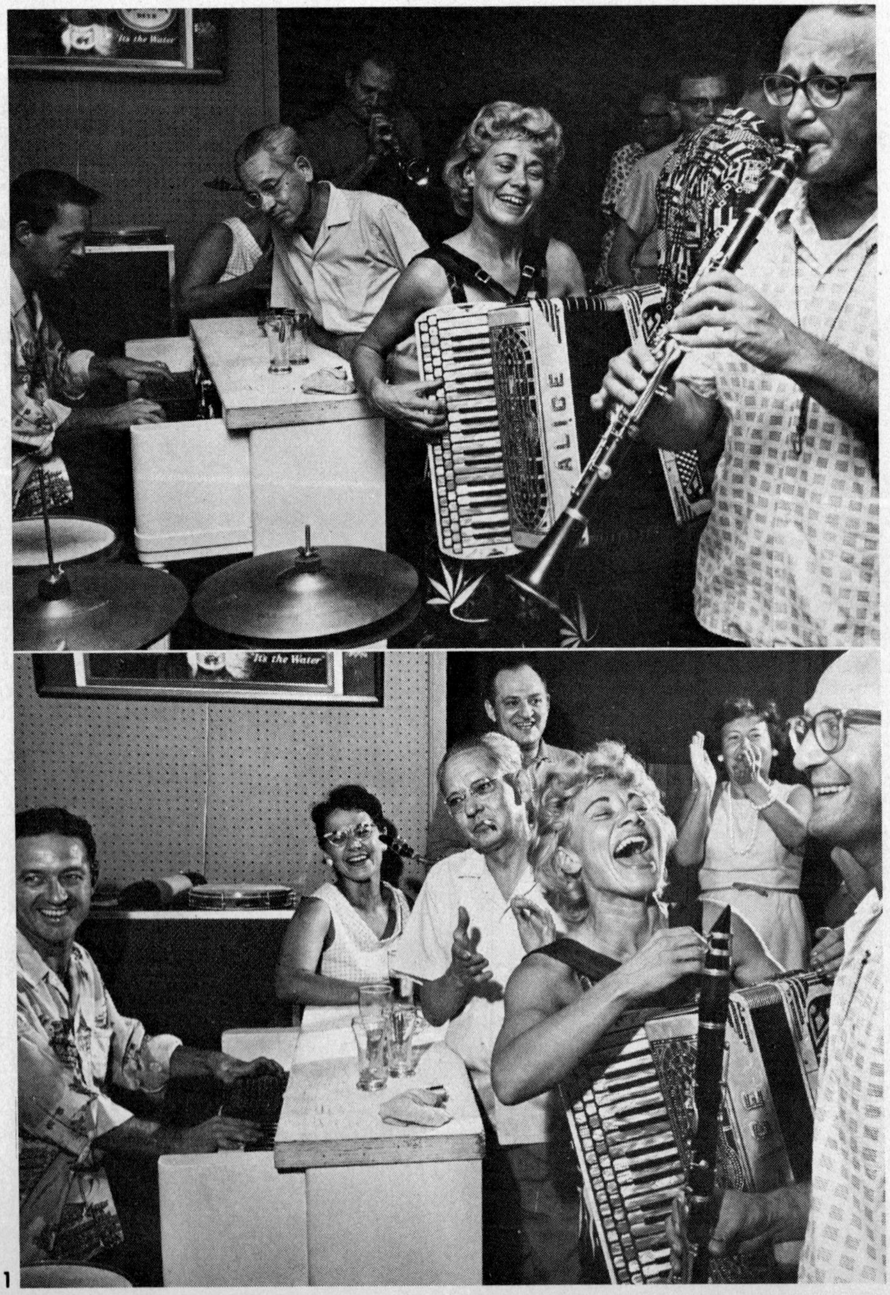

1

1. Comparison of bounce flash and multiple flash techniques. Happy musicians were first shot with small bounced EF unit and 35mm lens at f/8 on Tri-X rated at EI 1000. A second unit was added off-camera, activated by a photo-eye, and the on-camera unit was used directly for multiple-flash shot with exposure between f/11 and f/16.

2. Since manufacturer's recommended guide number for EF unit may be a bit optimistic, it is a good idea to test your unit's guide number. Set up a model holding a series of cards with f/stops in half-stop increments marked on them at a distance of 10 feet from your flash unit. Shoot a series of exposures at half-stop intervals, with the model holding the appropriate card. for each exposure. (A color slide film is best for this test.) When the film is processed, you'll get results that look something like the illustrations here. Pick the best exposure, multiply the number on the card in that exposure by 10 (the flash-to-subject distance), and you have the honest guide number for your electronic flash unit.

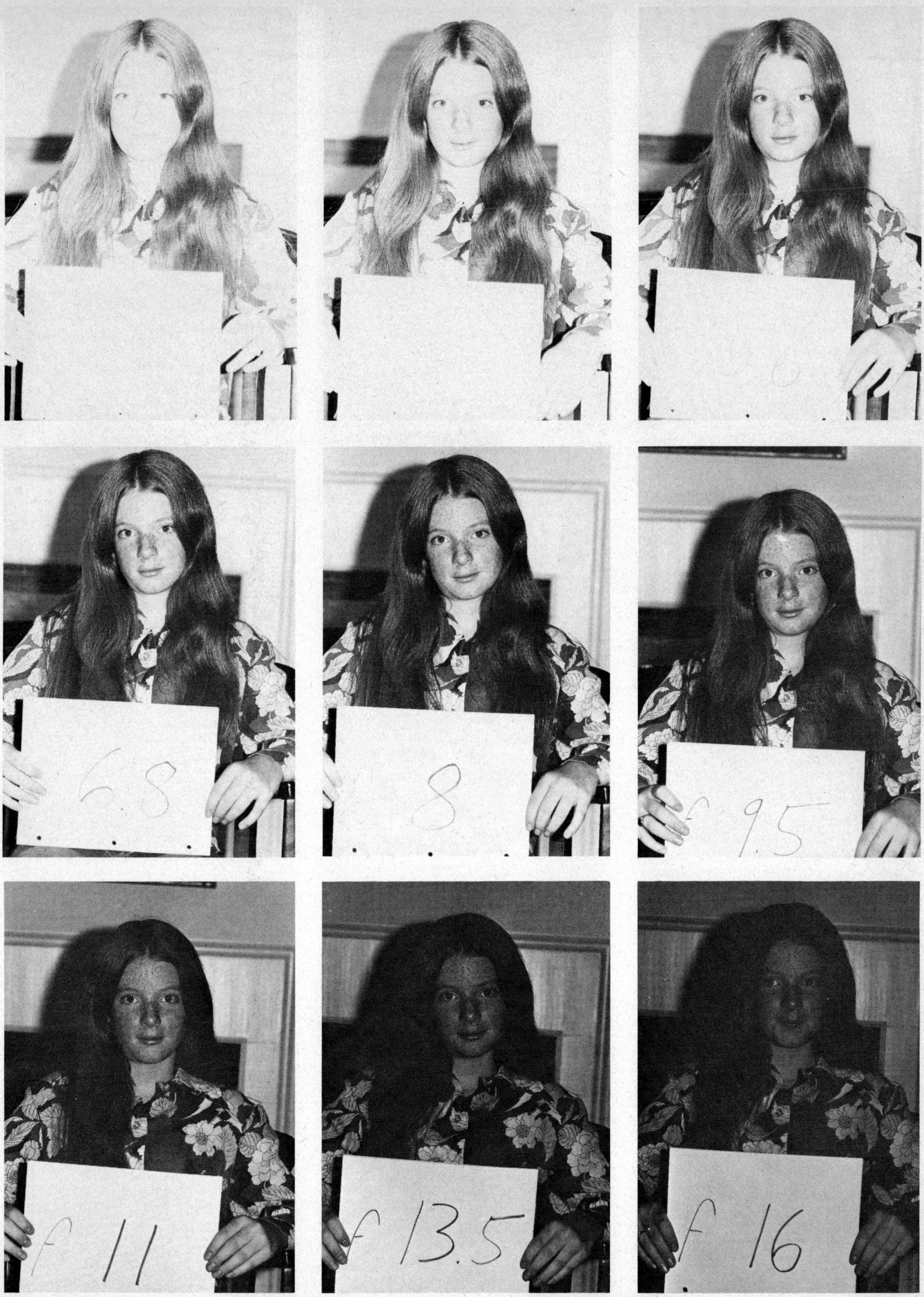

2

bright, each unit is built for a specific light output; this is rated either in watt seconds, beam candle power seconds (BCPS) or effective candle power seconds (ECPS). You may only need these numbers for finding guide numbers on film instruction sheets, because most portable EF units are rated according to those guide numbers.

A guide number is a figure into which you divide the number of feet from camera to subject in order to ascertain the aperture setting for a given film. Most manufacturers use the guide number for Kodachrome II (ASA 25) as a comparison standard. For instance, the Kodachrome II guide number for a small inexpensive (about $20) EF unit may be 30. One costing $30 might have a guide number of 35, and at $40, the guide number may jump to 40. These number-to-price relationships vary considerably between brands, but enable you to compare power along with other features.

Exposure by guide number, or by built-in exposure calculator on most units, is reasonably simple, but can be influenced by several factors. First, a room with light-colored walls and ceiling will reflect more light than average, and you can use half lessop or a full stop less than the guide number or calculator indicate. Conversely, a room with dark wood paneling calls for half a stop or a full stop more exposure, as does shooting outdoors at night where there are no reflecting surfaces.

Second, though many manufacturers recommend guide numbers or design exposure calculators for the average room, some tend to exaggerate or inflate these ratings, so you should test your unit at first. Keep careful notes on camera-to-subject distances and lens openings. Third, the design of EF light reflectors varies; some are more efficient than others.

It is well to compare exposure by guide number with exposure by the calculator in the unit. If the latter is accurate, you can ignore dividing footage into guide number and decide exposure by a twist of the calculator dial.

Note: All flash exposures are based on the physical principle that the intensity of light decreases as distance from light source to subject increases. When you double the distance, the formula states that only one-fourth the amount of light strikes the subject. If, for instance, an EF unit with a specific film calls for f/16

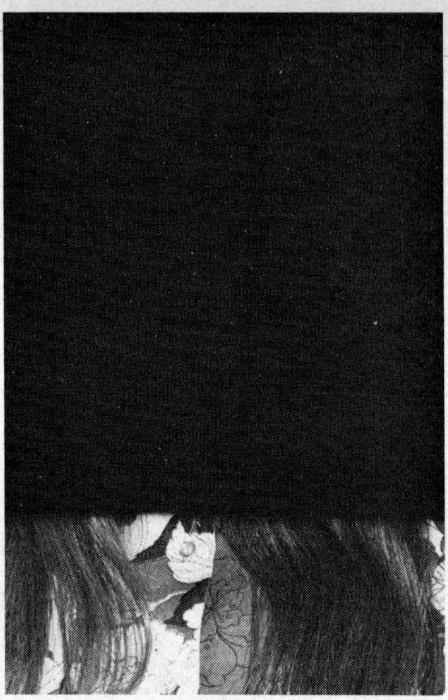

at 7 feet, the correct exposure would be f/11 at 10 feet, f/8 at 14 feet and f/5.6 at 20 feet. It is useful to know this principle, but with an exposure calculator or an automatic unit, you won't have to do math problems in your head.

AUTOMATIC EF UNITS

A few years ago the progressive photographic industry introduced automatic electronic flash. Here's how it works: Added to the normal EF circuitry is a sensor (operating through a small opening in the front of a unit) that measures light reflected from a subject and relays this information to a tiny computer. When the computer senses that enough light has been reflected back from the subject for proper exposure, according to a specified f/stop setting and film speed, a quenching circuit instantly cuts off the remaining light. All this happens at incredibly high speed *during* the flash, on calculations based on the speed of light.

In other words, automatic EF units eliminate calculating and guide number division to determine lens openings. Whether a subject is two feet or 12 feet from the camera, the film will usually be exposed correctly. Since a preselected f/stop is maintained, the unit quenches the light proportionately for near or far. This is particularly effective in close-up photography where it is often difficult to decide on correct flash exposure.

Since an automatic unit operates by varying its light output, the flash duration may be 1/500 second decreasing to as little as 1/70,000 second at minimum distances. You don't very often shoot something moving quickly close to the camera, but if you want the ultimate in action-stopping, an automatic EF unit is it.

Just as an automatic camera requires manual adjustment for high contrast subjects, an automatic flash unit may also be fooled in certain circumstances. For instance, if you are photographing a man in a white shirt against a white background, you are likely to get underexposed flesh tones. To correct this, you open the aperture one stop, and shoot without changing anything on the EF unit.

Recycling time on automatic units can be very short, as little as one-half second in some cases with fresh batteries. In addition, the latest models include a small capacitor (known technically as a thyrister), which stores unused energy resulting from less-than-maximum flash duration. Units without this feature merely drain off excess electrical energy, so the new thyrister design conserves battery power, making possible as many as 500 flashes per set of alkaline cells, rather than an average of 125 to 150 flashes.

Note: Now coming onto the market are separate sensors that trigger manual EF units automatically. If you own an EF unit you like, check into the cost of a separate sensor instead of buying a new automatic unit.

EF SHOPPING POINTERS

How powerful an EF unit should you buy? The answer depends on how much you wish to spend, how much weight you want to carry and what sort of picture situations you anticipate. More powerful units with

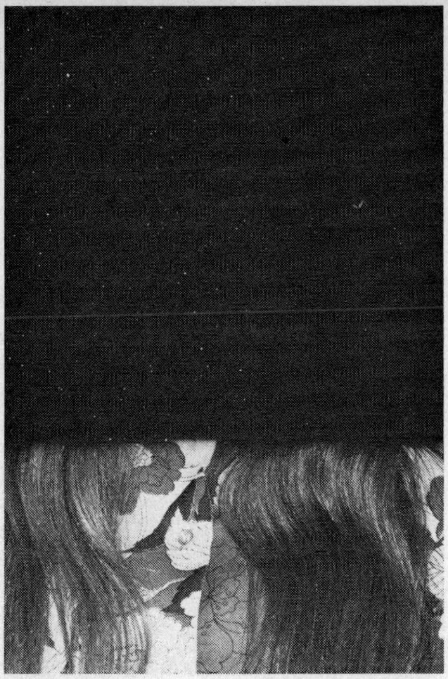
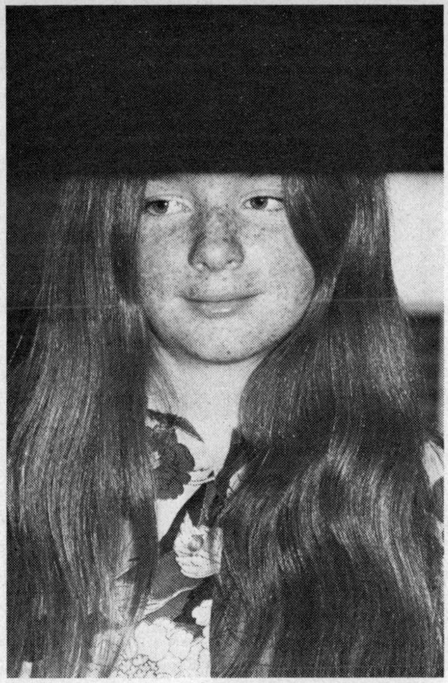
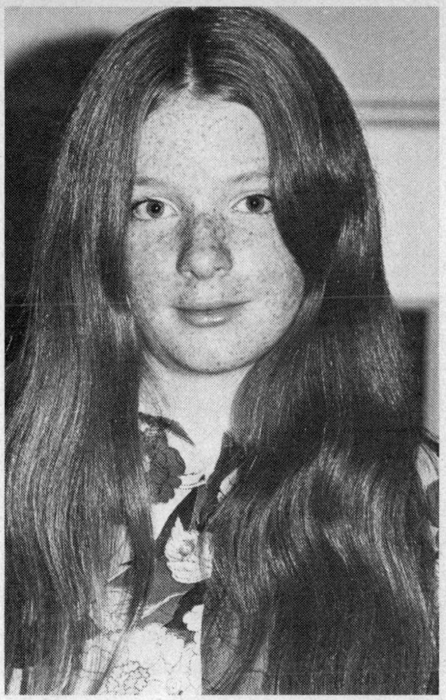

higher Kodachrome II guide numbers allow you to shoot groups of people from greater distances, using smaller lens openings. If the KII guide number of a unit is 30, you'll have to shoot at f/2.8 from 10 feet with Kodachrome II. There's not much depth of field with a normal lens at that aperture. You could, of course, use High Speed Ektachrome with the same unit, and have a guide number of 75. More powerful units cost more and offer proportionately more latitude to cover varying situations. Here are some other items to consider when buying an EF unit:

1. Small units with approximately the same power differ in price because of other features, such as type of battery power. A few dollars more invested may pay interest in the future in terms of lighting versatility.

2. Some units include accessories, such as filters, to cut the light. Others have separate battery chargers. Some require sync cords between unit and camera, while others also include a hot-shoe that connects directly to the camera by contact, without wires.

3. A unit that cannot be used on AC current should be avoided.

4. Most units have a storage area for PC cords, or camera-to-unit connector cords, which can be very handy.

5. A rechargeable unit that includes an indicator light to remind you the unit is fully charged is a convenience.

6. Some units take overnight to recharge, but many can be fully charged in an hour or two. A few recharge enough in 15 minutes to shoot a 20-exposure roll of pictures.

7. A unit with a lighted calculator dial makes it easier to see in a darkened room. The same light can be used to illuminate camera controls.

8. More powerful units are made with high and low power settings, so you can match light output to film speed and picture situation.

EF BRANDS

In alphabetical order, here are most of the electronic flash brands now available. Some manufacturers make a number of models, varying in price, power and features. Brands with both manual and automatic units are marked with an asterisk (*): Braun Hobby*, Capro, Hershey*, Honeywell*, Kako, Metz*, Minolta*, Spiratone, Rollei* and Vivitar*.

SPECIAL FLASH TECHNIQUES

Flash fill/ Aso called fill-in flash, this technique is used outdoors in sunlight to illuminate shadows. The trick is to pop flash or EF from the camera at the intensity, or distance, that will lighten shadows, but not make them brighter than sunlit areas. Here's the way to calculate exposure: Set your camera's shutter speed and f/stop for the proper exposure as if you were not using flash. Divide the flash guide number by the f/stop you have set. This will give you the flash-to-subject distance for *bright* fill. For example, if your film speed is ASA 25, and normal outdoor exposure is f/8 at 1/60 second, using an EF unit with a guide number of 40, you divide 8 into 40, and place your flash five feet from the subject. However, this may be too close, and that's O.K., because bright fill is often too obvious. Tonal or color balance is

Exposures with electronic flash and camera with focal-plane shutter at 1/1000, 1/500, 1/250, 1/125 and 1/60 second show why slow shutter speed is necessary with focal-plane shutters.

more normal at half again the distance at 7½ feet, for example, and the flash is barely perceptible at 10 feet. Make some flash fill tests, measuring distances carefully. Then decide how bright you prefer shadows to be for your own taste.

If you wish to shoot flash fill closer than normal, diffuse it with a layer of white handkerchief or facial tissue to cut the light about one stop. Two layers may be used at very close range. One or two fingers over the flash also reduce its intensity. I once read about a whole system of finger-diffusion worked out by a news photographer, and it sounded nicely predictable. If you shoot flash fill consistently, you might experiment with fingers or tissue to develop a reliable system of your own.

Because SLR focal-plane shutters synchronize with electronic flash and some flashcubes at relatively low speeds, flash fill with these cameras is somewhat discouraging. A few 35mm cameras sync at 1/125 second, which is an advantage, but shooting fast films in sunlight is normally impossible at 1/60 second or even 1/125 second because most lenses only stop down to f/16. To get around this, either use a neutral density filter to reduce the speed of fast film, or switch to a film no faster than ASA 64. At that speed, exposure and synchronization will be under convenient control. Of course, a camera using a leaf-type shutter (most rangefinder 35mms without interchangeable lenses, and many 2¼x2¼ cameras) can be set at any speed for flash or EF.

Open flash/ At night, or anywhere there is almost no ambient light, you can open a camera shutter on the B setting, and leave it open while you fire flash or EF one or more times on a subject. This is called open flash, and if you want to shoot the interior of a large building (that would require many floodlights and would hardly be seen at all with one flash), set the camera on a tripod. Set the lens according to the film guide number, open the shutter, and lock it open with a cable release. Pop your flash or EF in enough areas to illuminate the room adequately, realizing the light will overlap. Wear dark clothes and duck away from the flash so your own image doesn't show. When you close the shutter, the film will have recorded the series of flashes, and the room will have been "painted" with light.

You can use open flash for a variety of creative effects as well. For instance, while the shutter is open, film records any images that can be seen

1. Author's case of lights includes four stands, two quartz lights, three reflector floods, three sockets with clamps and extension cords. Case was made to fit the equipment.

2. Simple basic lighting setup here consists of reflector, two floodlights, extra bulbs, clamp, folding white background and umbrella reflector.

3. Front light—the same effect you get with on-camera flash—is expedient but not extremely flattering.

4. Direct sidelight, with no fill on shadow side and no background light, is more interesting than front light, but still leaves much to be desired.

5. Backlight, slightly from side, is shown here as part of exercise, but not as most exemplary portrait lighting.

6. This is 45-degree sidelighting, variations of which are often pleasant for portraits. Note triangle of light on left cheek of model Barbara Doyle.

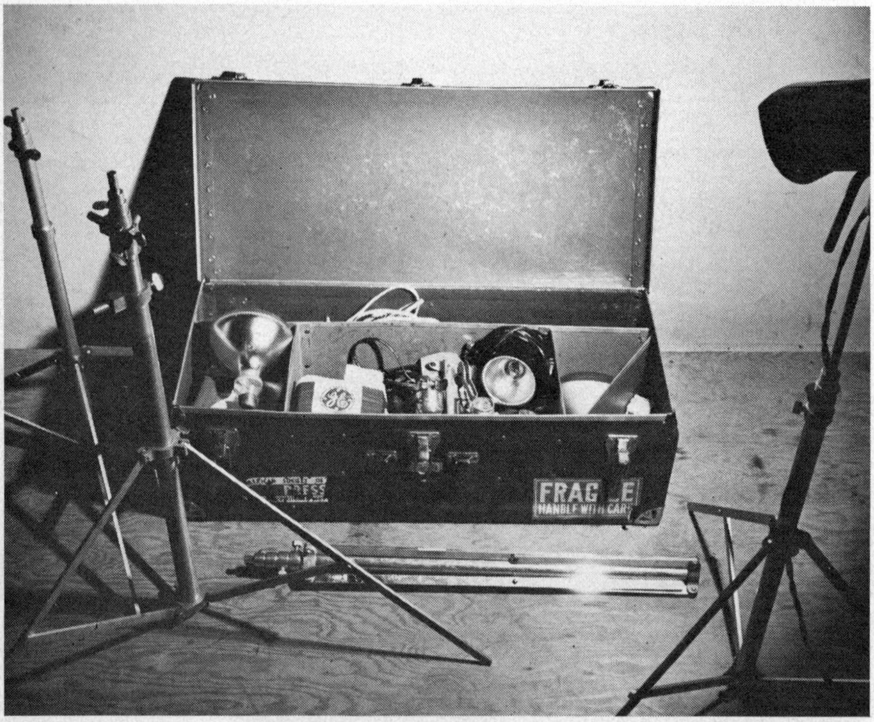

1

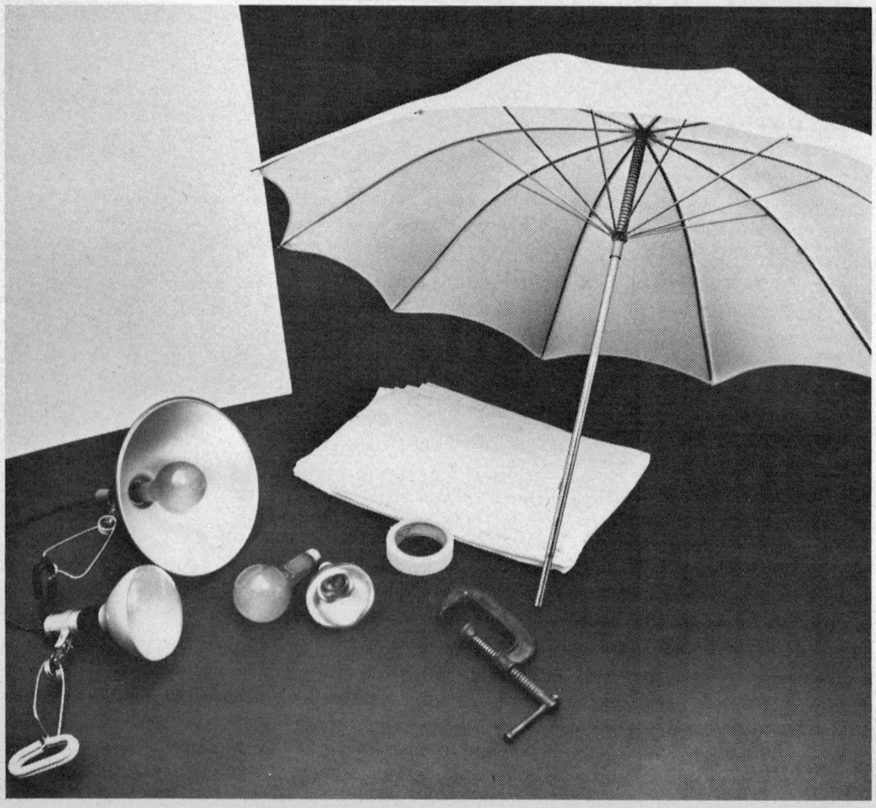

2

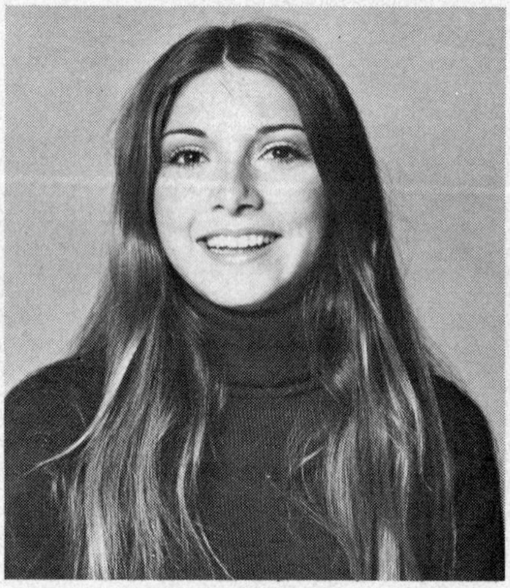

3

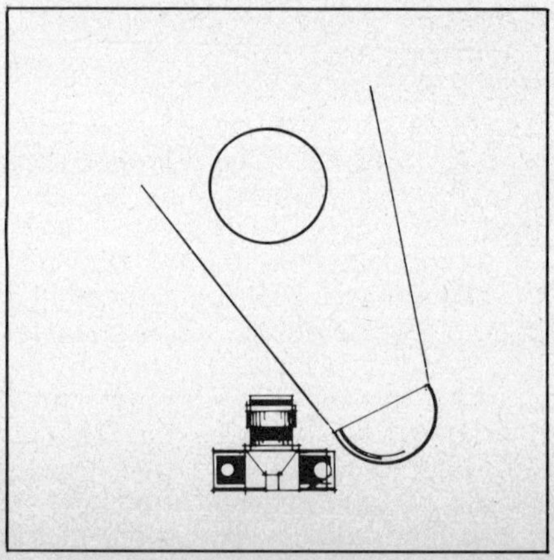

by existing light, plus images lit by flash. These may overlap or be separate. You can capture both a blurred and a sharp image in the same picture by having a model move slowly in existing light, and also be seen in one or more sharp images lit by flash. When you get blurred images you can't explain recorded while a shutter is open, they are often called ghost images.

Exciting montages can be created by repeated flash exposures of a moving model or object. Perhaps you have seen pictures made by fast repeating EF, called a stroboscopic effect, typified by a golfer seen in two dozen stages of his swing. By planning a model's movement, you can shoot overlapping action or portraits using open flash. Side lighting is recommended for this type of photography because overlapping images will register more effectively.

Multiple flash/ This merely means the use of two or more flash sources, EF units or bulbs, synchronized to fire simultaneously. Lights should be positioned by the same principles described later for floodlights. Multiple flash is particularly useful when floodlighting is not strong enough to shoot indoor action or expressions.

EF units can be connected by electrical cords to fire at the same time, but it is easier to attach an electronic eye "slave" triggering unit to the remote unit. The slave unit reacts instantly to light from the camera-attached flash, and fires a remote unit to which it is connected. Using such a wireless slave trigger, an off-camera light can be 15 or 20 feet away, and flash along with the main light. Various slave units are available at your photographic dealer.

Exposure for multiple flash is determined by the main light only, i.e., the light closest to the subject. More distant lights will be less intense and are used to illuminate shadows or background. However, if several lights are placed at about the same distance from the model(s), use a smaller aperture than indicated by guide number or calculator because the amount of light is compounded. If you haven't made tests, you had better bracket exposures for insurance.

Note: Bounce lighting is discussed later. It is hardly a "special" technique for flash because it proves useful so often.

FLOODLIGHTS

Before delving into indoor lighting techniques, let's investigate floodlighting equipment, which you can buy ready-made, or assemble yourself. Here are the components:

Reflectors/ They are made in several diameters for the bulbs mentioned following. Most are aluminum and include wood handles to manipulate them when they get very hot. Reflectors are equipped with a socket that fits to a light stand, or may be attached to stands or other objects with clamps. If you use reflector flood bulbs, it is not necessary to buy separate reflectors.

Flood bulbs/ There are two main types in two "flavors," which relates to their color temperature to match Type A or Type B color films. Standard photoflood bulbs are No. 1 (250W) and No. 2 (500W), and burn at 3400°K. That K stands for Kelvin temperature by which the color of light is measured. Type A Kodachrome is balanced for standard flood bulbs, which have a life span of about six hours. When a bulb begins to look gray or discolored, it's O.K. for black-and-white film, but should be replaced for use with color.

The second type of bulb, made in the same No. 1 and No. 2 sizes, is called a 3200°K bulb, has a much longer life span and is made to match Type B color film, namely Ekta-

4
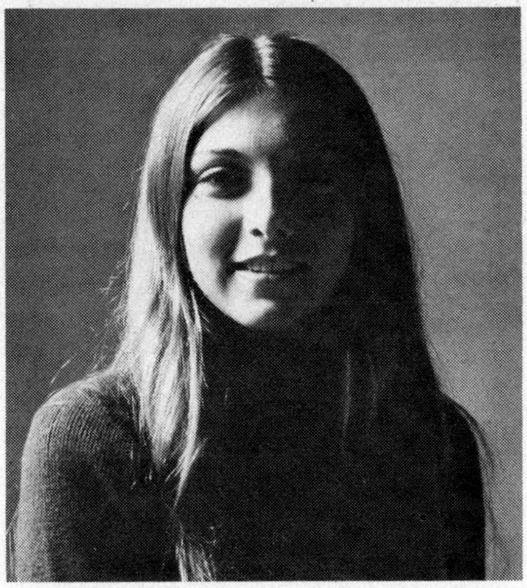

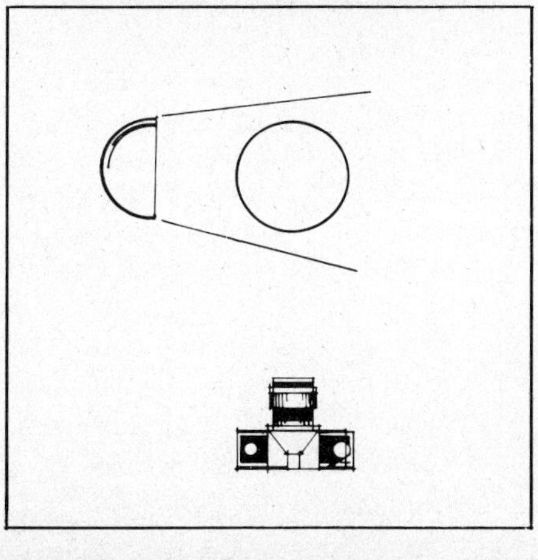

5
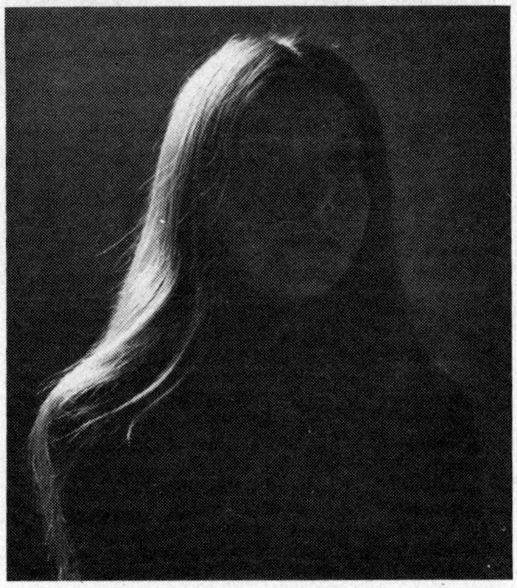

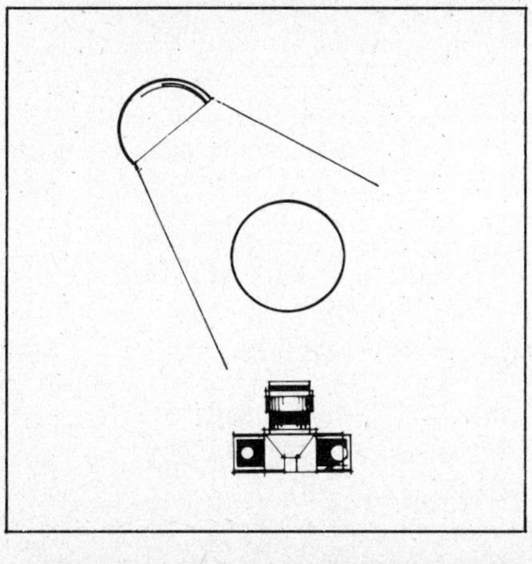

6
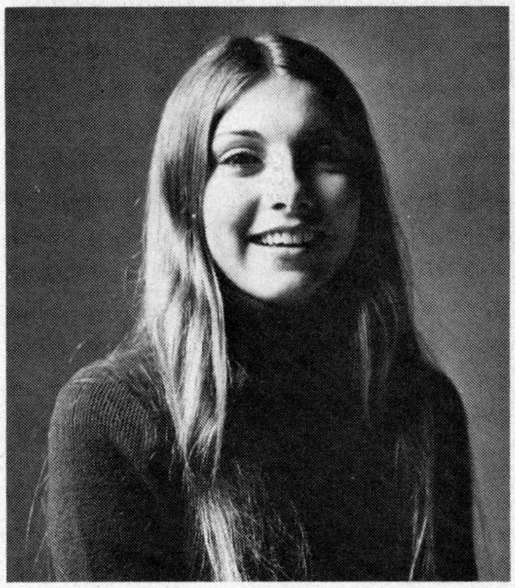

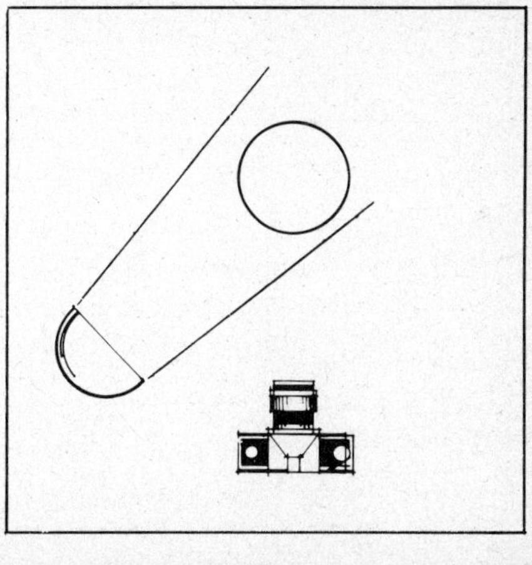

chrome. The slightly higher price of 3200°K bulbs is worth paying if you want flood bulbs for black-and-white, because they last indefinitely.

Reflector flood bulbs/ These self-contained units including an interior reflector in each bulb, are made in both 3400°K and 3200°K. Smaller 150W reflector bulbs are often screwed into hand-held bars used with movie cameras. Large types are 500W and cost considerably more than mere flood bulbs, but take up less room than separate reflectors, and are quite adaptable to the following compact kit. Reflector spots (150W) are also available. (Spotlights cast a concentrated beam, while floodlights spread their beam over a greater area.)

Quartz lights/ Also neat and portable for a homemade lighting outfit are self-contained quartz lights. A whole quartz unit is only a four- or five-inch cube, and more powerful (650W) than a flood bulb. Quartz lights cost $20 or more each, but two of them throw almost as much light as three reflector flood bulbs. If you are just getting started with floodlighting equipment, investigate quartz lights; they are made by several companies.

Make-your-own-lighting-kit/ If you choose to use reflector flood bulbs, it is easy to assemble individual lighting units. At a hardware store buy a socket with off-on switch, a wood handle made for files, and a brass threaded connector to screw the handle into the socket. At a photo supply store buy an Alligator clamp (a brand name), an arm of which fits around the socket. The jaws of this versatile clamp allow you to fasten it to a light stand, a door, or almost anything solid. The clamp can also be set firmly on the floor.

Attach 20 feet of electric cord to the socket, and put a plug on the opposite end. With a reflector flood completing each unit, you have a practical, economical homemade light. Three such lighting units, or several quartz lights, plus stands, an extension cord or two, some masking tape and a few extra bulbs can be carried in a fiber case made to hold everything. In Los Angeles, Industrial Fibre Products, 3680 S. Main Street, makes such cases to order, and similar services should be available in other cities. Ready-made cases may also be found at camera shops to hold your lights efficiently.

LIGHT STANDS AND BOOMS

The best stands are made of aluminum and come in several styles; they telescope two, three, or more sections compactly. There are other types in heavier materials that are quite suitable if you don't intend to carry them around very often. A light stand may cost $15 to $25, but it should last a lifetime. Some models have small projections in several places that are useful for attaching quartz lights.

To elevate a flood bulb over someone's head, you might buy a boom arm that has a socket at one end and a weight at the other. The boom attaches to a light stand and projects out three or four feet. Boom lights are standard equipment in portrait studios, but accessory equipment for the average photographer.

BASIC LIGHTING TECHNIQUES

The directional categories of light were discussed in Chapter 5 in relation to sunlight outdoors. The same principles apply indoors with flash or

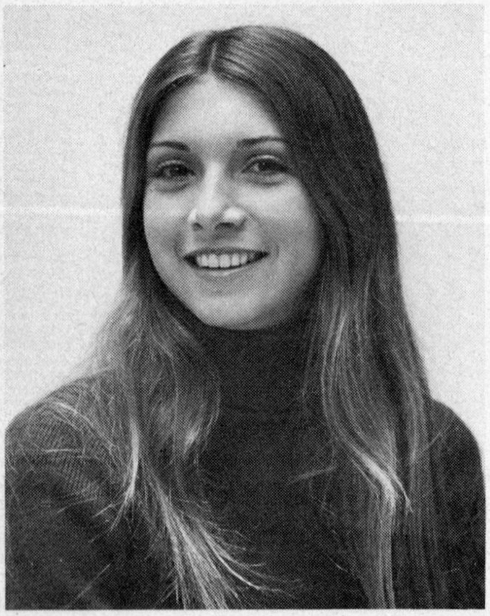
1

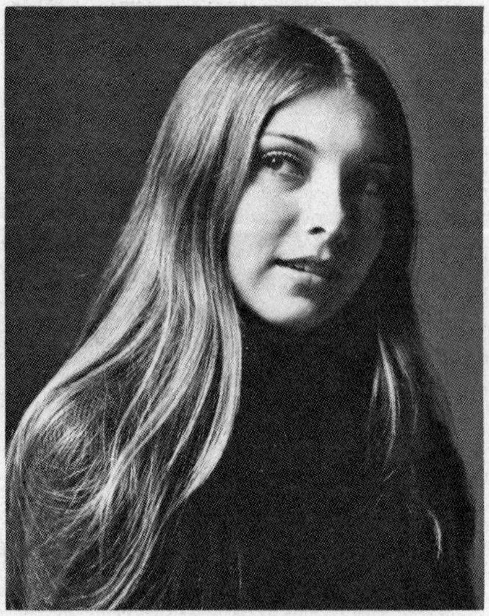
2

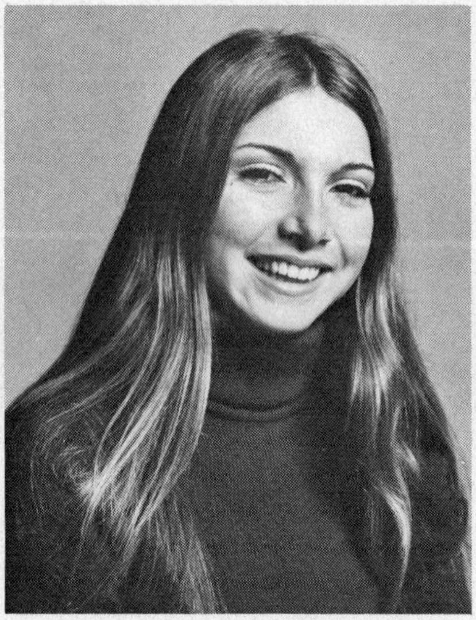
3

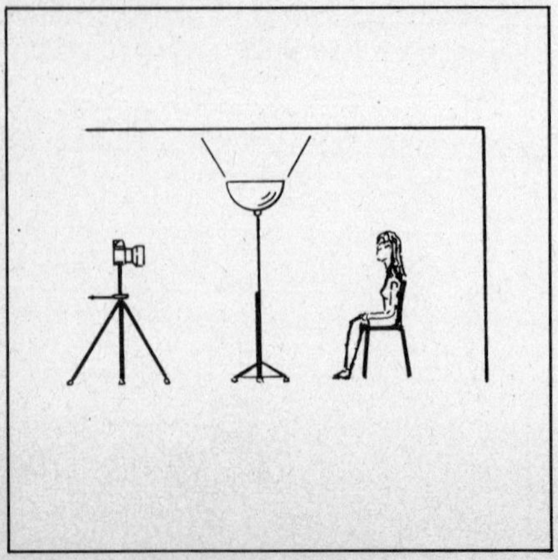

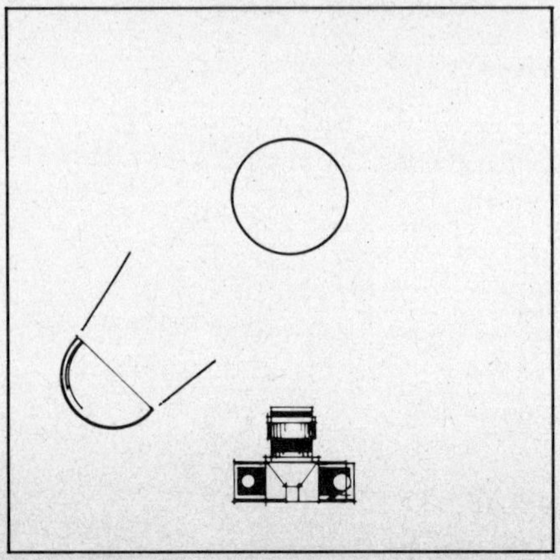

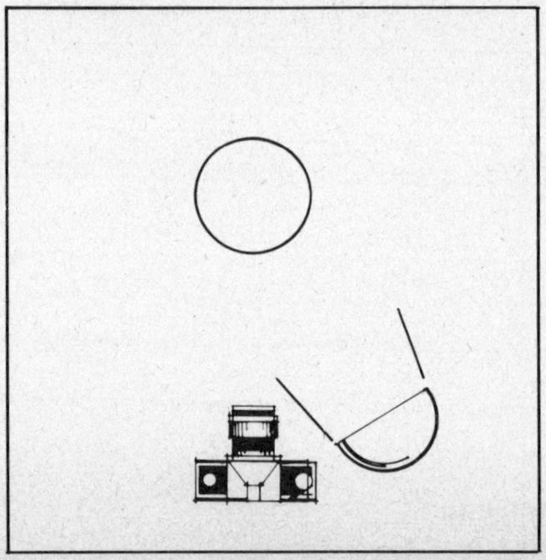

flood, expect that with artificial light, you have control over its placement. It is my impression that people shy away from using floodlights in favor of flash, because it takes a few minutes to set up the floods. This prejudice can easily be overcome, once you learn the simplicity of floodlighting. With it you can not only shoot a portrait or a room full of people, but you can *see* the effects of the light *before* you shoot.

Note: Some electronic flash units made for AC-use only include modeling lights, which are built-in incandescent bulbs that show how the flash will fall. They cost $75 to $100, but are very convenient for portraits when EF assures complete sharpness, spontaneity and consistent color.

If you have never played around with two or three floodlights and a model, you are in for a photographic treat. Observing small and subtle changes of form, dramatic contrasts and various lighting effects is both enlightening and fun. As you learn to control artificial light gracefully on a model or still life, you really get the feel of photography.

Let's review lighting practices with floods (or quartz lights). The demonstration photographs illustrate the various types of lighting.

Front light/ It's flat, and in flash it's expedient. Flash attached to the camera is mobile but not artistic. Front light is also "fill" light in conjunction with another light closer to the subject from the side or back.

Sidelight/ If you hold a flash or EF off the camera at arm's length (or place it on a light stand), you get a variation of sidelight, which is more attractive than light from the front. A floodlight on a stand at about a 45-degree angle to the subject is a good start for portraits.

Backlight/ In portraiture a light from an angle behind the subject creates drama and separation—if you can keep the light from shining into the lens. Light on a background will often reflect on the neck and face of a model, becoming a soft backlight.

Bounce or reflected light/ Just as reflected sunlight is soft and flattering outdoors, reflected flood or flash is a delight indoors. In color there may be an exposure problem, since reflected light is much weaker than direct light, so fast color films are necessary to arrest subject movement and assure reasonable depth of field. Most small EF units are not powerful enough to use in a reflected mode, but you can diffuse a direct light for a similar soft effect. Quartz lights or 500W floods are quite adaptable to black-and-white film or fast color, and by reflection are a means of achieving beautiful portraits.

Photographic umbrellas and cardboard reflectors all work well with artificial lights. The trick is to place the reflector close enough to the subject for maximum intensity and at an appropriate angle—without having the reflector cut into the picture. Experi-

1. Diffuse lighting (in this case, photoflood lamps bounced off white ceiling) produces soft effect.

2. In typical four-light portrait lighting setup, main light is at left of camera, producing this effect.

3. Fill light in four-light portrait setup is near camera, on right.

4. Background light is behind subject, aimed at background.

5. Fourth light is hair (accent) light.

6. Turn on all four lights at once, and you've got a portrait.

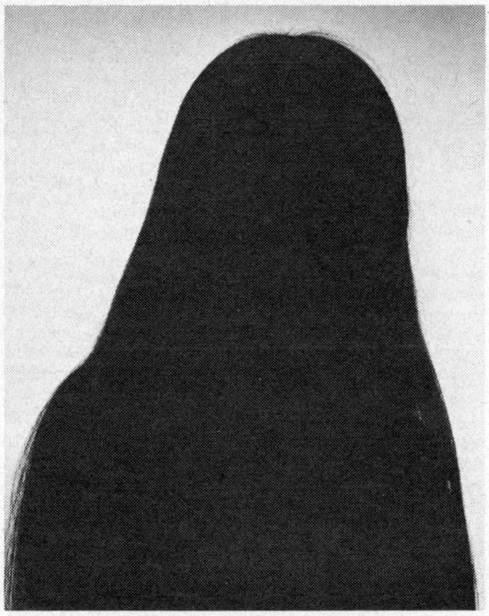

4

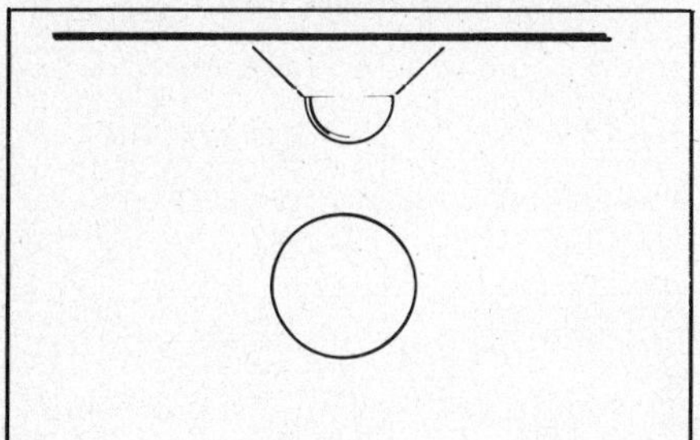

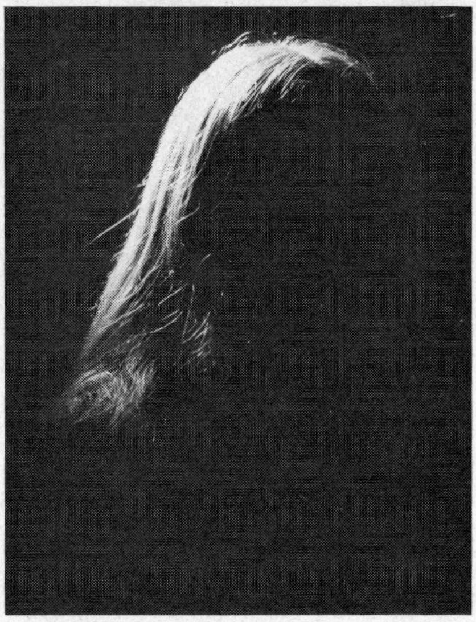

5

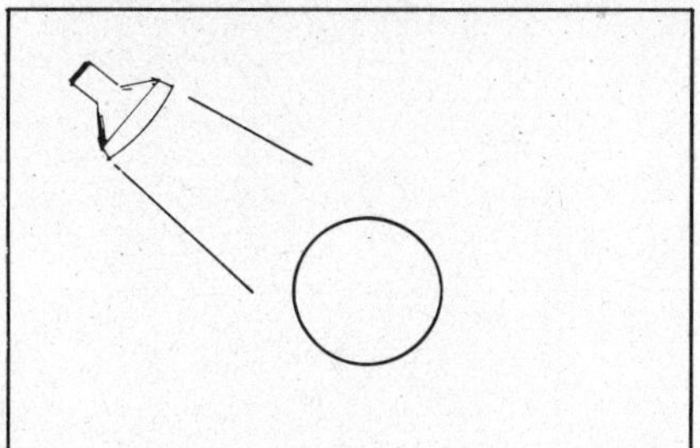

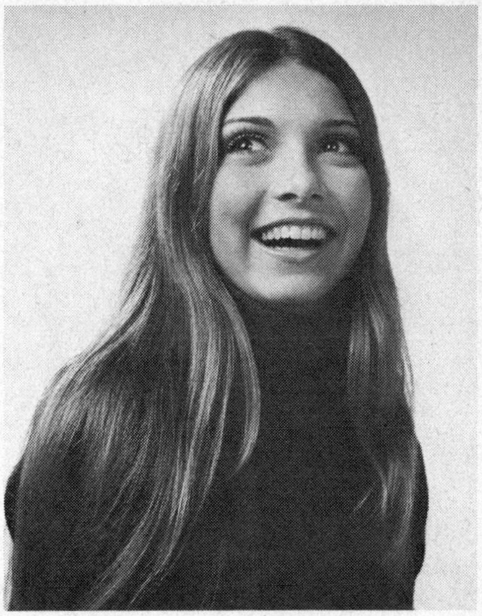

6

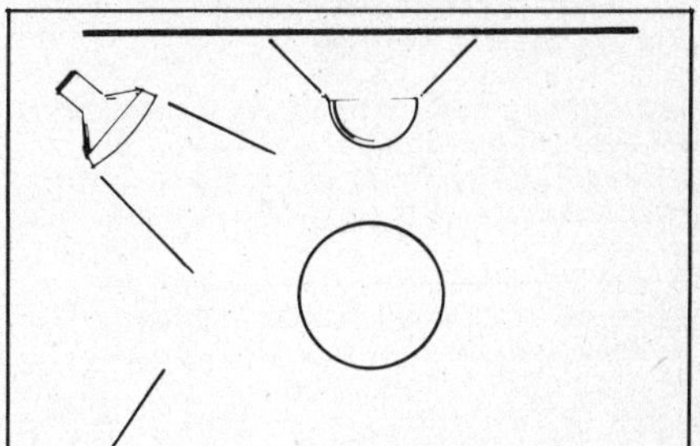

Indoor Lighting

ence at manipulation will solve the problem, for the glowing effects of reflected light are worth taking a little extra trouble.

Bounce light is also a term referring to use of flash or EF pointed at a slight angle at a ceiling in front of a subject, or occasionally at a wall. Bouncing a couple of floods or an EF unit increases the light level of a room, and helps maintain the natural feeling while filling shadows and making faster exposures possible. Of course, a white or light-colored ceiling is necessary in order to produce efficient bounce lighting.

Bounce flash or EF can be the most valuable way of using this light source. A ceiling spreads light which is reflected gently on subjects, and can cover evenly a much wider area than direct flash. Two floods or two EF units on stands on both sides of a group will enable you to cover everyone evenly because bounce light blends uniformly from its ceiling reflector. I carry a small EF unit on many jobs, and use it with Tri-X to give me a consistent light level in homes, offices, etc., for individuals or several people. The unit is attached to an extender atop the camera, and can be set to point at a ceiling or wall. Some EF units have pivoting heads, which make bounce light easier to achieve.

There is a simple rule for bounce exposure. Divide the guide number for your unit by 10, and open the aperture two stops more for the average 8- or 9-foot ceiling. Example: A guide number of 160 divided by 10 is 16; two additional stops means exposing at f/8. With a small EF unit and Tri-X film rated at EI 1000 (developed in Acufine), my average bounce exposure is f/8 or f/9. I have plenty of depth of field with a 35mm lens, a 52mm lens, or even a 100mm lens for portraits.

Experiment with bounce light. It can convert average pictures by di-

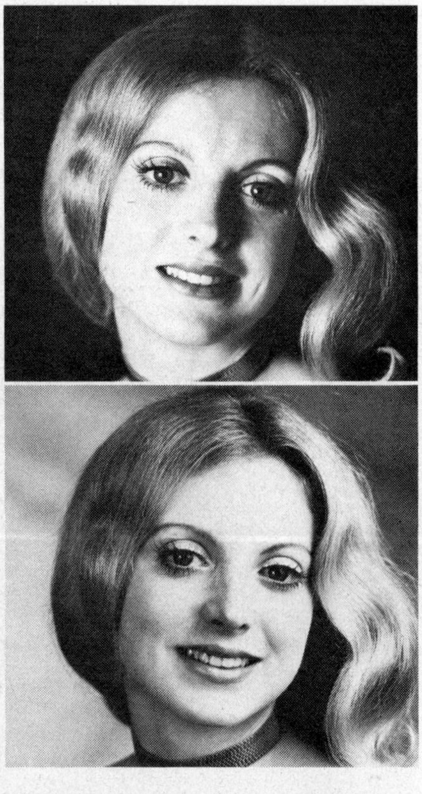

1

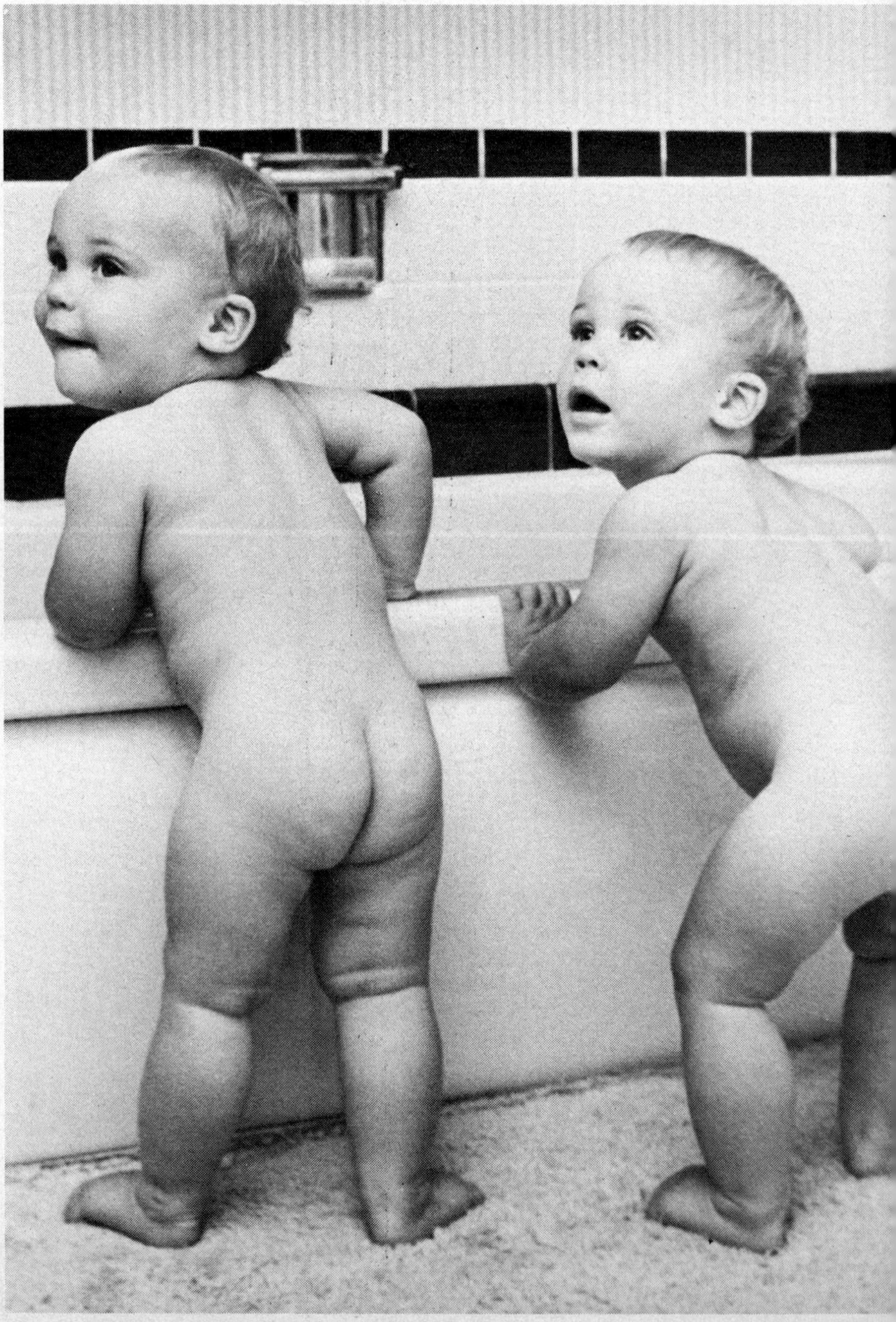

2

1. Though the main light on model shifts from left to right in these two pictures, they demonstrate effectiveness of background light. A dark-haired person might benefit by contrasting with light background even more. Photos by Jim Cornfield.

2. Bounced electronic flash, especially in light room such as bathroom, is ideal for many kinds of subjects, giving soft shadows and even illumination.

3. Gil Smith set razor and blade on sheet of glass and curved a sheet of white cardboard underneath as background and as reflecting canopy. Shadows were thus eliminated by technique popular with commercial photographers for small objects.

4. Using 50mm lens, author was close enough to singers that man is slightly out of focus at f/8 with bounced electronic flash in living room. Effect is far more pleasant than direct flash.

rect light into unusual prints or slides.

Background light/ Behind a portrait subject it is often good practice to light the background with a separate light (which is why you probably need three floods in your kit). Unwelcome shadows from front and side lights falling on the background are subdued or eliminated. A background light also sets up contrast for skin tones and makes a neater-looking portrait. Naturally, pictures of people are often taken against black or gray backgrounds as well as light-colored ones, but even so, in the Karsh tradition, light may glow from a background light placed behind a model's neck. You should be familiar with background lighting effects as you play with floods or flash.

HAVE FUN WITH LIGHT

See what happens when you put one light behind objects, some of which are translucent (such as bottles) and some opaque. You can create all sorts of unusual effects with just one light.

Discover the pleasures of placing small objects on a piece of glass and lighting them from below (keep hot lights far enough away from the glass, please).

Combine direct and reflected light for a variety of shadows and highlights on a portrait or still life.

If you want to bring out form in a piece of sculpture, place a reflector spot bulb above it at an appropriate angle. Fill the shadows with light reflected from an umbrella.

Try shadowless lighting of small objects, especially those with reflecting surfaces such as metal or glass. Place the objects on a piece of cardboard or heavy paper that curves up in the background to eliminate any horizon line. Suspend another piece of cardboard or a reflector umbrella above the objects or from the side. Bounce your lights in a way that shadows are almost nonexistent.

Look at lighting effects in pictures everywhere—in magizines, exhibits, advertising, etc. Simulate effects you like, and try some far out experiments as well. Make mistakes and discoveries. Enjoy the beauty that light creates under your careful control.

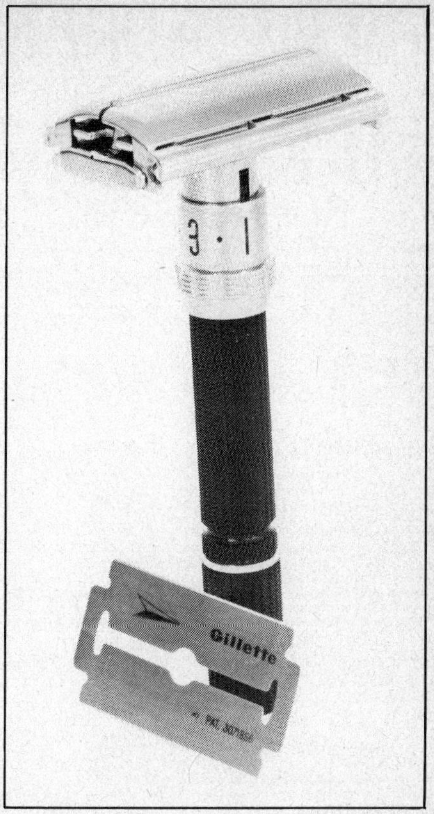

3

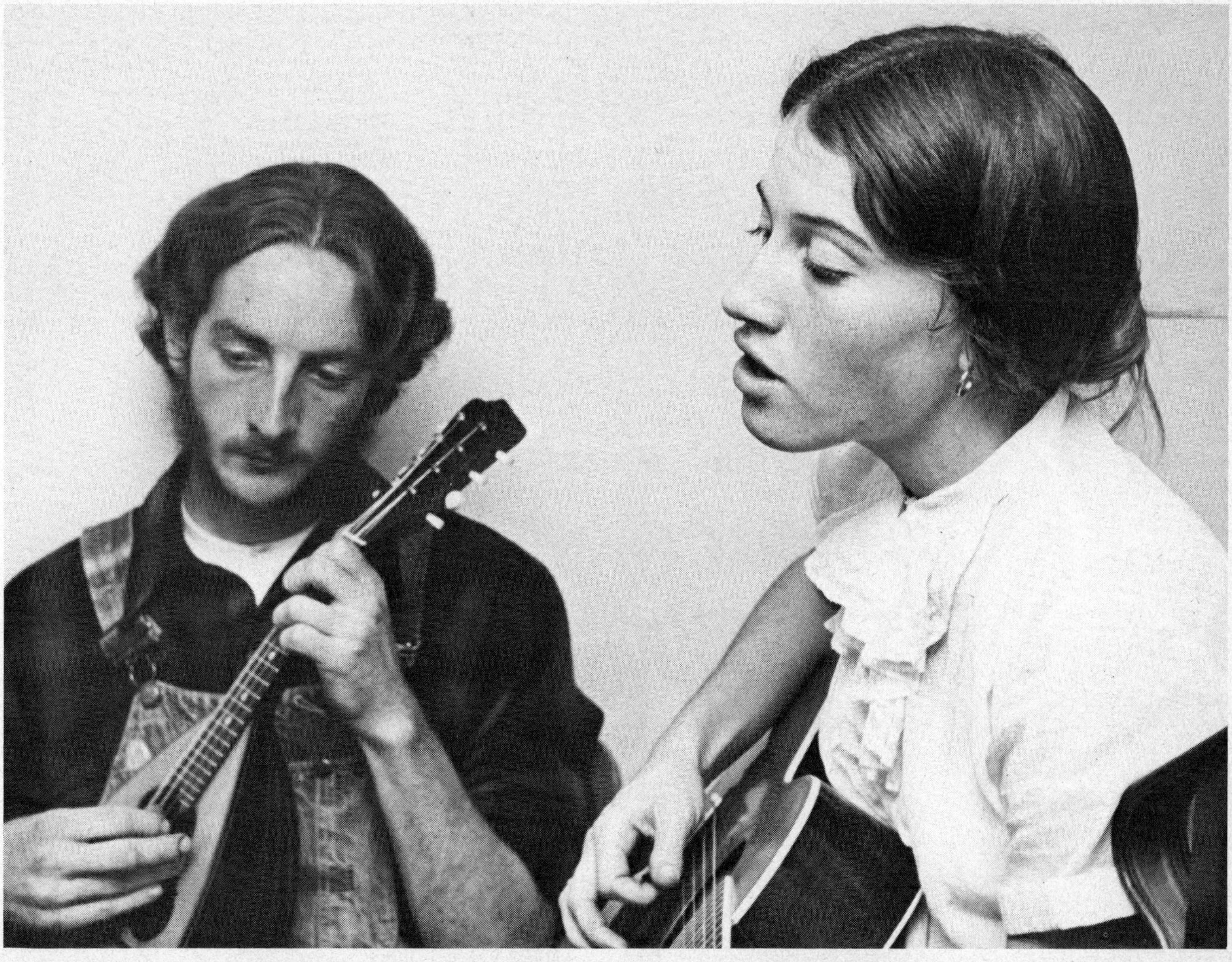
4

CHAPTER 7 Composition--the Way We See

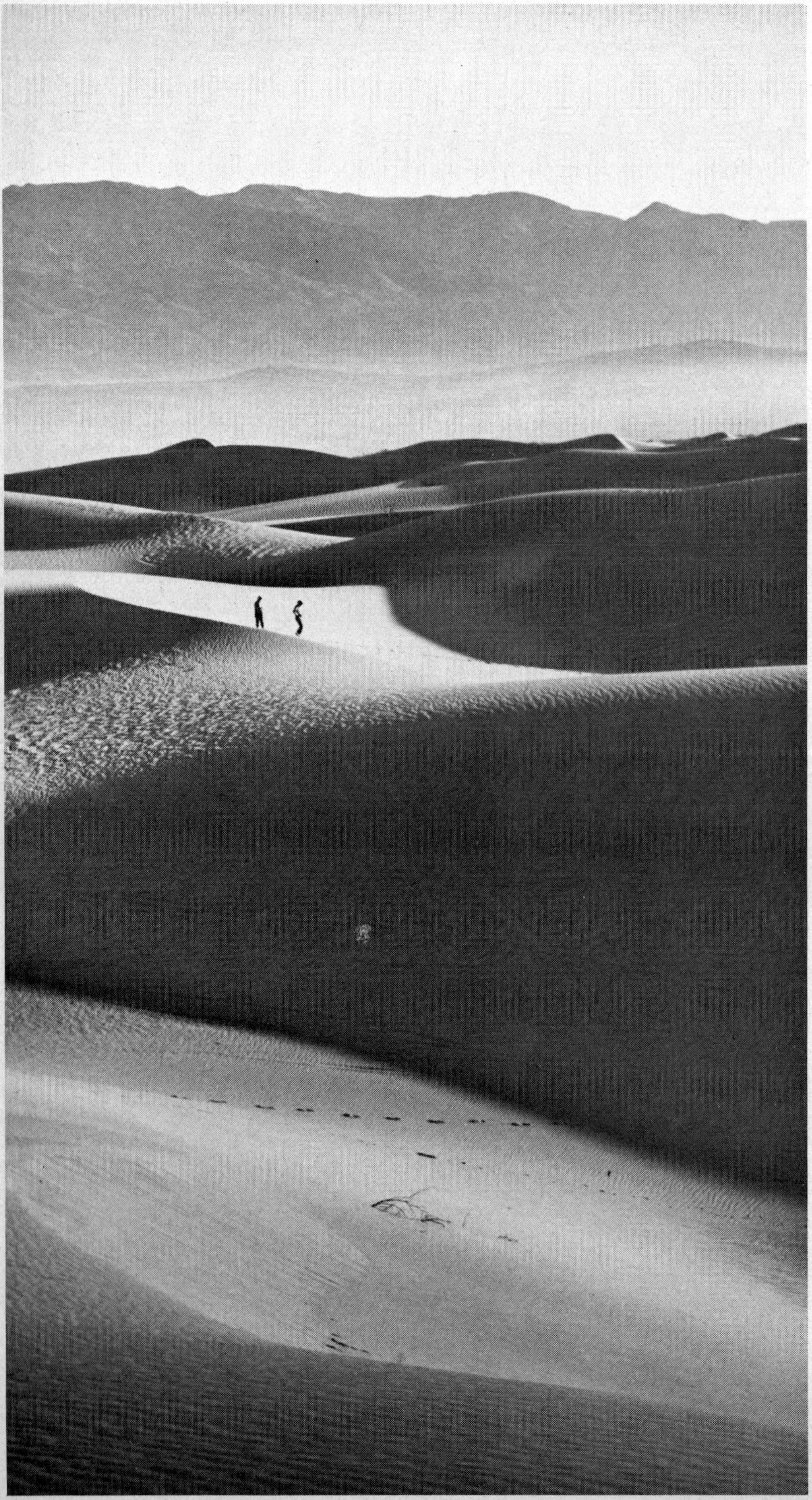

1

In this automated age when pictures telecast from the moon may be more creative than ones we snap at the Grand Canyon, it's child's play to ''compose'' a photograph. Simply point the camera, focus, set the exposure, depress the shutter release and you have—an image. It may be orderly and exciting or inane and worthless, depending on how you see. An image recorded largely by default is hardly a valid, hard-earned composition. The latter requires conscious, sensitive arrangement of pictorial elements, for you must be aware of how to see effectively to get real satisfaction from photography.

This may sound like a sermon, but composition is a subject about which I feel strongly. You can learn a lot about equipment and lighting, or tricks of exposure, but until you learn to *see* composition and translate it to film and prints with uncommon impact, everything else is just an exercise and experimentation.

A while back I was talking about this subject with the editor of *PhotoGraphic Magazine*. He brought up what he calls the ''dead center syndrome,'' which he says, ''is suffered by people who focus on a face, for instance, in the center grid of an SLR finder, and just snap the subject in that position.'' He wished there was a way to divide a camera finder with faint grid lines to remind photographers to shift the camera and keep the main subject away from dead center in photographs. ''It would result in a lot more interesting pictures,'' he added.

I agree completely, and therein lies an important principle of composition, namely *balance*. Some photographs are far more pleasingly balanced than others. A picture may entertain, in take down form, delight or shock you, but why is one pictorial arrangement fascinating and another one dull? The answer lies in basic design, a series of fundamental tenets by which we see, compose and judge graphic images such as paintings, sculpture, drawings, buildings or photographs.

The elements of design will sound familiar to you: lines, forms (shapes), texture, space and color. We'll deal with these shortly, but first I want emphasize a natural law which states that equal-size shapes, or a composition that is divided into equal segments, is likely to be boring. The human aesthetic sense craves change of pace, variety and contrast, just as normally as men enjoy looking at women and women enjoy looking at clothes. The same natural law helps us avoid monotony in our lives, as it encourages us to try to shoot images that both impress the eye and challenge the mind.

This explains why a diversity of pictorial balance is more attractive than dead-center dullness. One common name for a picture so afflicted is "snapshot." The word infers that someone snapped or exposed an image with minimum awareness of what composition is all about. From a semantic viewpoint, photographers are those who are conscious of design and composition, while snapshooters just don't know any better.

ELEMENTS OF COMPOSITION

In some books the principles that define composition are called "rules." I have never liked that word in this regard because it implies rigidity. Fixed rules are fine for football games or traffic control, but in aesthetics, rules are meant to be observed and interpreted in highly personal ways (called style), which means they are often broken by visual pacesetters and experimenters. With this in mind, let's talk about other precepts, or principles, by which we compose and evaluate a composition.

Dominance/ The largest, brightest or most favorably placed object, shape or person in a composition is the most dominant. It is the element you see first, such as the eyes in a portrait, the main action of a football scrimmage or the tallest building in a skyline. You may set out to make something dominant in a scene, or it may simply end up that way because it was naturally the most important element. The dominant may appear anywhere within the frame of a picture, and the eye will go to it first automatically because of its outstanding qualities of size, color, position or human interest.

Subordination/ The remaining shapes in a composition are subordinate to the dominant one, perhaps not in storytelling character, but in visual priority. Some subordinate shapes or figures may be almost equal to the main one, and there can be a wide spectrum of secondary components that work with and support the primary one in a photograph.

Eye Flow/ This refers not to tears but to the path by which the eye views and flows in, through and out of a picture, from left to right, top to bottom, etc. There is no specific direction in which a composition must flow to make it effective, and we are usually not conscious of eye flow as we take pictures, but it influences the success of the total image. Look at a few pictures; decide how your vision moves from one area to another. Is your eye stopped somewhere and blocked? Are there several paths by which you can explore the composition? An abrupt visual halt may call attention to a dominant subject or activity, or it may be awkward. Several interconnected patterns of eye flow are also normal in many successful compositions.

A traditional form of visual move-

2

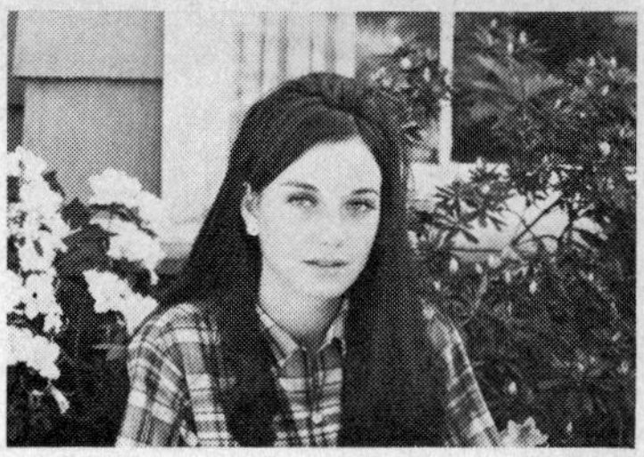

3

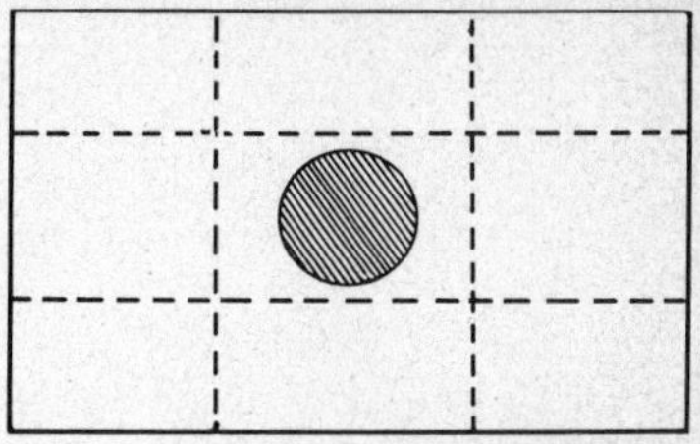

4

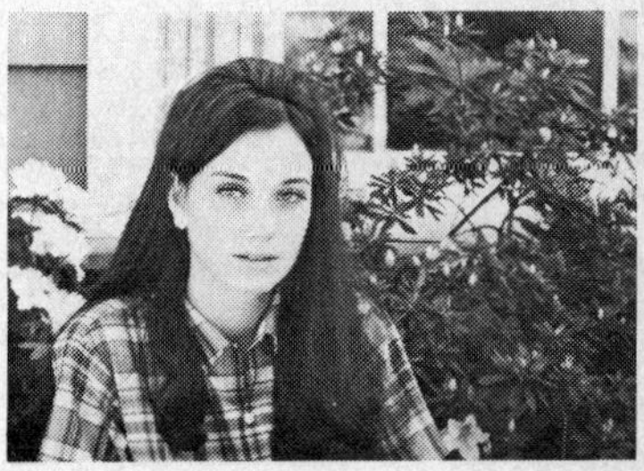

5

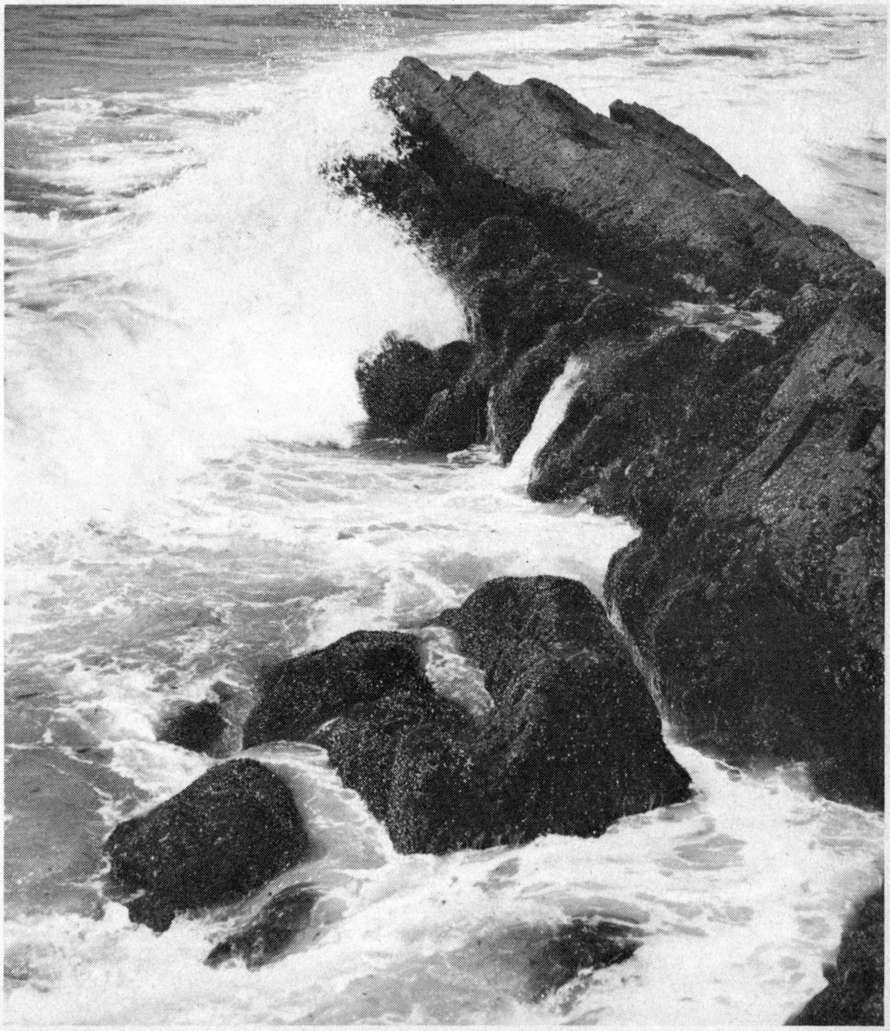

1. Composition depends on many elements which we arrange visually in the finder, and perhaps rearrange later by cropping a print or slide. The exciting forms of Death Valley dunes have been composed to please the eye according to guidelines in this chapter. Shot taken by Bronica, Tri-X, 135mm lens, 1/250 second, f/16.

2. Centering a model is often a monotonous placement that can also be static.

3. If the ground glass of a single-lens reflex had a grid pattern within it, photographers might be reminded to shift camera after focusing to avoid "dead center syndrome."

4. A more pleasing off-center arrangement of model and background results from shifting the camera to one side.

5. Balance, harmonious or distracting for a purpose, is an important principle of composition. In this seascape the thrusting rock at top center is balanced by the opposing angle of surf and secondary rocks at bottom center. Taken with view camera, 8-inch lens, 1/100 second, f/32, Tri-X film.

ment in a picture is called the S-curve, which indicates that the eye flows in an S-shape. This configuration may serve you well at times, but the S-curve theory has been greatly overblown. It was an old standby of salon photographers, but now the S-curve is only one of many ways to structure a photo.

Lines, forms, texture, space and color/ These are visual ingredients of which pictures are made; aware photographers learn to recognize and use them. You see a picket fence and integrate its lines into your composition, or you photograph the form of a lovely girl, and make her dominant within your space. You can shoot a portrait, landscape or action shot without thinking where you are placing its lines, forms, colors, etc., but if you are analytical, your compositions are likely to improve. Soon you will stop analyzing consciously, and structuring a photograph will become personal technique.

One or a combination of lines, forms, etc. may be dominant or subordinate in a composition. Painters are probably more aware of using these elements because they draw them on canvas in precisely the position they wish, to tell a story or make a visual point. Photographers have to arrange what's there to coalesce harmoniously to please the senses or even create surprise. We can move people and things sometimes, but usually we move ourselves to achieve better compositions, more effective angles, stronger patterns, etc. Essentially, we strive for a picture that intrigues the eye, is entertaining, imaginative or emotionally dramatic.

Texture is a part of form, but a pattern can become a dominant theme. Texture of nature or man-made things is usually subordinate to other elements in a composition, but it can serve to catch the eye, and must be managed to enhance or be functional in a photograph.

Space is a somewhat elusive element because it is only implied in a print or slide. Conventionally, space is shown by the relationship of foreground and background objects, via prominent perspective or the placement of people and things. Space is often associated with distance, but there can be a spacial feeling in a picture of two people in a room when nothing is very far away.

Painters use a technique of implying space by placement of colors. The eye will move from an area or spot of color in the foreground of a picture to the same color at the top or side. This manner of suggesting space without accenting perspective was pioneered by painter Paul Cézanne. Note in some of his land-

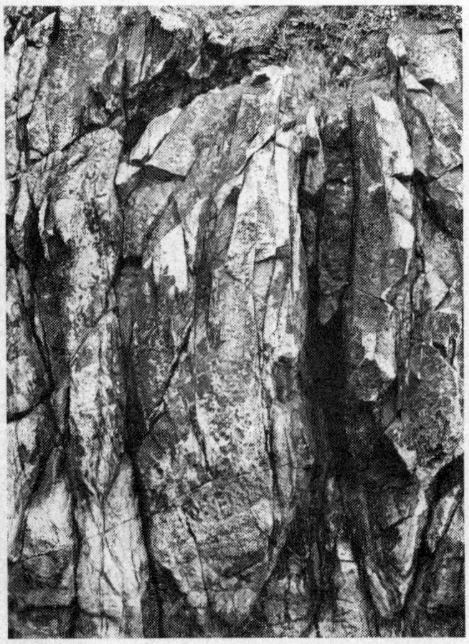

1

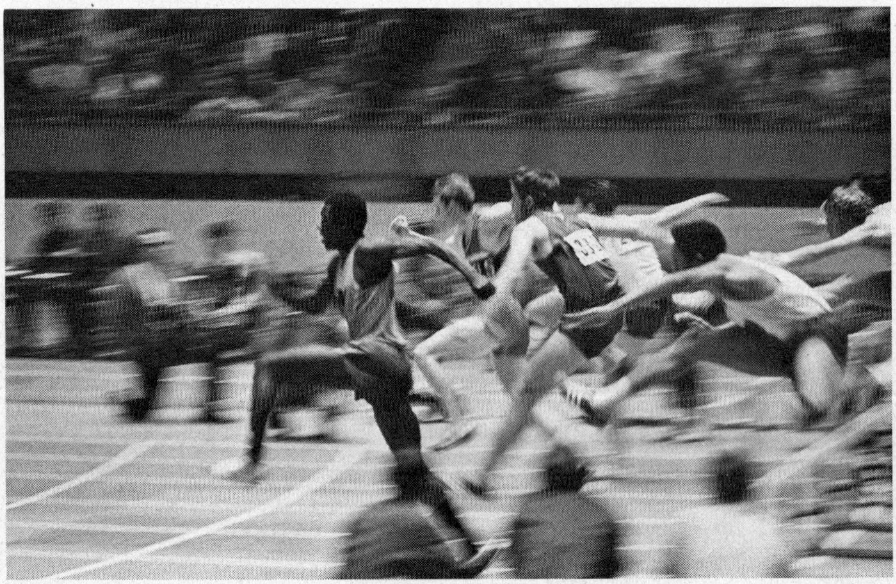

3

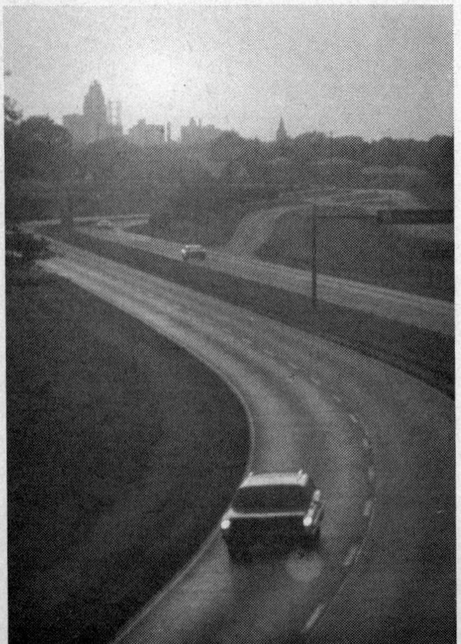

2

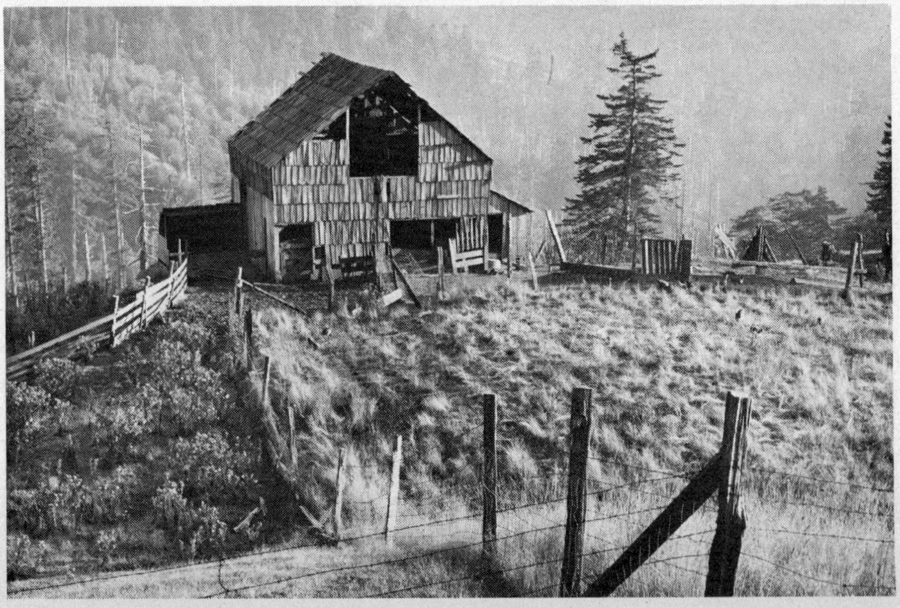

4

scape paintings how colors offer the impression of space without traditional lines or forms receding from front to back. Artists call this flow of color, form, lines, etc., plasticity. When handled deftly, plasticity can be a dynamic pictorial force.

PICTORIAL ELEMENTS OF COMPOSITION

Backgrounds/ Messy backgrounds are responsible for as many image failures as camera movement and faulty timing. It is obvious that backgrounds should be as simple and unobtrusive as possible, unless they are salient to the theme of your pictures. All sorts of junk seems to turn up behind people you photograph, usually because you are so intent on getting a good expression that the background is ignored. I continually find myself shifting the camera, trying to place faces, figures or objects against plainer backgrounds. If I cannot move, I try to shift the subject, and if all else fails, I use a large enough aperture to throw the background out of focus. This may be difficult with fast black-and-white or color film, which is a good argument to use slower films in order to retain aperture control over backgrounds that may divert the eye.

When the background adds something to your picture, you are more likely to keep it organized. Photographs of people in settings where they live or work may be enhanced when you can see their surroundings. Can you think of a portrait you shot in which the background contributes to the overall effect? Can you think of other integrated backgrounds you tried to achieve?

Contrasts/ These have been mentioned before in terms of large vs. small, light vs. dark, etc. Various elements of design are used to provide contrasts that make a composition more attractive. Perhaps you have made a landscape photograph that might have been improved by a figure or object in it to give the scene a sense of scale, of perspective. Contrasts contribute to composition in direct or subtle ways.

Expression and emotion/ These are not part of the structure of a composition, but can be integral to the content of a picture. When something happens to make people react as you shoot, their faces tell a story, and you are challenged to expose at the decisive moment (a la Henri Cartier-Bresson) when an emotion, movement or expression is most striking.

1. Composition and choice of subject can ally photography closely with painting in terms of artistic expression. This wall of rocks has a cubist feeling; shot taken with 4x5 view camera and an 8-inch lens.

2. The S-curve is a traditional form of composition illustrated in Mark Packo's Scholastic/Kodak Award winner. An S-shaped composition is an old standby of salon photographers, although it is only one of many ways in which a photograph can be organized or arranged.

3. Lines and forms in this dynamic shot by Robert Lewis (another Scholastic/Kodak Award winner) combine to dominate the composition as a visual mixture. The eye is forced to move in the direction of the sprinters.

4. Some elements of composition are demonstrated in photo shot in Northern California by the author with a 4x5 view camera. The rectangle was visualized with the barn as dominant because of its size and placement. Other subjects are subordinate in visual priority, but support the dominant by placement; fence posts lead to the barn; tree, textured earth and background are all integral. Eye flow, which is the path by which the eye views and flows through a photograph, is along the lines of objects that lead to the barn.

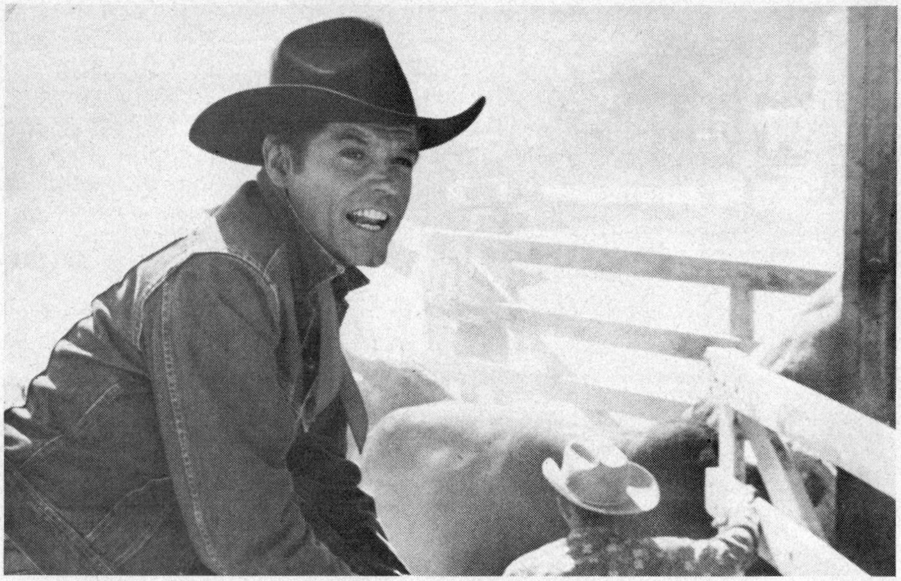

5

5. A fortunately simple background strengthened this picture of actor Jack Lord in a scene from the Stoney Burke TV series. The dusty, sunlit corral provided a natural contrast to Lord's face, in the shadow. He is off-center in the composition and lines in the background lead to his face.

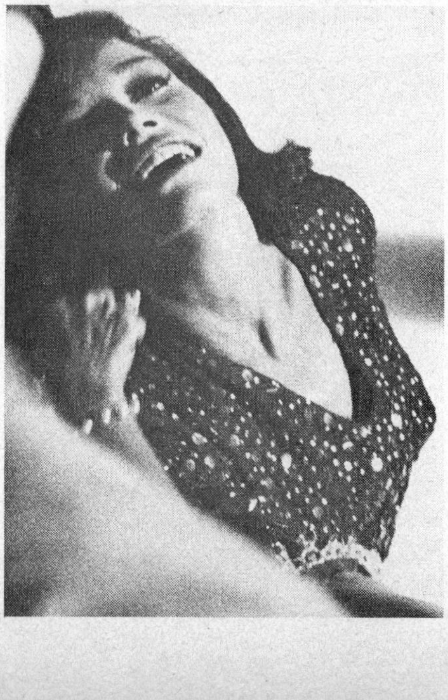

6

6. Expression of happiness or joy is the key attraction in this experimental photo of Mary Tyler Moore by Ken Whitmore. Though not part of compositional structure, emotional impact is very important to many pictures. Enlarged grain texture was intentional, accomplished by making huge blow-up from 35mm original negative.

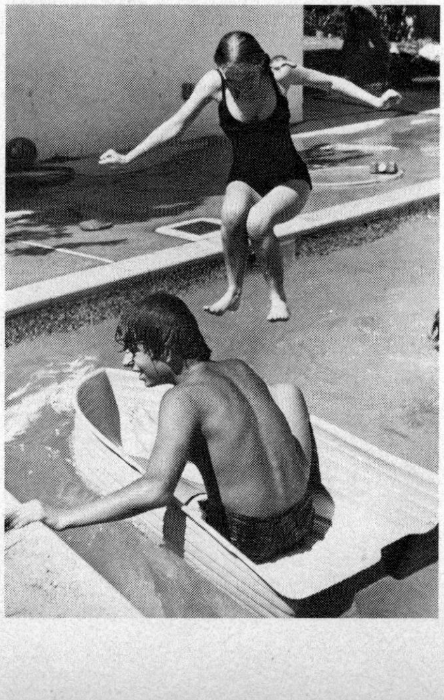

7

7. Space is implied and apparent here as the eye moves from bottom foreground to top background, and accepts illusion of impending collision between young lady and young man. (She actually landed in water.) Both the action and its perspective dominate this picture shot with a 35mm lens, 1/1000 second, f/16 on Tri-X film.

Composition

Your instinct for timing as well as your involvement with people are responsible for success in capturing human interest. There are pictures that may not be ideally arranged, and yet have impact because of human values. What I mean is, composition is always important, but in certain cases it can be secondary to the content of your pictures.

Framing/ Familiar techniques include looking through, under, around or over a foreground shape that partly or totally frames something more important behind it. Hanging branches make a sky more interesting as they frame a landscape or seascape. A porch may frame activity in the nearby yard, an overhanging roof adds its accent to a street scene, or the lines of a jungle gym can interrupt the foreground in a shot of kids playing. Framing adds drama and may help furnish an otherwise bare scene.

Framing also includes using an "interrupting object" or figure in the foreground over which you see the dominant area of a picture. Perhaps you have shot across somebody in a crowd, and found that a head, or an arm, even out of focus, adds a sense of visual impact.

A feeling of motion/ When you capture action sharply on film, it is often the dominant of a composition. However, if you allow action to blur via a slow shutter speed, it may contribute a vivid sense of movement which can be more important visually than the action-story itself. The eye is entertained by decorative blur which allows the imagination to speculate. Blur may not be literal, but it can be dynamic symbolism. Have you seen Ernst Haas's bullfight pictures in color? He eschews sharpness to achieve images closely related to paintings.

Mood/ This quality of a composition may be real or fantasy. Mood can be an ethereal thing, or a strong essence of photographs. Lighting and tonality often influence mood, along with human interest, color, etc.

Point of view/ Commonplace scenes can be interpreted with a visual thrust when they are shot from a viewpoint that is different from the average. I once heard a photographer tell of an assignment he shot when a couple of celebrities were posing for the press. "There were about eight guys with cameras," he reported. "I decided it was silly to line up with them and take the same pictures, so I roamed around the edges, and even went behind the subjects, looking for an unusual point of view. A lot of my shots were spoiled by unmanageable backgrounds, but I did get an edge-lighted series that was different."

Point of view is worth remembering when you travel, shooting new places and things that many others have photographed before you. It is easy

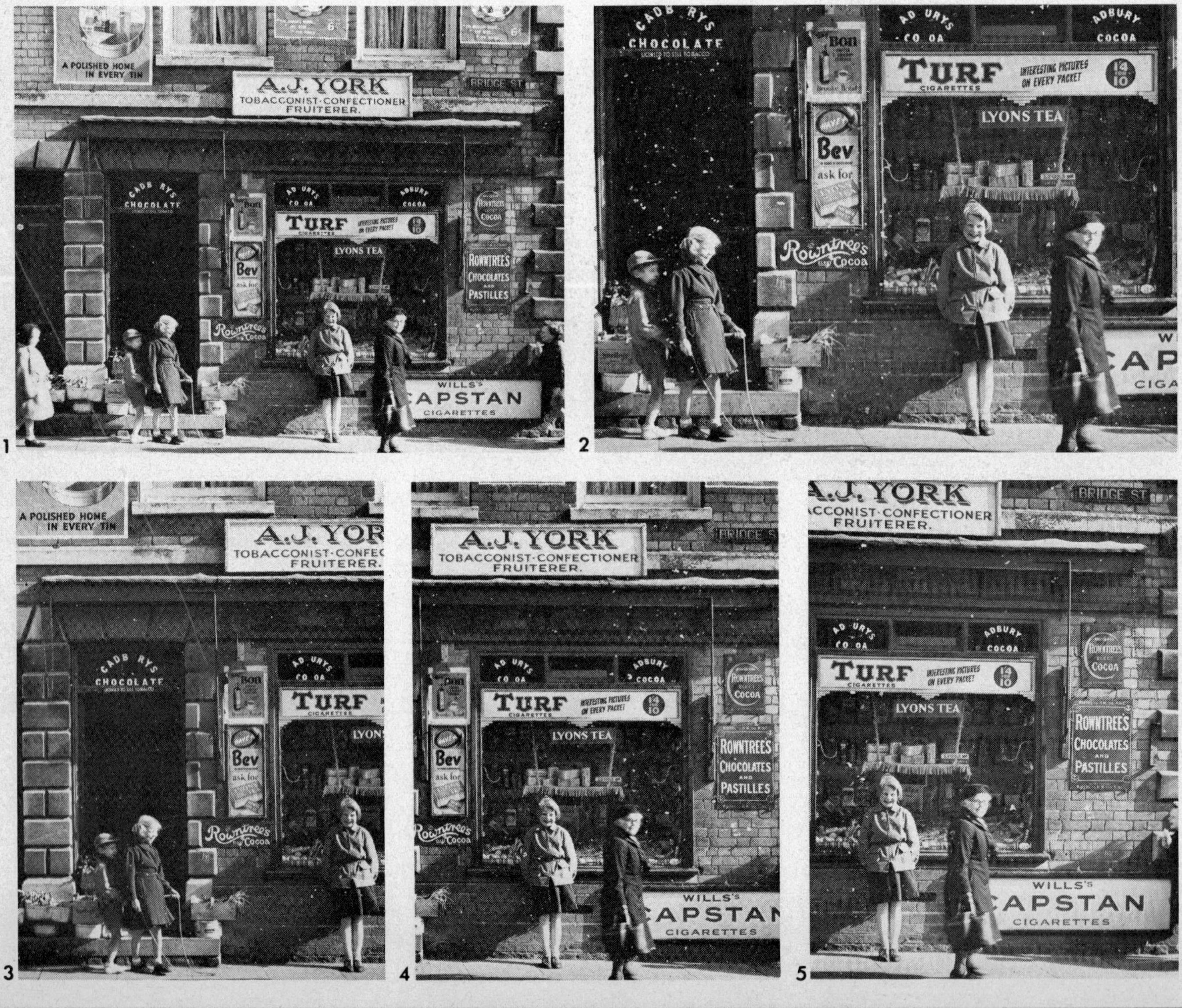

1 2 3 4 5

to stand by the "shoot here" sign and get a conventional composition, but look further. There *must* be some other spots from which to see the same scene with a visual twist, in a different light, with a longer or shorter focal length lens, or vertically rather than horizontally. Exploration occasions its own rewards.

Simplicity/ When you put all the elements of composition together, they should spell "simplicity." The most direct, restrained and uncomplicated way you can see a subject through your finder will usually create the most fascinating pictures. Study magazine covers and posters. They have to be simple and strong. Look carefully at pictures you see everywhere, including your own. Notice that the ones which leave a lasting impression are usually simply composed.

COMPOSITION BY CROPPING

Edward Weston shot his marvelous studies of nature and man-made articles with an 8x10 view camera, and disdained any cropping when he made contact prints of each full negative. Similar discipline is a great method of training yourself as you learn photography with a 35mm camera, but it is hard to be as much a purist as Weston was. Most of us find that negatives and slides can be improved by cropping, which means to cut off extraneous parts of an image as it is printed or projected. Through sensitive cropping, you concentrate on the essentials, and eliminate everything that does not support your story or theme.

The easiest way to crop a print is with a pair of "L's" made from thin cardboard. Cut each L long enough to cover the size print you are cropping. Move the L's in and around the frame, deciding when you have just the image you want. Then trim off the edges, or mask a slide with black tape.

In your own darkroom, cropping is part of the fun and creativity of enlarging. Make preliminary crop marks on a proof or contact print with a red grease pencil if someone else does your printing, but you are in a better position to select your image than are most outsiders. Composition is personal, and the best exercise of your own taste.

In a cropping exercise in this chapter, I demonstrate how one picture can be seen in several ways. Use one of your own photographs to crop other images from it, or at least improve it. Eliminated areas strengthen those that remain.

TOWARD BETTER COMPOSITION

How does one learn to compose in the finder and to crop more effectively? The process might be compared to learning to cook. You gather the ingredients and blend them, following a recipe. You taste the concoction, make corrections, and give it an aesthetic touch if possible when you serve it. You cook new dishes and go back to improve old ones. Eventually, you have a touch, an instinct, that comes from experience, persistence, ingenuity and whatever talent you were born with.

In photography the ingredients are visual and often gathered for you before you shoot. You blend them through the finder and "taste the concoction" via your aesthetic sense, with which you also make corrections before you depress the shutter release. Afterward, you can add other improvements, the "seasoning" of cropping. Your instincts improve as you see, feel, think and shoot regu-

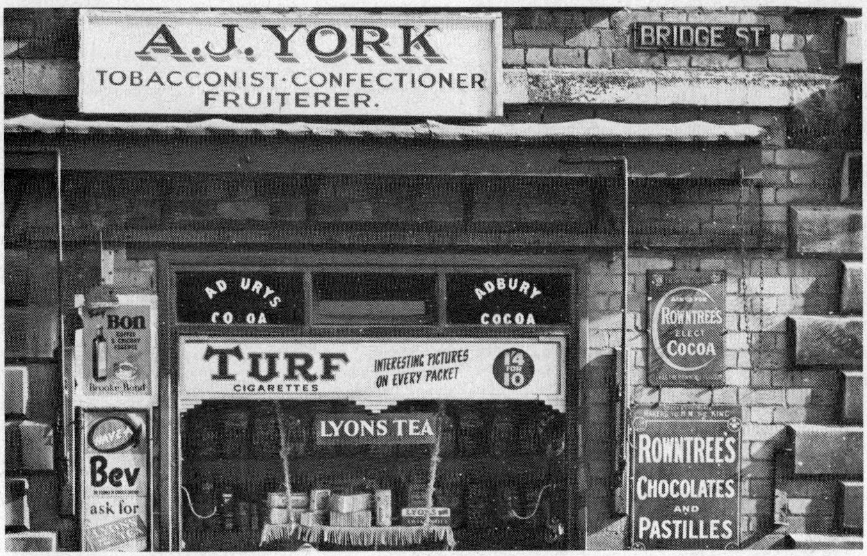

6

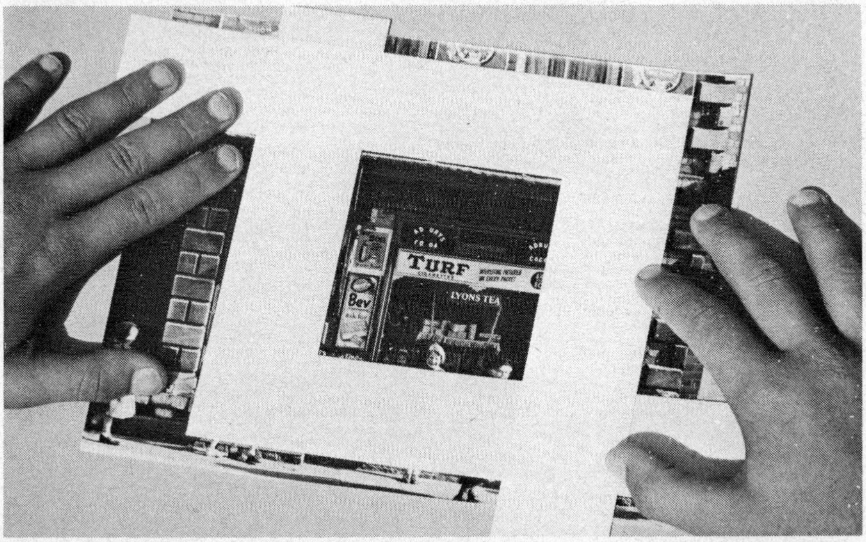

7

1. This is the full negative shot in a small English town, from which cropping produced five different aspects. View camera on a tripod, f/22, 1/5 second, slow pan film.

2. The main figures and a section of the store front are interesting enough to stand alone.

3. Shifting to a vertical, there is still a nice balance of rectangles around and above the children.

4. Variation of the vertical theme works, even though figures are low in the picture. There is impact in this off-beat composition.

5. In this vertical, notice how the horizontal sign near the bottom is balanced by the "Turf" sign near the center and "York" sign at top. The eye steps either up or down.

6. This cropping is pure geometry, a pattern of rectangles. Although a dark horizontal area divides the picture in the center, top and bottom seem to be suitably connected to each other.

7. A pair of L-shaped pieces of cardboard make excellent cropping devices. Composition will be improved by anything you can crop out that seems to be extraneous to the main subject.

larly. Thus photographic composition is blended like a gourmet dish with concern, training and sensitivity.

Studying art and/or design, or reading about them in books, are definite assets to aesthetic development. Don't get bogged down with "rules" or "laws" that seem inflexible. Talk about pictures with friends. Expose yourself to fine art at museums, galleries and in books. Take a painting or drawing class.

There are millions of graphic images available to study these days, by your contemporaries and by outstanding painters and photographers who have left us a pictorial legacy. As you learn and reflect, you will realize how much composition is a product of individual taste interpreting certain principles to imbue photographs with beauty, impact and drama. Try to decide why some compositions you enjoy are successful. Criticize photographs that do not impress you to discover why. Eventually, as your awareness improves, you will find that you have unconsciously gained a sense of composition.

Composition is the way we see, and anyone can increase his visual perception. No one has a monopoly on talent. When you get the feel of it, you'll take pictures through sheer instinct that you may not be able to see today.

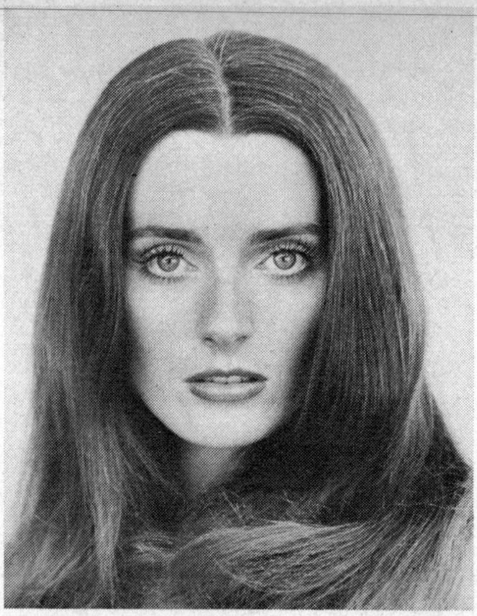
1

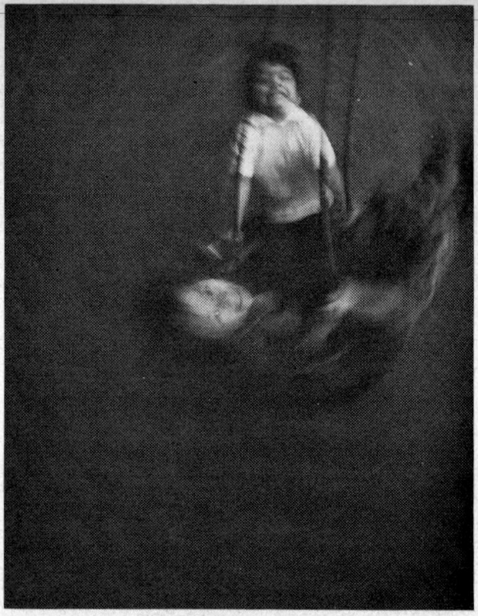
2

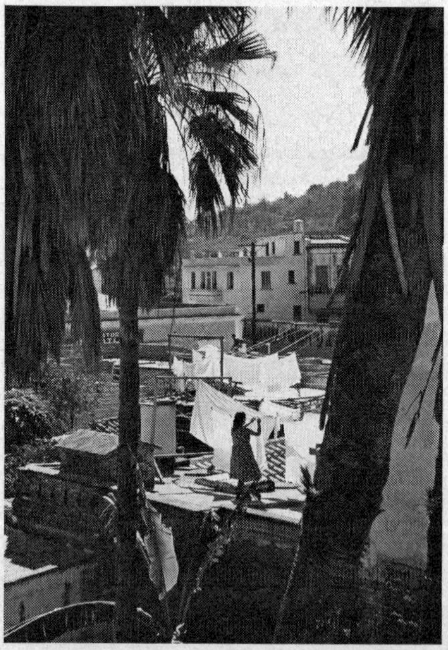
3

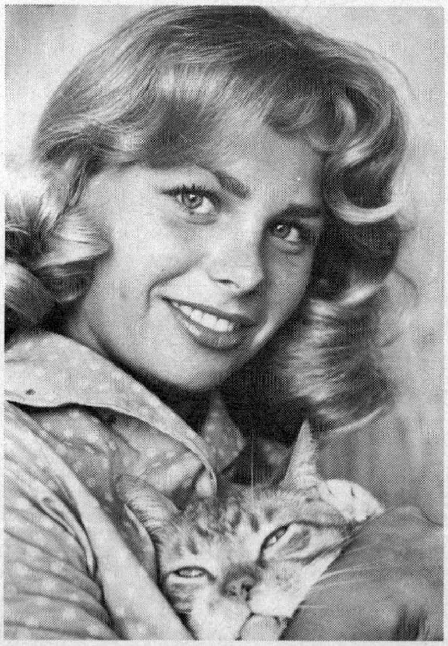
4

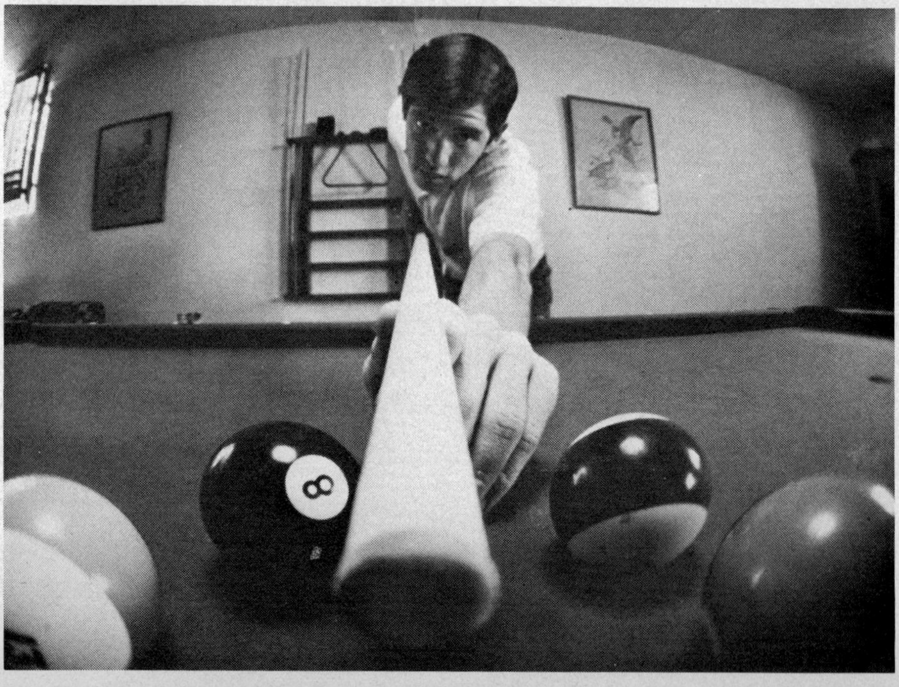
5

1. Though the model's face is centered vertically, her eyes are above center and her hair is fuller at bottom right. Looking directly at the viewer, the expression is attractive and appealing. Shot with 100mm lens, 1/250 second, f/11, Tri-X film.

2. Mood and motion both dominate this low-key shot by Gil Smith, a Scholastic/Kodak Award winner. Placement of figures in top right segment of the frame underlines the unconventional approach taken by the photographer.

3. Framing is a standard compositional device. Trees frame the woman hanging laundry, increasing pictorial interest. Without the trees, the scene might have been rather bare.

4. Simplicity of composition helps make this photograph enjoyable. The girl's face and eyes are dominant and above the horizontal center of the frame for more interesting balance. Cropping into her hair maneuvers the eye to her face more deftly. Close cropping at left bottom, at bottom, and into the hand at right make these elements more subordinate. In a portrait you usually don't want to include shapes that compete with your subject. The background is also simple and not at all distracting to the eye.

5. John Barringer's 18mm point of view is unusual and striking in this Scholastic/Kodak Award winner. Camera was about 12 inches from the pool cue, which is greatly enlarged at the tip because of its proximity to the lens.

THE PLEASURES OF COLOR

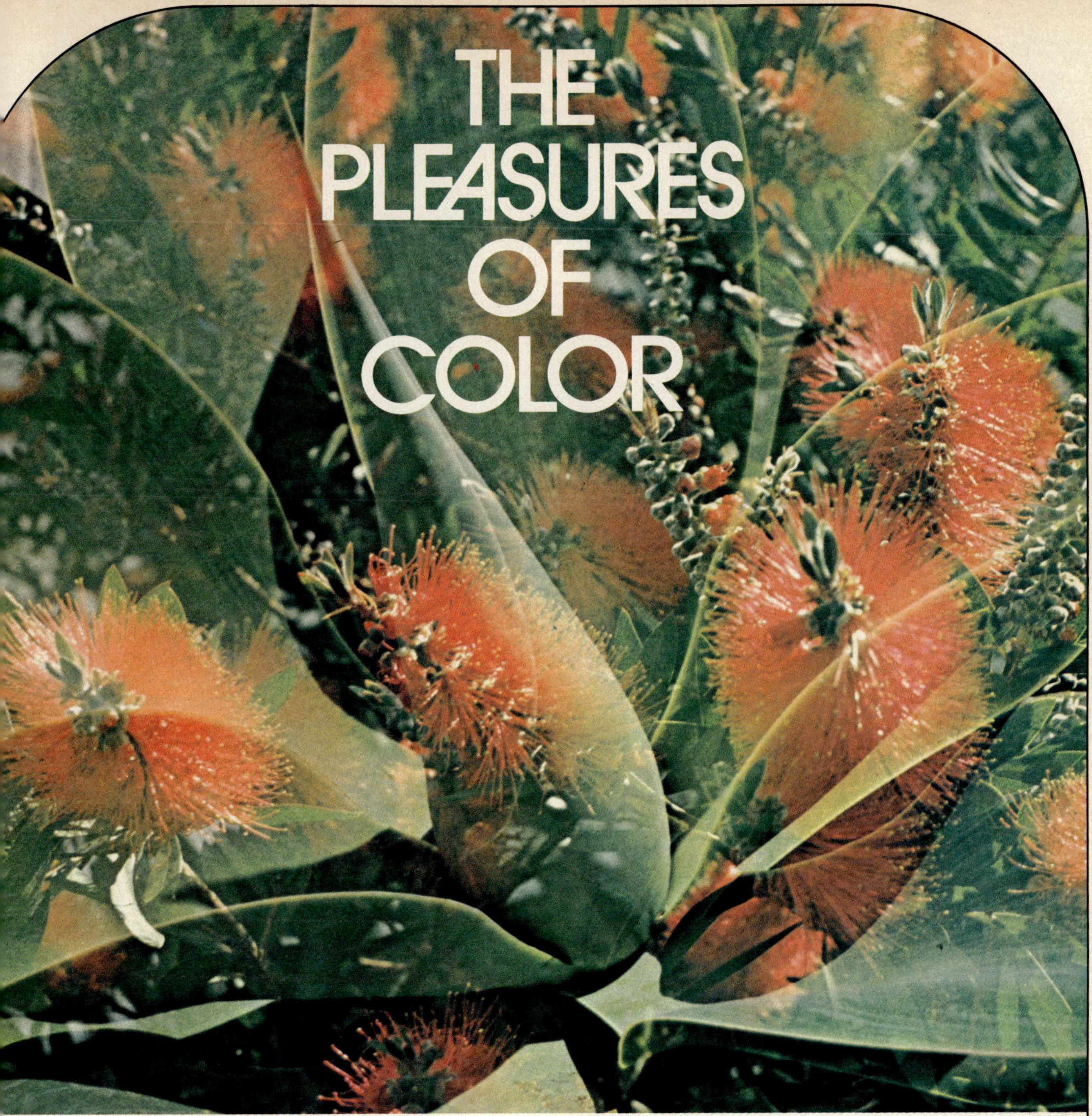

Intentional double exposure in camera of flowers and green plant was made on Ektachrome-X film.

Throughout this book color photography is discussed in many technical and aesthetic aspects, since color is not an isolated topic. More people shoot slides and color negatives than they do black-and-white, and why not? However, these pictures are often what I call *record shots*. By that I mean they are a record of people, places and things, which might be borderline artistic, but are not particularly interpretive or creative. In this chapter I'll concentrate on the significance of color beyond the literal record, and add a few guidelines for approaching color photography without frills.

SEEING IN COLOR

There is no reason to make an odious comparison between color and black-and-white, for each has a valuable place as a photographic medium. In that black-and-white came first, many fine photographers and most of the general public have been conditioned to see the world in monochrome. Prints may be tinted or toned, but essentially, black-and-white photographs translate what we see into a gradation of tones from white through grays to black. The outcome is a kind of abstraction that we readily accept, and black-and-white photography will always offer a potential for beautiful, delicate tones and exciting contrasts.

If you do your own black-and-white printing, this approach to picture-taking might well be considered more challenging than color in terms of achieving image quality. In color,

THE PLEASURES OF COLOR

1. Arrival of Queen Mary at Long Beach was shot from another ship with 135mm lens on Nikon SP, Ektachrome-X / 2. Three floodlights were used for portrait of late actress Sharon Tate: main near camera, fill at left of camera and hair light behind her / 3. Backlight dramatized waterfall at Yosemite, shot on Ektachrome-X / 4. Light reflected from deck gave model sparkle in shot on High Speed Ektachrome / 5. Actor Sam Broome was photographed on hazy day at beach on Ektachrome-X / 6. Author's son Barry Jacobs used 135mm lens on Nikon SP rangefinder camera to shoot racing cars rounding turn, on High Speed Ektachrome.

your control usually ends when the picture is taken. Of course, if you can develop your own color film and make your own color prints, you have a wide spectrum of manipulation techniques (filters, timing, composition, etc.) at your fingertips.

How does the above situation influence the way we see color? Well, to begin with, most of us shoot color in and for its literal appearance. We try to capture the vivid reds of a sunset, the subtle pastels of an overcast day, the bright hues of a landscape or of people doing things, or the pleasant skin tones of a portrait. With only a Skylight filter to warm the bluish cast of a cloudy day, we can usually rely on modern color films to record images with fidelity. Slides may give "truer" color than prints, and we will make comparisons of films and color quality later in the chapter.

The meaning of color/ Books and essays have been written on the psychology of color and how it may be individually interpreted. The topic can become heavy and confusing; it is enough to analyze color briefly according to its emotional, literal and decorative qualities.

Emotional connotations of color are well known. Red signifies danger and is an advancing color, one that pops out to meet the eye. Blue symbolizes calm, among other things, and is a retreating color that usually keeps its place in a picture. Yellow is cheerful, orange is warm and friendly, green is the primary color of nature, purple stands for royalty, brown is burned, white is virginal and black is funereal. These word-color descriptions are oversimplified, but can trigger other

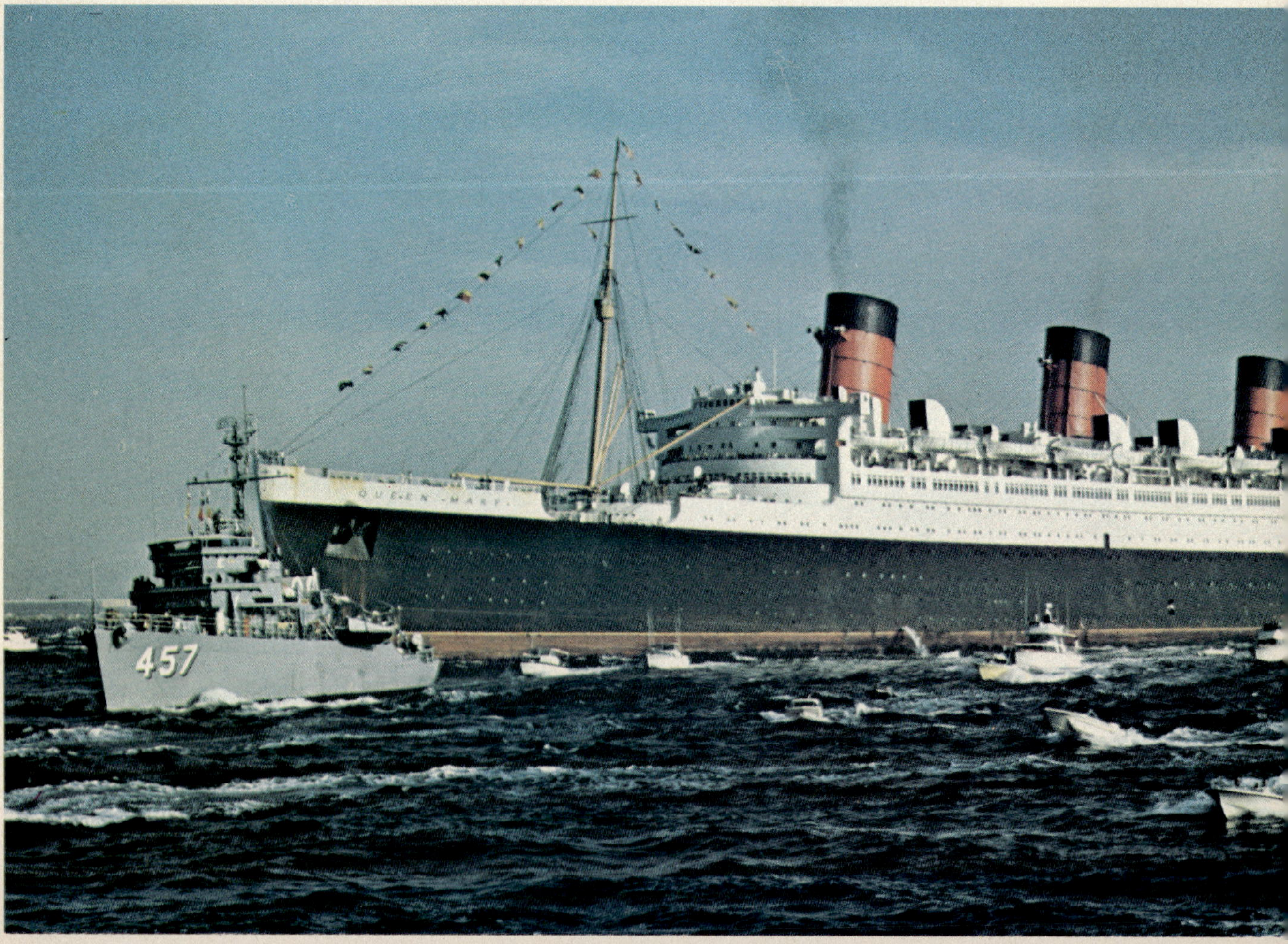

1

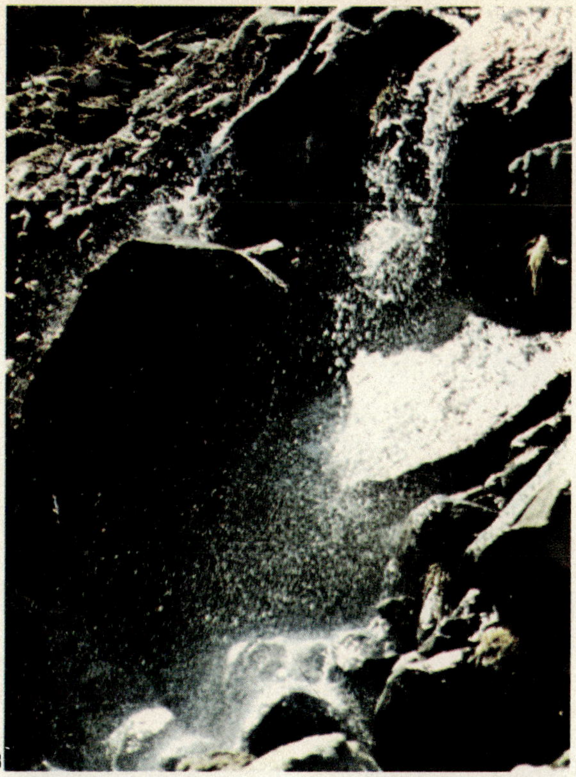

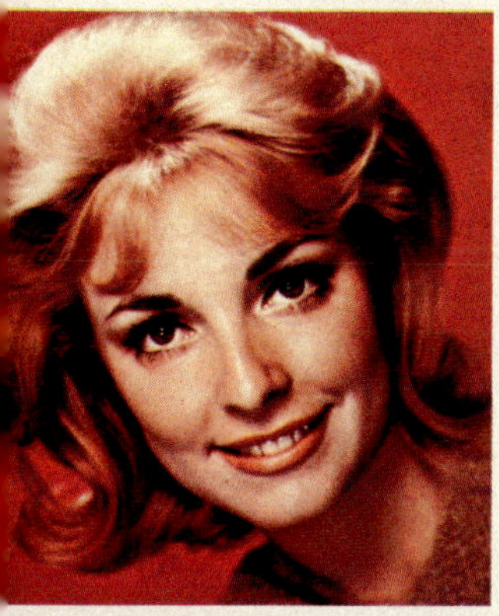

3

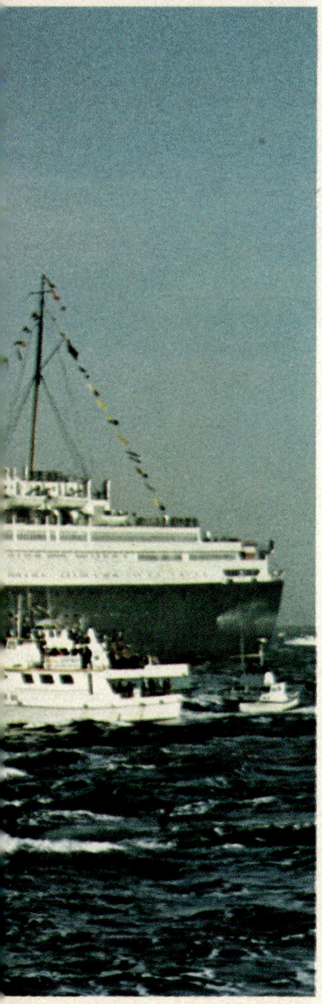

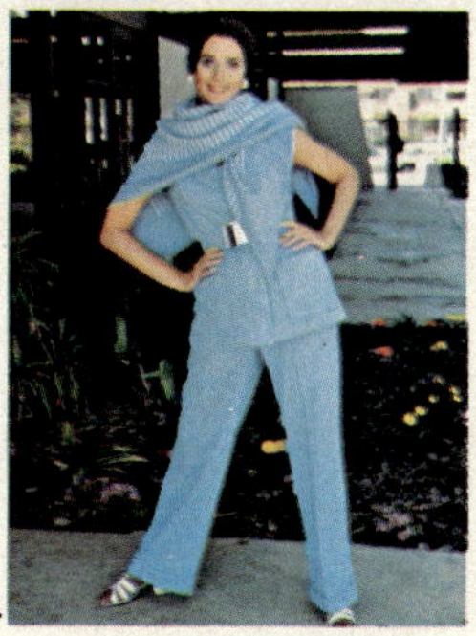

4

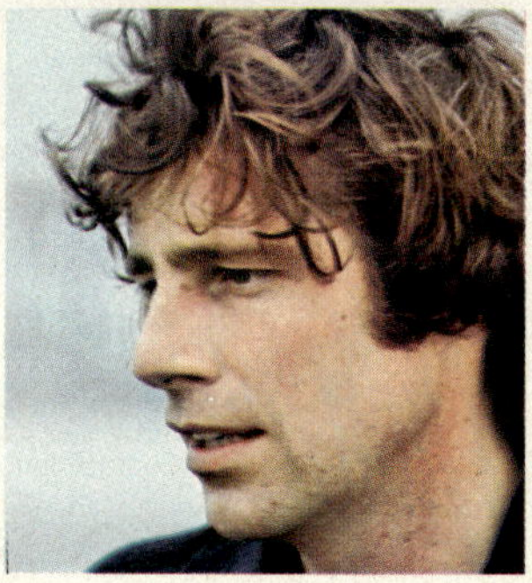

5

interpretations of your own. Unless we are color stylists, we do not photograph colors for specific reasons, though it is useful to realize how color is related to emotion and the effect it can have.

In a literal sense, color is simply there. The advertising photographer in his studio may choose colors carefully for backgrounds or subject matter, for mood or message, but in general we photograph people, places and things as we find them. If the slide or print is close enough to the way we remembered the color, it is usually satisfying.

Color can also be decorative. A field of flowers is a pattern of brilliance with its own pictorial impact. A sunset may be composed without great skill, but the color itself impresses the viewer. There is nothing wrong with depending on chromatic excitement as long as you exercise your visual skill as well, if color dominates a composition.

COLOR IMPRESSIONISM

There are various methods of influencing color in order to create a visual impression that is *not* literal, but translates imagery to film in ways rarely or never seen in reality. For instance:

Color blur/ Mentioned before, blur is a result of slow shutter speeds during

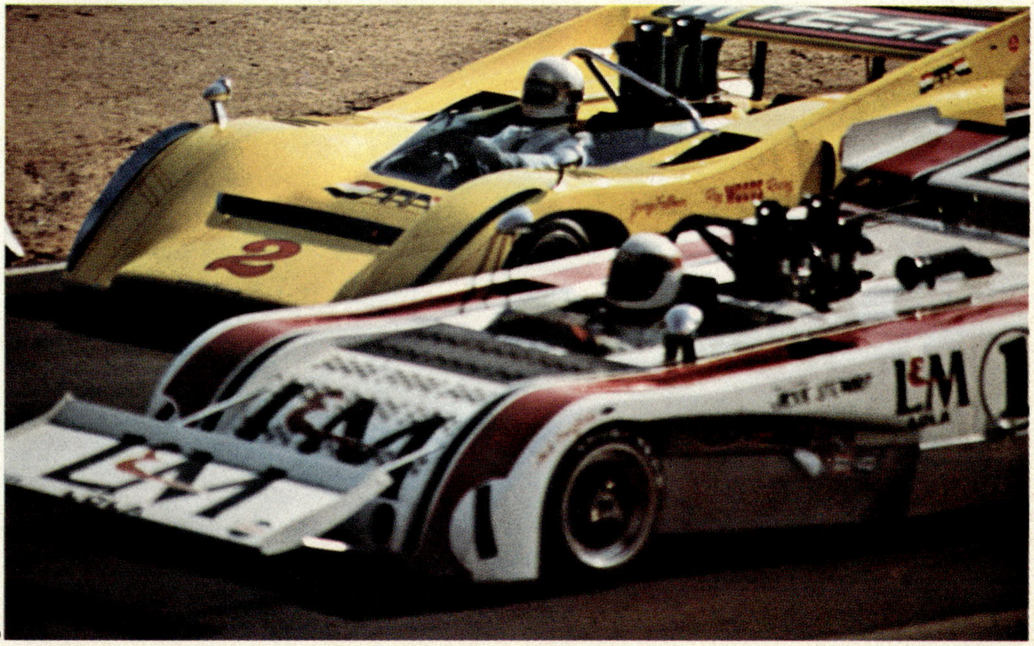

6

THE PLEASURES OF COLOR

1. Barry Jacobs panned camera in direction of car to produce blurred background in Ektachrome-X shot / 2. Backlighted bougainvillaea flowers were shot on Ektachrome-X / 3. Lamp cast yellowish pool of light, adding warmth to Ektachrome-X portrait / 4. Planned double exposure of clouds with nude produced subtle hues / 5. Rescue scene from TV series Police Surgeon *was shot on Ektachrome-X / 6. Portion of Oregon coast was photographed from hill on Ektachrome-X / 7. Brightness of cotton-tuft clouds dominated exposure in this scene in which figures are semi-silhouette. Ektachrome-X film, 21mm wide-angle lens recorded shot.*

which moving objects or figures are seen softly or indistinctly on film, often evoking delicate or dynamic feeling. Since blur is somewhat unpredictable, it is advisable to shoot a number of exposures to assure a selection of images. The camera should be on a tripod or otherwise secured, and you should experiment with various shutter speeds to vary the blur effect. This sort of color impressionism in fortuitous circumstances is fun, and your pictures may assume the qualities of paintings.

Color filters/ Using a colored filter with color film distorts the hues in a print or slide, but with a purpose. I once used a light yellow filter to shoot some kids in a rowboat at a very colorless spot on the Sacramento River. I shot against the sun, and the kids were silhouetted. The filter tinted the speckles of sunlight on the water, and captured the mood of the moment more graphically than it would have been without a filter.

Orange and red filters heighten the effects of a sunrise or sunset when natural colors are not strong enough. A blue filter may emphasize a cold day or a snowy scene. You must be careful that the filter does not distort other subject matter (such as people) so it looks ridiculous, but exposure for land and sky may make other subjects subordinated.

Indoors, using a colored filter on the camera or colored gels of plastic over floodlights can also create striking effects. You can tint a white background, or one side of a face in a moody or decorative way that raises pictures above the ordinary.

Expect disappointment along with triumph when using colored filters. As

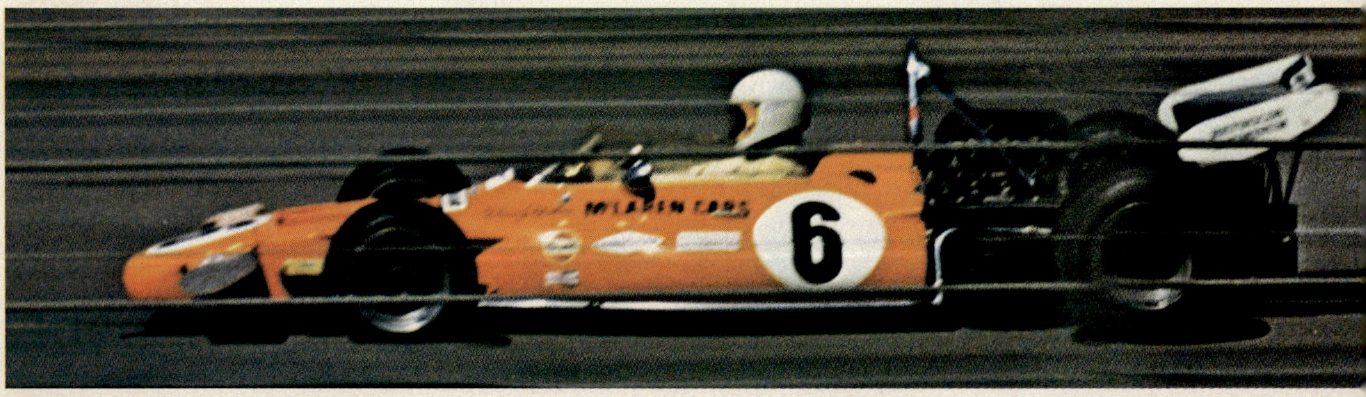

1

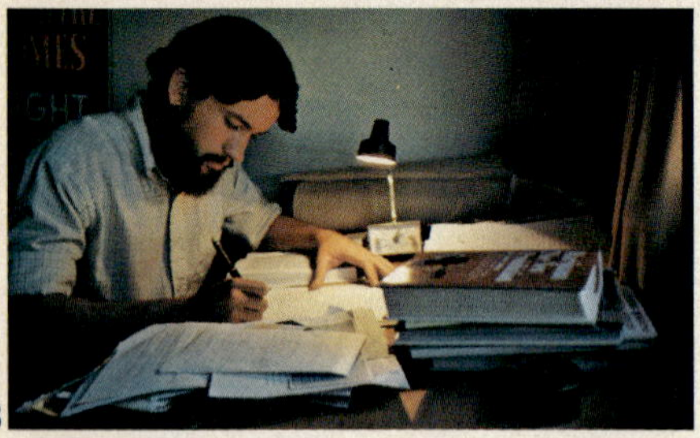

3

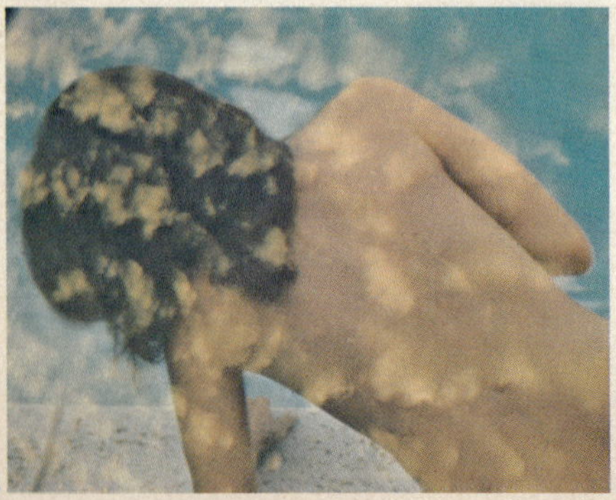

4

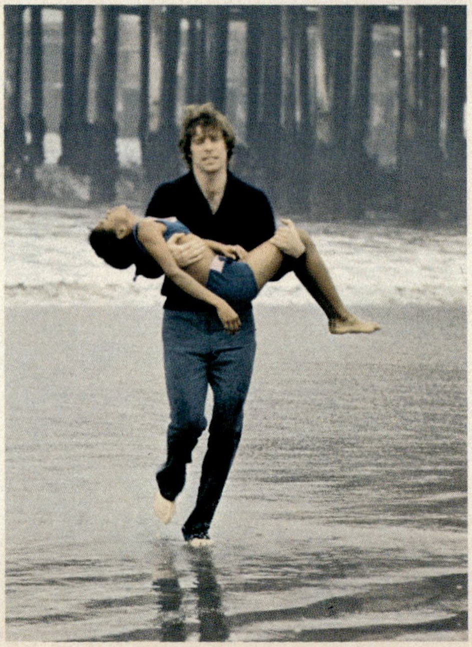

5

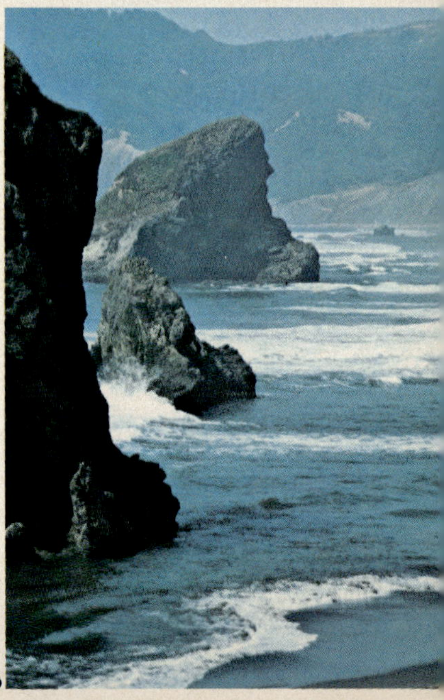

6

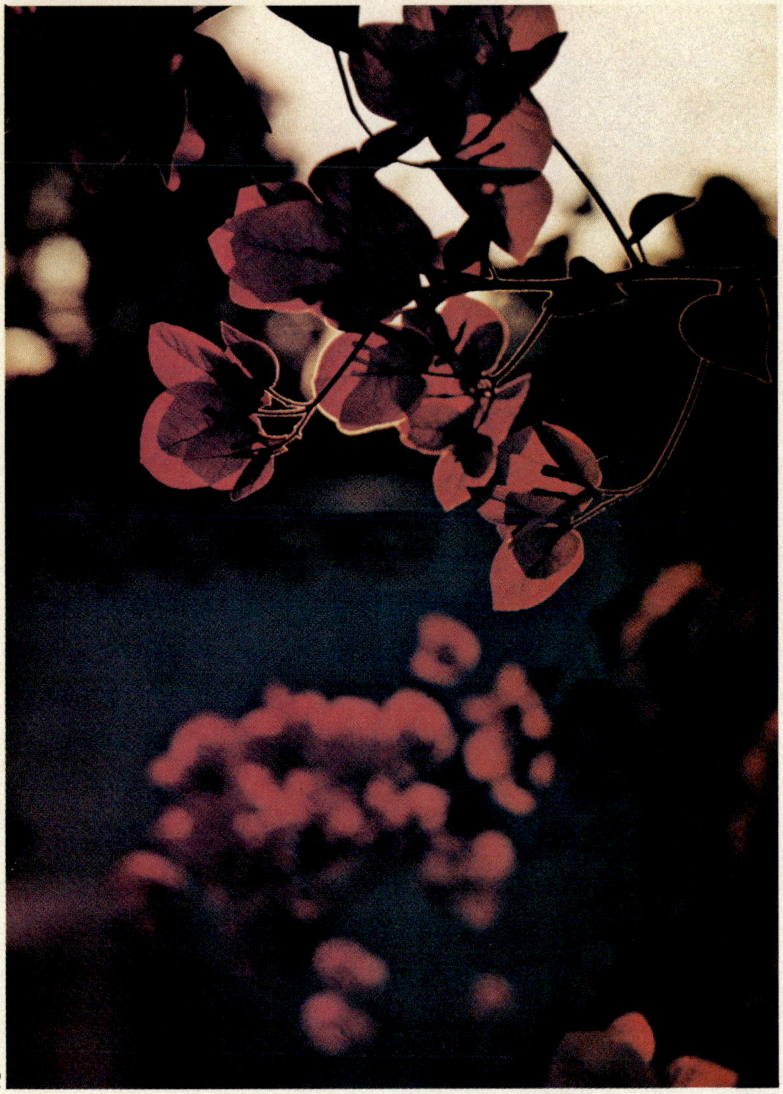

2

the fortune cookie might say, experimentation can be enlightening and interesting.

Double exposures/ While must SLR cameras are designed to prevent double exposures, it is possible to cock the shutter without winding the film by using the clutch on some models. Check the camera instruction booklet, or ask advice at a camera shop for specific techniques.

If you intend to expose one frame of film twice, cut each exposure time in half. In other words, if the camera meter indicates f/8 at 1/125 second, use f/11 *or* 1/250 second for each of the exposures. In this way the film will receive the proper exposure for the combined image to be viewed as a single picture.

Double exposures should be planned with some accuracy, though the element of chance is always present. Remember how your first image was composed as you superimpose the second one. Colors will blend and relate in surprising and delightful ways. Unnatural overlapping and juxtaposition of color images make attempts at color double exposures worthwhile, if you care to take the time to plan each exposure.

Note: The main drawback in double exposing with most 35mm SLR cameras is lack of registration. You must draw the film tightly with the rewind knob before the first shot, and hold

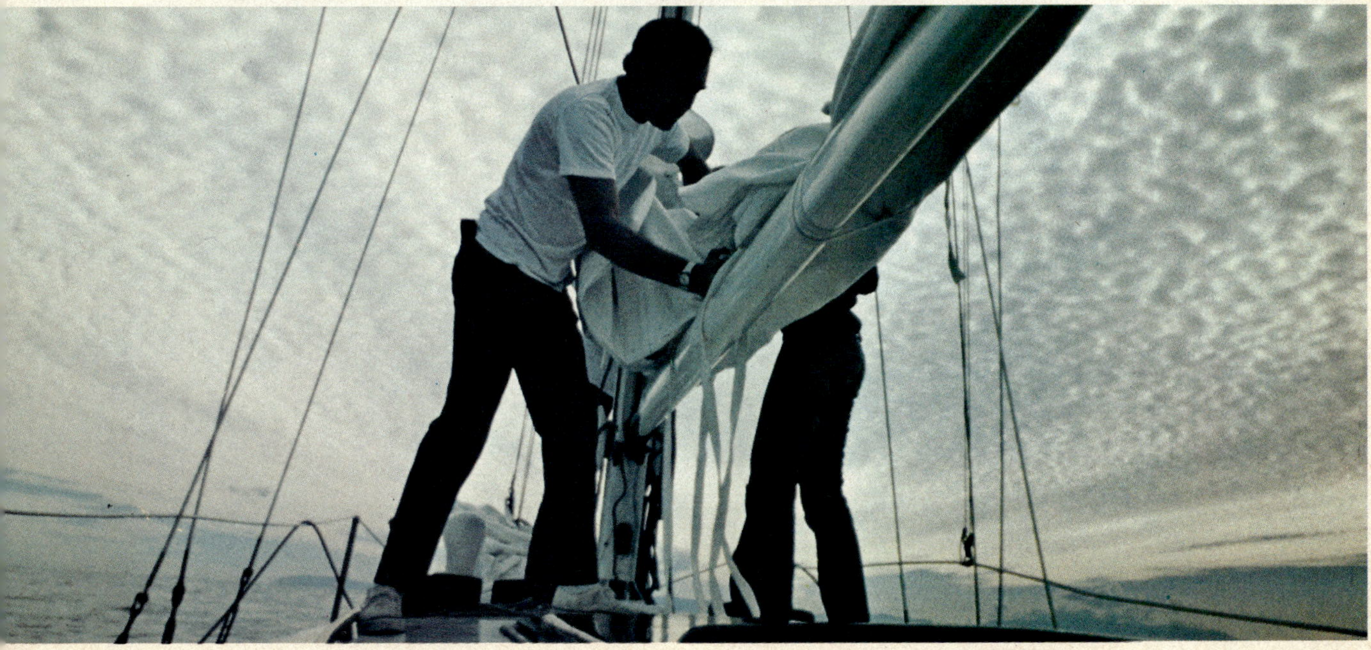

THE PLEASURES OF COLOR

1. Appearance of afternoon sun was produced in drab scene by yellow filter over lens with Ektachrome-X / 2. Palm Springs Aerial Tramway recedes in distance in Kodachrome II shot / 3. Twirling teacups at Disneyland were photographed from Skyride at night on Ektachrome-X / 4. Boat and sailors were semi-backlighted at Lake Arrowhead, Calif., recorded on Ektachrome-X / 5. Actress Mitzi Gaynor posed by window at her home for daylit portrait on Kodachrome II / 6. Surfer cutting through waves was photographed with 300mm lens on Kodachrome-X, with author standing on beach.

the knob firmly when you cock the shutter to prevent the film from shifting even slightly. Some camera manufacturers say this cannot be done successfully. A few may be right!

Color printing tricks/ As you may know, making a color print entails the use of color filters that translate a negative into hues on paper. If you set out to vary or distort a print, unconventional filtering will provide decorative, weird or dramatic coloring for various effects. Once you know the correct technique for printing in color, you can deftly choose filters that provide strange and stimulating creative impressions.

PRINTS VS. SLIDES

There is no controversy in your choice of negative or transparency films, because either can eventually be converted to the other. However, if you prefer color prints as the most convenient way to show pictures, you will start with color negatives. Prints have the advantage of instant availability, and many people prefer them for pictures of domestic events (parties or new babies, for instance), as a travelogue, etc., because friends and relatives can view them immediately and carry them easily.

Slides projected in a darkened room are seen on a screen much larger than the average print, which is a distinct advantage. The size and detail of a slide show can be enjoyable home entertainment—if you first edit your pictures and store away the duds. One can have negatives and prints made from favorite slides, and have the best of both worlds of color photography.

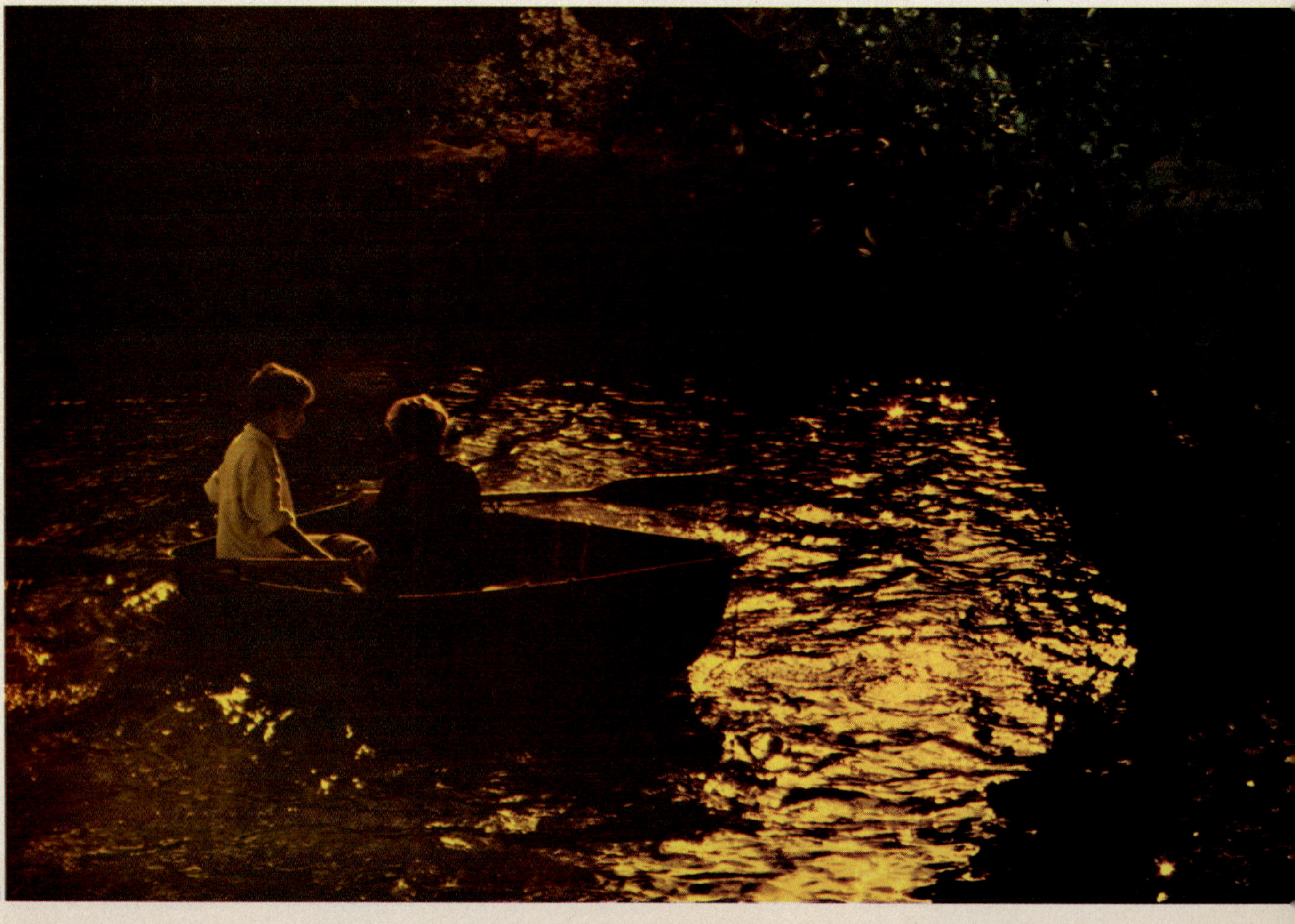
1

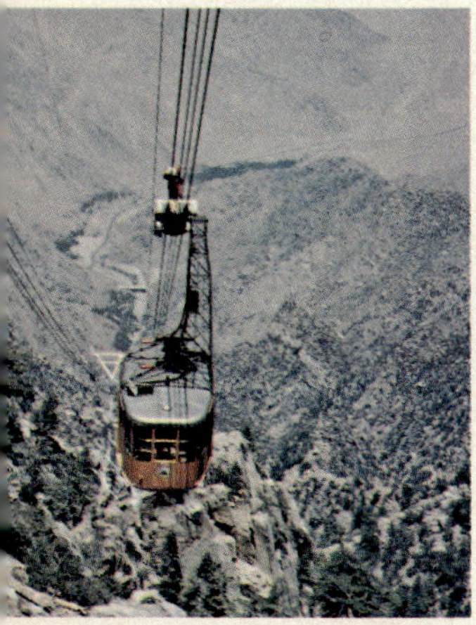

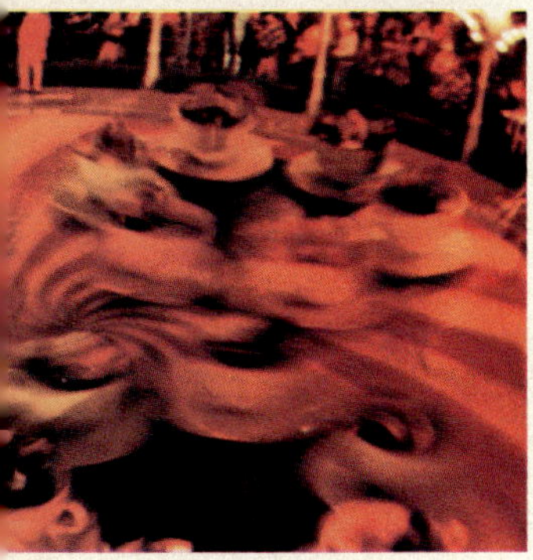

4

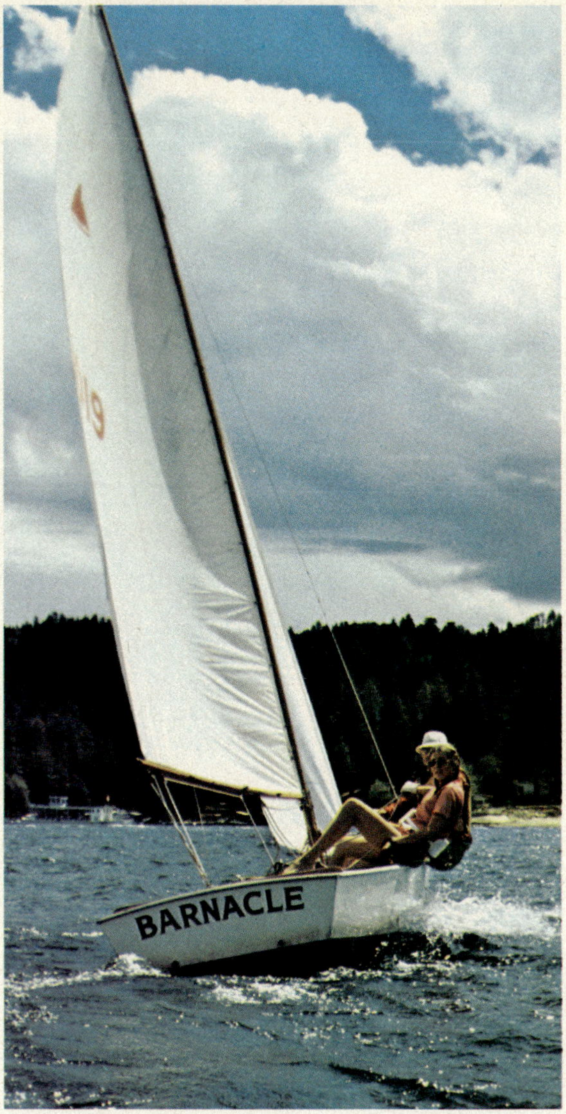

COLOR FIDELITY

"True" color in film or print is usually in the eye of the beholder. Perhaps you have seen a single scene or portrait shot on a number of different color films and reproduced in a magazine or book. Certain brands of film, you may have noted, tend toward warm or cool rendition, and each has chromatic characteristics. Some films render color with more intensity or saturation, while others are more literal with either flesh tones or the green hues of nature. However, all popular color films have acceptable fidelity. See for yourself by shooting several different films and compare the results, choosing according to your own taste.

Color variations in prints exist more in terms of the processing lab than in the film brand. You could have a single color negative printed in five different cities or five different labs, and get five slightly different color renditions. If you are not satisfied with the fidelity of the color prints you are getting, switch from one lab to another. The color processing and printing business is highly competitive.

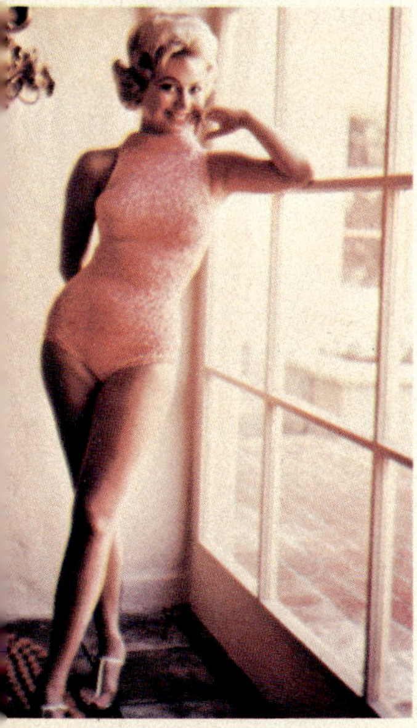

6

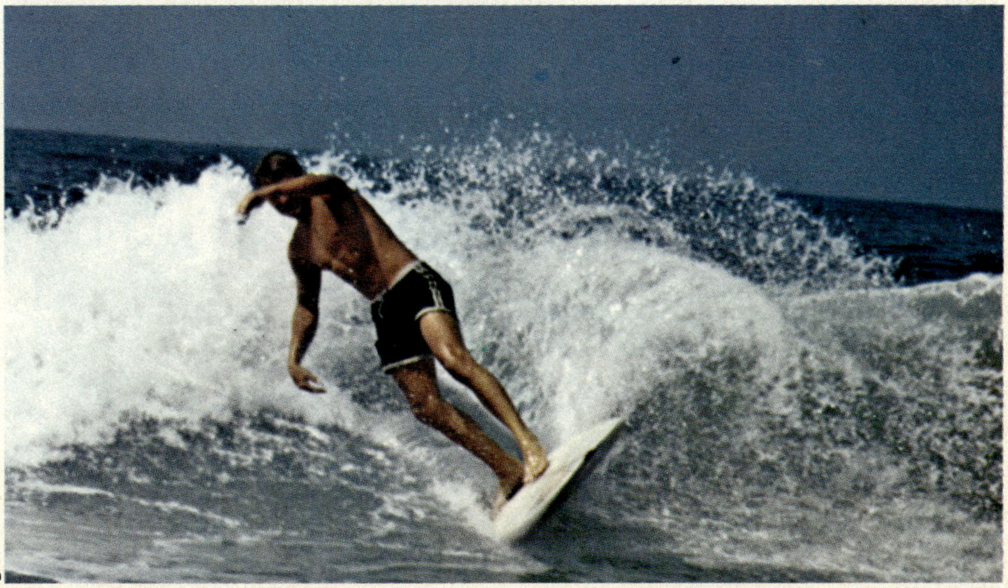

THE PLEASURES OF COLOR

1. Sunset over San Diego Bay was shot from tripod with 80-200mm zoom lens set at about 180mm, using Ektachrome-X, ½ second at f/6.3 / 2. Using High Speed Ektachrome (Tungsten) on a rainy day provided impressionistic blue cast to photo from front seat of moving car. Exposure was 1/125 second at f/8.

If the color in prints or slides is not accurate, it may be for one or more of the following reasons:

1. An error of exposure. Overexposure results in pale, washed out color, and underexposure makes color appear dark or obscure.

2. The light did not match the color film. Colors are too warm when daylight-type film is shot in artificial light without a correction filter, and very blue when indoor (tungsten) film is exposed outdoors without a conversion filter. These aberrations refer to transparency films, since negative color can be partly corrected by the lab in printing.

3. Faces are often green when color film is exposed by fluorescent light without a correction filter.

4. People or objects in the background of flash pictures may appear brownish because the light level was too low for proper exposure.

5. High altitude or snow pictures may be too blue because of excess ultraviolet light. A UV filter is advised to prevent this.

1

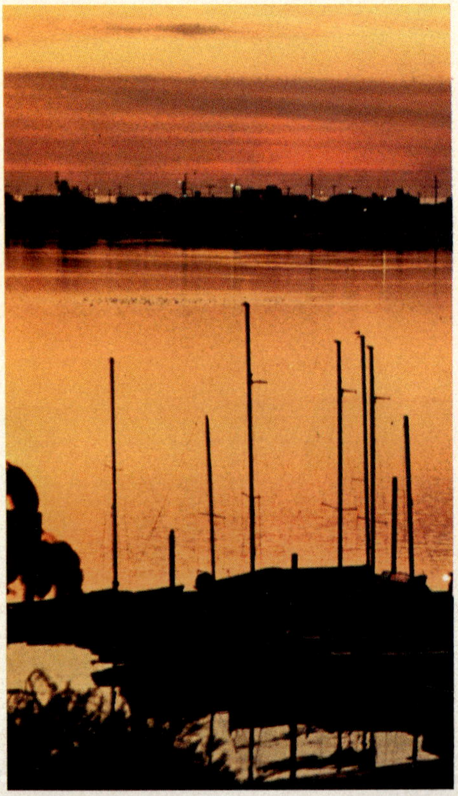

6. Laboratory processing was faulty in some way. Transparency film is usually developed properly, but color prints may suffer from careless printing or hasty judgment. If people were more critical of their color prints, it might make them more careful with exposure, lighting and choice of processing.

Note: Kodachrome II is processed automatically by elaborate machines, and is likely to be more consistent than other color materials. However, I've heard professional photographers comparing Kodachrome processing from Honolulu, New York, Los Angeles and Paris, and slight variations seem to occur!

Shooting color can be easy and literal, or more complex and interpretive. In either case, color gives the photographer pleasure without strain. Polaroid color prints are fully developed in 60 seconds in case you can't wait to enjoy more conventional picture-taking!

2

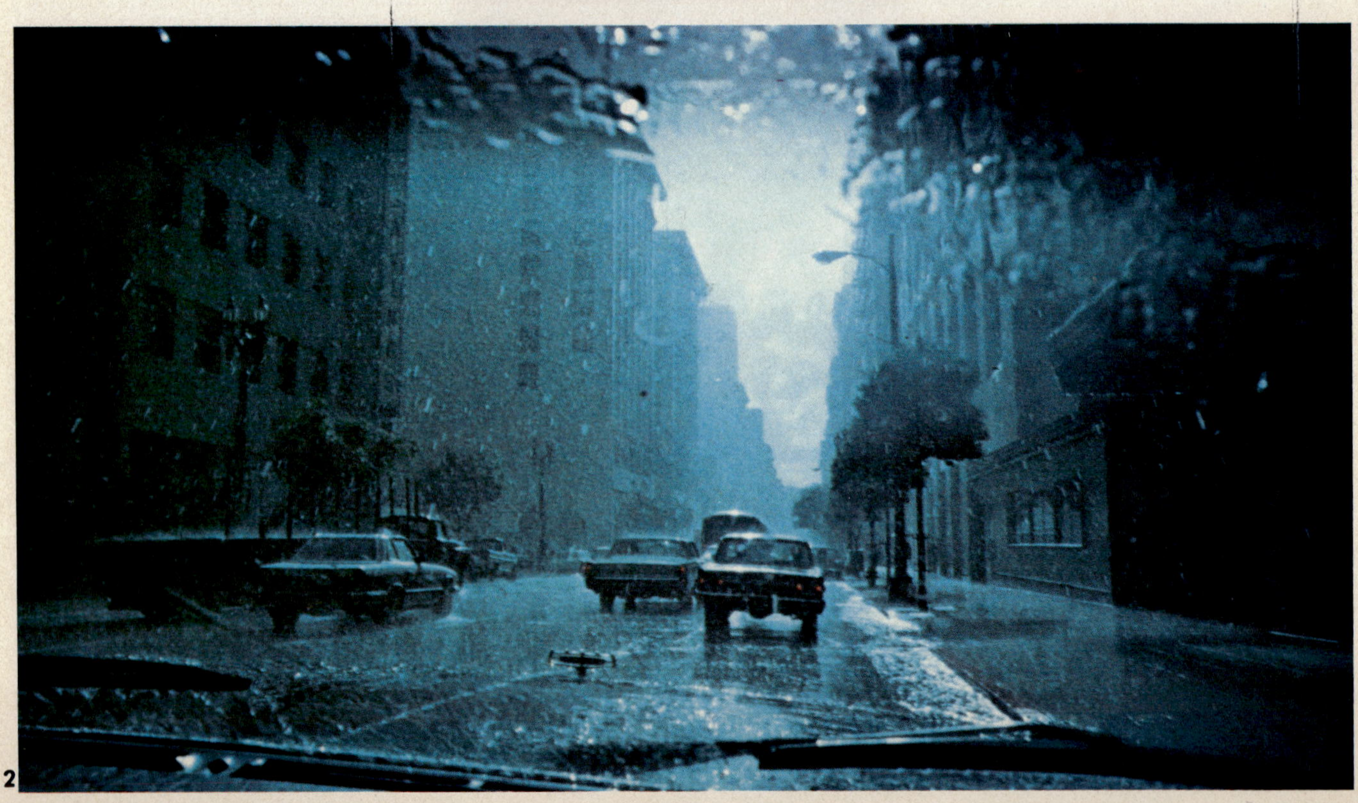

CHAPTER 9 Special Problems

Photography is a blend of ideas and techniques. Ideas may be expressed in reportage, impressions, humor, darkroom manipulation, or anything that turns you on to thinking in images. Through the tools of the world's most popular hobby we translate our ideas to paper and film. We may communicate with simple snapshots or via artistic images worth enjoying indefinitely. As I've said before, success in photography comes from preparation, thinking, instinct and practice. Success is not a gift, but is often earned as you tackle special problems with your camera.

Some of the collection of pictorial approaches in this chapter have been touched on before and need elaboration, while others are variations to encourage versatility and confidence. I've chosen to present them as short case histories which I hope will inspire you to your own twists and turns into unexplored territory.

THE ALPHABET OF ACTION

Action is not as simple as ABC, but is a matter of timing in relation to the direction a subject is moving—which influences sharpness as much as shutter speed does. If the action is going *across* the film plane, parallel to the film in other words, you need the fastest shutter speed to stop it because the subject covers a greater distance across the film than if it were coming toward you or approaching at an angle. For instance, the picture of kids playing touch football was shot at 1/1000 second with a Konica Autoreflex T. I used the Hexanon zoom lens ranging from 80 to 200mm, and it was stretched to its focal limit for this shot. By following the game patiently and remaining alert for the best activities, I was ready at this moment. (You know the definition of luck: when preparation meets opportunity.) Film was Tri-X and aperture was f/11 on an overcast day.

On the other hand, the shot of a car streaking across the track was made at 1/250 second with the intention of symbolizing speed via blur. I also meant to establish the contrast between a static figure and the 150-mile-per-hour car. You can read several meanings into this story, trying to explain why the guy isn't shooting with all that equipment!

When the movement of a subject is *toward* or directly *away* from the camera, a shutter speed of 1/250 or 1/500 second will often catch it sharply. You may even freeze a figure running toward you at 1/125 second with a little bit of luck, though arms or legs might blur slightly. In many cases, blur suggests motion better than a totally sharp image.

Subject movement at an angle requires medium-to-fast shutter speeds, similar to those mentioned for across the film plane, though not necessarily as high. If you have a choice of angles, choose one which presents the subject more in a head-on position if the top speed of your camera is 1/200 or 1/250 second.

You may have heard the expression *peak action,* which refers to snapping a picture when a motion is at its apex. The leaping whale is an example, shot at 1/500 second of f/16 on Tri-X. I waited for the animal to reach the full extent of its jump,

Action moving across the film plane requires fast shutter speed such as 1/1000 second used to stop action here.

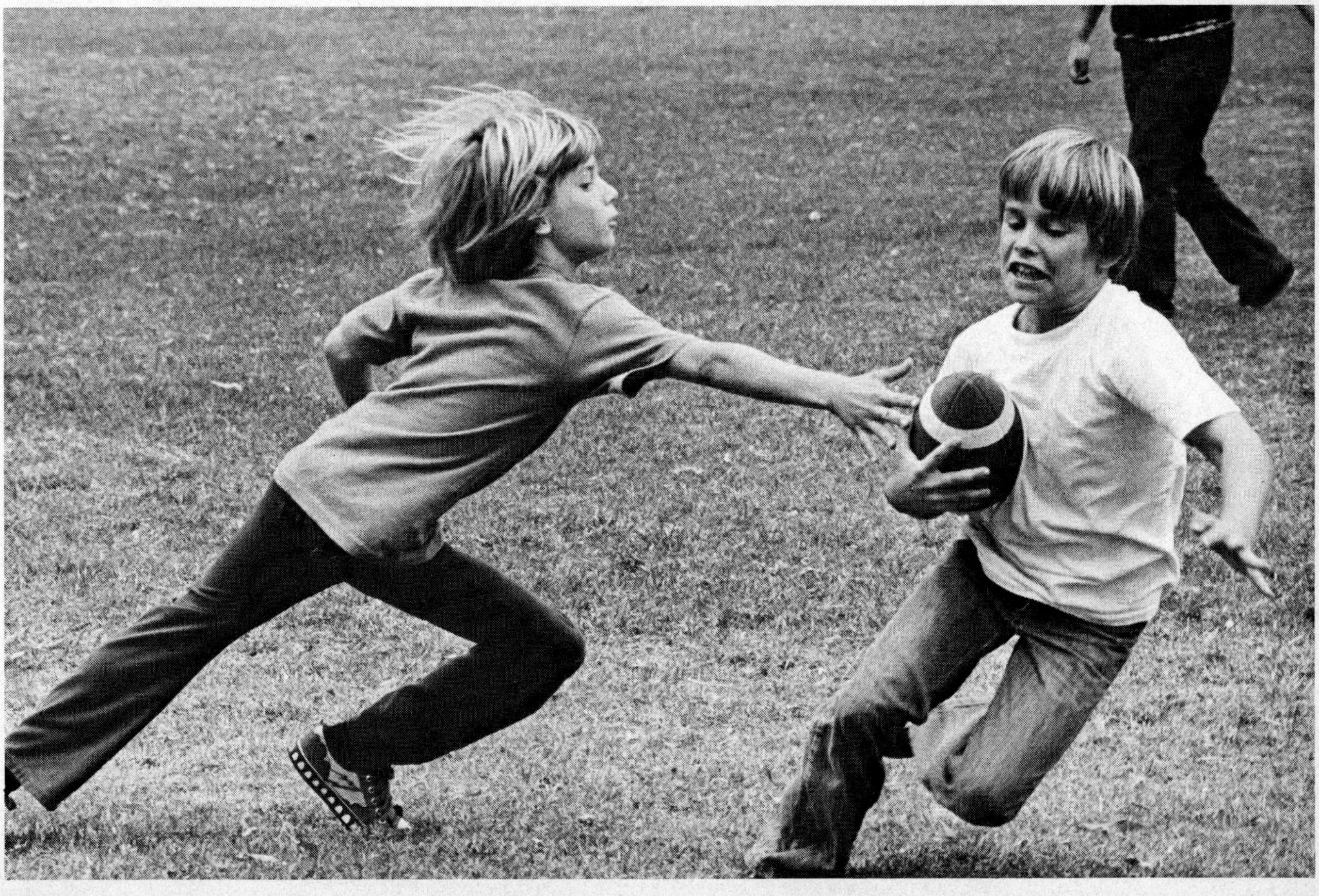

and as it hovered for a fraction of a second, I fired. Anticipating peak action enables you to achieve sharp images even at slower shutter speeds. I once shot a series of pictures (with my 35mm SLR on a tripod) of businessmen speaking to an audience. The light level (from bounced quartz lights) dictated 1/60 second at f/4.5 on Tri-X rated at an EI (exposure index) of 1000. By waiting for facial expressions to pause momentarily between sentences, I was able to get reasonable sharpness to satisfy the client. One of the pictures is shown on these pages. Of course there were a number of frames when faces blurred, but I shot enough to assure the quality necessary.

A third way to tackle fast action is by *panning* the camera, which means swinging it horizontally or vertically with the subject as it passes. Ron Contarsy shot the motorcyclist this way at 1/500 second. He followed the action and anticipated the moment when his composition was right, and his picture won a Kodak/Scholastic award. A blurred or streaked background and foreground is indigenous to panning, and adds a neat out-of-focus effect that helps eliminate confusion behind the dominant subject. Even when panning is not necessary to freeze fast action, it might be considered as a means of background control.

SLOW SHUTTER SPEEDS

In contrast to using high shutter speeds for fast action, there are also useful ways of employing slow shutter speeds for a variety of results. For instance James J. Thacker (a Kodak/

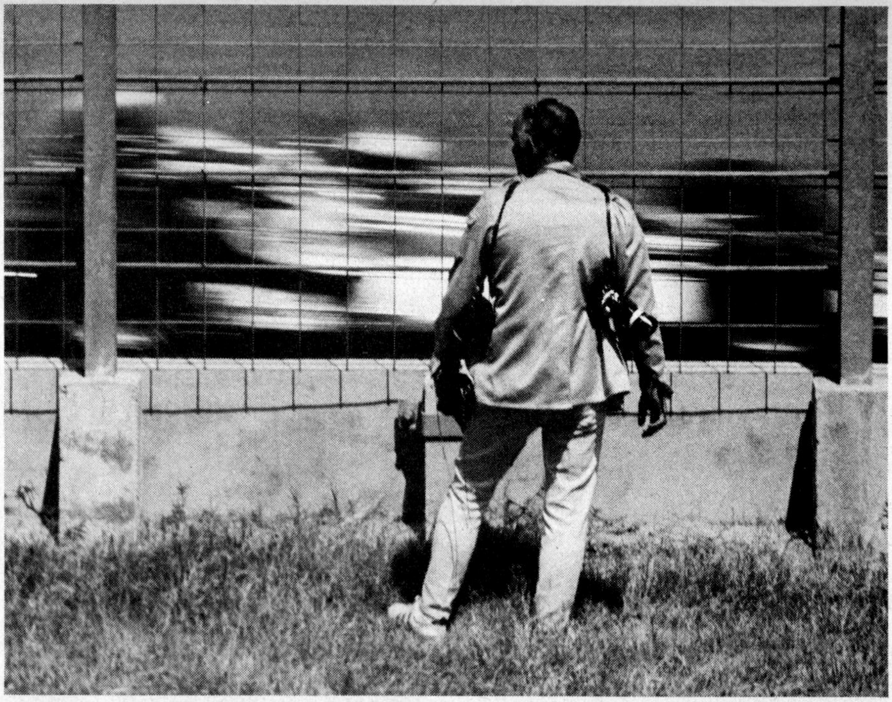
1

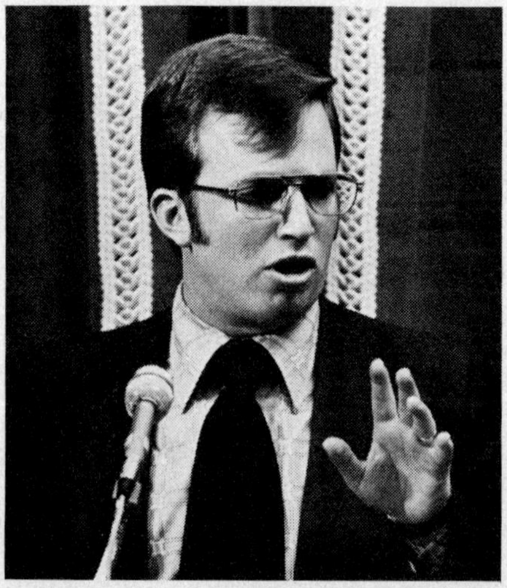
2

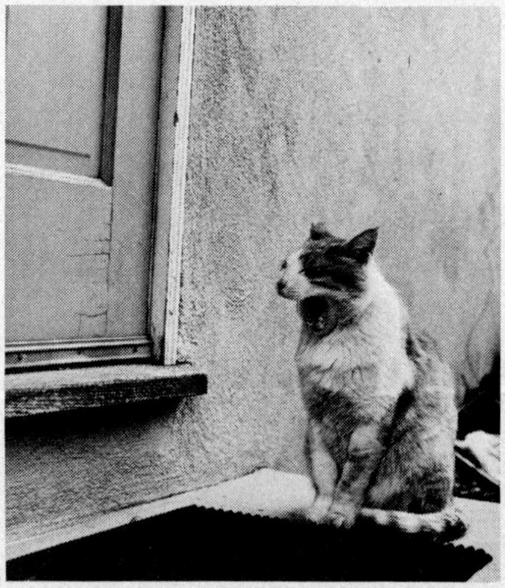
3

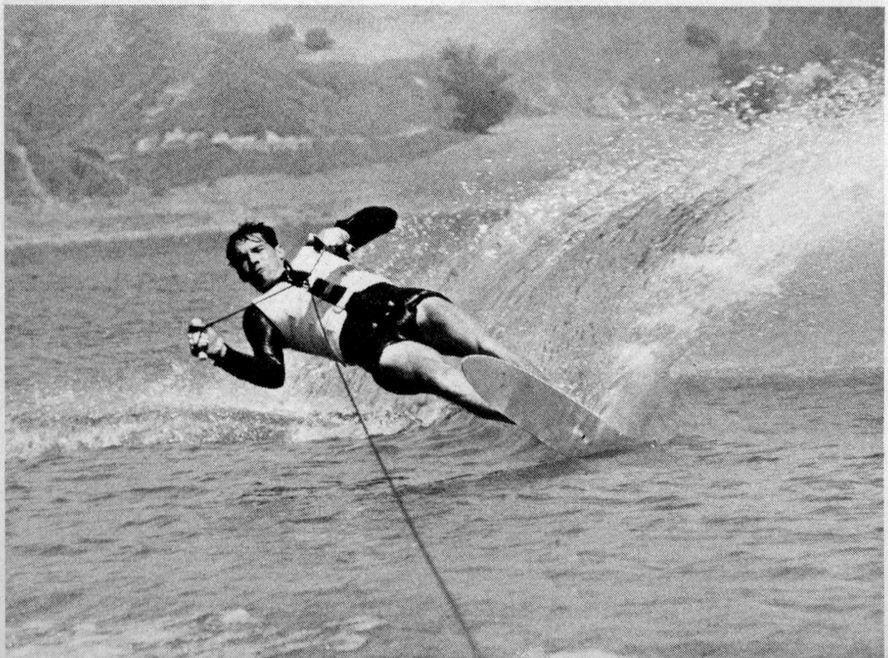
4

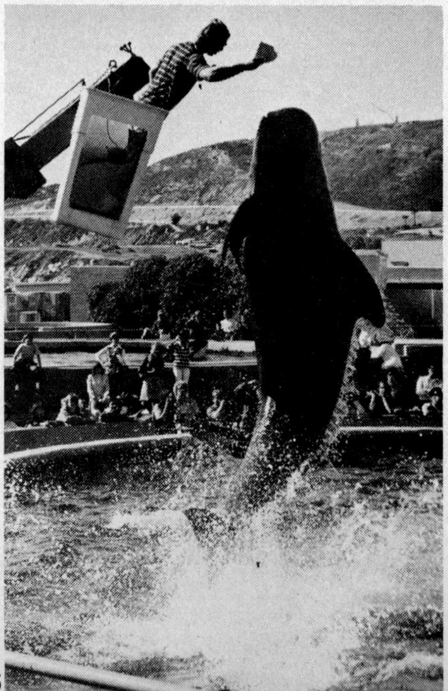
5

Scholastic prize winner) set his 35mm camera on a tripod, chose an uncluttered series of bowling lanes as a background, and shot the foreground figure at 1/2 second at f/16 on Plus-X. Here is an unusual way to symbolize action when there's no need to identify the subject. This, and some of the other uses of slow shutter speeds, approach the photograph as a design more than a record of places or events.

1. Fast race car moving across film plane became blur at 1/250 second, a speed chosen to accentuate movement.

2. By anticipating peak of a motion, such as phrase being spoken, a shot like this can be made at 1/60 second.

3. Capturing peak of action requires some anticipation and quick finger.

4. Water Moccasin water ski manufacturer Alan Pittman was frozen in action by 1/1000 shutter speed.

5. At peak of its leap this whale was caught sharply at 1/500 second.

6. Panning camera with fast-moving subject is a popular way to freeze action and blur the background.

You are probably familiar with pictures made by zooming a lens during an exposure of ¼, ½ or a full second, especially in color. Effects can be quite decorative, and the element of chance is a challenge, since you are never precisely sure what will happen on the film. With the camera on a tripod, you may zoom the lens in either direction for equally strange streaks and blurs of highlighted subject matter. The burst of light in my photograph came from a background hamburger stand as a figure crossed the film plane.

The longer the exposure, the more extended the zoom effect will be. In dim light, fast films are okay because you can stop down comfortably. In bright light, you must either use slow films or neutral density filters in order to accommodate aperture settings to slow shutter speeds. Experiment with zooming during slow exposures for surprising and fascinating results.

Another more functional place for slow shutter speeds is a dimly lighted room or area where the film will register more than the eye can see. I photographed a banquet with my Bronica on a tripod, exposing at ½ second and f/5.6 with Tri-X rated at ASA 400. I guessed the exposure because my meter didn't register, but one more stop would have given me greater shadow detail as light collected on the film. A further extension of this is to shoot by the light of a full moon, stopping down to about f/6.3 and timing the exposure for 5 or 10 seconds. With some films and subject matter your pictures may seem to be made in daylight!

Normal night pictures call for shutter speeds ranging from perhaps 1/60 second down to several seconds. Since the camera meter only registers the brightest lights, you will usually increase exposure from that indicated by one or two stops to assure some detail in dark areas. The downtown street scene was shot hand-held at 1/15 second and f/4 with a 35mm lens on Tri-X rated at ASA 400. At night the contrast range is extreme, which often adds up to dramatic pictures.

Color at night can be especially rewarding, strange or downright eerie. For instance, water fountains with colored lights playing on them turn unusual hues as colors blend if the exposure is long enough. Even overexposure can create pastels you

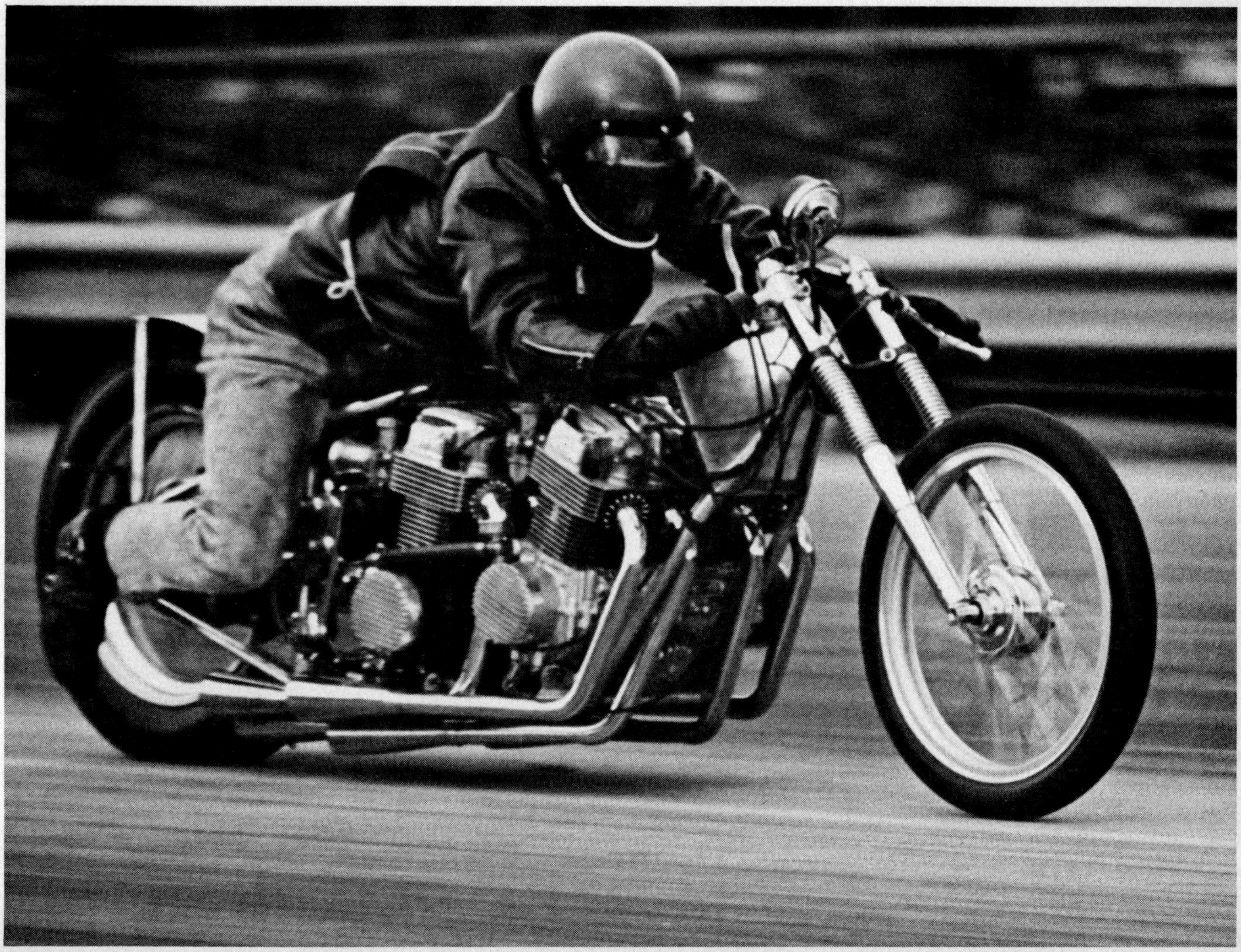

6

don't expect. Daylight films render some colors, such as electric signs, more accurately, but Type A or Type B films are more likely to capture the hues of the city with fidelity. Expose by meter, and if the needle fails to move, take several guesses to assure proper color saturation.

The slow shutter speed is a tool often forgotten or ignored, but it adds dimension to photography when you can relax and play around.

MULTIPLE EXPOSURES

I mentioned double exposures in the camera in Chapter 8, but I want to underline a few special pleasures and variations. Photographer-editor Jim Cornfield planned the double portrait of a girl against a black background, and shot with a Hasselblad, removing the back and cocking the shutter (without advancing the film) between each shot. He used electronic flash, though floodlight would have given him equal control to maintain a dark background. Try your own variation of this using a couple; put him on one side and her on the other, their shoulders growing out of each other. If your camera does not make double exposures easily, use the open flash technique in a darkened room, and cover the lens between exposures. In color or black-and-white it can be quite an adventure.

Remember Duchamp's *Nude Descending A Staircase,* a painting still famous after more than 60 years? The artist seemed to anticipate the stroboscopic effects of multiple sequential electronic flash pioneered by Dr. Harold Edgerton. With the same technique Jim Cornfield did a sort of "nude crossing the film plane," using an inexpensive repeating strobe light that flashed twice a second as the model moved. The shutter of Jim's Hasselblad was open during the entire movement. Since the light built up negative density at the left, this area is lighter than at right where the arm registered only individual flashes. Variations of multiple strobe are another stimulus toward creativity.

Gil Smith won a Kodak/Scholastic award with his moon/orange over the Sunkist building in Sherman Oaks, California. He shot the night-lighted structure with a 4x5 view camera and made the second planned exposure of an orange at home on a black surface. Using a view camera it is easy to reinsert the sheet film and plot

1. With his camera on tripod, James Thacker shot at ½ second to intentionally blur the bowler.

2. Unpredictable blurred effects are possible by zooming a lens during a short exposure such as ½ second or even one that is longer.

3. Slow shutter speeds pay off in dimly lighted rooms such as this banquet hall where ½ second at f/5.6 was exposure used for shot.

4. At night, exposures longer than one second produce beautiful photos.

5. Night photos generally consist of bright areas against black areas.

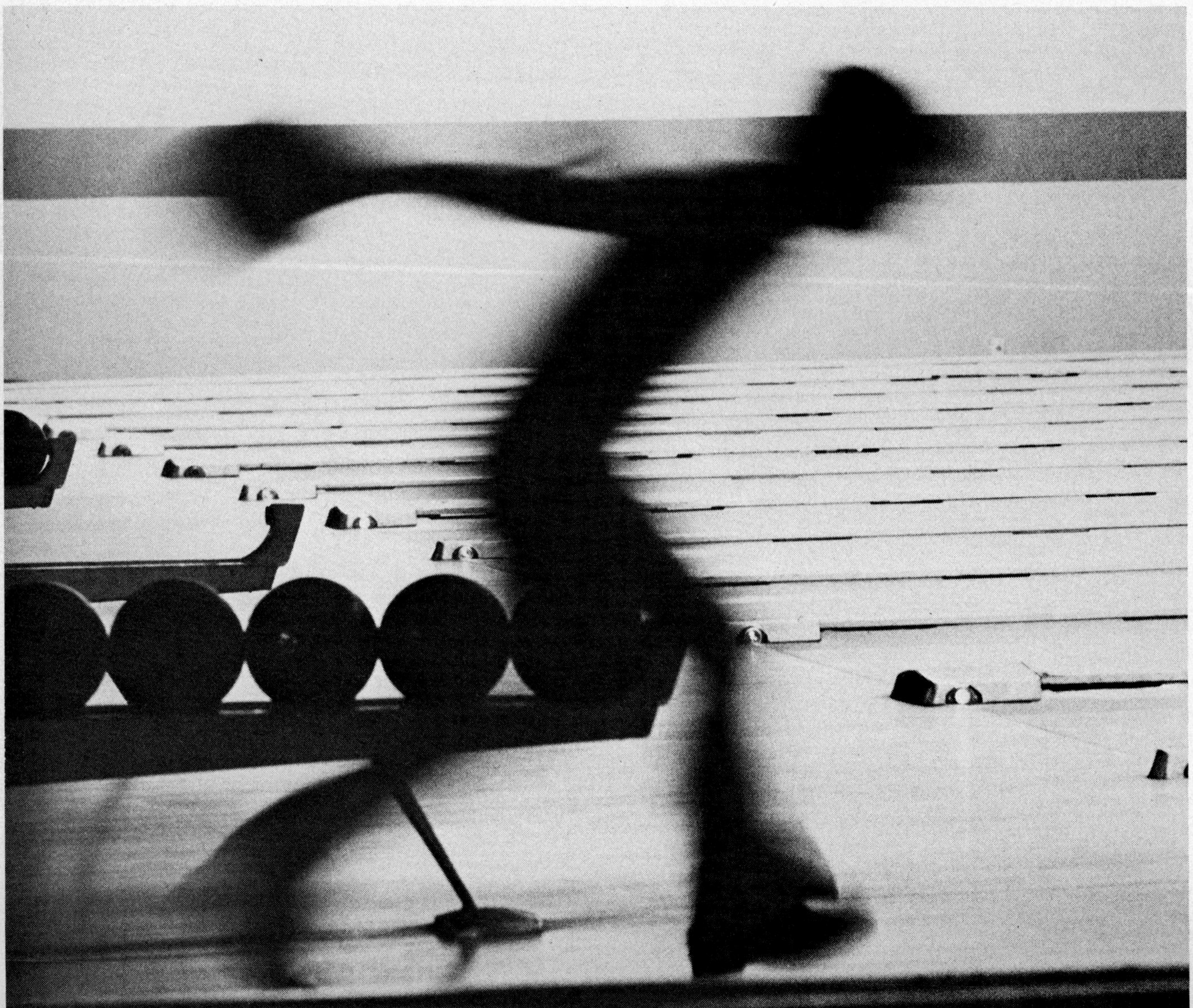

1

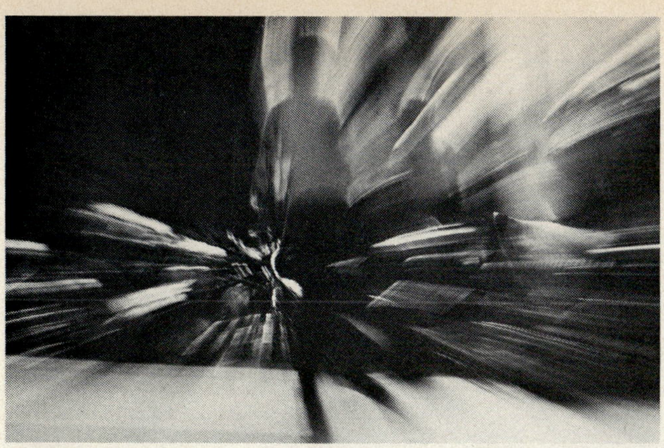

2

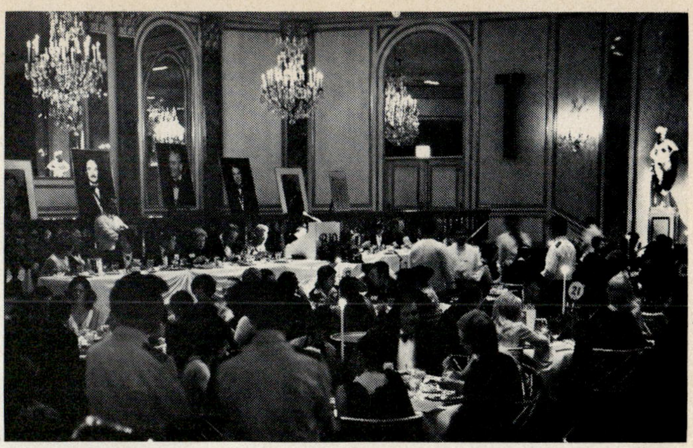

3

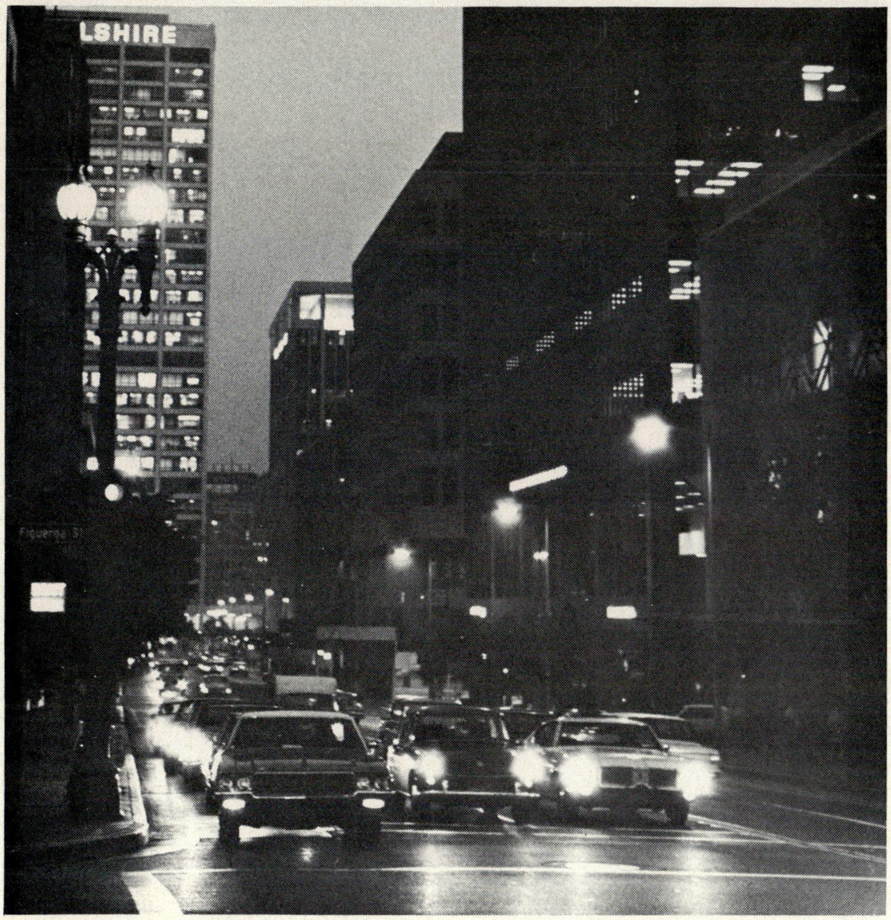

4

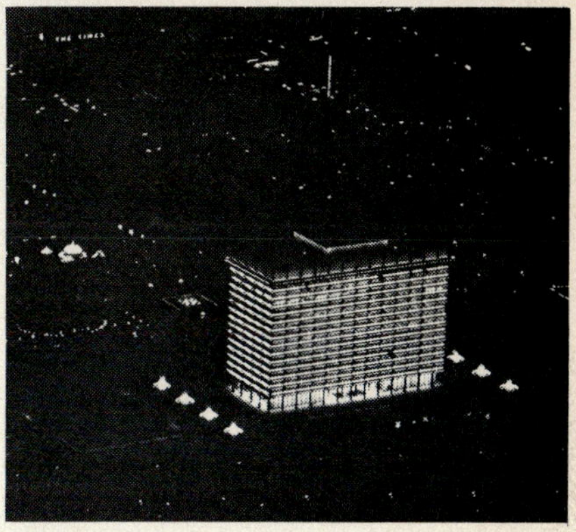

5

composition by marking the original building on tracing paper held against the ground glass. Using this sketch to guide him, adding the orange was easy.

When you first attempt multiple exposures, stick with dark or black backgrounds because they make it more comfortable to blend several images that retain their identity. Later you can experiment with completely overlapping images as I did with the Air Force officer over whom I superimposed a shot of a globe. You can see his hand resting on the same globe at bottom center which I shot against a medium gray wall. When I made the exposure of the globe close-up, its details registered lightly, because they were partly blocked by the density of the wall.

AGAINST THE LIGHT IS ALL RIGHT

Shooting into the light can be a special problem in two ways: (a) you may get flare from light rays into the lens, and (b) exposure may be difficult to judge. However, neither of these conditions should bother you when brilliant, natural backlighting is waiting to be captured.

The sun's glitter on water comes from what is called specular highlights, which means they are reflected in the manner of a mirror. Guy Draughon made the picture of a tiny sailboat on a calm sea almost lost in the light. He shot from a light airplane using Plus-X in a 35mm camera and exposed at 1/500 second at f/11.

I once asked Edward Weston about an unbelievable shot he made at Point Lobos on the California coast, looking down on a bed of kelp visible only by specular highlights. I told him I assumed he had waited for that moment which passed quickly, and he confirmed my guess. Such jewels of light are fleeting and treasured by aware photographers—with patience.

Guy Draughon also shot the entirely different backlighted picture of still life on a shag rug near a large sliding glass door. His exposure was 1/60 second between f/8 and f/11 with Plus-X, to provide a negative that included enough shadow detail and plenty of texture in the background. Using the clear glass sphere gave additional contrast to the other objects, all of which glow in the picture because of the directional light he chose.

INFRARED IS WILD AND WEIRD

Unmentioned in Chapter 4 are color and black-and-white infrared films—because they are rather "special." By that I mean infrared is temperamental, frustrating and wildly unpredictable—but capable of producing very exciting photographs. *PhotoGraphic* staffer Guy Draughon, surveyed infrared films in the June, 1972 issue, and here is a digest of his findings.

Special Problems

So-called infrared "light" is really infrared energy which is invisible to the eye, but which infrared film can record. By using a red filter such as the No. 25 over a camera lens, you can photograph a scene by infrared energy *and* by the part of the red spectrum which the filter transmits. Though infrared film is used for scientific purposes and aerial surveillance, don't be awed by it, since it is processed as easily as Ektachrome-X or Tri-X. Most photographers use infrared film for special effects and offbeat colored scenics. It is available as Kodak High Speed Infrared film for black-and-white work and Ektachrome Infrared for color. Should you want more information about these films than you find here, Kodak technical publication, M-28, *Applied Infrared Photography,* has the data.

If your camera is light-tight, chances are it is infrared-tight. Older cameras with rubberized focal-plane shutters or plastic shutter blades are possible exceptions. A focal-plane shutter which leaks infrared will leave streaks across the film.

Black-and-white infrared film can be stored like any pan film, so long as it isn't near a heat source, because it is sensitive to heat. Refrigerate the film which *must*—Kodak says—be loaded and unloaded from the camera in total darkness. Don't even open the can the film comes in unless you are in a darkroom, closet or changing bag, as the lips of the film cartridge will not block infrared energy. Use a changing bag in the shade. Store the film in its light-tight can until you are ready to process it.

The pictures Guy Draughon took that illustrate this section were processed in D-76 for 11 minutes at 70°, which Kodak recommends for "normal contrast." With infrared this means considerably more contrast than an ideal negative with conventional pan films. For higher contrast still, try D-19 for 7½ minutes at 70°. It is contrast that makes infrared prints spectacular, and at best, you will see grain because it is inherent in the film.

Grass and foliage will appear extremely dense on an infrared negative, while sky and water will be very clear. In a finished print, therefore, chlorophyll-rich materials come out as white, while the sky is very dark. Sky has little infrared radiation present and its blue is held back in a negative. If you want to experiment with somewhat reduced contrast, use an orange filter, which allows more visible light rays to affect the film. With an orange filter, infrared film picks up some of the green light and

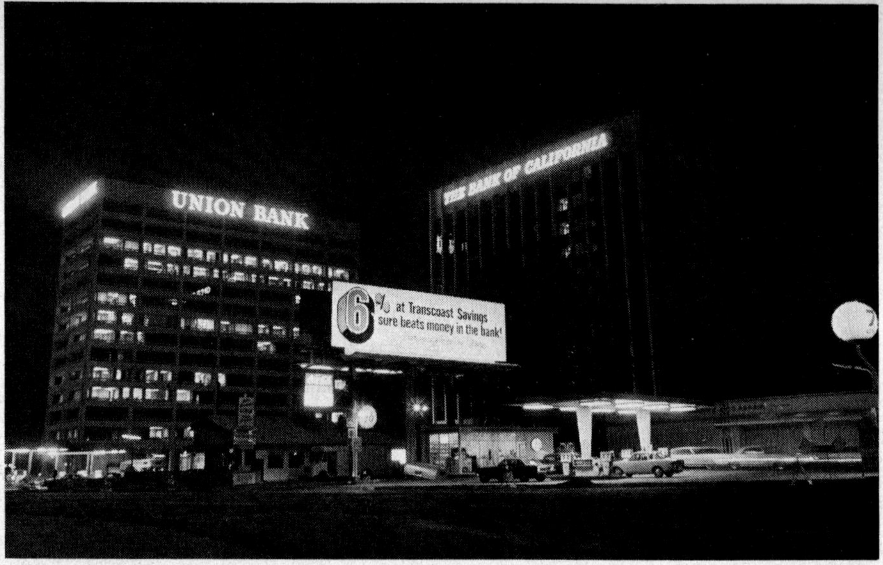

1

SUGGESTED EXPOSURES FOR *KODAK* FILMS

Picture Subject	KODACHROME-X EKTACHROME-X KODACOLOR-X ASA 64	High Speed EKTACHROME—Normal Processing VERICHROME Pan PLUS-X Pan ASA 125	High Speed EKTACHROME—with ESP-1 Processing for 2½ times normal film speed TRI-X Pan ASA 400	ROYAL-X Pan 2475 Recording (ESTAR-AH Base) ASA 1000
Home Interiors at Night—Areas with bright light	1/15 sec f/2	1/30 sec f/2	1/30 sec f/2.8 ↓ 4	1/60 sec f/4
Areas with average light	1/4 sec f/2 ↓ 2.8	1/8 sec f/2 ↓ 2.8	1/30 sec f/2	1/30 sec f/2.8 ↓ 4
Candlelighted Close-ups	–	1/4 sec f/2 ↓ 2.8	1/15 sec f/2	1/30 sec f/2 ↓ 2.8
Indoor and Outdoor Christmas Lighting at Night, Christmas Trees	1 sec f/4	1 sec f/5.6	1/30 sec f/2	1/30 sec f/2.8 ↓ 4
Brightly Lighted Downtown Street Scenes (Wet streets add interesting reflections.)	1/30 sec f/2	1/30 sec f/2.8	1/60 sec f/2.8 ↓ 4	1/125 sec f/4
Brightly Lighted Nightclub or Theatre Districts—Las Vegas or Times Square	1/30 sec f/2.8	1/30 sec f/4	1/60 sec f/4 ↓ 5.6	1/125 sec f/5.6
Neon Signs and Other Lighted Signs	1/30 sec f/4	1/60 sec f/4	1/125 sec f/4 ↓ 5.6	1/125 sec f/8
Store Windows	1/30 sec f/2.8	1/30 sec f/4	1/60 sec f/4 ↓ 5.6	1/60 sec f/8
Floodlighted Buildings Fountains, Monuments	4 sec f/5.6	1 sec f/4	1/15 sec f/2	1/30 sec f/2 ↓ 2.8
Skyline—Distant view of lighted buildings at night	4 sec f/2.8	1 sec f/2	1 sec f/2.8 ↓ 4	1 sec f/5.6
Skyline—10 minutes after sunset	1/30 sec f/4	1/60 sec f/4	1/60 sec f/5.6 ↓ 8	1/125 sec f/8
Fairs, Amusement Parks	1/15 sec f/2	1/30 sec f/2	1/30 sec f/2.8 ↓ 4	1/60 sec f/4
Fireworks—Displays on the ground	1/30 sec f/2.8	1/30 sec f/4	1/60 sec f/4 ↓ 5.6	1/60 sec f/8
Fireworks—Aerial displays (Keep shutter open on "BULB" or "TIME" for several bursts.)	f/8	f/11	f/16 ↓ 22	f/32
Lightning (Keep shutter open on "BULB" or "TIME" for one or two streaks of lightning.)	f/5.6	f/8	f/11 ↓ 16	f/22
Burning Buildings, Campfires, Bonfires	1/30 sec f/2.8	1/30 sec f/4	1/60 sec f/4 ↓ 5.6	1/125 sec f/5.6
Night Football, Baseball, Racetracks	1/30 sec f/2.8	1/60 sec f/2.8	1/125 sec f/2.8 ↓ 4	1/250 sec f/4
Niagara Falls— White lights	15 sec f/5.6	8 sec f/5.6	6 sec f/8	4 sec f/11
Light-colored lights	30 sec f/5.6	15 sec f/5.6	6 sec f/5.6	4 sec f/8
Dark-colored lights	30 sec f/4	30 sec f/5.6	12 sec f/5.6	4 sec f/5.6

From the Kodak booklet, *Adventures in Existing Light Photography* (Kodak publication No. AC-44, $1.25 at Kodak dealers, or write to Eastman Kodak Company, Consumer Markets Division, Rochester, New York 14650)

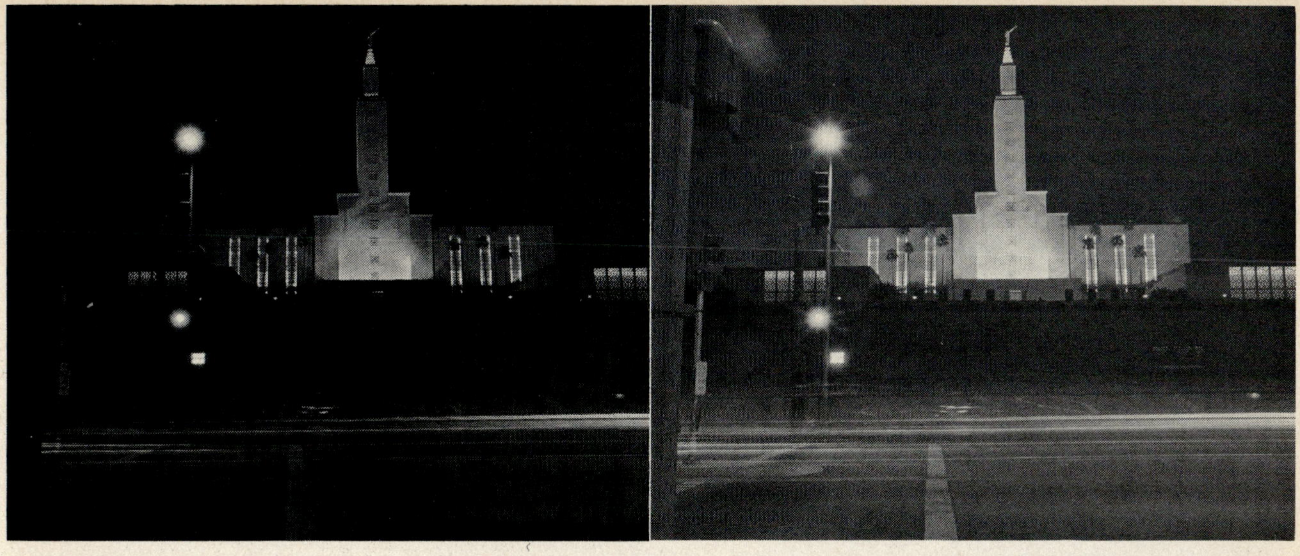

2

registers slightly more open shadows.

Infrared-sensitive film is sensational when it comes to cutting haze and is more effective in probing into distant scenes than normal panchromatic film with a red filter. There are three reasons for this: (1) infrared energy is scattered less than visible red light, (2) the contrast of the scene increases the apparent brightness, and (3) the average outdoor scene is usually highly reflective to the infrared radiation present.

Focusing is not as critical as you may think, although the longer infrared wavelengths do not focus at the same point as visible energy. If your camera has a red dot or line for infrared focusing, use it. Draughon tried focusing both ways and found little difference because depth of field was generally sufficient outdoors to

1. The secret of night photography is to bracket your exposures—whether you used the accompanying chart or a light meter, whether shooting color or black-and-white. After a while, you'll know pretty much what you'll get under various conditions. Bear in mind that the more exposure you give a night scene, the more detail you'll get in the darker parts of the scene, the less detail you'll get in the brighter parts of the scene, and the less your photo will look like a night scene. The less exposure you give the scene, the more detail you'll get in the bright areas, the less detail you'll get in the dark areas, and the more the photo will look like a night scene. Use Mark Hilburn's exposure/development chart (later in chapter) to compensate for reciprocity failure at long exposure times.

2. A compensating developer such as Ethol TEC will reduce contrast, help preserve shadow detail in night shots, if you want that effect.

3. Fast-repeating electronic flash created sequential series of images as model moved in front of Jim Cornfield's Hasselblad 2¼x2¼ camera.

3

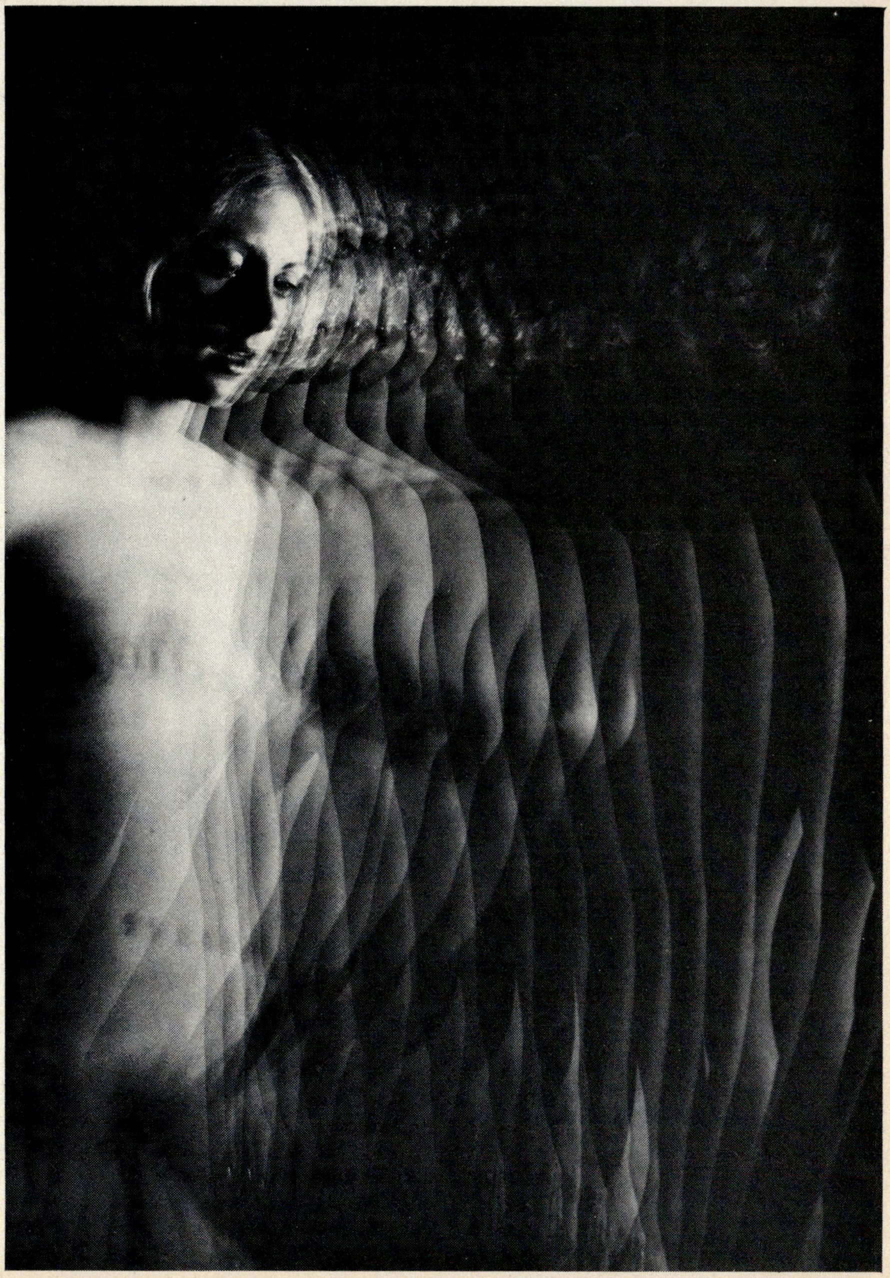

carry the difference in focus. He warns not to use the infrared focus mark when shooting infrared color film, since two of the film's layers are sensitive to light and only one layer is sensitive to infrared energy.

Sunlight is usually ideal for infrared work, and tungsten light is rich in infrared as well. As an indoor test, Draughon suggests using a pair of No. 2 photolamps in 12-inch reflectors and expose at 1/30 second at f/8 with the lamps 4½ feet away from the subject. Don't use infrared heat lamps because their radiation is inappropriate, and avoid fluorescent lights in this situation as they are deficient in infrared energy.

There is no established ASA speed for Kodak High Speed Infrared Film since the ratio of infrared to visible light is variable. An Exposure Index of 50 (using the No. 25 filter) worked well in Draughon's tests, and he bracketed his exposures between f/8 and f/11 at 1/125 second on a bright sunny day. On an overcast day infrared energy is extremely variable, so bracket an extra stop on both sides of the meter reading. Remember that your exposure meter is *not* sensitive to the infrared end of the spectrum, so you won't get a precise reading. Indoors under photofloods, start with an El of 125, since this light source has more infrared energy compared to visible light. Without a filter the film speed is 80 outdoors and 200 in tungsten light.

Infrared color/ For delightful "distortion" this film has no peer. When used with the recommended No. 12 yellow filter, the results are fairly predictable (by infrared standards), because this is the way it is used in scientific work. But when you substitute other filters (red, darker yellow, orange or whatever you choose), watch out! Unlike normal color film, infrared color has no yellow layer in the emulsion, and hence the use of a yellow filter. Green objects reproduce as blue, red reproduces as green and infrared-rich subjects photograph as red. Grass is one of the last, and comes out as red or magenta. Take away the yellow filter and use a No. 25 red or 15 orange or X1 green, and the colors indeed go wild.

As a general rule, if you shoot a neutral subject with a red filter, you will get a yellowish image; if you shoot with an orange filter (which lets in some of the blue-green light) you get a blue-green picture, and if you shoot with a green filter, blue predominates. Infrared mixing with visible light can record very strikingly.

Infrared color film should also be refrigerated, but it is not as sensitive to being loaded and unloaded in total darkness, although it is recommended. You do *not* use the infrared focusing mark with infrared color be-

1. Jim Cornfield made two exposures on one frame of film in his Hasselblad for beautiful double portrait.

2. Guy Draughon backlighted this attractive still-life for dramatic effect, and to set off textures.

3. One exposure for building and another later for orange gave Gil Smith an amusing photographic moon.

4. Beautiful specular highlights from the sea engulf tiny sailboat in Guy Draughon's striking photograph.

5. This multiple exposure was made with Rolleiflex and planned in the finder to symbolize the Air Force officer's global operations.

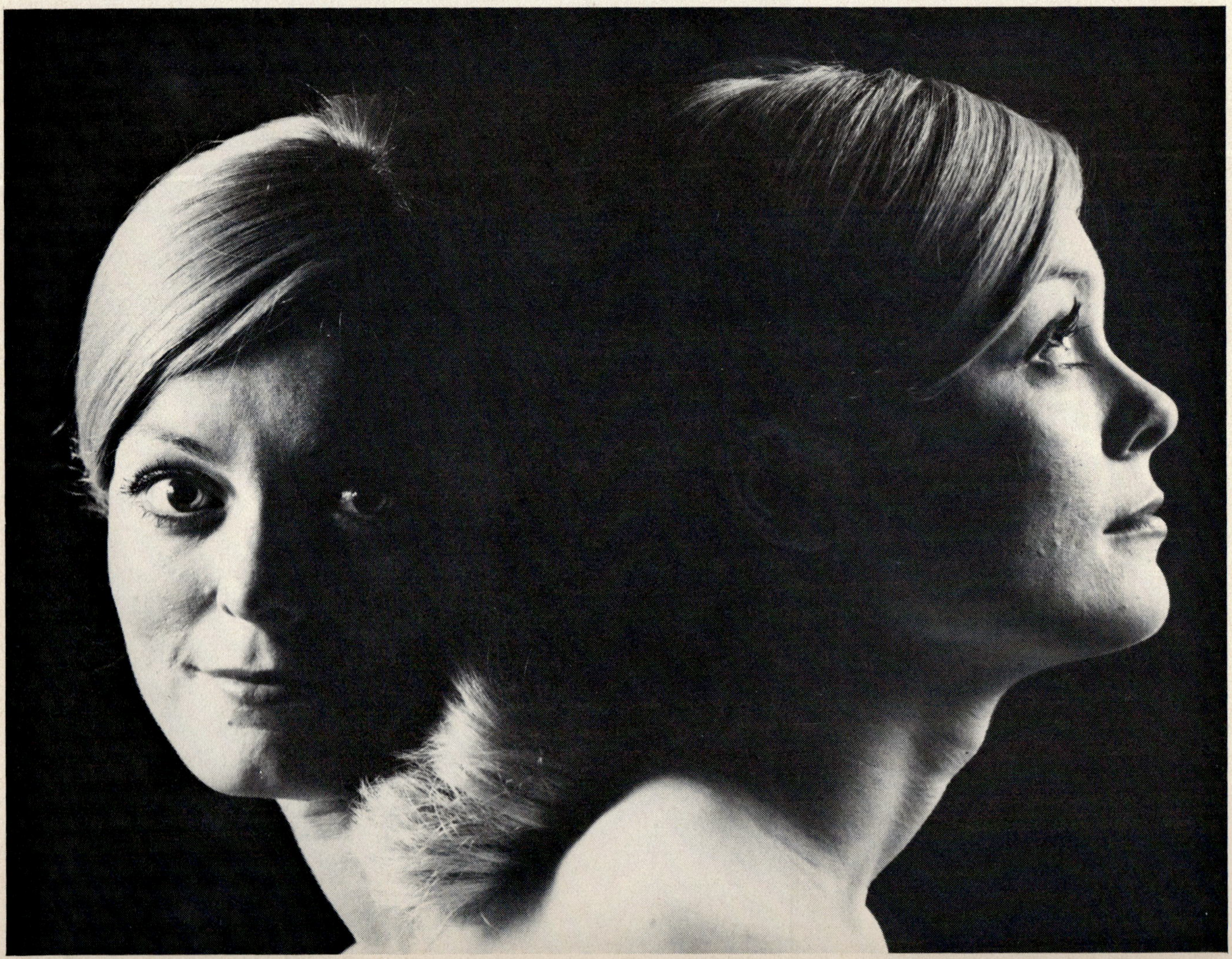
1

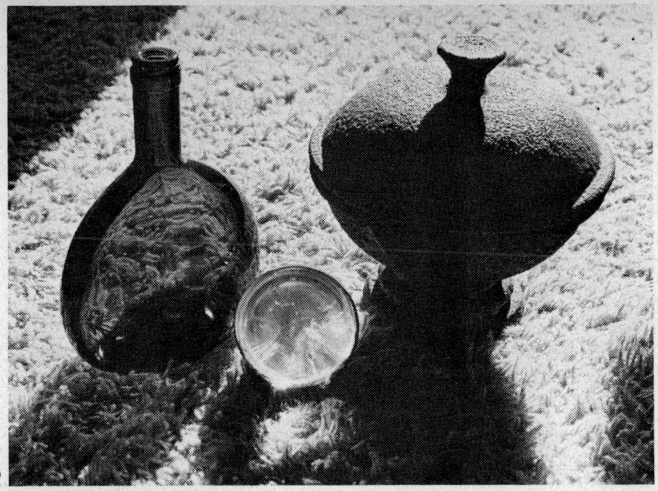

2

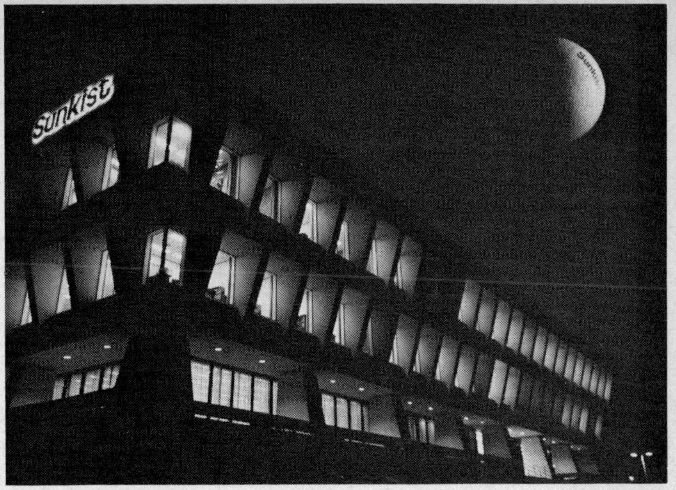

3

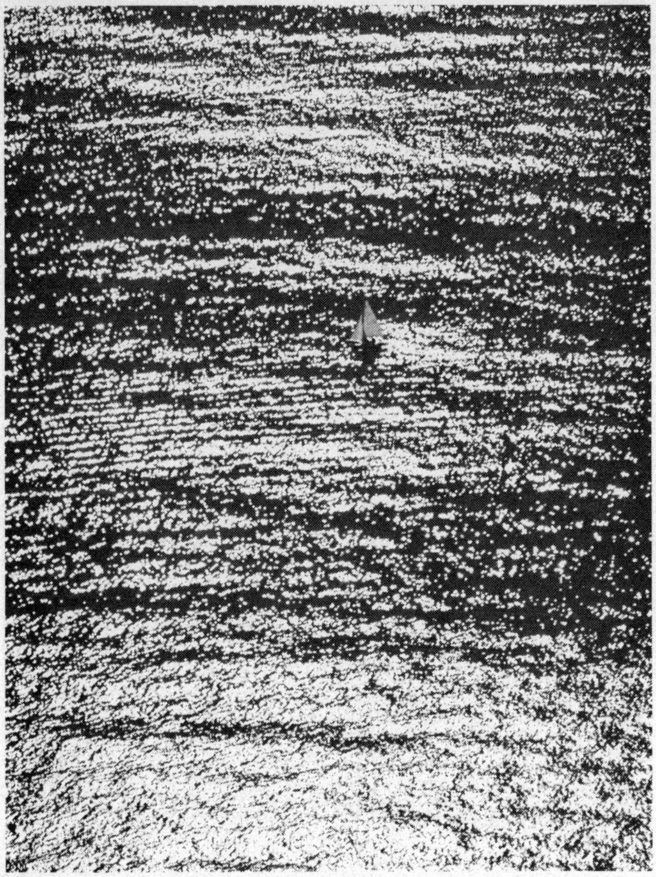

4

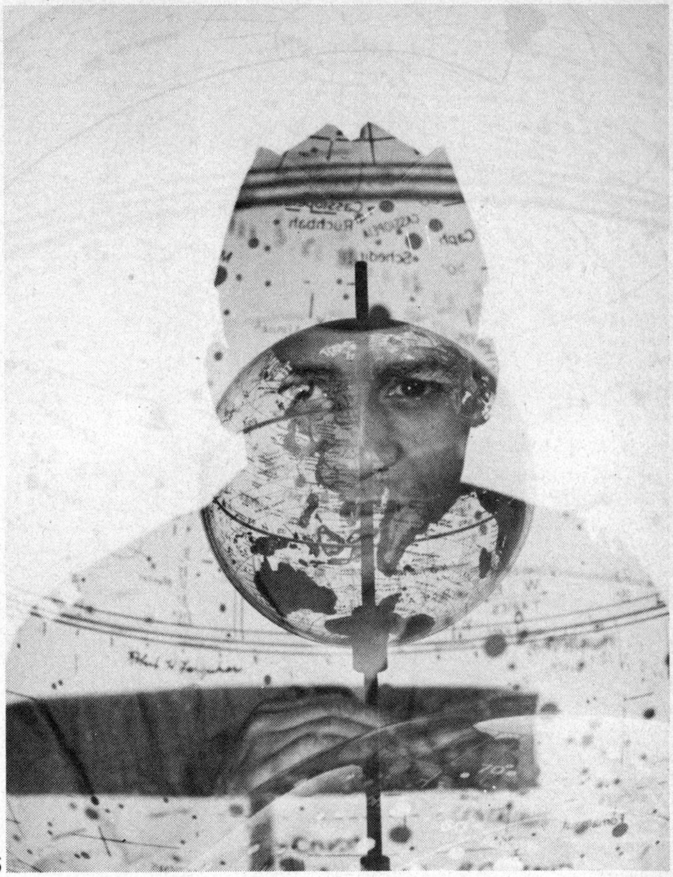

5

cause two layers of the emulsion are responding to visible light—green and red. It is recommended that you bracket every shot in half-stop increments. Guy Draughon found that the film has more latitude with a green filter than with orange or red. He also learned that backlighted situations produce vivid colors when the subject is rich in infrared.

Use an Exposure Index of 50 with the orange, red and yellow filters, and an EI of 20 with the green filter. Expect surprises, such as two rolls Draughon shot on a day when infrared energy apparently "wasn't working," and his scenes were puce-green. Ektachrome Infrared film can be processed in Kodak's E-4 kit just like Ektachrome-X, and it is fun to watch the weird colors pop up on the film as it is drying.

Even if you are not bored with conventional photographic effects, you might give infrared a try to stimulate your imagination and also extend your capabilities.

MORE DRAMATIC SUNSETS

A blood-red sun sinking out of sight behind clouds, below mountains or ocean horizon line, is a sight that few photographers can resist. Unfortunately, too many sunset pictures are not very inspiring because (1) you did not believe your meter and the color was washed out; (2) the sun itself was reduced to an insignificant size; or (3) foreground subjects were either lacking or dull.

Beginning with exposure, it is not "cheating" to bracket a sunset shot to assure yourself of beautiful color saturation in at least one slide of a series. Take a meter reading from the most important part of the sky and shoot accordingly. If you know the latitude of your film and the aptitude of your camera meter, one shot may be enough, but half a stop on each side of that indicated exposure could provide even better pictures. After all, the light is changing rapidly, and your judgment about the color can be reserved for when you see the finished pictures.

Point number two about the size of the sun can be influenced by using a semitelephoto or telephoto lens instead of a normal or wide-angle. Longer focal length lenses produce a larger image of the sun and zero in on the most brilliant area of the sunset itself. In most cases, using a telephoto lens at sunset-time makes it almost mandatory to use a tripod, monopod or *some* steady camera support. Lenses longer than 135mm begin to get heavy and unwieldy, and test results in Chapter 3 demonstrated how difficult it is to hold a camera with normal lens absolutely steady at even 1/125 second. Should you be using a very long lens, such as 500mm or longer, you may want to reduce vibrations on a tripod by draping something such as an overcoat over the lens. If the lens is supported on the hood of a car, for instance, place a shirt or a sweater or a piece of foam rubber beneath it to dampen vibrations.

A beautiful sunset can be enhanced by the foreground subjects silhouetted against it, such as figures, trees, buildings, etc. A totally blank horizon line won't have the same interest, even if the sky and clouds are vivid and dynamic. Choose a camera position that gives you a pleasant design or arrangement of subject matter that complements the sky and its blazing color.

Choice of film for sunsets is a personal matter, but since you are dealing with distance, and contrast is subdued by atmospheric conditions, a higher-contrast film is suggested. Kodachrome II, push-processed Ektachrome, Panatomic-X or Plus-X all lend themselves to the extra-contrast specifications.

If you are using a through-the-lens or hand-held CdS meter, take care not to point it at the sun for more than moments. (Turn the meter system off in the camera while composing.) Remember that a CdS cell, when exposed to very bright light,

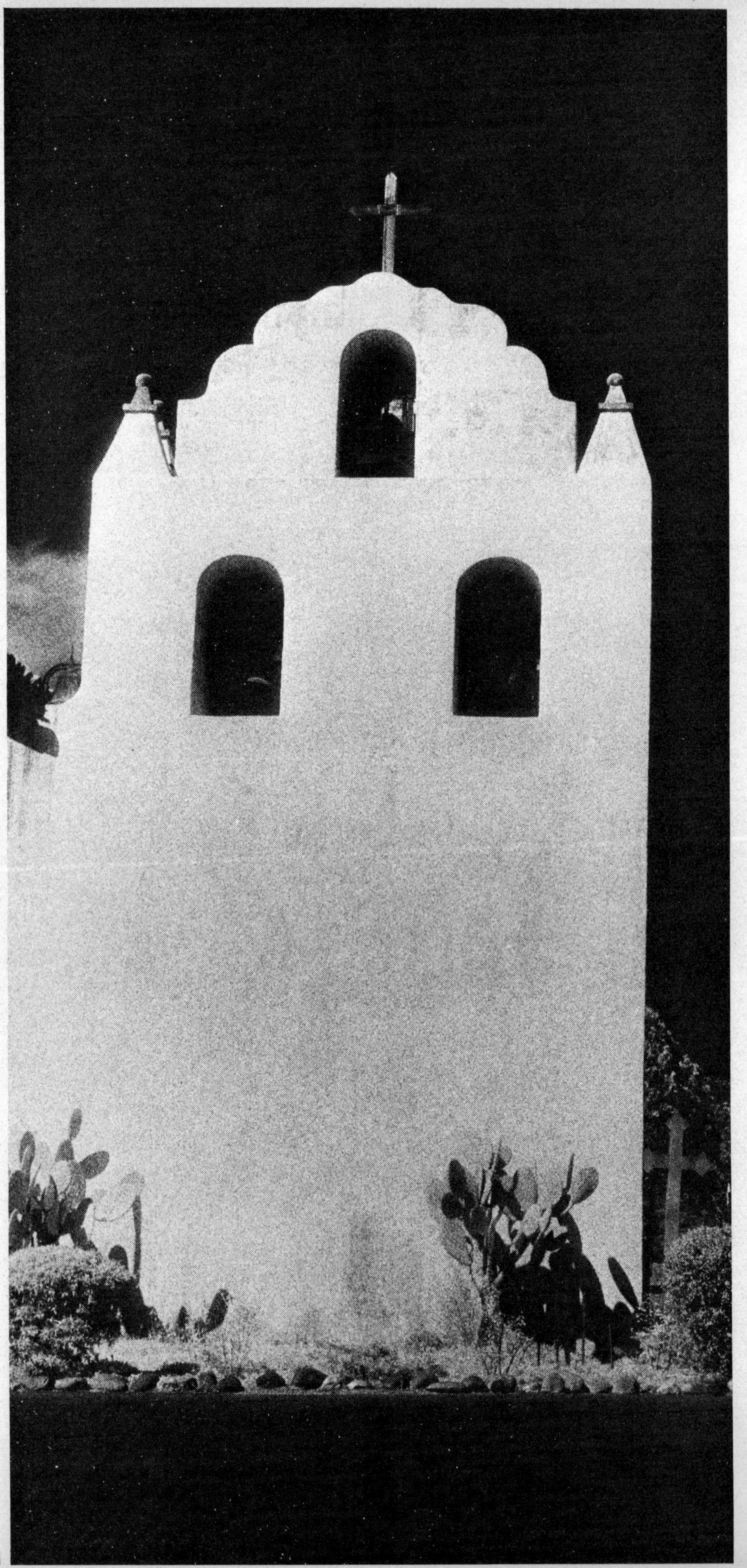

1

1. Stark white mission and deep blue sky produce high contrast through red filter and infrared film.

2. Infrared film produces dramatic black skies and white foliage.

3. Backlighted windmill stands out against white grass in infrared shot. Shot was made toward sun, so sky remained light gray instead of black.

4. Infrared shot of swimming pool area without red filter reproduces water in pool as clear, shadows light. Adding filter darkens shadows and turns water black.

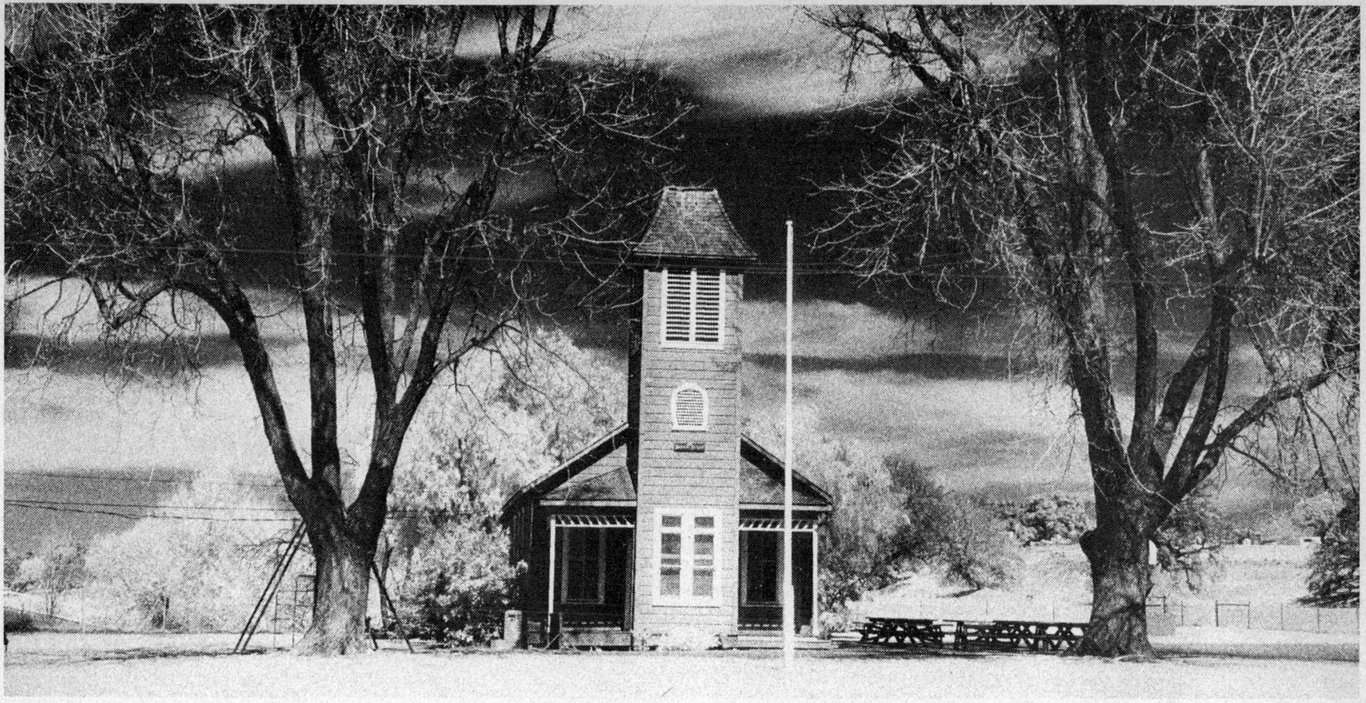

2

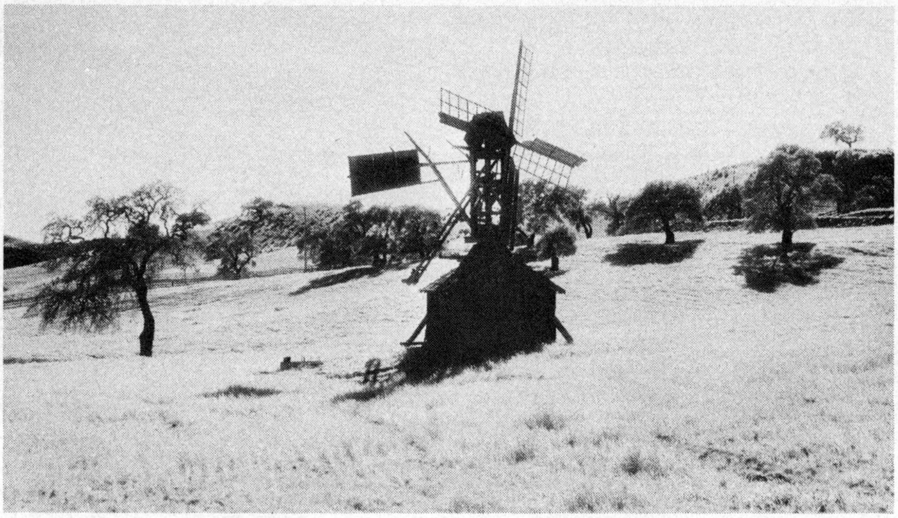

3

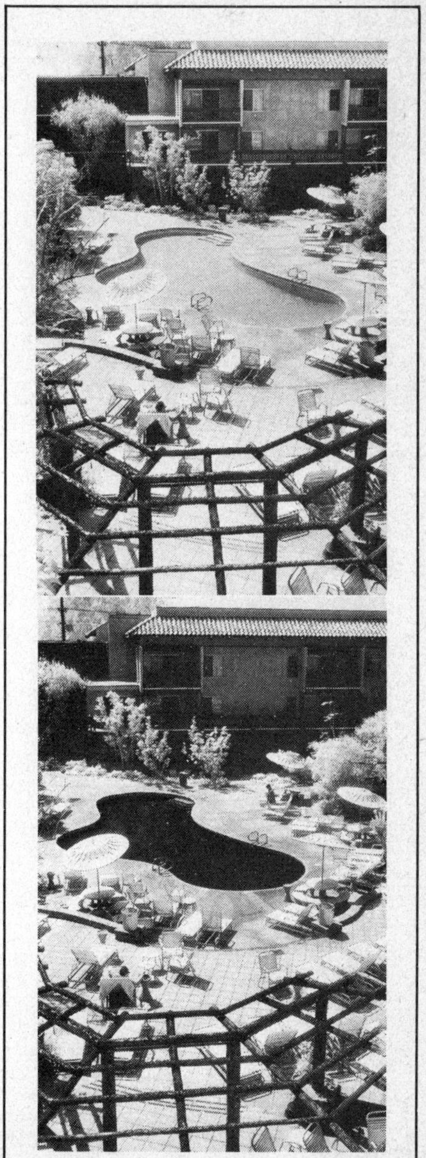

4

takes a while to recover. With a long lens such as a 1000mm on your camera, meter the sun quickly, for you can literally fry the CdS cell!

A word of warning before you start following the sun with a telephoto lens: Do not look directly at it unless your eyes are protected against its volatile UV and infrared rays which can cause permanent damage to the retina without your even being aware of it. Dark glasses won't filter the rays, nor will a piece of exposed film guarantee protection. You might hold a piece of paper behind the eyepiece of your SLR, and when the sun is in the picture, a disc of light will shine on the paper. Better yet, wait until the sun is filtered through clouds or disappears behind the horizon before starting to shoot.

SHOOTING A TV SCREEN

There are several reasons why you might wish to shoot images from a TV screen. First, to make a record of events, people or something you want to remember, pictures you can't get any other way as easily. In that case, it is simple to set your camera on a tripod, frame the screen carefully—and shoot. A normal lens is fine, and with black-and-white films, choose one that allows you to shoot 1/30 second at f/5.6 at least. I've used Tri-X successfully for this purpose.

Turn off room lights to eliminate unwanted reflections, take a reading with a separate meter or through the lens of the whole screen. Since TV images are composed of scanning lines that move across the screen, there is a limitation on shutter speed to 1/30 second or *slower* with a leaf-type shutter. I've used 1/30 second with a focal-plane shutter, but experts say 1/8 second is necessary to obtain uniform exposure. Faster shutter speeds will produce a dark diagonal band across the picture, which can be very annoying.

You may shoot color TV screens in the same way—with one important exception: the set may be tuned for literal color or for offbeat effects. Be sure the color is stronger than pastels, and let your imagination roam for a variety of rich and spectacular images. Shoot close-up sections of the screen, use slow shutter speeds for decorative blur or try some colored filters for psychedelic patterns. You will benefit from using a high-speed color film, and High Speed Ektachrome (Daylight) push-processed to an exposure index of 400 will give you an exposure of about 1/8 second at f/5.6. You will need a CC40R filter over the lens for literal color, but if you want the greenish cast from a TV tube, try pictures without the filter.

Those are the conditions for photographing a TV screen. Now all you need is a fine sense of timing to avoid subject movement at 1/8 second. Anticipate peak action or wait until people are still enough to be captured at that relatively slow shutter speed.

COPING WITH RECIPROCITY FAILURE

The next time you are in deep conversation with a fellow photographer and want to make a really heavy impression, mention reciprocity failure or reciprocity departure—but be sure you know what this phenomenon is yourself. Without getting too technical, these terms refer to a failure of the reciprocity law at very long or very short exposure times, resulting in underexposed negatives if the light meter's readings are followed.

The reciprocity law simply indicates that total exposure—the density of the image on a negative—is the product of the intensity of the light that hits the film and the amount of time it hits the film. In photography's everyday terms, it means that a shutter speed/aperture combination of 1/250 second at f/11 is the same as a combination of 1/125 second at f/16, or combination of 1/60 second at f/22, or a combination of 1/500 second at f/8, etc.—all these shutter speed/aperture combinations will produce the same exposure (image density) on a negative.

When you use exposure times longer than about 1/10 second, or shorter than about 1/1000 second, though, the reciprocity law fails to hold true. Most films lose speed—their ASA number decreases—when exposure times fall outside this 1/10-1/1000-second range. In working terms, this means that an exposure time/aperture combination of four seconds at f/16 will produce less density (exposure) on a negative than will a combination of two seconds at f/11.

There are two kinds of reciprocity failure. High-intensity reciprocity failure occurs when very high intensities of light are used—such as electronic flash—that call for very short exposure times. Such short exposure times are simply not long enough to allow a developable image to form on the film. Low-intensity reciprocity failure occurs when very low light intensities—such as indoor scenes at a bar—exist, calling for very long exposure times. When exposure times run into seconds, some electro-chemical reactions in the emulsion of the film result in underexposure.

What can you do about reciprocity

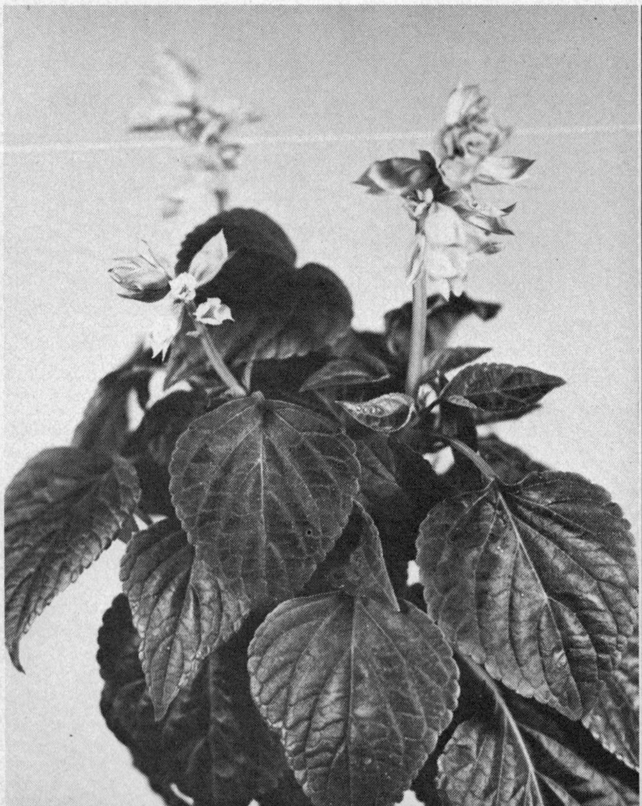

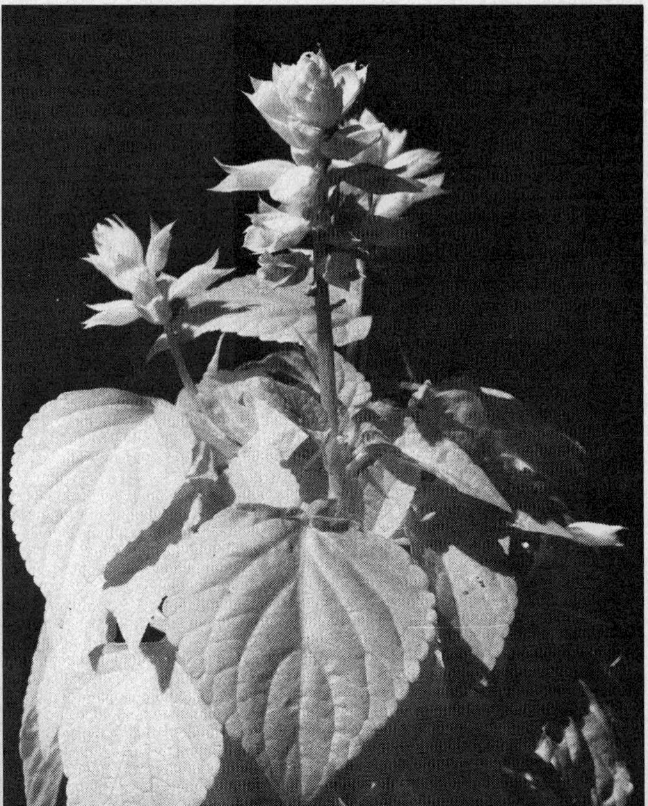

1

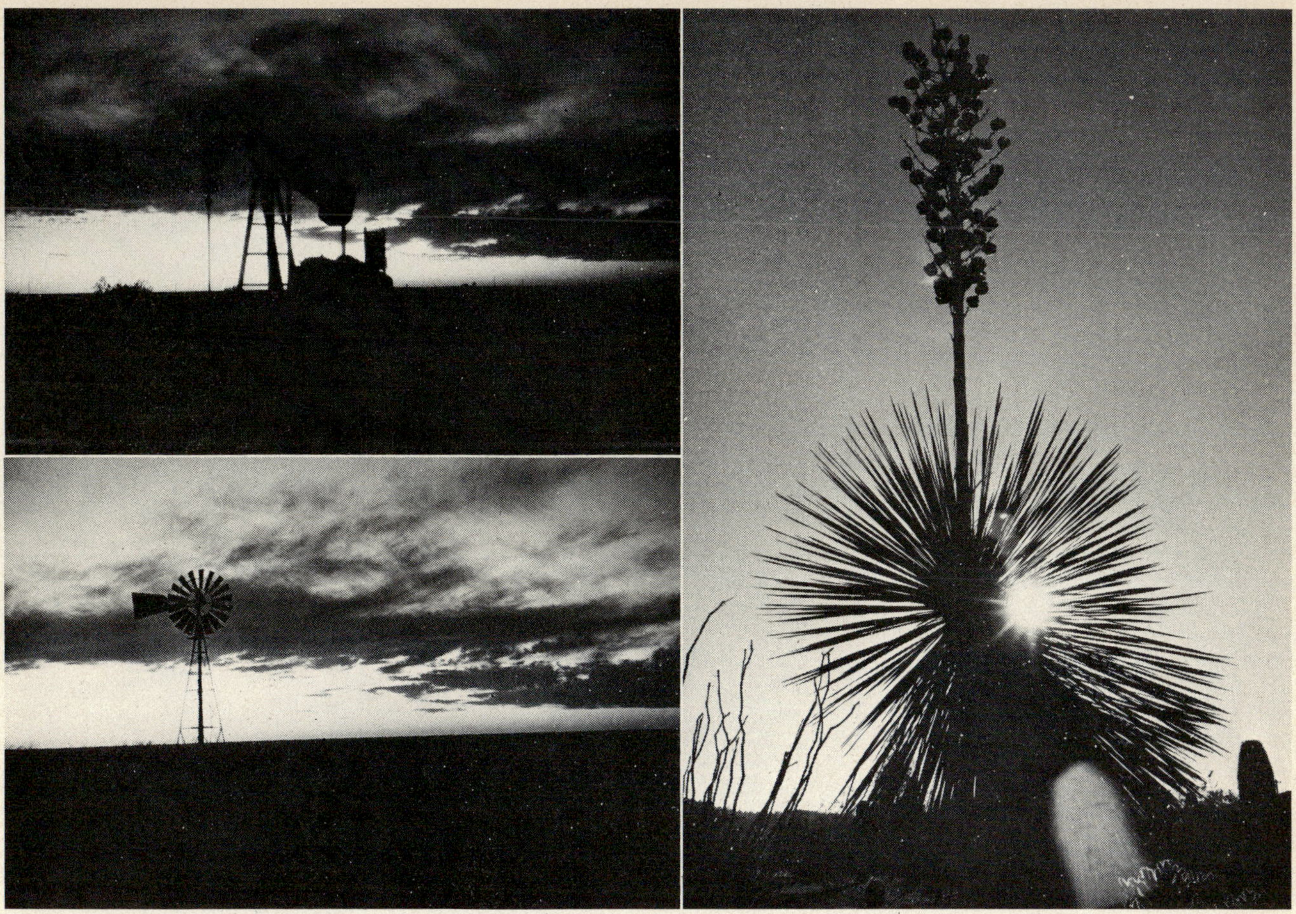

2

1. Panchromatic film registers red flowers and green leaves as we are familiar with them. Infrared film lightens chlorophyll-rich leaves.

2. Including foreground subject in sunset shots makes them dramatic.

3. Long telephoto lens, like this 1250mm Celestron, will produce big sun in your sunset shots.

failure? When using electronic flash, especially automatic units that have durations as short as 1/50,000 second, open the lens about half a stop or so from what your guide number calculations indicate, and develop your black-and-white film 25-50 percent longer than usual to get back the contrast lost through the high-intensity reciprocity failure mechanism. When using very long exposure times, expose the film longer than your meter tells you to—the accompanying chart from Mark Hilburn will give you some starting points for experimentation—and reduce your developing time to kill off some some of the excess contrast produced by the low-intensity reciprocity failure mechanism.

If you are shooting color film, you'll encounter another problem besides the speed loss when reciprocity fail-

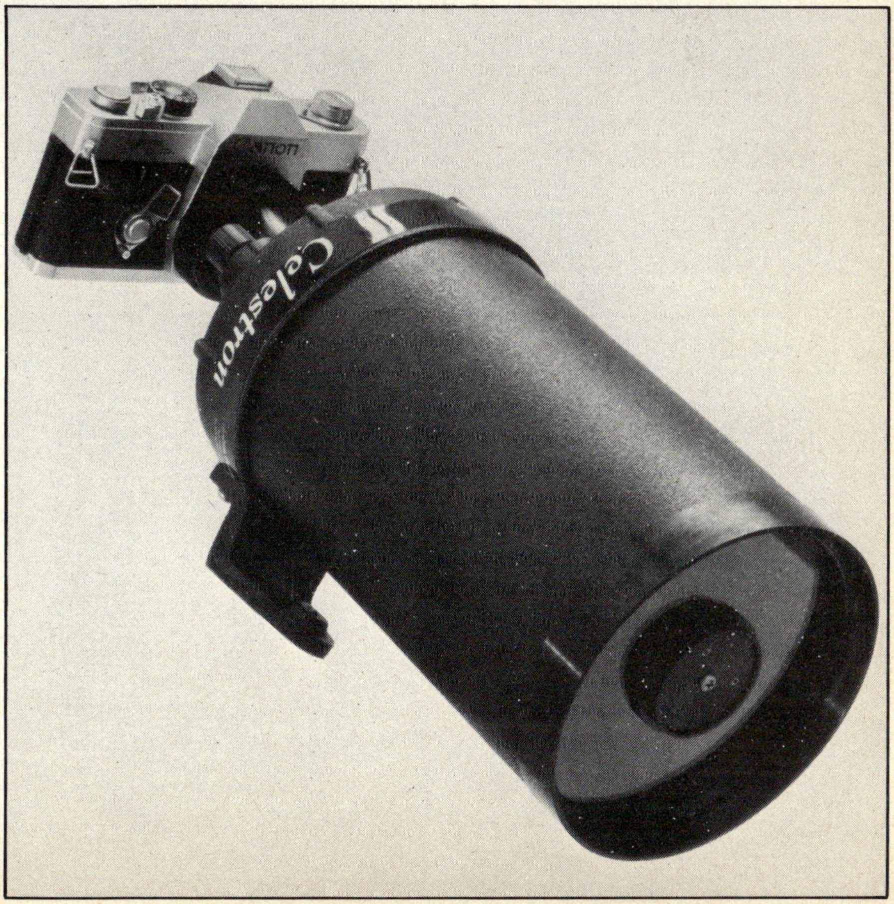

3

ure occurs, and this is a color shift. Color films consist of three emulsion layers, and they don't all lose speed at the same rate when reciprocity failure is encountered, hence the color shift. When using electronic flash, this shift is nearly always to the blue/cyan, and a No. 81B filter over the lens usually cures that. In the case of long exposure times (low-intensity reciprocity failure), you'll have to use color compensating (CC) filters to correct the color shift, as well as increase the size of the aperture or decrease the shutter speed. Some manufacturers will provide you with color shift data for their films, but this information is not always correct—films vary from emulsion batch to emulsion batch. The answer here, if perfect color rendition is critical, is to buy enough film of the same emulsion batch (the emulsion number is printed on the box along with the expiration date) to shoot a roll at progressively slower shutter speeds, using the f/stops recommended by the meter (or EF guide number, if applicable), and have the test roll processed. Keep notes, analyze the pictures for density and color balance, decide which CC filter(s) are needed and what exposure increase is needed, then shoot another test roll, using these corrections. Have this roll processed, then evaluate it, and apply whatever other corrections you deem necessary to the roll you are shooting the critical work with. That's the only sure way to get the results you want.

More special problems? Devise some of your own based on themes mentioned here, or invent variations on conventional situations which carry you into the unknown where imagination is your ticket to triumph.

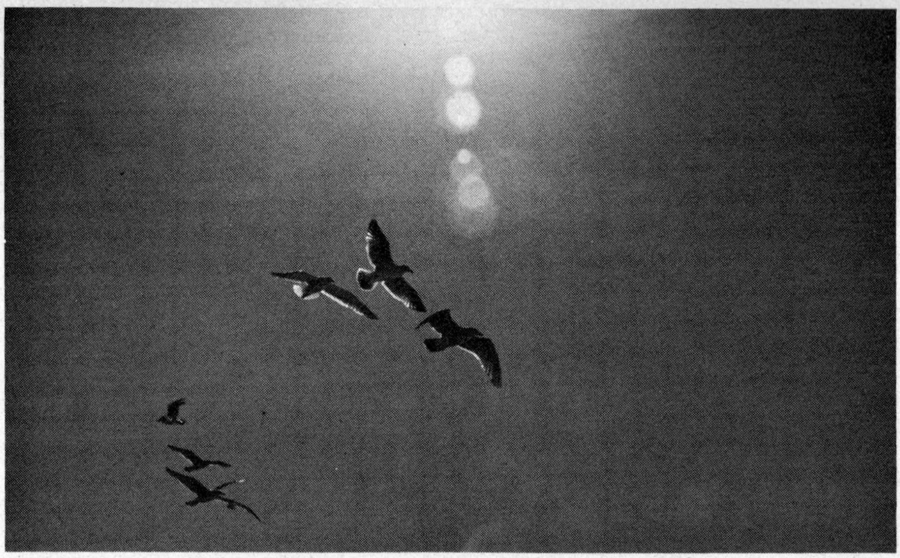
1

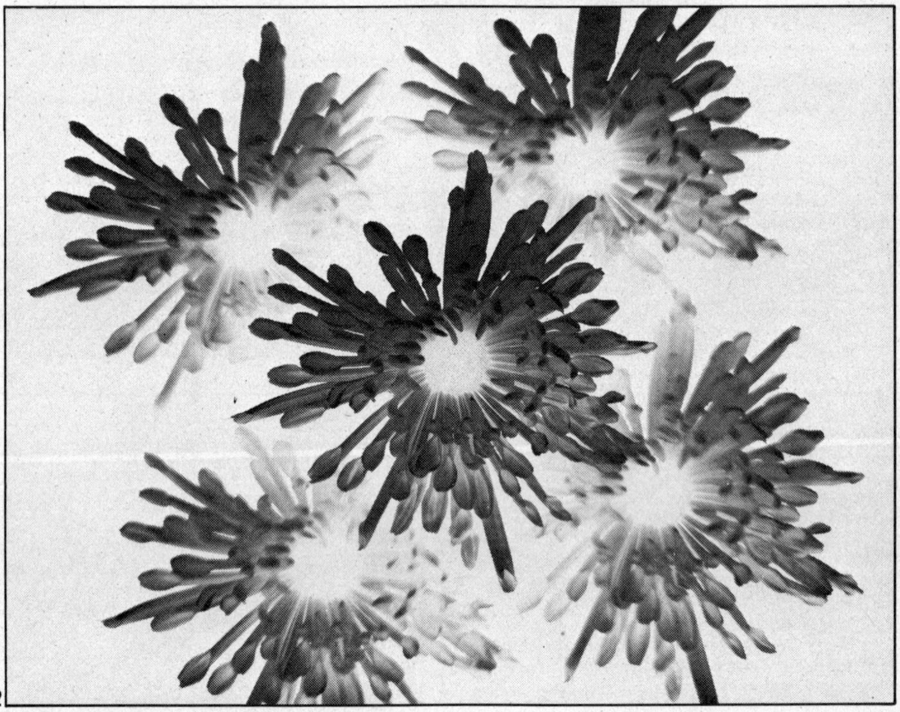
2

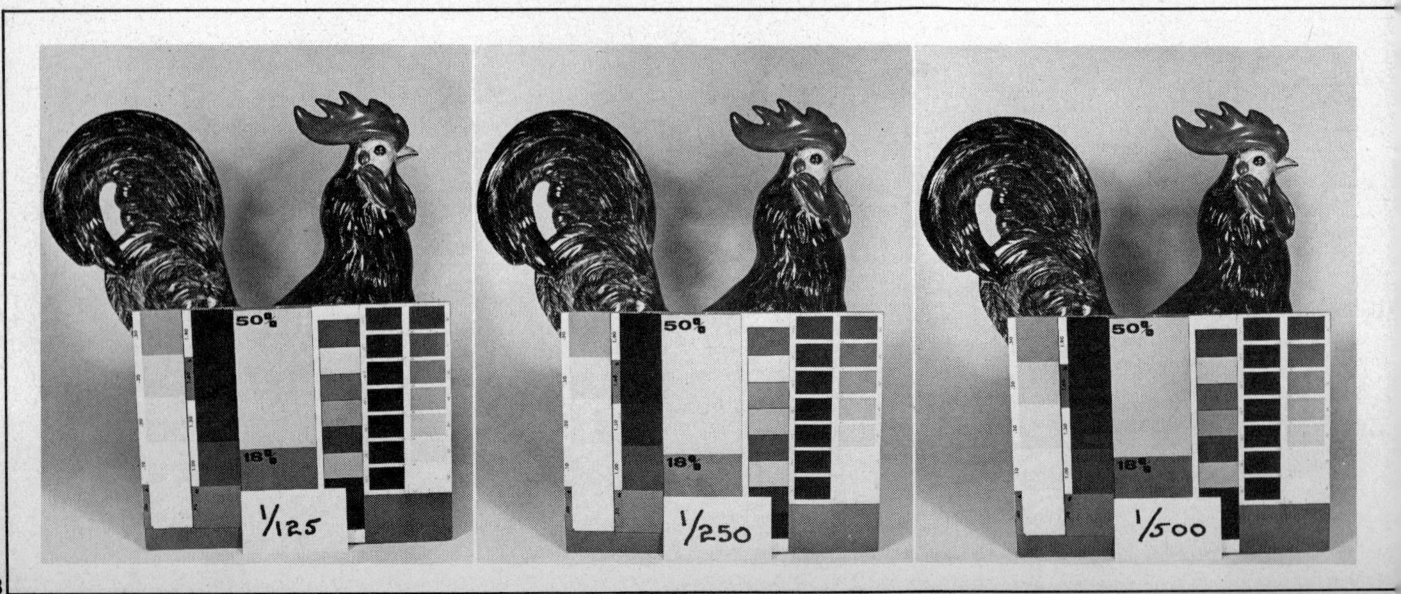

3

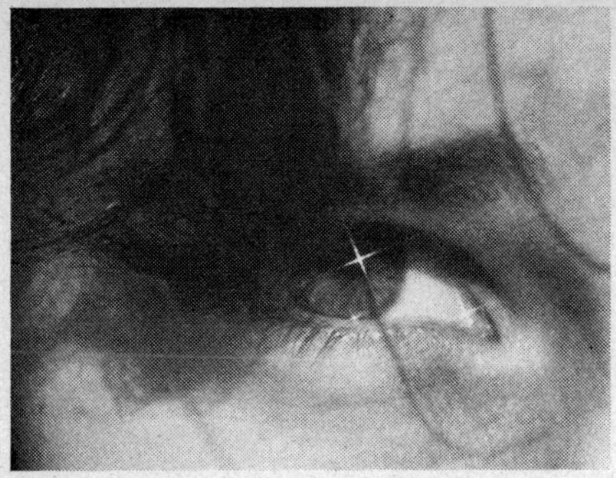

4

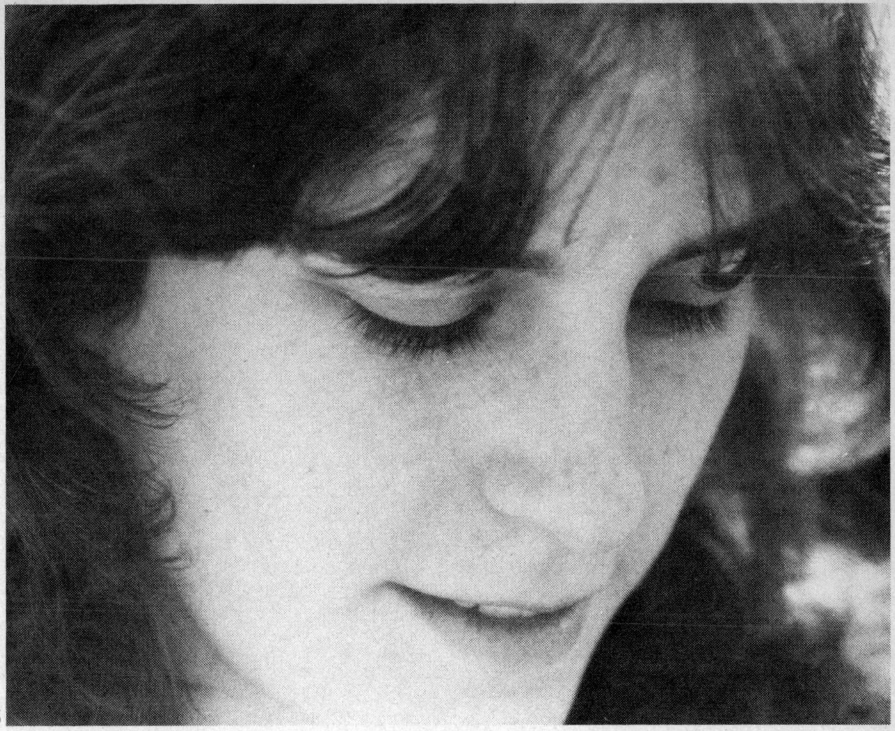

5

1. This effect is called halation. It occurs when you shoot toward the sun. To determine exposure, point your meter off to the side of the sun, then bracket your exposures. Large lens openings produce large hexagons; small apertures produce small ones. Wide-angle lenses will prevent the hexagons from fogging the whole frame.

2. Prism filter produced this star of flowers for photographer Ken Biggs.

3. Series of exposures made on Plus-X film demonstrates failure of reciprocity law for long exposures. Note how exposures are reciprocal for 1/125, 1/250 and 1/500 exposures (opening lens one f/stop each time the shutter speed was halved resulted in equal exposures), yet how loss of film speed becomes more and more apparent at 125, 250 and 500-second exposures. Note loss of steps in gray scale in 500-second exposure as compared to the shorter-duration exposures. When overly long exposures are made on black-and-white films, compensating exposure/development is called for. When long exposures are made on color films, compensating exposure and filtration are called for.

4. Cross-screen filter turns specular highlights into stars, can be used to put sparkle into eyes, add excitement to night shots, or do whatever your imagination can come up with.

5. Cross-screen filter can also be used for diffusion, as in this shot, although special diffusion filters are available for this purpose.

MARK HILBURN'S RECIPROCITY COMPENSATION TABLE FOR BLACK-AND-WHITE FILMS

Exposure time based on meter reading	Exposure time you should use	Development adjustment
½ second	1 second	93%
1 second	3 seconds	90%
2 seconds	8 seconds	87%
4 seconds	20 seconds	84%
8 seconds	48 seconds	81%
15 seconds	105 seconds	78%
30 seconds	240 seconds	75%
60 seconds	540 seconds	72%
120 seconds	1200 seconds	70%

Example: If the meter says to expose for 15 seconds at the f/stop you are using, you should expose the film for 105 seconds, and then develop it for 78% of the time you'd normally develop it.

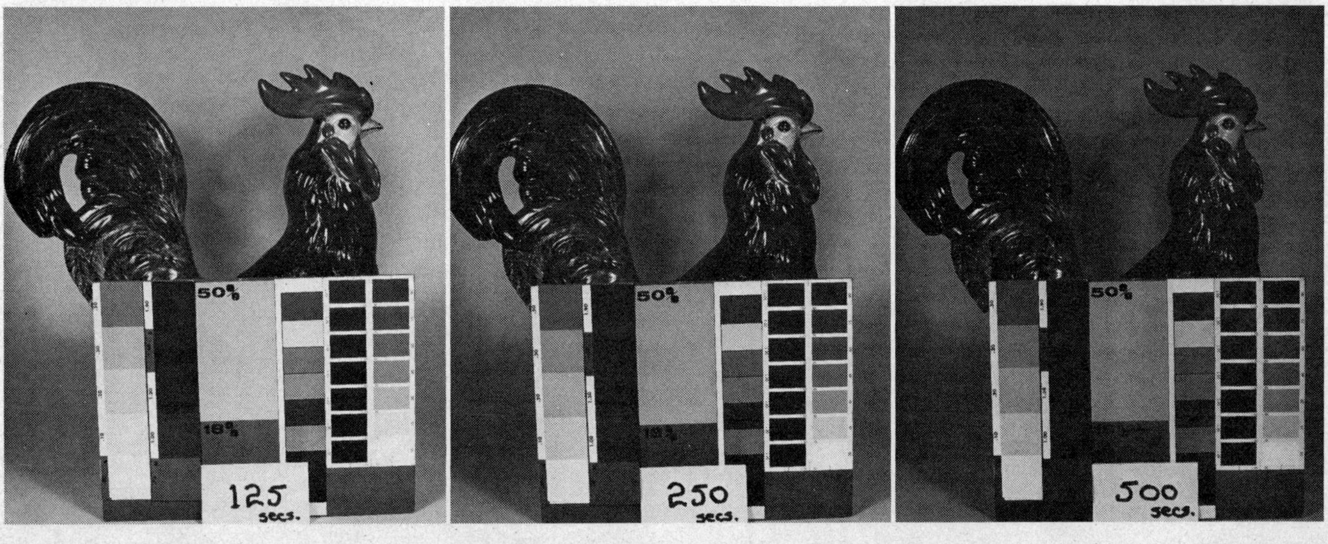

CHAPTER 10 Close-Up Photography

In researching my photo files for this chapter, I came across some long-forgotten prints shot about 1951. At that time rangefinder 35mm cameras were big, and there were only seven or eight SIRs on the market, most of which have since disappeared. I was using a Contax II which focused to about three feet. In order to shoot close-ups with an RF camera, you need a separate finder system and a method of extending a normal lens to make larger, closer images. When a Los Angeles company began making a device called a Speed-O-Copy, I got one for the Contax, and was able to shoot close-ups with minimum complications, accounting for the enlarged pictures of seashells and tree bark I discovered in my files. The Speed-O-Copy, which included a small ground glass finder that hinged out of the way to be replaced by the camera body, still works. But single-lens reflex cameras make close-up pictures so much easier that adapting a rangefinder camera seems unnecessary.

There are four types of close-up accessories from which to choose for your SLR: attachment lenses, extension bellows, close-up rings and macro lenses. In general they all accomplish the same ends with more or less dexterity, versatility and cost. I will describe each system separately and briefly, but first there are a few principles for close-up photography that need explanation.

CLOSE-UP THEORY

Most normal-focal-length reflex camera lenses focus to somewhere between 18 and 24 inches, depending on the brand and design. (Short focal-length lenses such as the 21mm or the 28mm may focus as close as 10 inches without attachments, but they are less suitable for close-ups because of their wide field of view.) Close-up photography is usually defined as taking pictures at distances closer than normal lenses permit in order to extract details of a subject, such as the human eye, still life and hundreds of other possibilities. Copying documents, pictures, etc. often requires close-up photography as well, and many scientific subjects such as insect studies, depend on images magnified larger than life size in color slides or black-and-white prints. In other words, you may be shooting closer than normally for the design possibilities, for functional reasons or merely for fun.

Depth of field/ This is one of several items that must be considered in using close-up lenses or devices. As you know, the closer you are to a subject, the less depth of field you get at any given aperture. By the time you are very close to a subject, just inches away, depth of field is being measured in fractions of an inch. Thus, the combination of nearness and the use of even small apertures results in such shallow depth of field that focus is critical. If you photograph a flat surface, there are few problems, but when you zero in on a three-dimensional object, being able to judge depth of field in the finder is very important to overall sharpness. For this reason, depth of field tables are usually supplied with close-up lenses and devices. Of course, the smaller your aperture, the greater your depth of field, and the more latitude you will have to compensate for tiny focusing errors caused by visual limitations that are only human.

A steady camera/ It follows that when an image is magnified, even the slightest camera movement will also be enlarged in the finished picture. Shooting close-ups from a tripod is therefore a necessity, except when you are outdoors using shutter speeds of 1/250 second or faster. In addition, using a tripod makes composing easier, because even minor shifting of the camera can throw you off target.

Lighting/ When you move very close to shapes and textures, detail is magnified, but even the surface of a sliced orange looks pretty smooth unless you light it in a way that accents its miniature topography. Therefore lights should be placed almost at the same level as the subject, from the side or behind it, in order to see form more clearly. If a surface is rough enough, the light source may be higher, but when you zero in on a smooth surface, you will benefit by placing your floodlights or electronic flash at a low angle. In sunlight, early morning and late afternoon offer the same kind of accent for textures.

At times a lens may be so close to a subject that it is difficult to place a light conveniently. In such cases, for

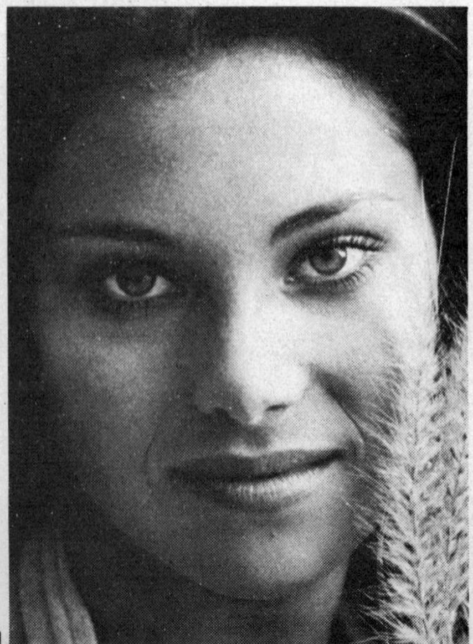

1

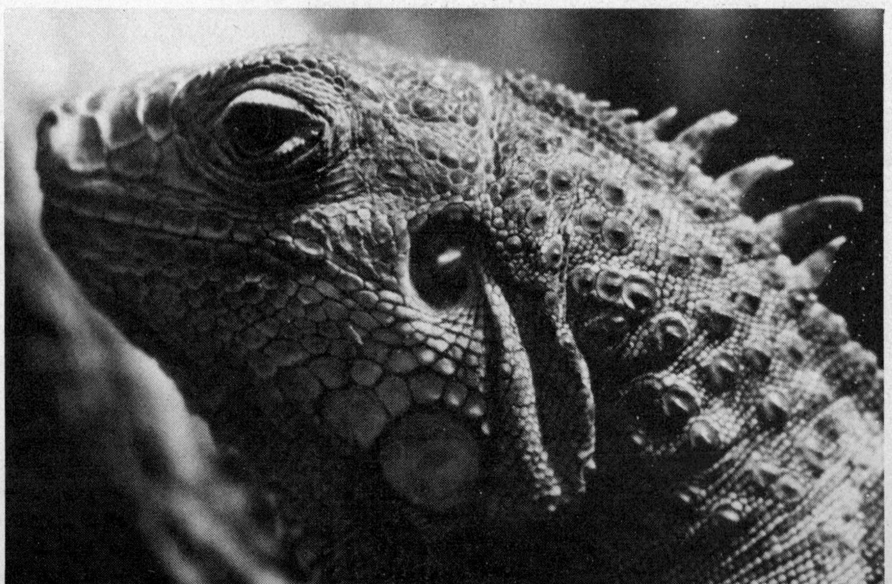

2

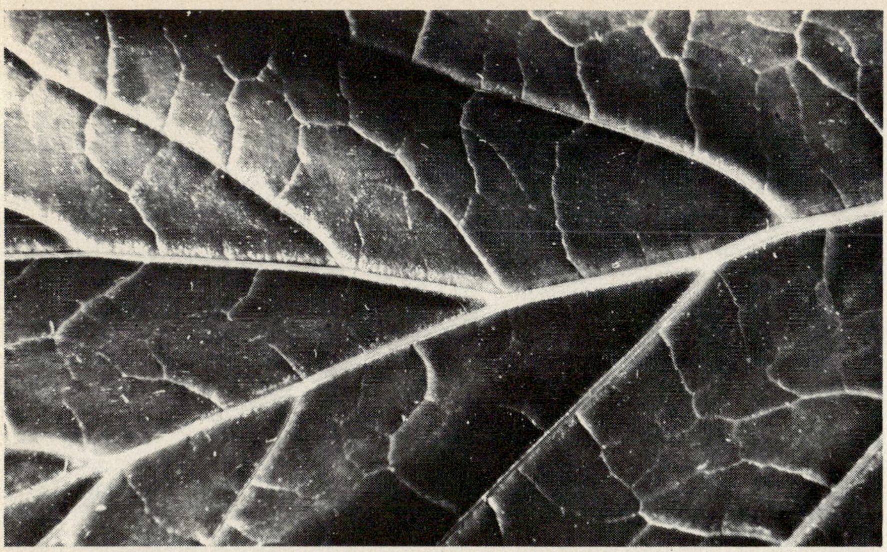

3

example when a dentist photographs a patient's mouth and teeth, there are special electronic flash units made in circular tube shapes which surround the camera lens. These close-up units offer a flat light with minimum shadows, but they avoid the heat of floodlights which might be uncomfortable or damage certain materials.

Lenses/ One way to open the space between the camera lens and the object you are shooting is to use a lens that is longer than those in the normal 50mm range. An 85mm, 100mm or 135mm lens can be adapted for close-up work with attachment lenses, rings or bellows. However, these longer focal-length lenses offer less depth of field at a given aperture, so a normal lens is usually preferable, and even a 35mm lens might suit some subject matter where depth of field requirements are greater.

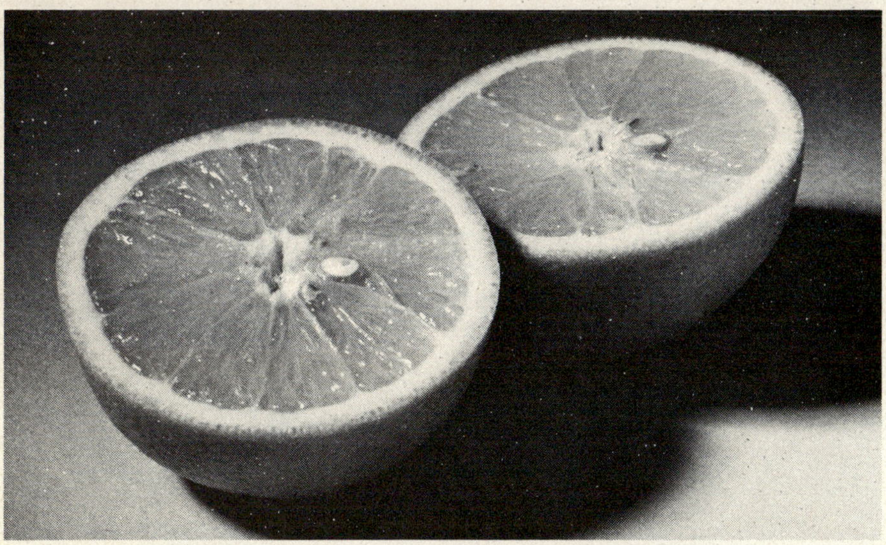

4

CLOSE-UP EQUIPMENT

Attachment lenses/ These are least expensive and most expedient for close-ups. Various camera and lens manufacturers make sets of three close-up lenses which act as magnifying glasses when screwed into the front of a camera lens. Exposure with the camera meter is set in the usual way. In a set of three lenses, #1 may allow you to focus down to 12 or 15 inches, #2 down to 9 or 10 inches and #3 down to 6 or 8 inches. Combining two or all three of the lenses may allow you to shoot only 4 or 5 inches from a subject.

The oranges and the enlarged sur-

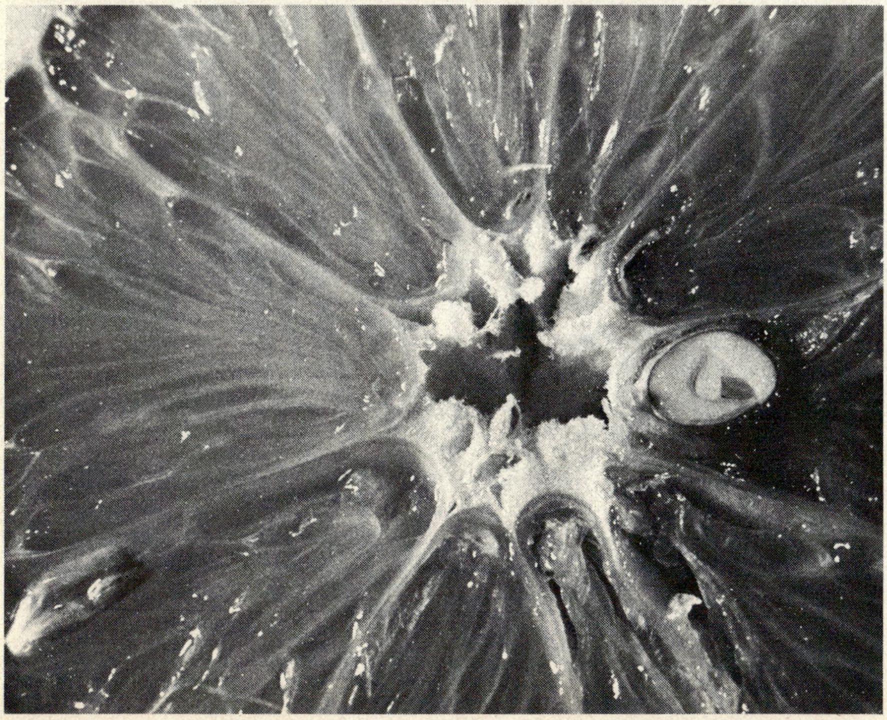

5

1. Some normal SLR camera lenses allow you to focus sharply as close as this, but Jim Cornfield used a macro lens on his camera, which gave him wide range of close-up image sizes.

2. Depth of field is always a consideration in close-up work because even at small apertures it is often measured in inches or fractions of inches. Dennis Krukowski's close-up of iguana is sharp except at nose and along rear edges where his depth of field did not carry. Photo won Scholastic/Kodak Award.

3. Low-level lighting helps accentuate texture in close-ups, especially when surfaces are nearly flat. Section of leaf was shot by sunlight that emphasized form, with 55mm macro lens about four inches away from subject.

4. One close-up attachment lens on normal 52mm SLR lens was sufficient for picture of oranges lighted with single 150W photospot bulb from back left.

5. Full set of three close-up attachment lenses was used for segment of orange, using same 52mm camera lens. Front lens was about three inches from orange, which was lighted with same photospot bulb as longer shot.

face of one orange illustrated in this chapter were shot with a set of $13 close-up lenses. Optically, they may not be as sharp as a camera lens or a macro lens, but the results are quite acceptable. The orange pictures were shot with one 150W photospot bulb, a useful light source for small objects, sculpture and even for certain portrait effects.

Variable focusing close-up lenses are also made to screw into a camera lens or directly into the camera body. Operating on a kind of zoom principle, these lenses change magnification, and therefore image size, as you adjust them. Check your photo supply dealer for the pleasant variety of close-up lenses available, including a special lens that enlarges up to 10 times by itself.

Close-up rings/ Also called extension rings or tubes, these are usually sold in sets of three. One or more rings can be screwed or bayoneted into the lens mount of a camera with the lens screwed or bayoneted into the end ring. Be sure you buy a set of rings made to fit your automatic diaphragm mechanism, or else you will have to open and close the lens by hand before and after exposure. Rings and tubes cost slightly more than attachment lenses, but allow use of the superior camera lens alone.

Bellows/ Extension bellows for close-up work can be bought for $20 and up. The less expensive types operate on a single rail on which you focus and enlarge by running the bellows back and forth to obtain the image you want in the finder. For additional money you can buy a bellows on a double rail (and double extension bellows as well) which offers more stability, especially when extended to some length. You attach the camera lens at one end of the bellows, which is screwed or bayonet-mounted to the camera body at the other end. Use of a bellows offers an infinite latitude of lens-to-subject distances and greater magnification than rings or attachment lenses. There are also slide-copying devices that fit onto bellows. Check the instructions with your bellows to discover if reversal of the camera lens is recommended for more efficient operation.

More elaborate bellows equipment may include provision for automatic diaphragm control, since this feature of a camera is disconnected by a standard bellows. In fact there are some fancy bellows assemblies on the market which cost as much as a medium-priced SLR camera. These are made for very precise photography, and include a series of accesories or adaptors.

Macro lenses/ The word "macro" is borrowed from the Greek and means "large" or "long." In relation to a camera lens, macro indicates a special ability to focus very closely to a subject with no need for attachment rings, lenses, etc. Many camera manufacturers make macro lenses to fit their SLRs, and these lovely optics are usually rated about 55mm and f/3.5. You can recognize a macro lens easily because the front element is usually deeply inset to form a lens hood. While a macro lens may cost $200 or more, it serves many purposes. You can carry the lens on the camera as your normal lens and be able to shoot close-ups with it at any time.

Some macro lenses are made with an adaptor or extender which is attached between the lens and the camera body to make photography possible down to about one inch from a subject. Using a macro lens assures excellent optical qualities, no problems with automatic diaphragm or built-in meter operation and an infinite range of image sizes as large as 1:1. With my macro lens I have photographed a postage stamp actual size, and I also use it to make black-and-white negatives from color slides. I merely set the slide against an opal glass light box, and with my Konica Autoreflex T on a tripod, I can

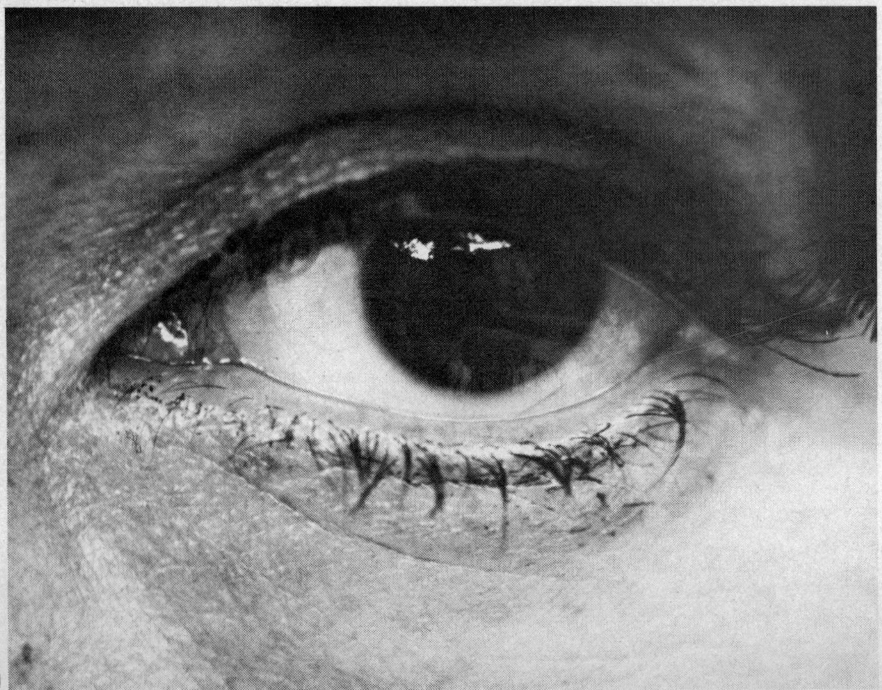

1

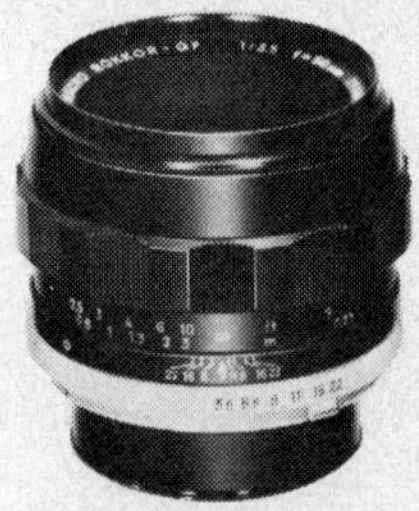

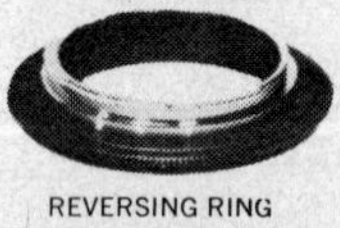

REVERSING RING

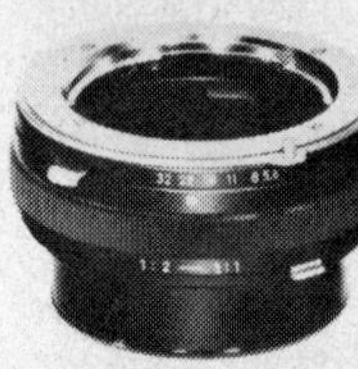

INTERMEDIATE TUBE

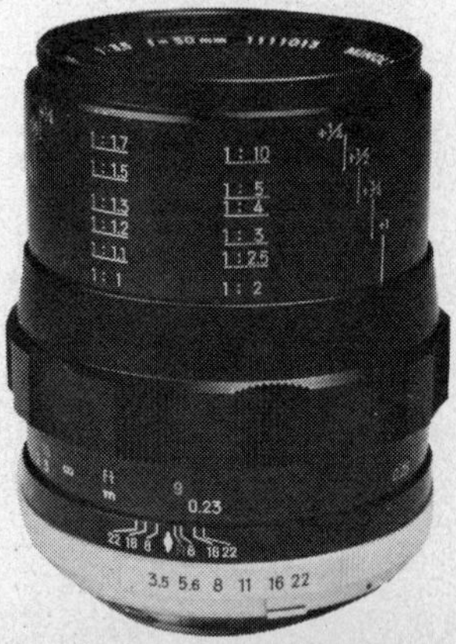

LENS BARREL ENGRAVINGS PROVIDE ALL INFORMATION NEEDED TO DETERMINE MAGNIFICATION RATIO, EXPOSURE FACTOR AND EFFECTIVE APERTURE FOR MACROPHOTOGRAPHY

2

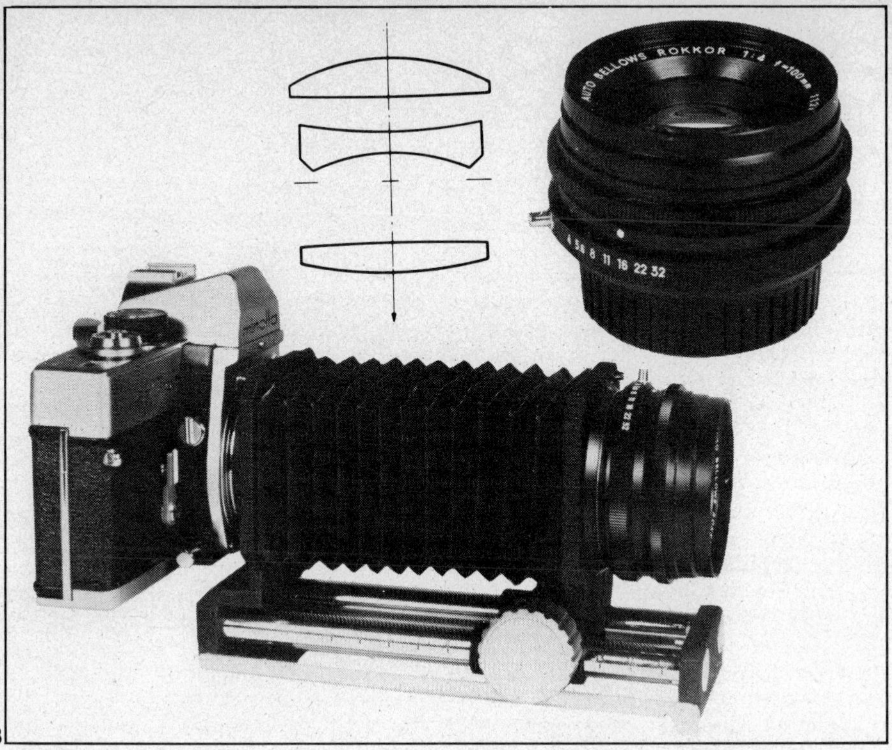

3

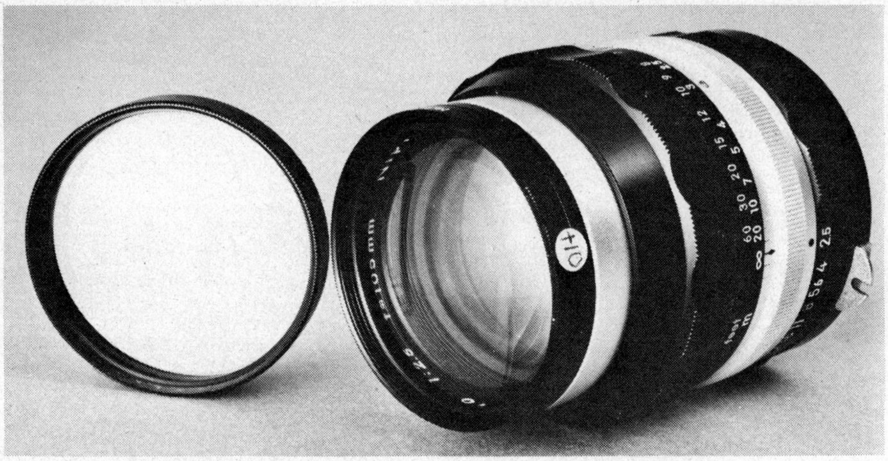

4

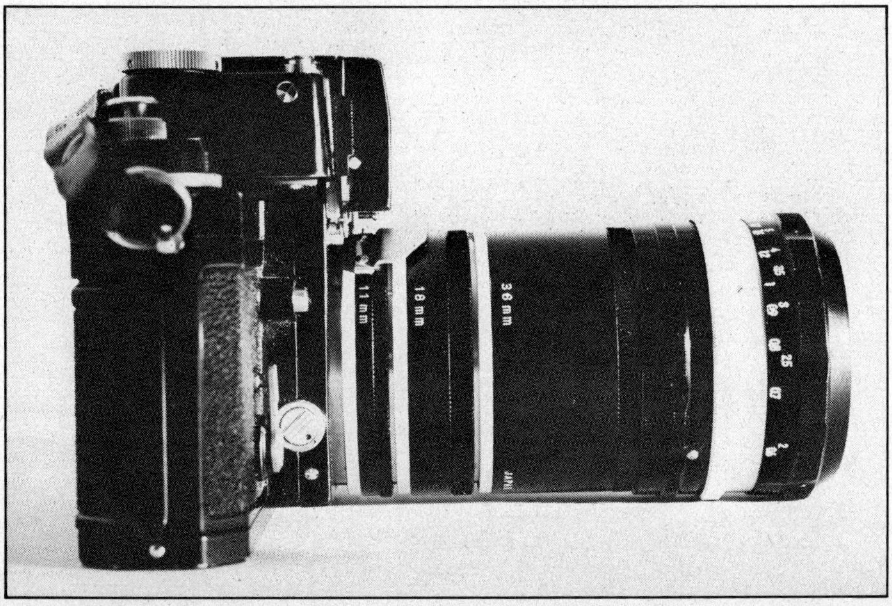

5

reproduce the slide on a full negative. Be sure to keep the slide very clean of dust, and use a medium-contrast film such as Tri-X, since contrast builds up slightly during any copy process.

On the barrel of a macro lens are usually engraved a series of numbers representing distance, magnification and aperture scales to allow compensation for extreme close-up exposures. It is an optical principle that as you focus closer to a subject, you must increase exposure since the *effective* aperture is altered as a lens is extended. Through-the-lens meters make this adjustment automatically when using attachment rings, extension tubes and bellows attachments.

COPYING

Special slide copying attachments are available to fit most SLRs. Some models include a simple lens within, and others are made for use with the camera lens. A copier sets the slide at the proper distance for 1:1 magnification. Check your photo supply dealer for information about copiers, lighting and films. In general the use of electronic flash and low contrast color films gives the best results.

To copy flat materials such as photographs or documents, inexpensive copy stands are available. These include a base and a pole similar to those found on an enlarger. A camera mount slides up and down on the pole, and with some stands it is possible to use a bellows assembly on your camera. You may choose a stand with arms and light sockets for photoflood bulbs at each side, or simply set a couple of your own floodlights to illuminate the material being copied.

Close-up photography is a varied world of its own into which you should venture for the fun of it. With a small investment you will be seeing many common objects and surfaces in new and intriguing ways.

1. Macro lens focused at two inches produced negative of just the eye. Camera was hand-held, so f/8 at 1/250 second allowed minimum depth of field.

2. Typical macro lens with accessories is Minolta/Rokkor 50mm f/3.5. Figures on lens barrel indicate magnification ratio for extreme close-ups.

3. Minolta/Rokkor 100mm f/4 Auto Bellows lens is made especially for close-up work using bellows.

4. Close-up attachment lenses look like filters and are attached to lens like filters—very simple set-up.

5. Extension tubes are a relatively simple way to extend lens-film distance.

CHAPTER 11 The Pleasures of the Darkroom

Throughout this book I have emphasized the desirability of *control* over exposure, composition, print quality, etc. It is one thing to shoot pictures and hand them off to a processor, and quite another experience to handle them yourself. I am not suggesting that you worry about developing color negatives or transparencies, but I do feel that color printing is being enjoyed by more hobbyists, and will touch on these subjects later.

What I *am* suggesting is that in order to better grasp the fine points of photography, and get more satisfaction from camera work as well, if you develop your own black-and-white film and enlarge your own black-and-white prints, this involvement will inevitably stimulate your growth as a photographer. You will build skills on a foundation of mistakes corrected by your own hands and eyes. Your training will lead to discoveries of the nuances in printing and composition, resulting from negatives as excellent in quality as you can produce. When you are really serious about photography, having a darkroom in which to work will become a compulsion!

THE DARKROOM

Darkrooms may be built in various places: in a basement, a section of a garage, on a service porch, in a bedroom, in a spare room or structure, or by temporarily converting a bathroom or kitchen. (Note the photo of my friend Harvey Hill's portable setup.) My first darkroom was in a basement, and my second one in a wine vat adjacent to my work as a topographic model-maker in a small Algerian town about 1943. Since then I've converted several bedrooms into darkroom-offices, carrying water from nearby bathrooms. Today I have a custom-built darkroom with running water. Though it is only a modest 5 by 12 feet, I know from experience that one can turn out professional work in less convenient circumstances than he might think.

No matter where you settle or reconcile yourself, there are several basic requirements for a darkroom:

1. It must be blacked out completely by light-proof shades, baffles over windows or any method that is convertible or permanent.

2. Ventilation is necessary, often provided by a special light-proof exhaust fan set into the wall between the darkroom and an adjoining indoor or outdoor area. Photo supply shops carry such fans.

3. An air conditioner may substitute for the fan, and can be a blessing in the summer. In winter a heater is essential unless your air conditioner includes a heat pump.

4. The space need not be large nor the furnishing elaborate. You need tables for an enlarger, paper, trays and film developing (the kitchen sink will do when there is proper light control), plus storage for materials, and

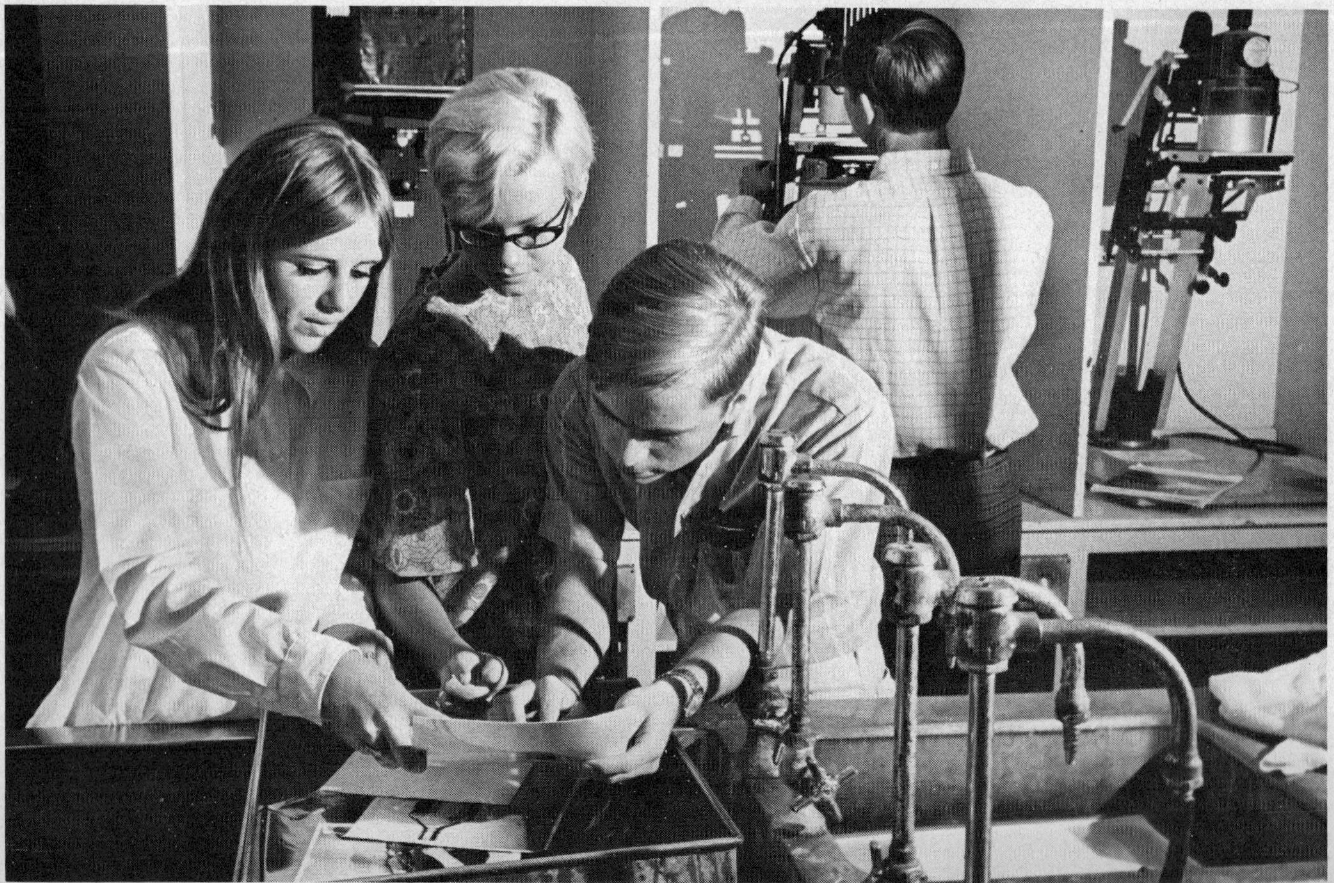

1

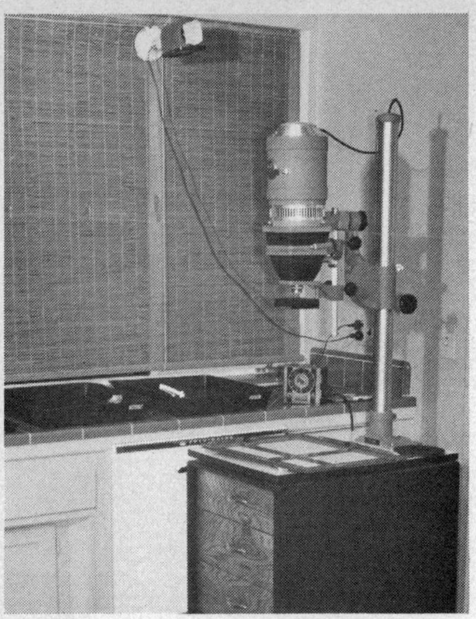

2

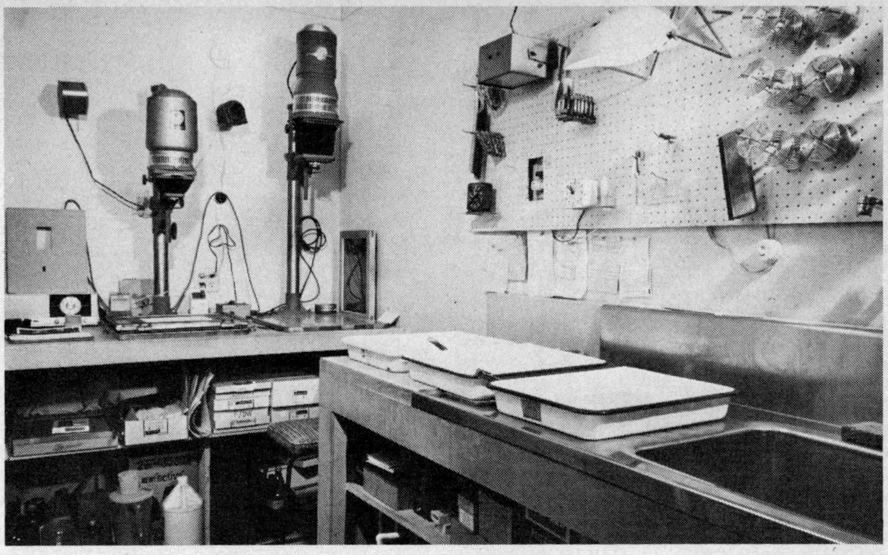

3

1. These high-school teens have the advantage of working in a darkroom to polish photographic techniques they learn in class and on location. Photo was made with one electronic flash unit on long extension at right, 35mm lens.

2. Author's friend Harvey Hill built rolling unit with drawers for paper and equipment, which he uses in blacked-out kitchen at night. Safelight is hung from top of blind; trays are in and on sink. At right of sink is electric timer for enlarger.

3. Author's darkroom is 12 feet long and 5 feet wide. Sink is former restaurant equipment; inspection light over hypo tray uses 40W bulb. Developing equipment hangs on pegboard.

4. All the equipment needed to process your own film is shown here. After initial investment (which can be somewhat reduced by using materials found in the home), you need only periodically replace the fixer and developer.

5. Developing tanks come in many varieties. In front row are stainless steel types professionals prefer. In back row are less expensive plastic tanks. Both types are good.

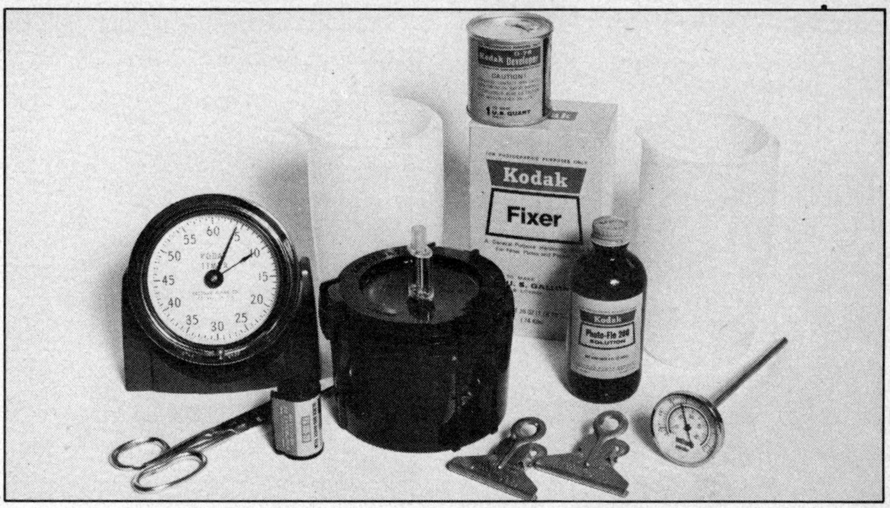

4

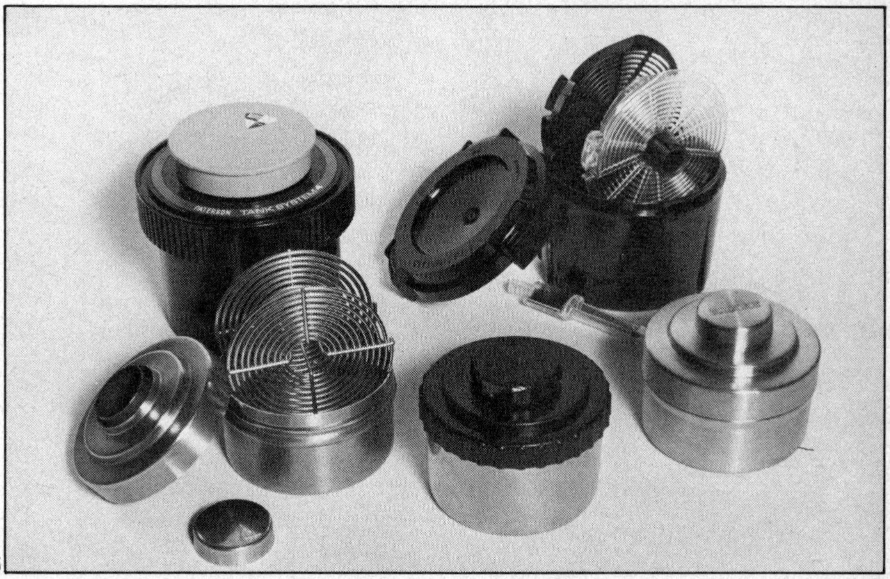

5

enough room to circulate between work surfaces. A sink in the darkroom is lovely, but you can prepare chemicals and wash prints or films in adjacent bathrooms, laundry sinks, and the like.

If the room you convert is carpeted, throw an inexpensive or used rug on the floor, or take up the carpet and store it. Throw rugs or padding are welcome on concrete or hardwood floors, and asphalt or vinyl tile floors are ideal because they clean easily.

Darkroom layout/ Location of work surfaces depends on the space available. Draw an informal plan to scale and fit the table sizes to the room. In my darkroom it is three feet from the sink to the opposite wall, which is plenty of room to walk, even when film is hanging to dry from wires extended along the black wall. Ideally, the table on which you enlarge should be apart from the surface where you develop film and prints. In other words, it is helpful to have separate wet and dry areas.

Darkroom tables must be quite stable (no card tables), and may be built of 2x4s, either attached to walls or free-standing Tops may be plywood at least half an inch thick, either coated with chemical-resistant paint or covered with a material such as Formica. Design table height to your own convenience. Mine are 38 inches high, 24 inches wide on the wet side and 27 inches wide where I enlarge. Under the tables build suitable storage shelves and compartments for bottles, cans, trays and gadgets. Plan the wet side long enough to accommodate three 11x14 trays in a row for developing prints, plus room for another tray in which to store prints until they are washed. The latter tray can be placed in the sink if you are lucky enough to have one.

On the dry side you need room for an enlarger and a box of paper, plus space to sort and handle negatives. My table is five feet wide, but I have two enlargers on it. Paper boxes and a small paper cutter are placed on the base of one enlarger while I'm printing with the other.

As for a sink, you can build a trough from plywood at least 2x2½ feet and 8 to 12 inches deep. Coat the surfaces with a liquid fiberglass material that is waterproof and fills the corners. (Check camera or paint stores for this.) You can also buy various sizes of new or used sinks in porcelain or stainless steel. (Mine is used restaurant equipment six feet long including aprons.) A faucet should be high enough to place a gallon bottle beneath it. You don't need a thermostat to control water temperature for black-and-white work, but such equipment is useful for color processing.

You need at least two safelights in convenient sizes with filters to match the papers in use. Fasten one safelight above your dry area and the other over your developing tray. Even if your room has a ceiling fixture, you may want to add a couple of work lights: one above the dry area for preparation of negatives, etc., and the other over the fixer tray by which to inspect prints. For the latter, a 40W bulb in a fixture between 24 and 30 inches above the tray is best.

There are many kinds of ready-made tables, cabinets, shelves, etc. that can be adapted for a darkroom. Check used furniture stores and even so-called junk shops where you may find bargains.

Outfitting the darkroom/ Some basic equipment may be more economical to buy in combination kits including trays, so inquire at your friendly neighborhood camera shop. Mean-

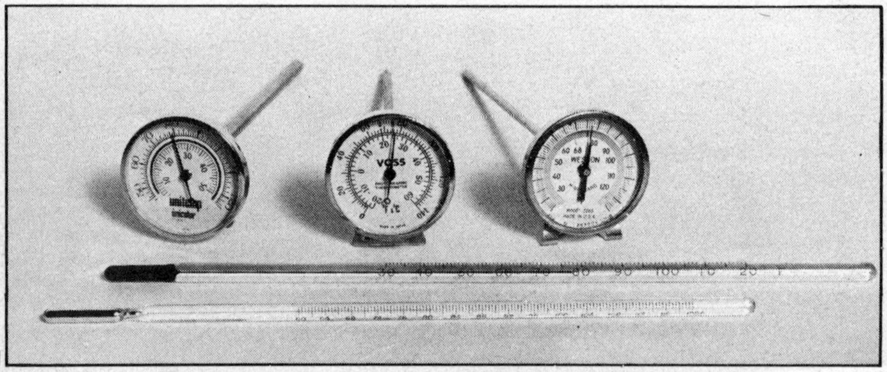

1

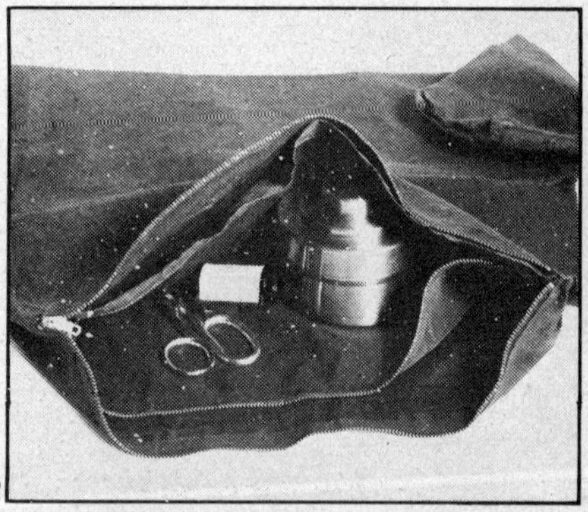

2

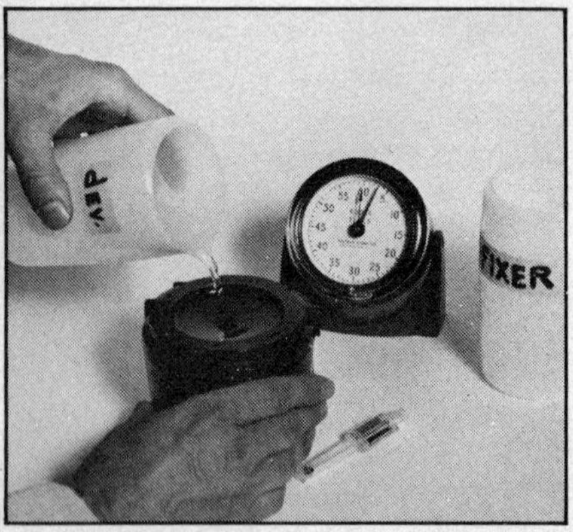

3

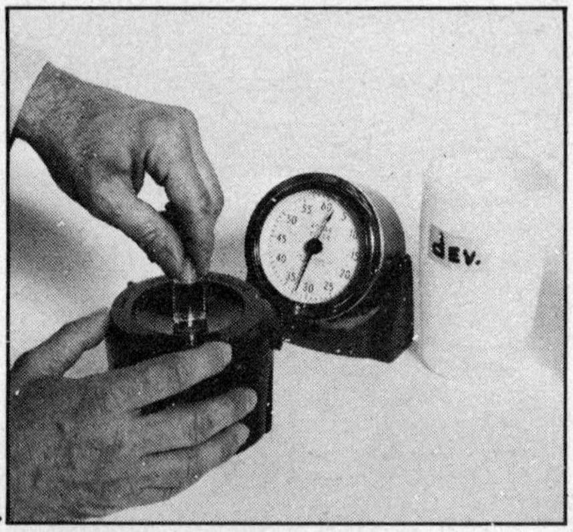

4

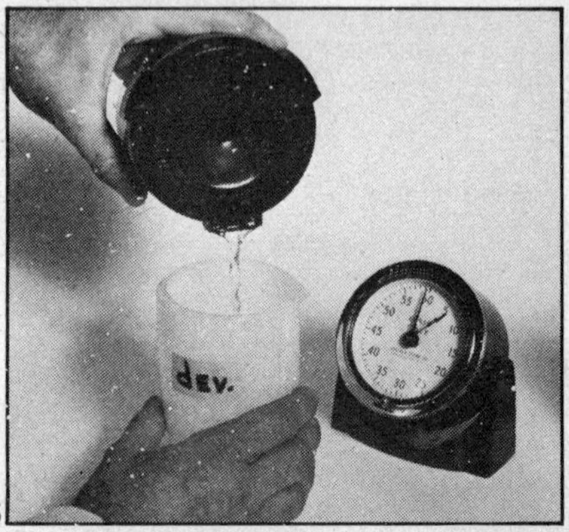

5

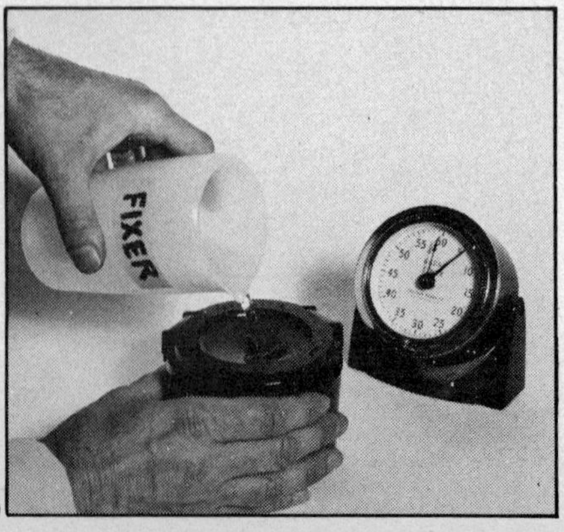

6

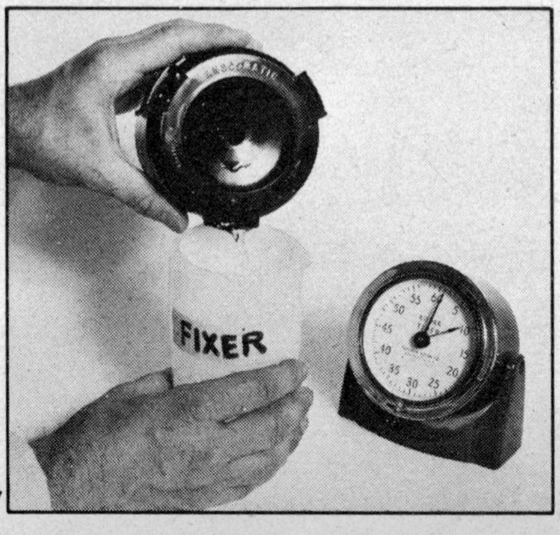

7

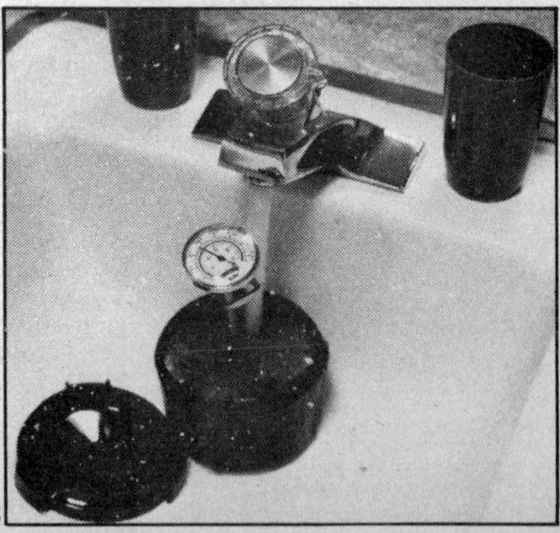

8

DEVELOPING BLACK-AND-WHITE FILM

IN LIGHT

1. Prepare chemicals and bring them to proper temperature (see manufacturer's instructions)

IN DARK

2. Load film into developing tank and put lid on tank

IN LIGHT

3. Pour developer into tank, agitate as per manufacturer's directions for length of time recommended by manufacturer, then pour developer out of tank
4. Rinse film in running water for 30 seconds
5. Pour hypo (fixer) into tank, agitate as per manufacturer's directions for length of time recommended by manufacturer, then pour hypo out of tank
6. Uncover tank
7. Wash film in running water according to film manufacturer's directions
8. Hang film up to dry

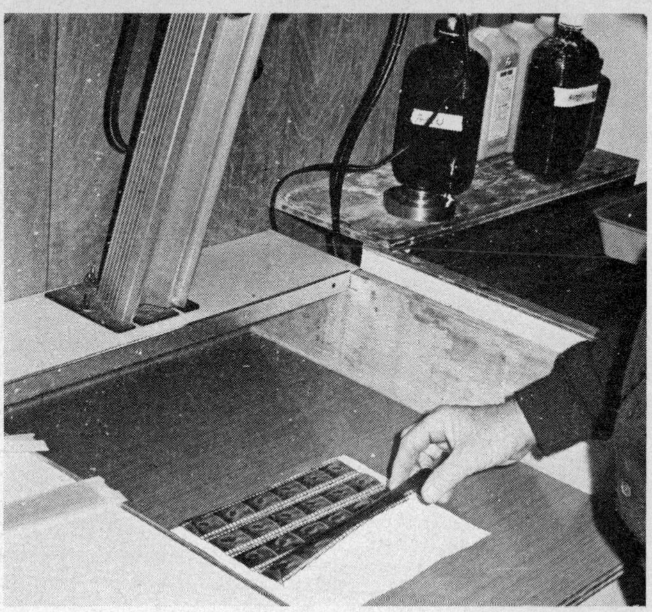

9

1. Capillary type thermometers (front) have alcohol or mercury columns, with mercury being preferred. Dial types are easier to read.

2. Darkroom is not a necessity. Most photo dealers sell changing bags like this one, which zips closed, allowing tank to be loaded in room light.

3. With film in developing tank, and all chemicals prepared and at proper temperatures, set timer to proper developing time, and pour developer into tank quickly.

4. Agitate the film in tank as per developer manufacturer's directions. This tank employs agitating rod; some have caps and are inverted several times to agitate film.

5. When timer tells you developer has been in tank long enough, pour it out.

6. Now you can (1) give film a 30-second rinse in running water, (2) use a stop bath as per manufacturer's instructions, or (3) just pour in the hypo, reset timer and agitate.

7. After fixing cycle is completed, pour hypo out of tank.

8. Remove lid of tank and place under running water. Use your thermometer to monitor temperature of water. All solutions should be within five degrees of developer's temperature.

9. To make contact proof sheet, lay out strips of negatives (under safelight illumination only) on sheet of printing paper, neatly.

10. In low light levels, such as this dimly lit stage, use of high energy developer allows you to use faster shutter speeds or smaller lens openings. Tri-X, 1/60 second at f/3.5 and 135mm lens were used.

while, here is a list of necessary items:

1. At least four plastic, enamel or stainless trays, 8x10 or 11x14. I usually use the larger size, even for 8x10 prints, because I can develop two at a time more dexterously.

2. An enlarger that accommodates the size(s) of film you use. There are many good ones on the market, some with automatic focus. A modestly priced enlarger may be quite adequate, but it is worth the extra money to buy a quality enlarging lens, because it will pay off in superior sharpness and tonality—which are inseparably linked. If you intend to print color negatives, inquire about enlargers with color heads.

3. A timer into which you plug your enlarger. The timer can be set for up to 60 minutes and automatically turns off the enlarger after the chosen interval of exposure time.

4. An enlarging easel, preferably one with four adjustable margins, that accepts paper up to 11x14 inches. Non-adjustable easels may be expedient, but allow for no cropping, which can be frustrating.

5. Stainless or plastic tongs to handle prints; one pair for the developer and another for shortstop and fixer.

6. An interval timer for developing film and drying prints; a clock or watch will do, but a timer reminds you more effectively.

7. A contact printing frame of which several types are made.

8. A paper cutter that may be stored on a shelf under the enlarging table, or brought to the darkroom from another part of the house.

9. A soft brush, or a blower or a can of compressed air to dust negatives (and the insides of cameras).

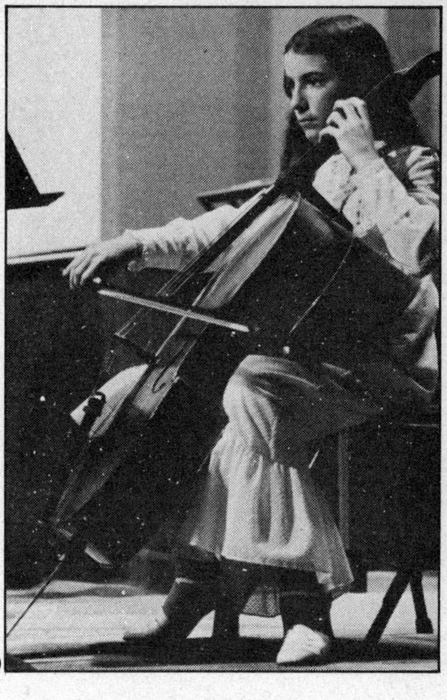

10

10. A reliable thermometer, preferably one with a long stem that inserts easily into chemical bottles.

11. A print washer, or tray siphon (made in several sizes and prices).

12. A print dryer, either flat or drum-shaped, and a squeegee to wipe excess water from prints before drying.

Most of the above equipment will be used for enlarging, and some for developing negatives as well. Following are additional items for film developing activities:

1. Tanks, either hard plastic or stainless steel, and reels of the same materials, made for each size of film or adjustable. Stainless steel is expensive, but will not break.

2. A container with drain holes at the bottom in which to wash films.

Special film washers activated by water pressure are also available.

3. A double squeegee sponge to remove water from the surface and sprocket holes of 35mm films, and an ordinary straight automobile windshield wiper blade for remaining moisture.

4. A place to hang film to dry, such as wires strung high enough in a low-traffic area where a minimum of dust will circulate. Fasten stainless clips as weights to the bottom of each roll of film to prevent curling.

5. A pair of scissors to cut film from spools, and an ordinary beer can opener to pry the bottom from 35mm cartridges.

Darkroom chemicals/ These come in several brands, and I have a certain degree of favortism toward some because they work for me:

1. Film developer(s) either recommended by the manufacturer of the film or by a camera shop, usually supplied in powder form. I use Microdol-X for normal development and Acufine for extra film speed, though other developers such as D-76 and UFG are also popular. Test any developer before using it to determine if the manufacturer's time and temperature charts suit your needs. I add about two minutes to Kodak's recommended time for Tri-X in Microdol-X because I prefer more negative contrast, but I follow the Acufine charts religiously when using that product.

2. Paper developer such as Dektol which I find works equally well on Kodak, Du Pont, Agfa and GAF materials. I mix my Dektol one part stock solution to one part water because I prefer the contrast properties it offers, but you may use two parts of water as well. To 12 ounces of water I add a heaping teaspoon of sodium carbonate which seems to give me better blacks and overall tonality.

3. Fixer (also called hypo), any brand, regular or fast; use one gallon or batch for paper and a separate gallon for film to assure cleanliness of the latter.

4. Acetic acid which you add to your water to make shortstop used between paper developer and fixer. *Use water only* to rinse film before fixing, as acid may cause tiny pinholes in the emulsion.

5. A hypo neutralizer in which to soak films and papers (in sperate batches again) before washing. This inexpensive chemical cuts washing time considerably and saves water as well. Kodak's Hypo Clearing Agent, Orbit Bath or Hustler Rapid Bath are all good.

6. A small squeeze bottle of hypo test liquid to check for exhausted fixing solution.

7. A wetting agent for prints, such as Flexigloss, whether you dry them glossy or not, to prevent curling. Orbit Bath and Hustler Rapid are sup-

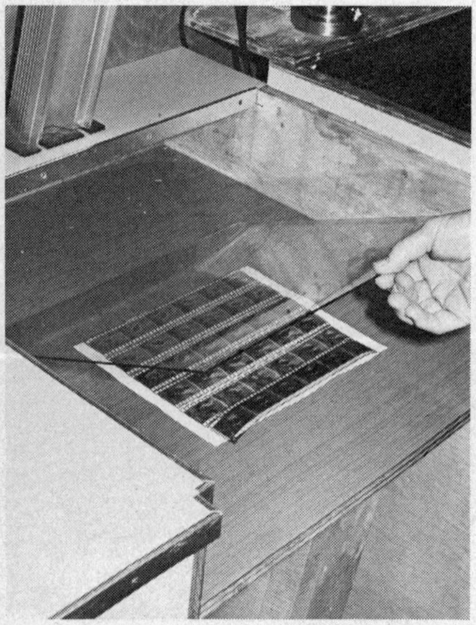
1

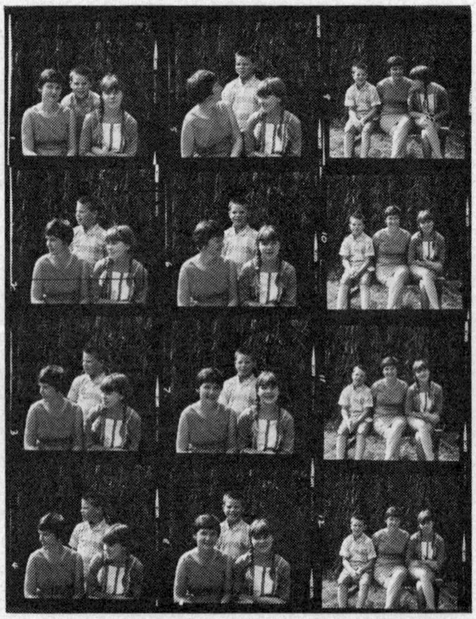
2

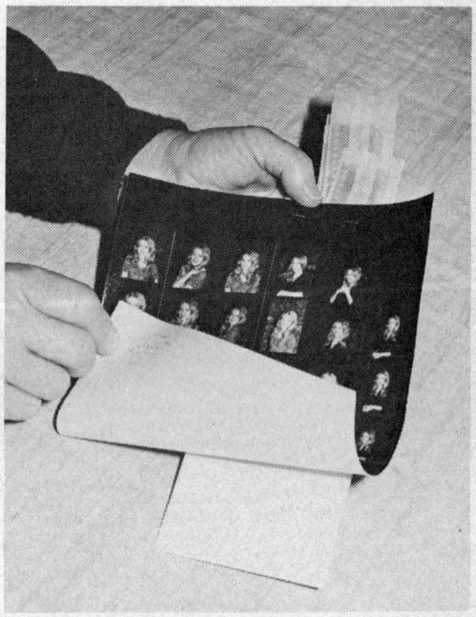
3

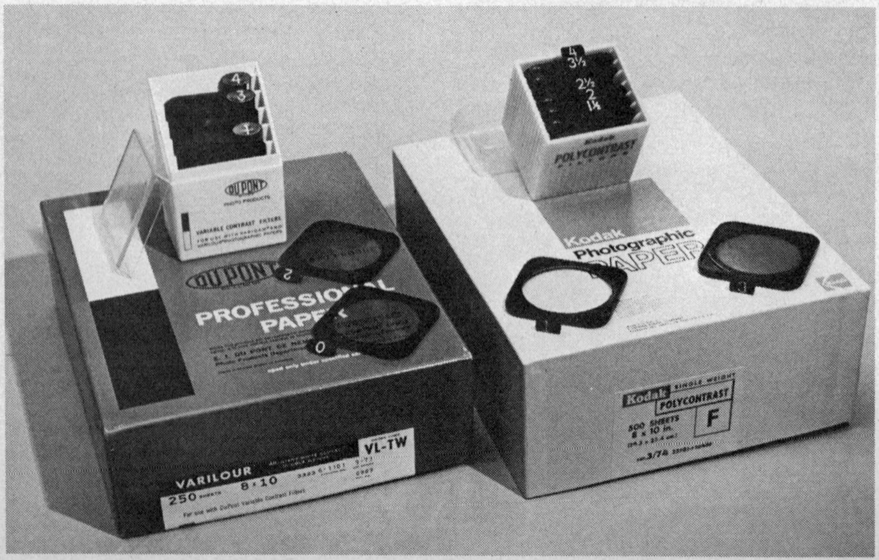

4

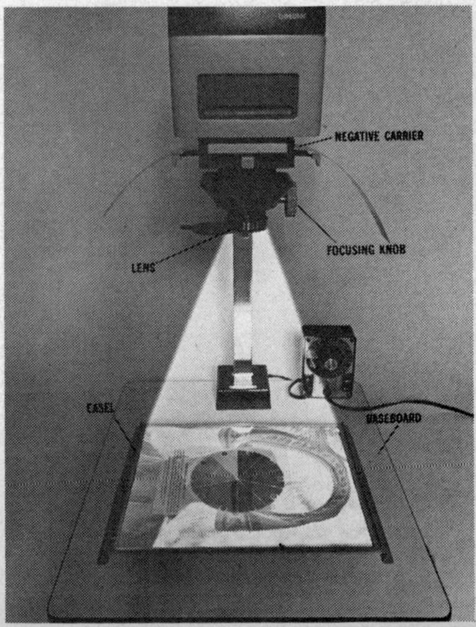

5

posed to do this job as well as neutralize hypo.

DEVELOPING FILM

This and the section on enlarging are necessarily digested, since whole books have been written on these darkroom arts and skills.

Loading a stainless spiral reel such as the Nikor can be tricky until you get the hang of it, after which it's a breeze. The one prerequisite for handling film is *never* to touch it except by the edges, though you can grasp the leading end surfaces when fitting it into a reel. Fill the tank before loading reels, after which you can load reels in a dark closet if necessary; after the tank is capped, the rest of the process continues with lights on. I rinse film in running water in the dark, and place it in already-poured hypo, but the same procedures can be accomplished in the original capped tank.

Agitate film 15 seconds at first, and 5 seconds each 30 seconds thereafter. Twirl the reel gently in a plastic tank. Lift a stainless tank, turn it upside down, and revolve it half a turn each time during agitation. In this way film develops evenly without streaks or overdeveloped skies.

Rinse film in running water or by filling the tank several times and emptying it. Agitate film for about 10 seconds when it is first placed in the hypo, and then agitate for a few seconds each minute. You may expose fixed film to light after only 15 or 20 seconds, but allow it to fix for approximately twice the time it takes for the milky backing to clear away.

Wash film five minutes after using a hypo neutralizer, and hang to dry. Yankee makes an alcohol solution called Instant Film Dryer which will dry film in 5 to 10 minutes depending on weather and temperature, if you are in a hurry.

Cut 35mm film into strips of six frames each and store them in envelopes. Cut 120-size film into strips of four at first. See Chapter 13 for filing details.

Keep some old bath towels and a good sponge handy to wipe water and chemical residue from darkroom work surfaces. Wash tanks and reels thoroughly. Dried chemicals show up

1. When negative strips are laid out neatly on paper, cover them with sheet of plate glass to hold them in flat contact with paper (otherwise they will be out of focus on proof sheet).

2. Typical contact sheet of 2¼x2¼ film allows you to view whole roll of film without printing each frame individually. Contact prints from 35mm film should be viewed with magnifying glass for details. Crop marks can be made on proof sheet.

3. If you don't shoot a lot of film, you might write data for each roll on back of proof sheet, put negatives in envelope stapled to back for storage. If you shoot a lot of film, see chapter 13 for filing and storage details.

4. Leading variable-contrast papers and their filter sets are shown here. Either set of filters may be used with either Kodak or DuPont papers.

5. Enlarger is basic piece of enlarging equipment. Easel holds paper.

6. Best timer for print making is enlarging timer with sockets for enlarger and safelight plugs.

7. Inexpensive enlarging computer is an enlarging luxury.

8. Kodak tray siphon is least expensive efficient way to wash prints.

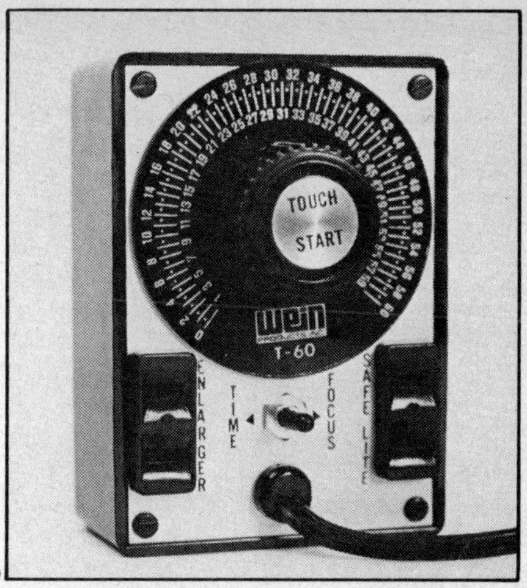

6

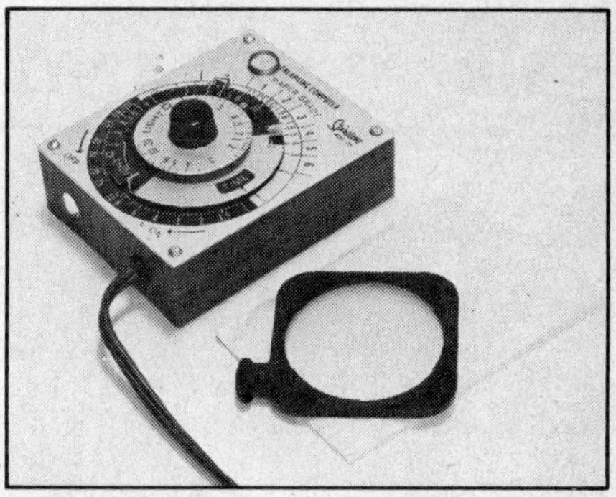
7

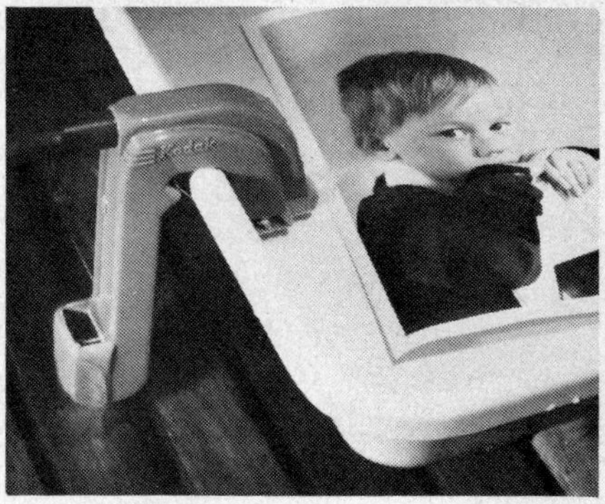

8

MAKING A BLACK-AND-WHITE ENLARGEMENT

IN LIGHT

1. Prepare chemicals and bring them to proper temperature (see manufacturers' instructions)
2. Select a negative to print, clean it with a Staticmaster brush, and put it in the enlarger's negative carrier

IN DARK (under safelight illumination)

3. Crop and scale negative by raising or lowering enlarger head and moving easel, then focus negative on easel, all with enlarger lens wide open
4. Set enlarger lens and timer to proper exposure time *
5. Put a piece of enlarging paper in easel, emulsion side up
6. Expose paper
7. Place paper face up in developer tray and agitate by rocking tray for 2½ minutes
8. Remove print from developer tray, let it drain into developer tray for a few seconds, then place it in stop-bath tray
9. Agitate print in stop-bath tray for 10 seconds
10. Remove print from stop-bath tray, let it drain for a few seconds, then put it into hypo tray and agitate for 30 seconds

IN LIGHT

11. Leave print in hypo tray, with occasional agitation, for 5-10 minutes
12. Remove print from hypo tray, let it drain, then put it into print washer, or water-filled tray with running water for washing. Wash for length of time recommended by paper manufacturer
13. Dry prints in print dryer, blotter roll, or just leave on tabletop (curl can be removed by carefully rolling dried prints against curl along edge of table)

* Proper exposure is determined by means of test strips. Cut a sheet of enlarging paper into narrow strips, stop the enlarger lens down halfway, and expose one strip for 5 seconds, one for 10 seconds, one for 20 seconds, and one for 40 seconds. Process the strips as described in steps 7-10 above, and examine. Determine proper exposure from appearance of test strips. If none of test strips seems properly exposed, make another set of them, first opening or closing the lens a stop or two. (Open the lens if all the test strips are too light; close the lens if all the test strips are too dark.)

as white, powdery stains which indicate sloppiness that may cause problems later. Cleanliness saves a lot of time and effort, avoids stains and dirt on prints and negatives, and reduces print spotting time to a minimum. If super-cleanliness does not become a darkroom habit, you're in trouble!

CONTACT PRINTING

Using either contact printing paper, which is relatively slow, or enlarging paper, which saves time, you place film against paper, emulsion to emulsion, and make one sheet for each roll in the printing frame you choose. Expose by room light, or better yet, place your frame under the enlarger and operate it via the electric timer. Wet or dry, you can then edit your contact prints and decide which negatives to enlarge.

ENLARGING

This is the nitty-gritty of darkroom work where aware judgment about printing and composition supports and displays your artistry with a camera. Here are a series of important points to help polish your techniques:

Enlarging papers/ There are two types, graded and variable contrast (VC). The former is made in grades numbered 1 through 6. Lower grades are softer, which means they are lower contrast, for use with higher-contrast negatives when the scale of tones needs to be softened or compacted. A somewhat overexposed negative with dense highlights will print better on a No. 1 paper, and a No. 2 is considered "normal," which is open to personal interpretation, but is a base for reference. No. 3 and higher numbers are called harder pa-

1. Kodak Projection Print Scale is inexpensive enlarging aid, helps you determine proper exposure. Place it on top of printing paper in easel, make one-minute exposure with lens at intermediate f/stop. Process paper, and read proper exposure time from circle in best-appearing segment.

2. Best appearing segment of Print Scale said 16 seconds, and here's print exposed for 16 seconds.

3. Comparison of variable-contrast papers: DuPont Varilour and Kodak Polycontrast, exposed without filters and through each of their filters.

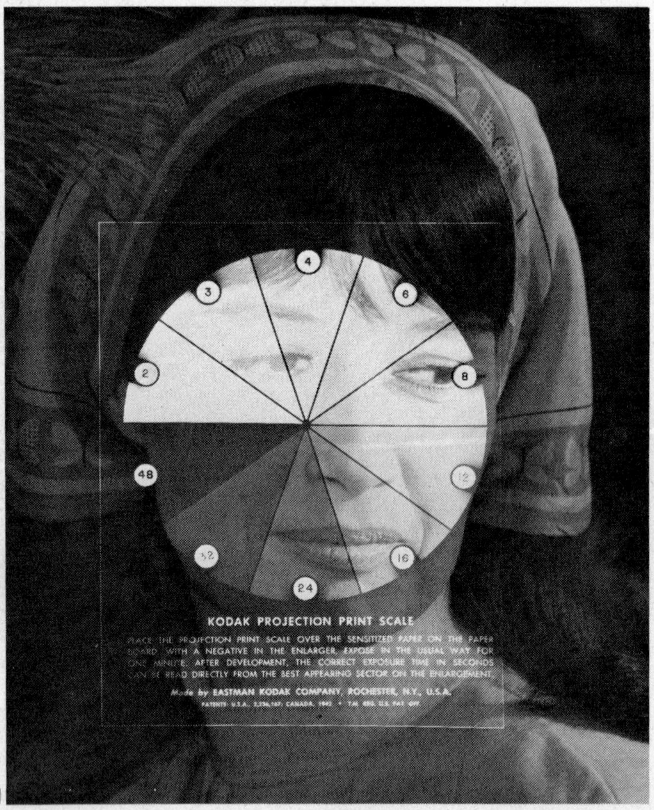

1

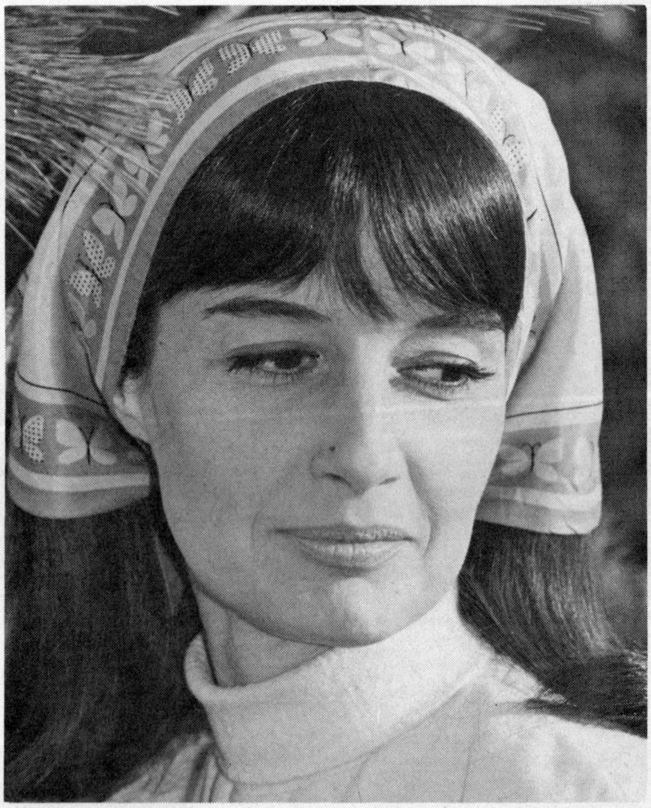

2

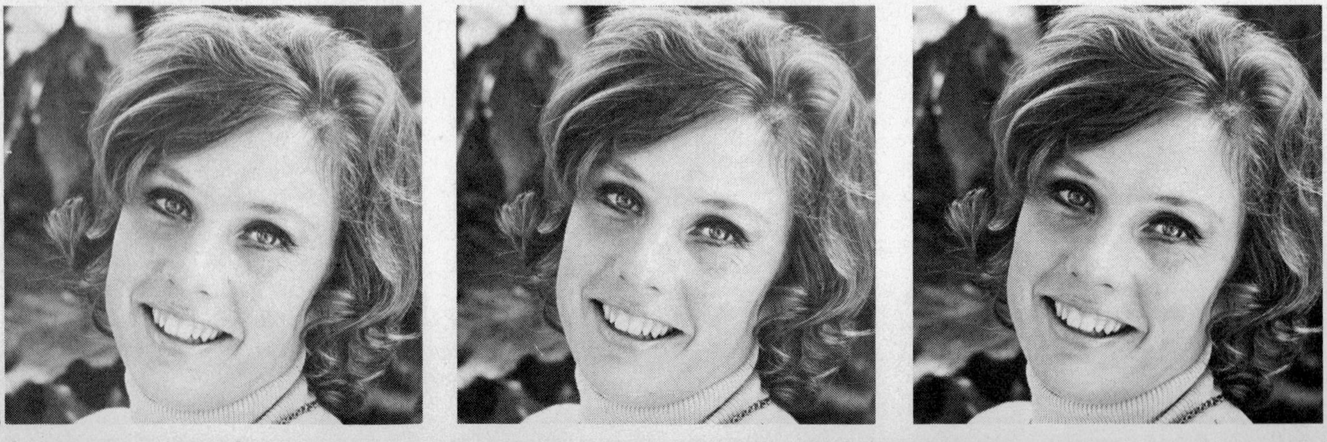

3

Varilour, No. 00 filter | *Varilour, No. 0 filter* | *Varilour, No. 1 filter*

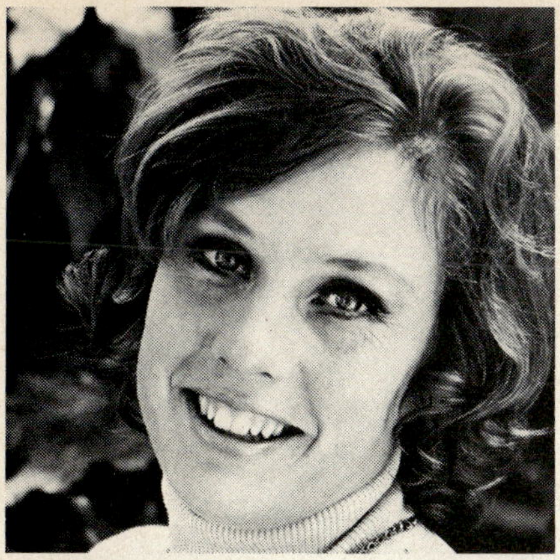
Varilour, no filter

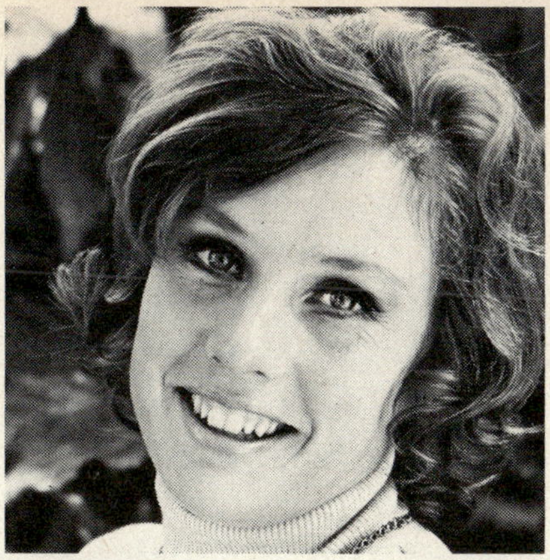
Varilour, No. 2 filter

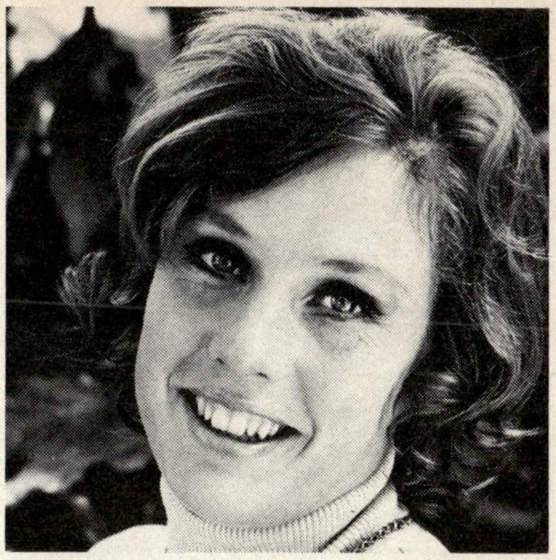
Varilour, No. 3 filter

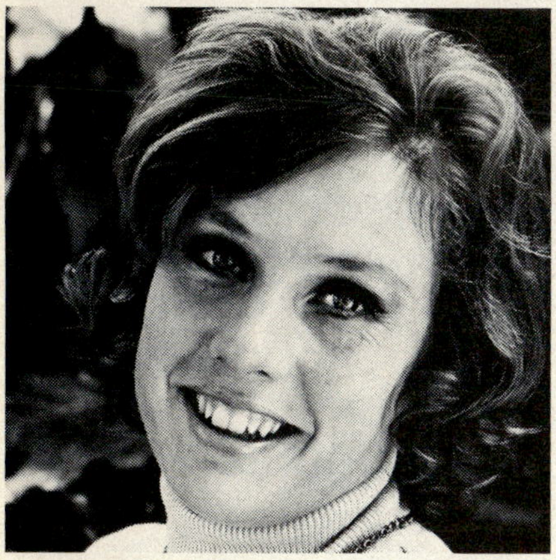
Varilour, No. 4 filter

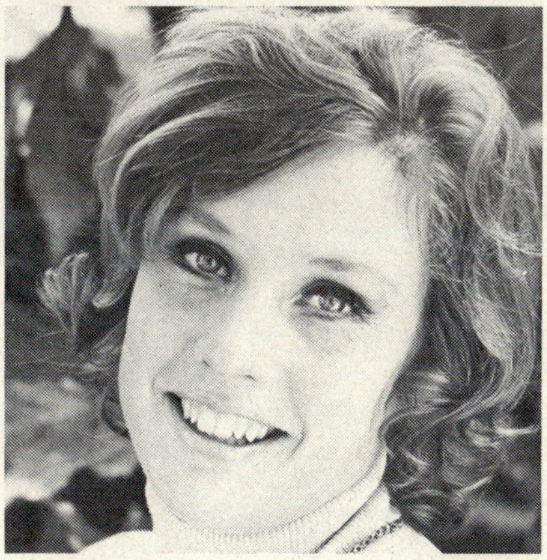
Polycontrast, No. 1 filter

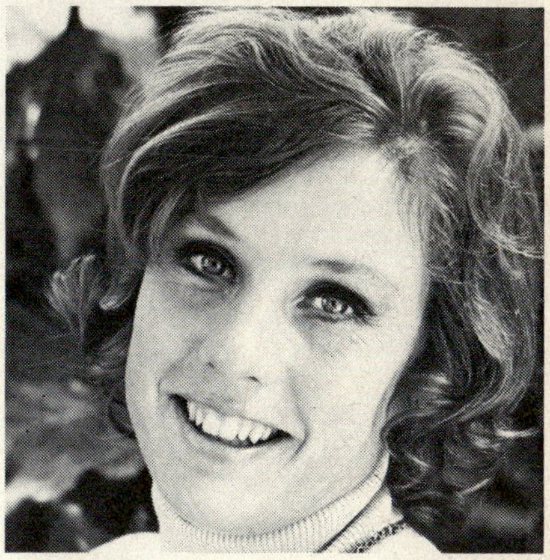
Polycontrast, No. 1½ filter

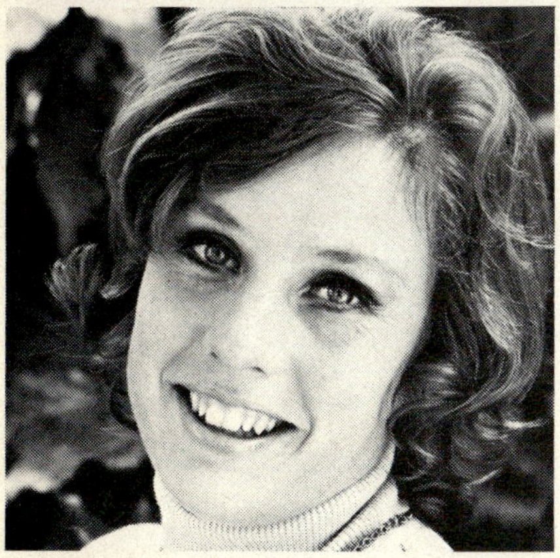
Polycontrast, no filter

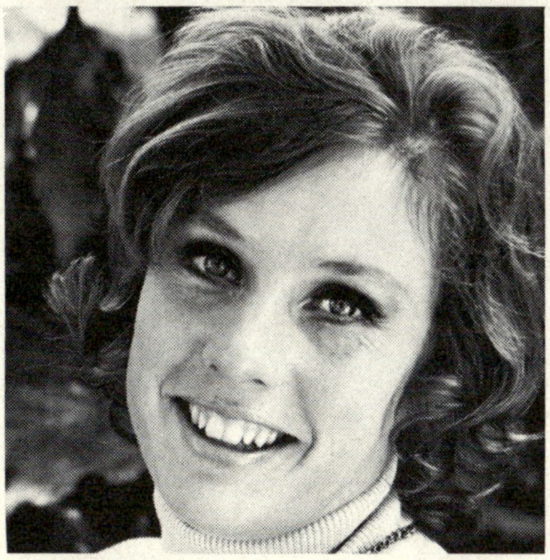
Polycontrast, No. 2 filter

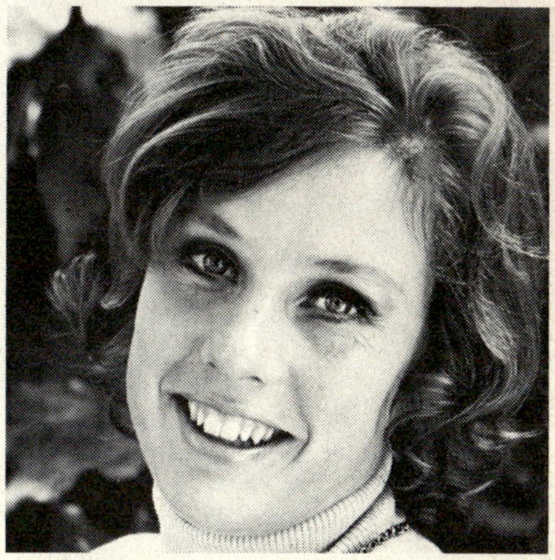
Polycontrast, No. 2½ filter

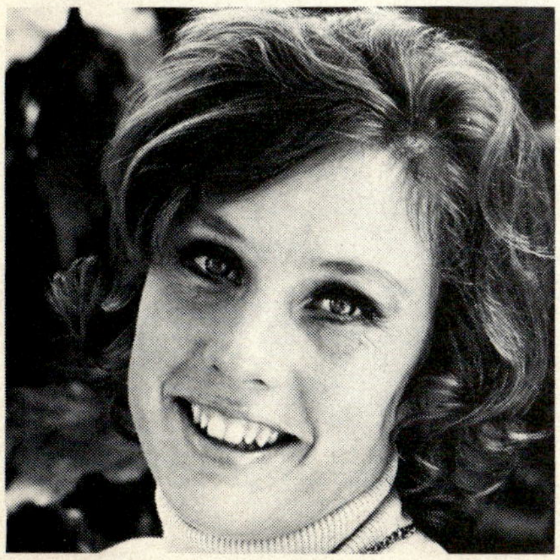
Polycontrast, No. 3 filter

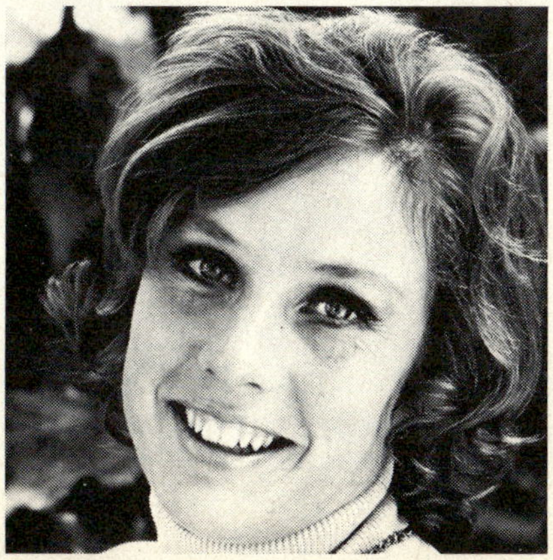
Polycontrast, No. 3½ filter

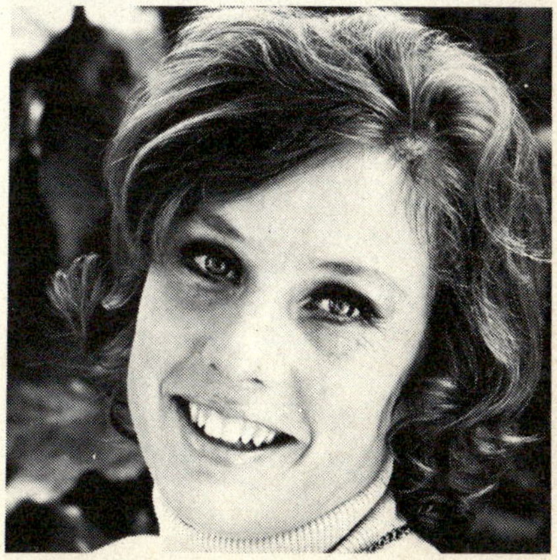
Polycontrast, No. 4 filter

pers, meaning they produce more contrast and are suitable for slightly thin to very thin underexposed negatives. Higher contrast grades expand tonality, producing both blacks and whites in place of dark grays and pale grays that might result from using softer papers.

It is so common to use a No. 3 grade of paper as "normal" that no stigma is attached. Nos. 4 through 6 will save your life with thin negatives, even at the expense of a slightly reduced scale of tones and a somewhat apparent grain pattern in Nos. 5 and 6. In general Nos. 1, 2 and 3 papers will be sufficient for the average printer.

Variable-contrast papers are made in one grade only, and respond to a scale of contrasts from No. 1 through No. 4 by printing through variable-contrast filters. Having written a book about VC paper *(How To Use Variable Contrast Papers,* AMPHOTO, New York, 1970), I admit prejudice, though many professionals prefer graded papers, and top-notch prints can be made on either type. Papers include Kodak Polycontrast regular and Rapid, Du Pont Varilour and Varigam and GAF VeeCee.

Kodak Polycontrast filters are made in a set of seven (1, 1½, 2, 2½, 3, 3½ and 4) and Du Pont VC filters come in a set of five (0, 1, 2, 3 and 4) with a very soft No. 00 available. Filters are interchangeable, meaning that you can use either set on any brand of paper. I used Polycontrast papers and filters for years until Du Pont improved Varilour and their fil-

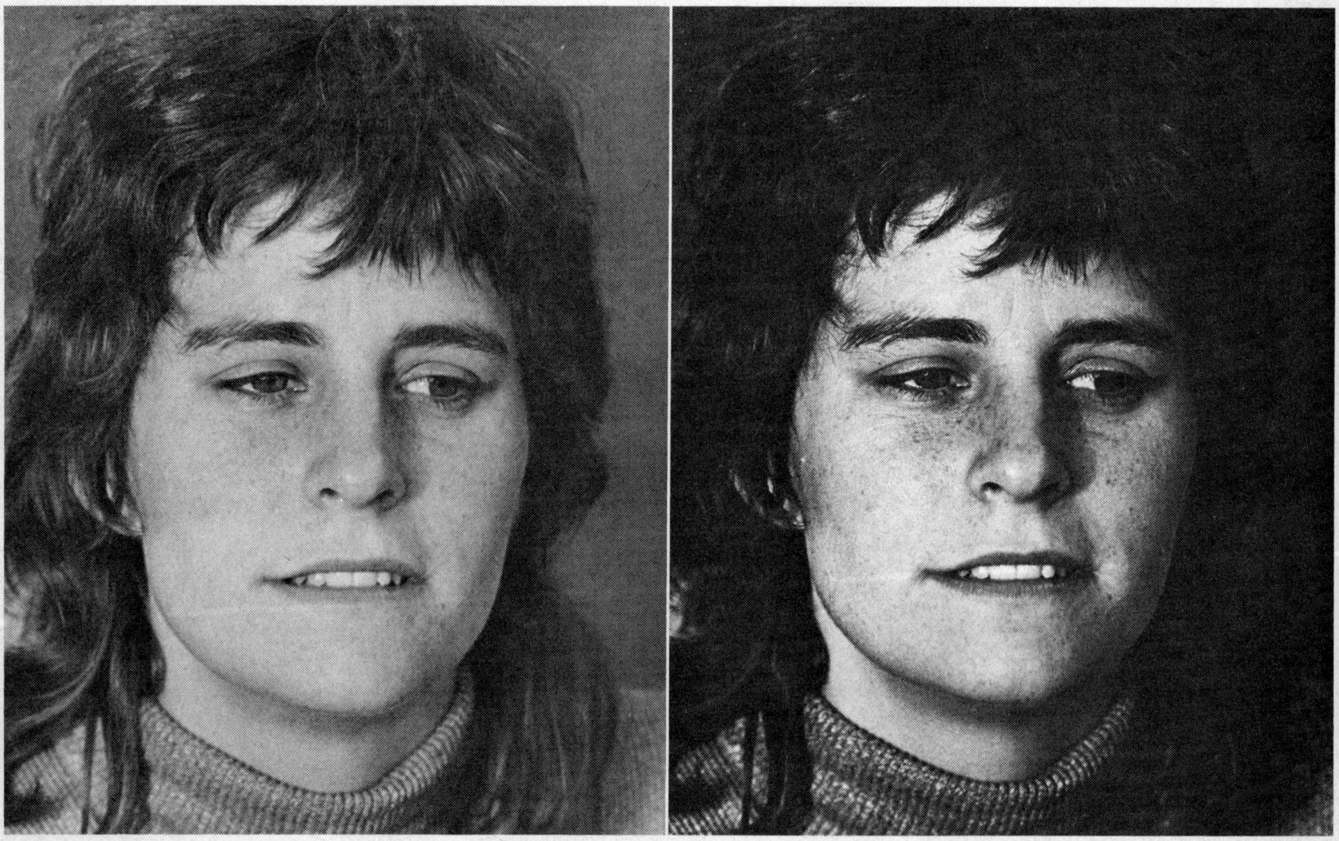

1

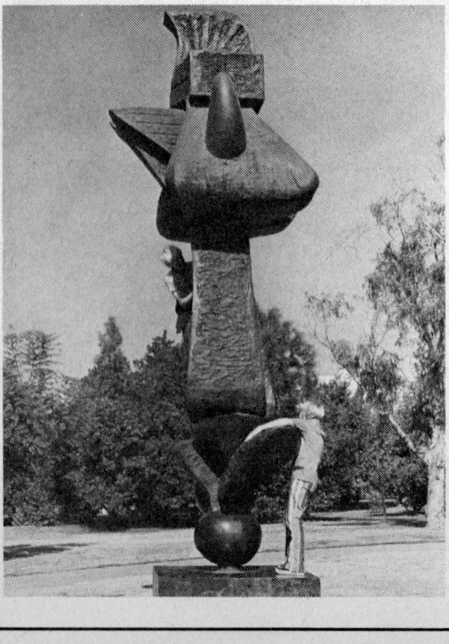

2

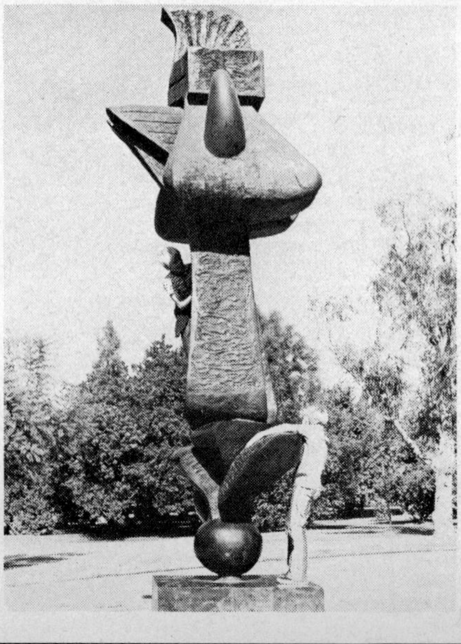

3

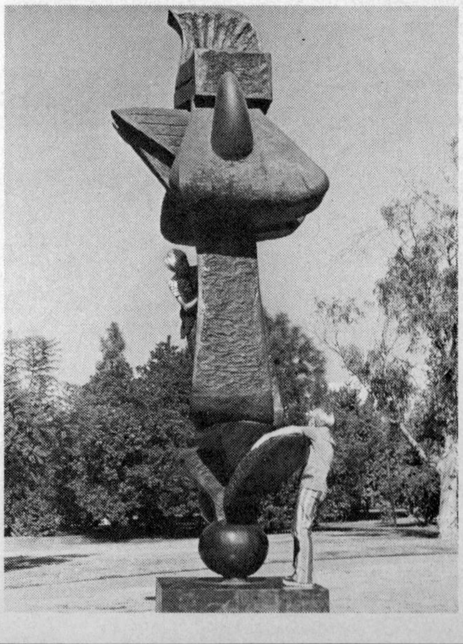

4

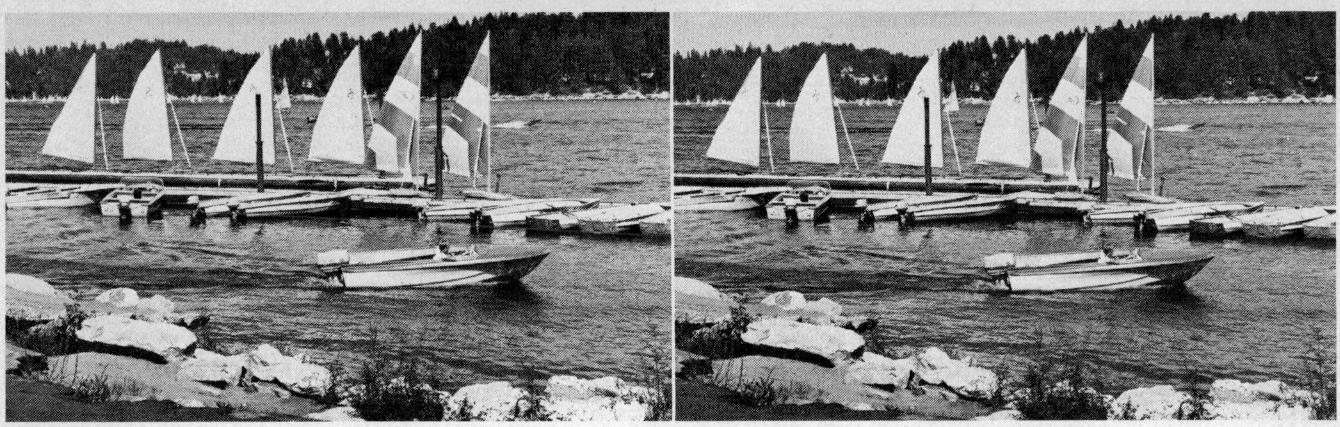

5

ters as well, and I switched. However, the properties of all five VC brands are similar enough to make any of them quite acceptable for excellent prints.

A No. 1 VC filter corresponds roughly to a No. 1 graded paper, a No. 2 to a No. 2 paper, etc., except that a No. 4 filter does not produce as much contrast as a No. 4 paper. I feel there are some distinct advantages to using VC papers as follows:

1. Half grades of contrast are possible using either Kodak's half-numbered filters or splitting exposures with Du Pont filters. In other words, you print half the exposure through one filter and the other half through another more or less contrasty.

1. The contrast range of enlarging papers is demonstrated here by printing a normal negative—one that prints properly on a No. 2 paper—on Varilour paper through a 00 filter and on Agfa No. 6 high-contrast paper.

2. Which grade of paper for which negative? No. 1 paper gives flat result—whites are light gray, darkest black is dark gray—with normal-contrast negative.

3. No. 3 paper gives too-contrasty result with normal-contrast negative. Lighter gray shades have gone white, darker grays have become black.

4. No. 2 paper and normal-contrast negative produce best result—print in which black is black, white is white, and all the shades of gray are also present on paper.

5. Modern enlarging papers have lots of latitude—one of these prints was exposed 11 seconds and developed for 90 seconds; the other was exposed for 15 seconds and developed for 45. There's very little difference.

6. Exposure latitude of modern papers is not infinite, though. Trying to save badly underexposed print by leaving it in developer too long results in light print lacking in detail. Trying to save overexposed print by pulling it out of developer quickly results in muddy, uneven print. Best way is to couple proper exposure with proper development time.

2. You can print a single negative with two or more contrasts by making an overall exposure with one filter, and localized exposure (such as a sky or foreground area) with another filter more or less contrasy.

3. By first exposing with a No. 1, 2 or 3 filter and then adding a touch of a No. 4 filter for a few seconds, you can accent blacks in a picture without appreciably affecting whites or light tones.

4. VC papers may be used without a filter, which makes them approximately a grade No. 2. This cuts exposure time in half (compared to using a filter) and is useful for many almost "normal" negatives.

5. It is not necessary to stock several boxes of paper in order to have a variety of grades when you use VC paper. This saves money and storage space, and may prevent wasted paper that becomes outdated.

Graded papers are made in more different surfaces than VC papers, but there are plenty of the latter to please the average hobbyist. I stock a glossy surface (in single weight and double weight) and a matte surface only. The former is used for reproduction and exhibition prints, and the latter for give-away pictures, portraits and personal photographs where the warm-toned, slightly rougher paper makes a better appearance. Both Kodak and Du Pont make sample booklets of their enlarging papers by which you can compare surfaces and weights.

Something special might be said for Agfa graded papers because of their lush printing qualities, especially in the higher grade numbers. I keep a box of Agfa No. 5 on hand to salvage those negatives which seem almost transparent, and the No. 6 is useful for high-contrast printing effects.

MISCELLANEOUS PRINTING HINTS

1. Both time and temperature govern the tonality of prints, just as they

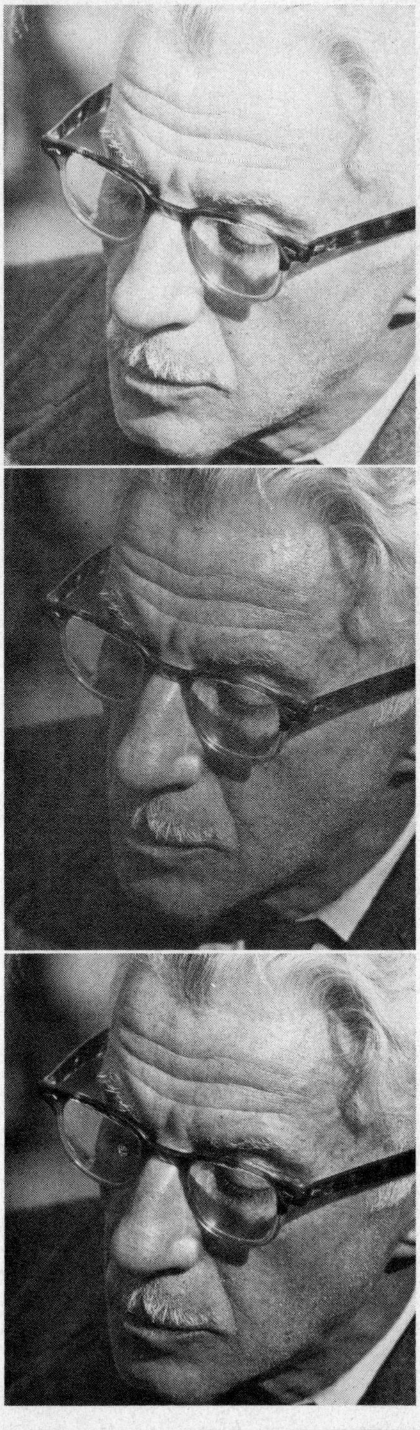

6

do negatives, via exposure and development. Paper developer should be 65 degrees or warmer, with 70 degrees ideal. You can stabilize temperature in winter to some extent by placing the developer tray into another tray of warm water which is renewed as it cools.

2. Enlarging paper has a lot of latitude, meaning that you can overexpose or underexpose it by a number of seconds, and still get acceptable prints by compensating in the developer. Ideally, a print should take about 2½ minutes to develop properly. However, many pictures are quite suitable at one minute, and three minute development often improves gradation and optimum brilliance. Longer than three minutes is also feasible for some negatives, but less than one minute usually means a somewhat degraded print.

3. *Black is the key to good printing.* As you learn to judge a print, you may discover that what you used to think was black is really only dark gray, and that a deeper black is possible in the darkest shadow areas of a subject. At the same time, a clean white should be retained someplace in most prints for the sparkle it provides, along with a full scale of intermediate gray tones. You learn to achieve these qualities through experience, after looking at and making plenty of prints while not being satisfied with compromise.

4. When enlarging, be sure to crop out all extraneous parts of a picture to retain the essentials that make a strong composition.

5. Experiment with printing techniques, paper surfaces, cropping, filters or paper grades. In the darkroom you should be having fun along with the work, and new approaches are stimulating.

6. To hold back or mask an area of a print during enlarging is called dodging. To do this there are simple tools you can make with wire coat hangers and cardboard shapes. To give a portion of a picture additional printing time while enlarging is called burning-in. You can use your hands, a piece of discarded photo paper or cardboard cut as shown in the illustration. I've found that most negatives need a little burning-in someplace, either in a corner, a sky, a bright object or wherever the highlights stand out particularly. Dodging is less frequent, and must be handled skillfully or an area will appear unnaturally light in comparison with its surrounding areas.

7. It is good parctice to cut a piece of enlarging paper into strips about 1½ inches wide with which to make test exposures before using a whole sheet.

8. Printing exposure meters are available which, when calibrated for your paper and techniques, indicate exposure time via a photo-eye for each specific negative. However, the variables involved have discouraged

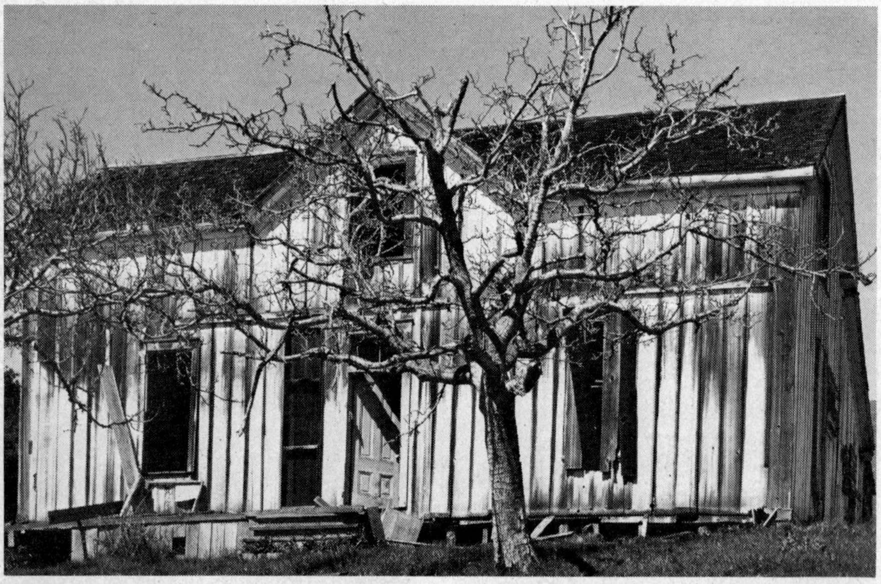

1

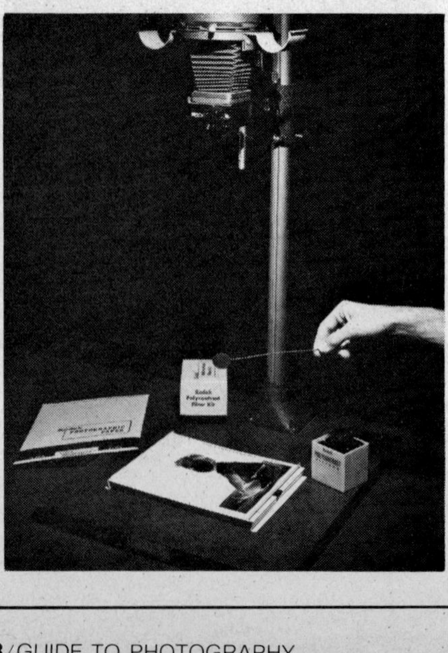

2

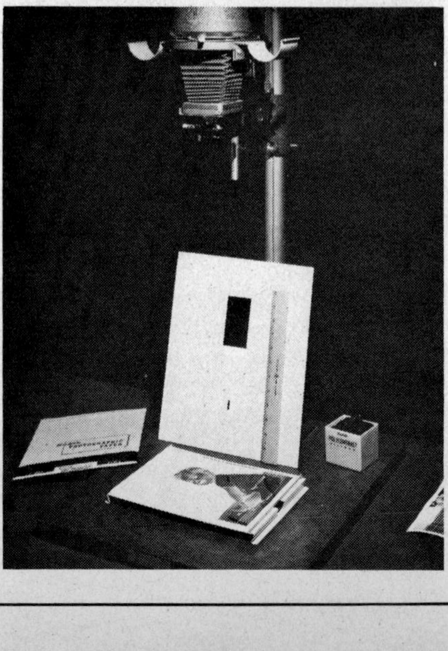

3

1. Full range of tones and print brilliance depend on both good blacks and good whites to set off middle grays inbetween. Shot with 4x5 view camera.

2. To hold back a section of a print during enlarging is called dodging. Dodging tool was made from wire coat hanger and cardboard.

3. Author uses piece of cardboard 11x14 inches in size with two rectangles cut from it, 2x3¾ and ¾x¼ inches for many burning-in operations.

4. You can make a "custom-fit" dodger or burning-in card by focusing image on easel, then putting stack of books on easel and tracing out-of-focus image part to be burned-in/dodged on piece of cardboard that comes in packs of printing paper. Cut out tracing and use small part as dodger, large portion of cardboard as burning-in card.

5. Burning-in card, shown in simulated use, cuts off light to all parts of print but that which needs burning-in (added exposure).

6. Model's fair skin was washed-out by harsh electronic flash exposure.

7. Burning-in restores face tones.

8. Keep dodger/burning-in card moving up and down an inch or so continuously or everyone will know you used it.

9. Scratched negatives can be saved if scratches are not too severe. A thin coating of Vaseline, or Edwal No-Scratch, or even skin grease, on both sides of the negative will hide the scratches while you make a print. Try to avoid dusty areas, as dust sticks to these substances. Be sure to remove the anti-scratch stuff before filing the negative.

me from using such a meter, and I have trained my own visual judgment instead.

9. Wash and dry prints carefully to avoid stains, creases, etc. Once you learn the correct methods, you should get consistently good enlargements—providing your judgement about tone quality matures.

10. Almost every print will have a few tiny white spots, no matter how carefully you dust the negatives before enlarging. These can be easily eliminated with a special dye called Spotone #3 used on a fine brush. If you must remove dark spots caused by holes or flaws in a negative, an etching knife is advised. Practice spotting and etching on rejected prints before trying on good ones.

Once you have a basic darkroom set-up equipping it may cost from $250 up, depending on the price of an enlarger and the amount of other equipment you choose. However, except for paper and chemicals, nothing else need be replaced.

CREATIVE PRINTING VARIATIONS

There a number of unconventional

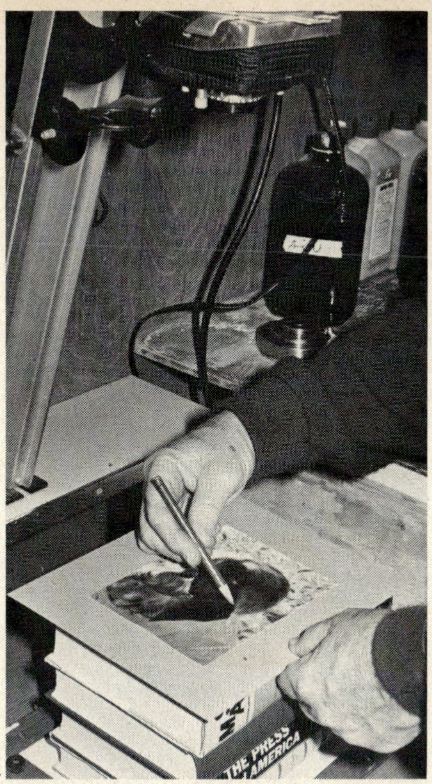
4

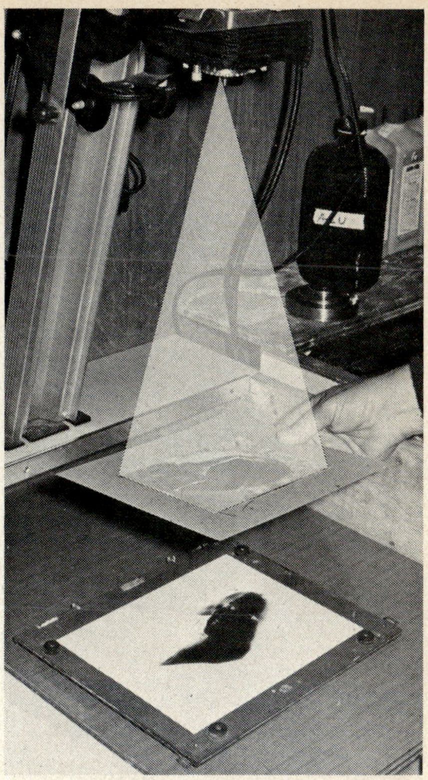
5

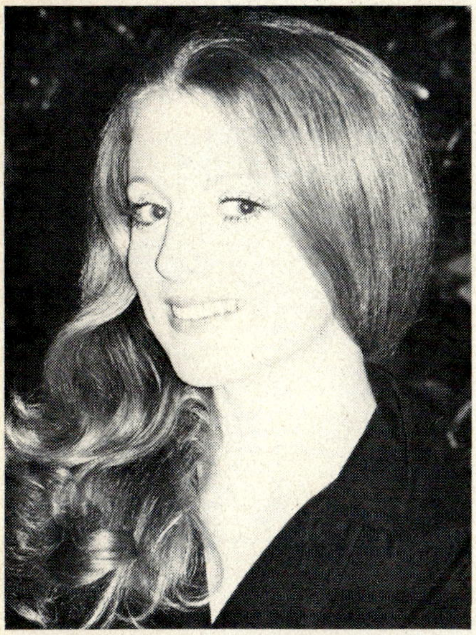
6

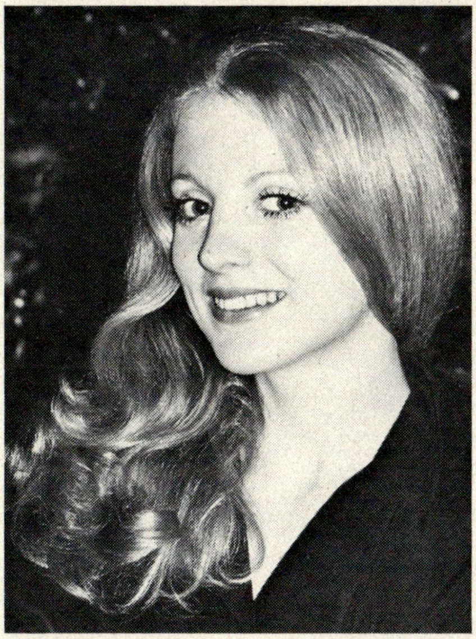
7

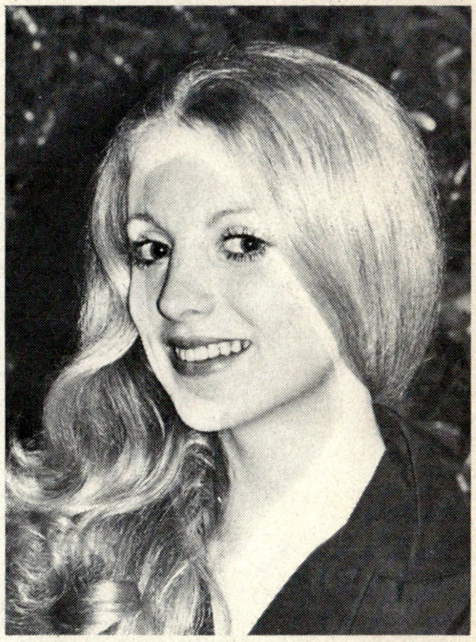
8

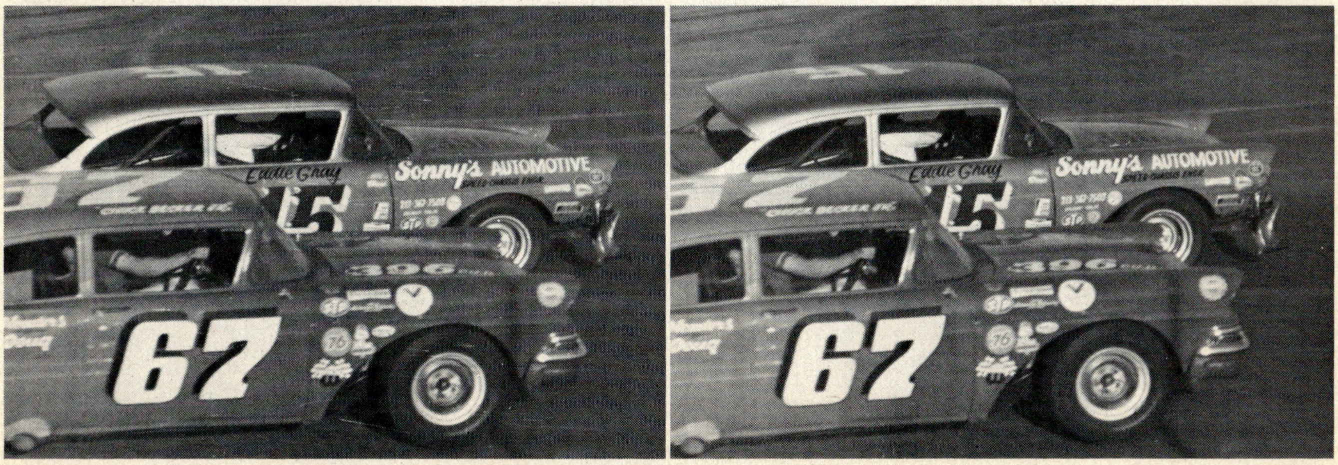

9

ways to create a photographic image on a piece of enlarging paper, of which I will mention only the most popular:

1. *Posterization* is a technique of transferring an image from conventional film to high-contrast film such as Kodalith. The latter is made in 4x5 sheets which are placed in the enlarging easel and exposed like paper. Sheets can be processed in paper developer under a red safelight. High-contrast film removes most of the intermediate tones in the original negative, leaving highlights and shadows, which suggests a poster-like appearance. The process must be taken through at least two steps by contact printing the first Kodalith positive (from your original negative) with another sheet of the same high-contrast film to obtain a negative. This eliminates more of the original gray tones, and when the resulting negative is printed, results are dramatic.

By enlarging a high-contrast positive and negative together, and slightly off-register, you get a bas-relief effect with varying decorative grays also possible. Posterization can be done with color negatives as well, or on tinted enlarging paper which offers an overall hue to a black-and-white scene.

2. *Texture screens* are available in two forms, either sandwiched with a negative or laid over enlarging paper during exposure. Screens come in a variety of textures such as linen, wood and bamboo. There is also a grain texture which accentuates the grain effect of film, and can enhance the proper subject.

3. *Double printing* has many variations. You can superimpose two negatives, or hold back a sky from one negative, and deftly print clouds into the same scene from another negative. Be prepared to experiment until you get the right combination of exposure and image placement.

4. Making a *photogram* is a darkroom exercise for which you don't even need a negative. Photograms are made by placing objects on a sheet of paper and exposing it to light—usually from the enlarger. In effect, you create designs, modified by the angle of the light, the placement, opacity or transparency of the objects, and especially their shape and size. Man Ray made photograms in the 1920s (and may have invented the technique) using window screen, other punctured-textured materials coiled 35mm film, transparent plastic blocks, flowers, the profile of a person, images of lenses, pipes, beads, and a lot of familiar things. His arrangements were artistic and often abstract, and you can imagine your own for added darkroom pleasure.

5. Though potassium ferricyanide is a powerful bleach (and poison) used to lighten tones in a photographic print on a localized basis, it can also be used for special effects. You use a dilute solution of ferricyanide in water on a thin brush or Q-tip to bleach shadow areas slightly, after which you dip the print in hypo immediately to stop the bleaching action. It takes time to master this skill because the chemical runs easily and bleaches adjacent areas you don't want affected. Practice on rejected prints, and see what happens if you use ferricyanide by letting it run or sprinkle it as an artistic destroyer!

Do be careful with chemicals; they can irritate the skin, stain the clothes and foul up negatives or prints if not contained properly and tossed out as they lose strength.

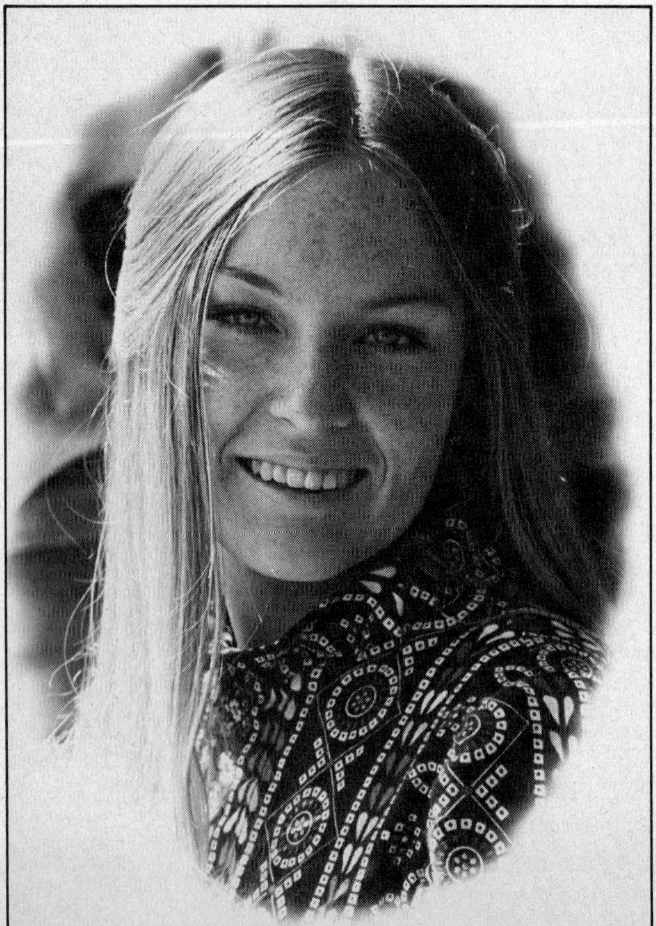

1

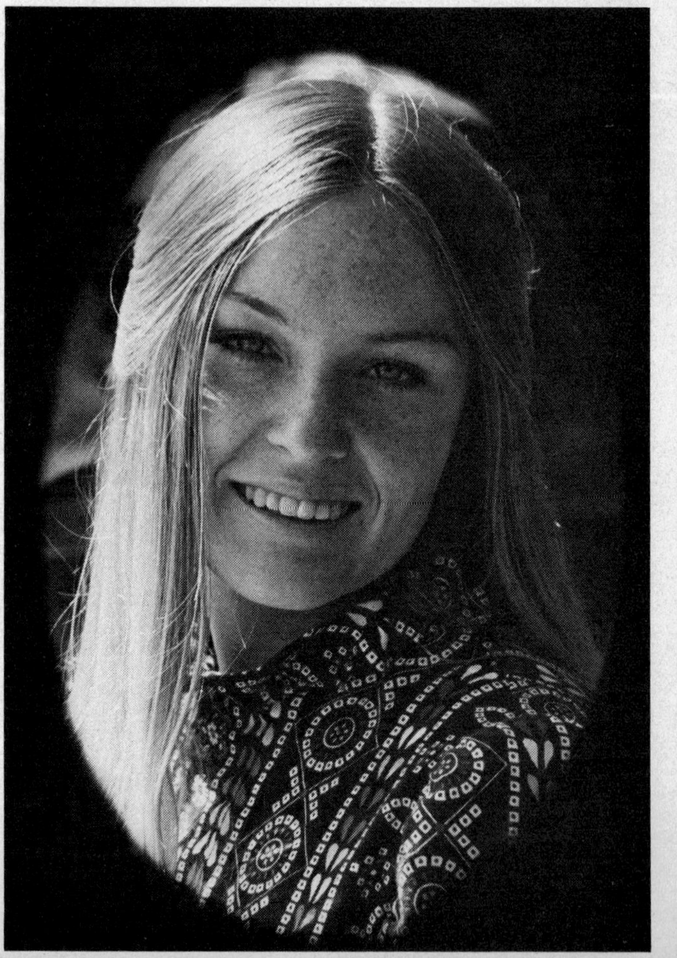

2

COLOR DEVELOPING AND PRINTING

Color film/ As I have stated, processing your own transparency film is rarely worth the trouble. Professional labs, often within a day's mailing distance, do the job consistently, and it's worth the money. However, if you wish to familiarize yourself with Ektachrome development, for instance, Kodak publishes booklets and instructions that tell how. The film goes through 13 steps in 9 different chemicals, is reversed, stabilized and finally dried. Then you have the dubious pleasure of mounting all those slides, which processors do at no extra cost.

If you shoot enough rolls of color to make the chemicals worth buying, you can save money developing your own film. In a fairly isolated area where mail service is slow, color film processing makes sense to save time. There are other methods besides Kodak's, and Paul Farber describes the Unicolor system thoroughly in the July, 1972 issue of *PhotoGraphic Magazine.* Unicolor Division of KMS Industires supplies reprints of the article in camera shops or by writing

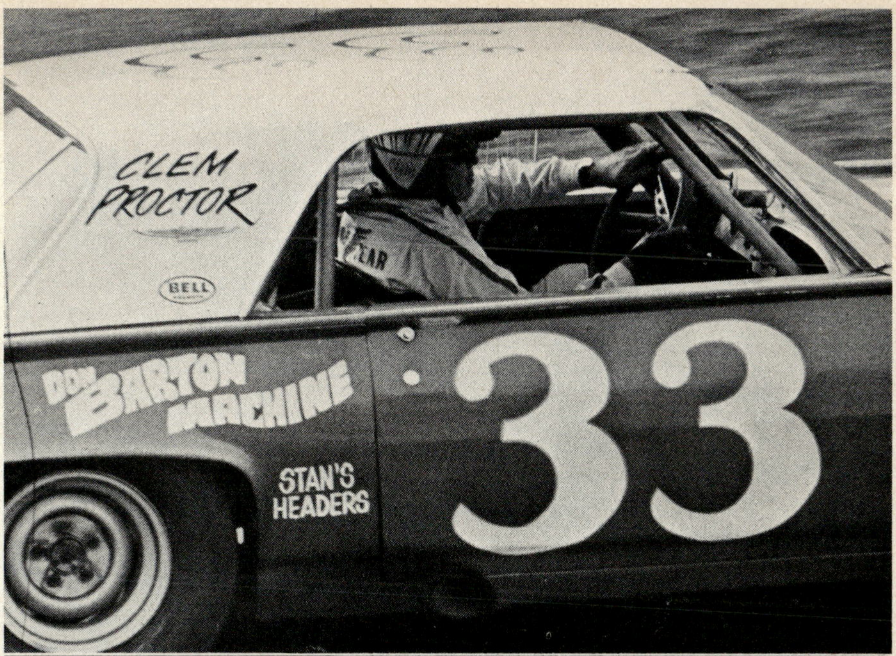

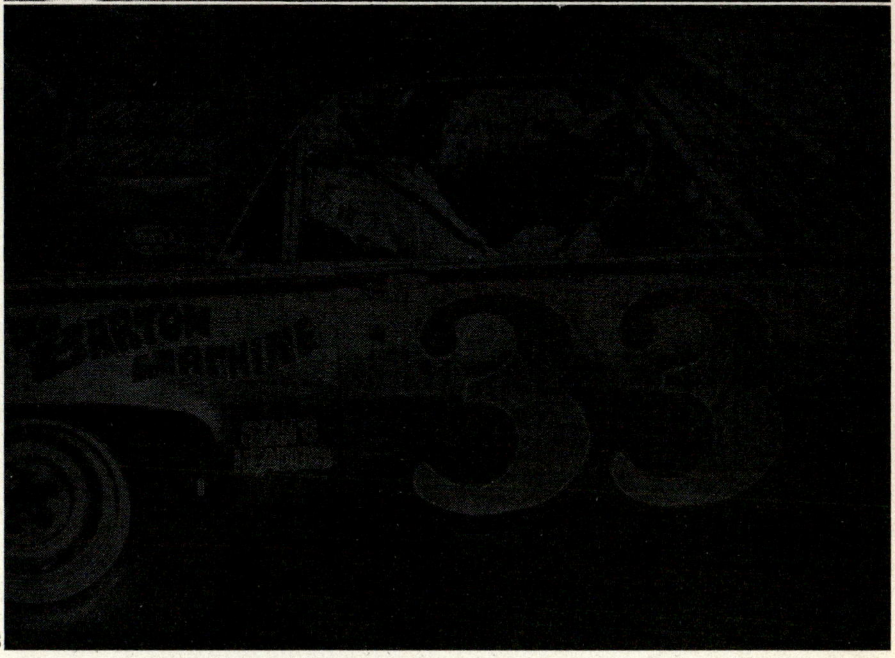

3

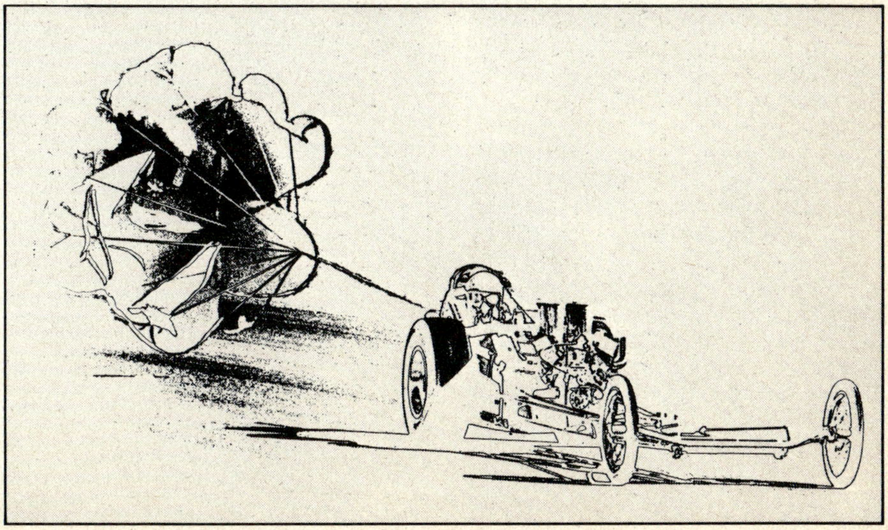

4

1. White vignette is effect produced by cutting subject-sized hole in piece of cardboard and holding cardboard over easel during entire exposure, allowing subject to be exposed through hole. If you want gentle shading of subject into white area, use hole with serrated edges, keep cardboard moving in small circles during exposure, and use lowest-contrast paper that will give acceptable print from negative.

2. Black vignette is produced by attaching cardboard you cut out of dodger used for white vignette to length of thin, stiff wire, then making normal exposure of whole negative, then placing piece of cardboard over subject and making 30-second exposure with lens wide open, moving cardboard in small circles with wire during exposure. Cardboard must be placed directly on enlarging paper for this step, or light will bleed under cardboard onto subject and fog its image.

3. Sabattier effect ("solarization") is partial reversal of image on print. Effect is produced by exposing paper to light (enlarger is good source) for two or three seconds after paper has been in developer about a minute. Be ready to pull print out of developer soon after exposure to light. Effect works best with contrasty negative and/or contrasty paper.

4. Posterization with high-contrast film produced this strange-looking picture for Ron Contarsy (a Kodak/Scholastic Award winner) who printed the positive image for a negative effect. In other words, blacks and whites are reversed from the way the original scene appeared.

The Darkroom

P.O. Box 306, Dexter, Michigan 48130.

Color negatives can also be developed in the home darkroom in fewer steps than transparency film if the effort seems worthwhile.

Color printing/ "It's easy," says a Unicolor booklet about their chemicals and equipment. Other companies also make kits for the home darkroom, including a processing drum in which you develop a print for about seven minutes. Kodak's Ektacolor papers and chemicals and their motorized Rapid Color Processor are also available for the serious amateur or professional. Kodak's Type C process is for color negatives, and Type R for printing directly from transparencies. Color quality of the former is superior to the latter.

Color negatives are printed through a series of separate filters which become a filter pack that translates the negative color image to positive paper in which there are dyes. Just as you must learn black-and-white printing skills with filters or graded papers, it takes time and experience to choose correct filters for color printing. There are both mechanical and optical aids for filter selection, some of which are modestly priced and some expensive. Processing steps for a print run 7½ to 23 minutes, and temperature control is critical. You cannot be sure your color print is accurate with some materials until the print is dry.

In my estimation, color printing is an adventure, and I recommended it to anyone who has the time, money and urge to explore the literal and impressionistic world of color photography. Strange, odd and curious effects are not difficult using the "wrong" filters at the right time, and discovering the correct filter pack for exacting color is worth the experimentation. Just be sure you know what you are getting into, and don't expect perfect results immediately. When you have mastered the techniques, making your own color prints can *really* save money, since professional lab charges are largely for labor.

In general, darkroom work is a pleasure, the final payoff in the creative sequence. If you don't enjoy it, it is likely you won't continue, but if you are having fun in either black-and-white or color, there is no limit to your photographic horizon.

SOME THEORY

So that you'll have some idea of what is going on when your chemicals are working in the developing tank or printing trays, here's some simplified exposure/development theory to consider.

Photographic emulsions contain silver salts, such as silver bromide. (Common table salt is a sodium salt, sodium chloride, if that helps.) Unlike other salts, silver salts do a funny thing when light hits them—they change into metallic silver, among other things. It is this habit of the silver salts, producing metallic silver when struck by light, upon which photography as we know it is based.

When light rays hit the silver halide in the film or paper emulsion, they cause little specks of metallic silver to appear. These little specks are so small that not even a microscope would reveal them, but they are very important to photography. They are called the latent image, and they become attack points for the developer when it is poured into the tank or the print is put into the developer tray. They are the "hidden" image that the developer will turn into a visible one.

Photographic developers can be thought of as amplifiers of a sort; they take those little specks of metallic silver and increase their size perhaps a billion times.

After development, unexposed and undeveloped silver halides that were not needed to form the image are still in the emulsion, and these would turn into black metallic silver if exposed to light. Washing the emulsion with water would remove the developer, but not these silver halides. This is where the fixer, or hypo, comes in. The fixer converts the "extra" silver halides into compounds that won't react with light to form black metallic silver, compounds that can be washed out of the emulsion with water.

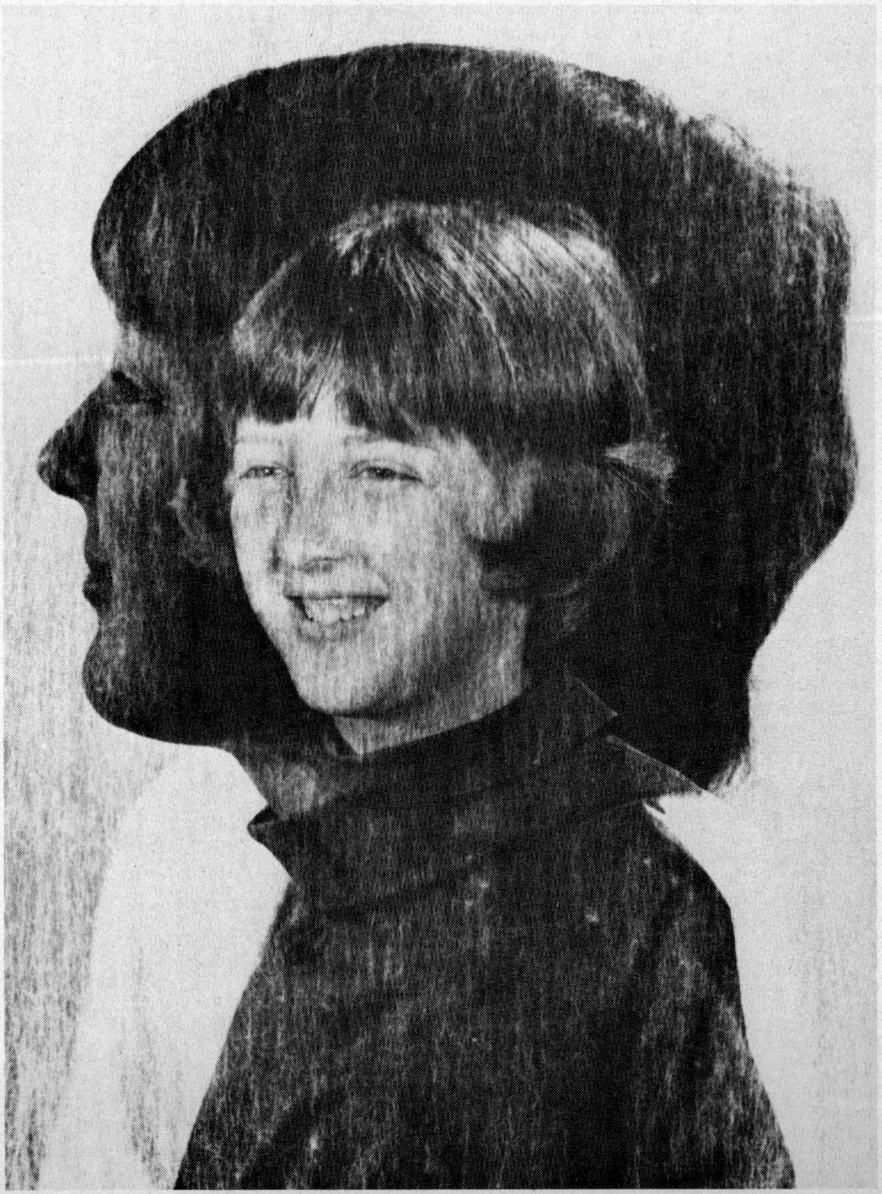

1

1. Robert Bush superimposed (sandwiched) two negatives for fascinating double print portrait, and won Kodak/Scholastic Award for his efforts.

2. Jim Cornfield laid texture screen over his enlarging paper when he printed girl's portrait for this very unusual effect.

3. Ron Contarsy enlarged 35mm negative on high-contrast 4x5 film and exposed it to light for an instant during development, partly reversing ("solarizing") the image. While printing, he dabbed the paper with weak potassium ferricyanide mixture to bleach a random pattern bit by bit. A Kodak/Scholastic Award winner.

4. Martha Grose laid a scissors, film developing reel, twine and odd bits of paper (removed part way through the exposure) on sheet of photographic paper to make photogram that won Kodak/Scholastic Award.

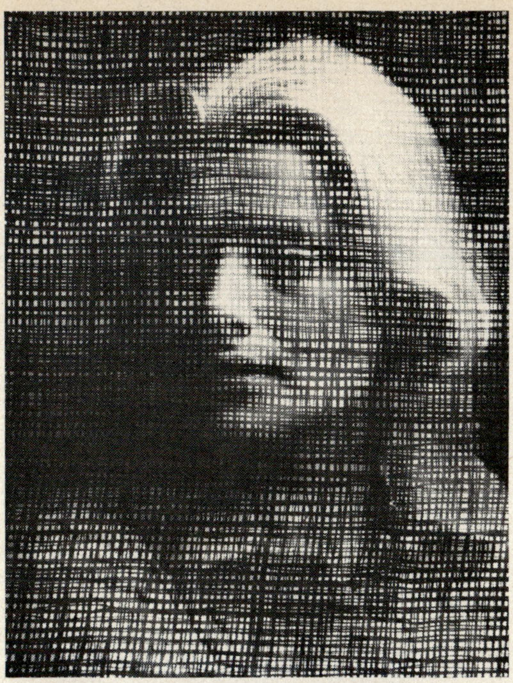

2

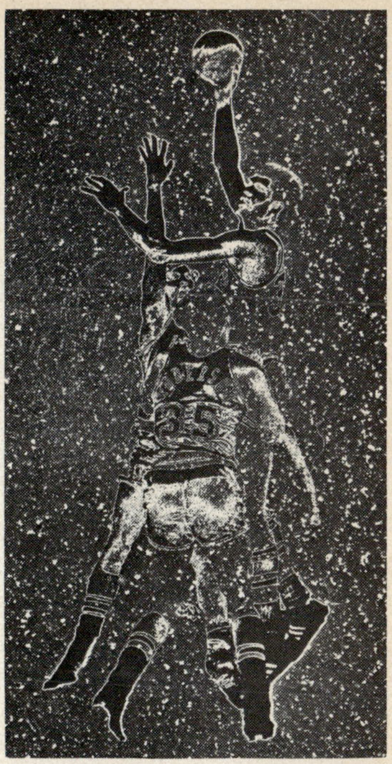

3

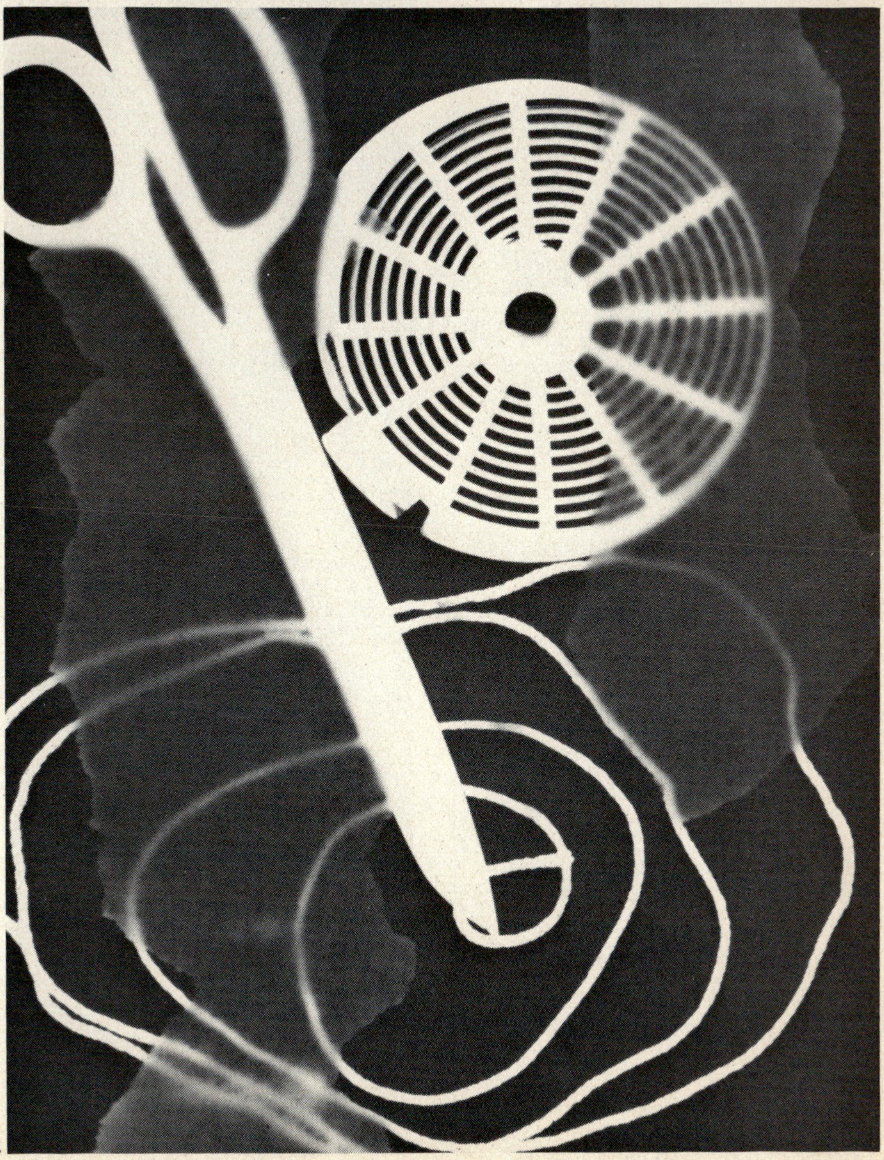

4

After fixing, the fixer and the compounds it forms must be washed out of the emulsion, or they will eventually react with the silver of the image to produce a yellow-brown stain, the same sort of thing that happens when silverware tarnishes.

Now you'll know that when you're shooting pictures, you're allowing the light reflected by the objects forming the scene you're photographing to form a latent image on the film. When your pour the developer into the tank with the film, you're amplifying that image, making it visible. When you pour the fixer into the tank, you're rendering the unexposed and undeveloped "left-over" silver halides insensitive to light. When you wash the film, you're removing all the unnecessary stuff from the emulsion. When you expose your enlarging paper, you're creating a latent image, which your print developer will turn into a visible one, and so on.

Bearing in mind the foregoing, think about this: When you "push" film by developing it for more than the recommended time after exposing it at a higher exposure index than its ASA speed (i.e., underexposing it), what is happening? If the shadow areas of the scene did not receive enough exposure to form a latent image, your developer cannot produce a visible image there; the shadow areas on the negative will be void of detail no matter how long you develop the film. Increasing the developing time in this case will only increase the density of the highlight areas on the negative, which in turn increases the contrast of the negative. But are you actually getting a higher film speed? Not without the shadow detail ...you're only getting more contrast, not more film speed.

CHAPTER 12 Building Your Own Photographic Equipment

Though I usually refer to buying photographic equipment in past chapters, many items mentioned can be built by the average photographer who chooses to use his manual dexterity with tools and materials. Often the main problem is finding plans and directions for the design and construction of equipment. For instance, you may need something as simple as a lens hood and not wish to pay $7-15 for one. Such an item can be machined from aluminum tubing, spun from flat aluminum over a form, turned from hard wood or made from heavy black paper and masking tape. If machines and tools are available, the build-it-yourself process can be very satisfying.

In general, a photographer stays away from trying to build cameras, shutters, lenses and electronic equipment, or anything that consists of specially designed components that may cost more separately than the finished product. However, if you care to make the effort, you can save enough money making photo equipment to buy ready-made things you might not otherwise have been able to afford, and you will have many items that you would not have invested in on dealer's shelves.

I am not a do-it-yourself expert, but I have the assistance of someone who is: Parry C. Yob. This chapter is a preview of his book in *PhotoGraphic's* series, titled *Photo Equipment You Can Make,* and it includes a few of his photographs of typical home-workshop projects covered in his book. He gives complete plans and instructions for often-costly pieces of darkroom and studio equipment you can build economically with ordinary household tools. Construction is largely from standard-dimension lumber and parts available from local hardware stores or home improvement centers.

SOME BRIEF DESCRIPTIONS

A camera dolly built from wood weighs less than ready-made dollies of metal, but offers all the mobility and ease of operation found in studio stands costing $300 or more. On this rolling dolly you can mount any camera from 35mm to 8x10, and it works smoothly enough that it is also quite adaptable for shooting with motion picture cameras.

A dry-mounting press large enough for 16x20-inch mounts can be built for about $30, and works as well as a commercial model costing 10 times that much. A few inexpensive welding and tin operations can be farmed out. This particular press has been used by Parry C. Yob to mount prints which have won many awards in local and national competitions.

A background stand holds seamless paper or a variety of other background materials on long or short rolls. The stand is easily taken apart for storage if you use your living room as a temporary studio. It takes

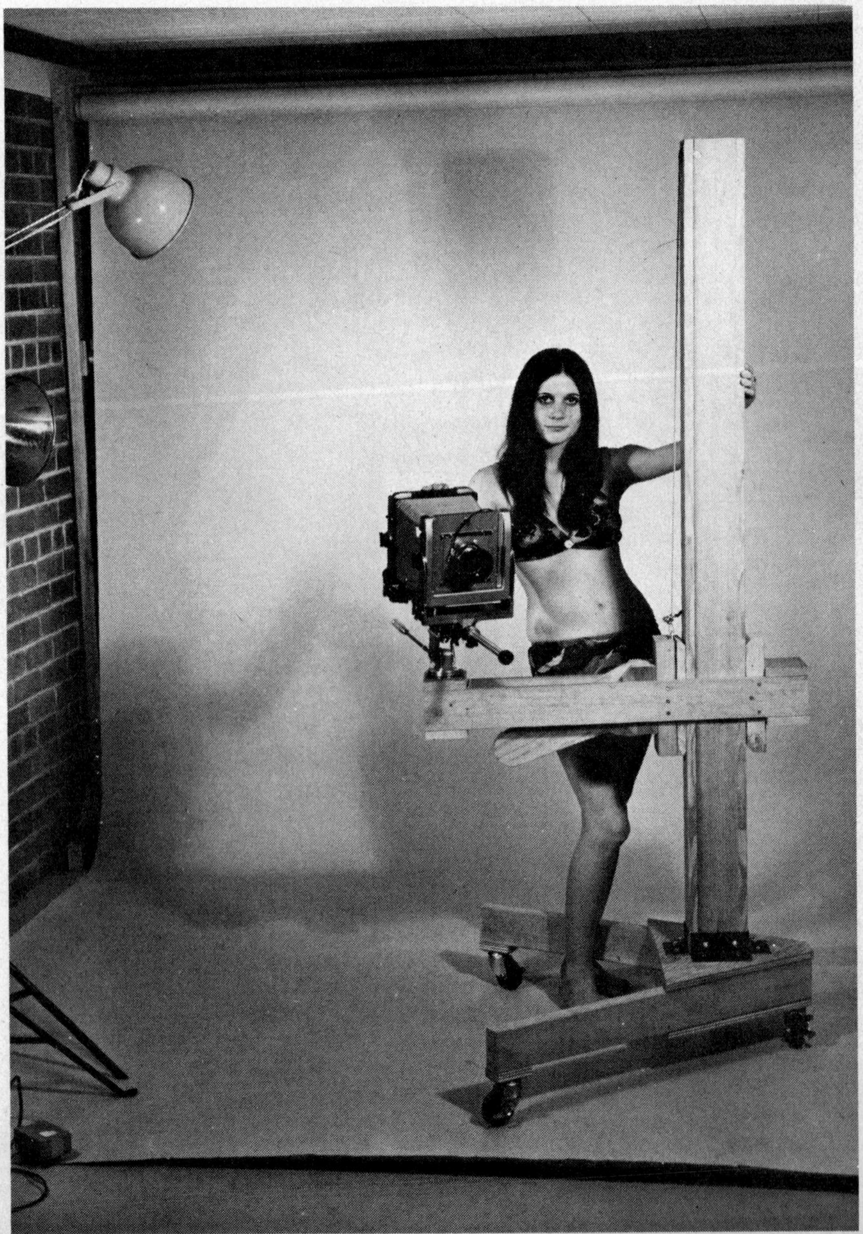

1

standard nine-foot-wide paper rolls.

A softlight can be a delight for portraits or still-life pictures because it diffuses the light and softens shadows. Using standard photoflood bulbs, this softlight will work with both color and black-and-white films, and its intensity is more than adequate for even the slower film speeds.

A darkroom timer is very handy for processing film, and its large sweep second hand is visible from quite a distance. This timer may also be used to time enlarger exposures, though it does not turn the enlarger off after set intervals.

A matte print dryer dries all sizes of paper up to large double weight exhibition prints. They come out absolutely flat in three to four hours without attention. It will take up to 40 16x20 prints or 200 8x10 prints at the same time. If you wash your prints at night, you can load them in the dryer and find everything ready to mount, send out or admire in the morning.

Home workshop enthusiasts should study Yob's book for fun and profit. In addition to the above, there are many other projects, and he has included sources of materials and tools, plus many shortcuts that will save work and money when building photographic equipment at home.

STOP-ACTION FLASH WITH A FIVE-CENT GADGET

Standard studio and darkroom equipment is not all you can make in the way of photographic equipment. With a little ingenuity, you can think up and build useful equipment that you can't buy in photo stores.

1. This camera dolly built of wood rolls smoothly and can handle any size camera, which is raised up or pulled down on a counter-balance.

2. For 1/10 the cost of a factory-made dry-mounting press you can make your own by having just a few welding and tin-forming jobs done.

3. This background stand holds paper rolls up to nine feet long, and it can be taken apart for storage or for work to be done on location.

4. Softlight on rolling stand is excellent for portraits or still-life photography with color or black-and-white films.

5. Large face of this darkroom timer is easy to see while developing film or making prints.

6. Plywood box with its own small fans will dry large number of prints in three to four hours.

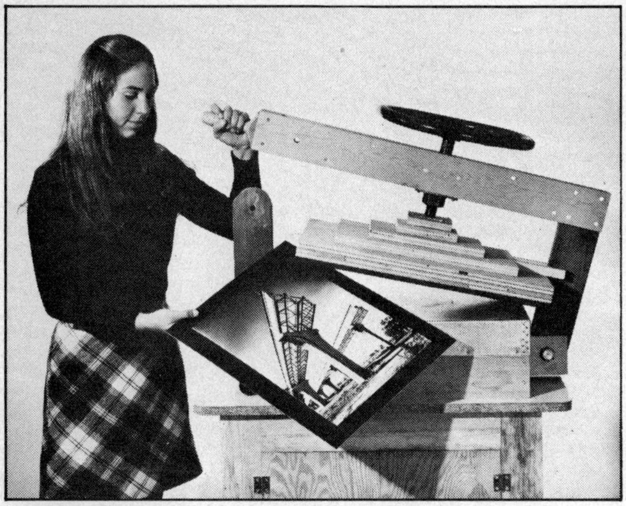

2

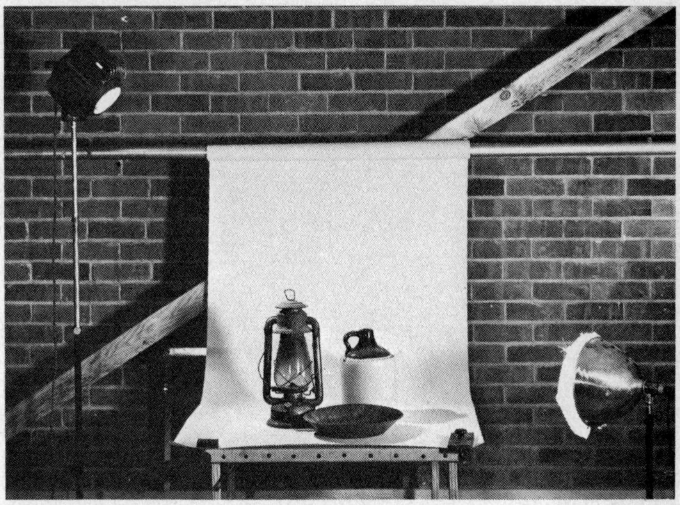

3

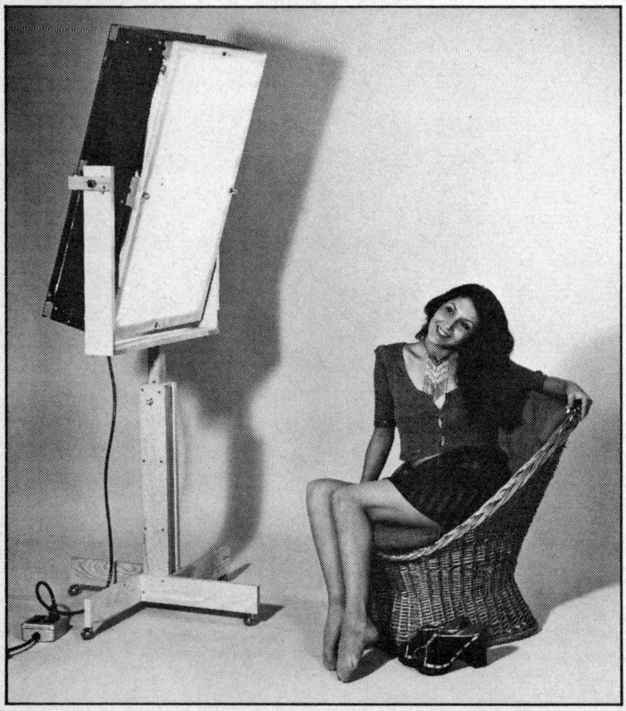

4

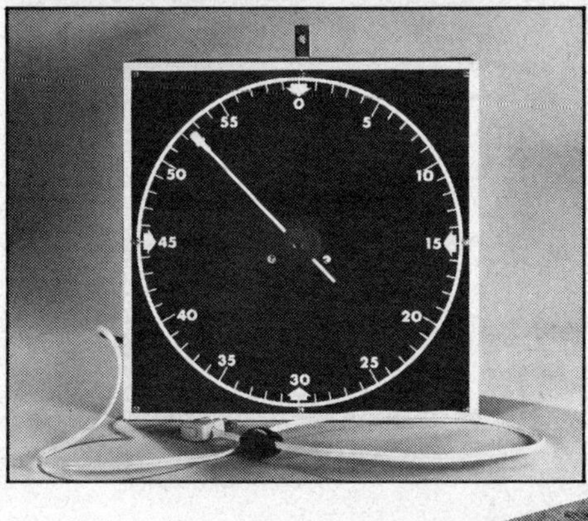

5

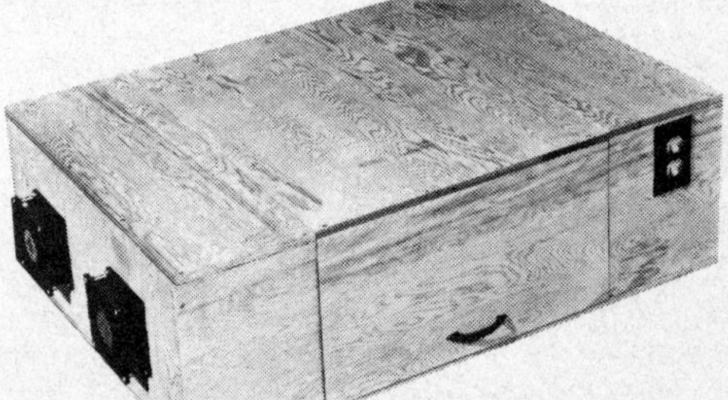

6

Hundreds of photographs have amply demonstrated that a wink of light—electronic flash—is faster than a speeding bullet, and that the same ultra-fast light can make sequence pictures with the right equipment and timing devices. Most electronic flash users have tried to snap peak action, such as a falling deck of cards, only to find that success depends on sheer chance because manual synchronization of trigger-finger to action is very tricky.

Paul Farber has devised a simple synchronizing gadget for use with your present electronic flash and camera, which affords about 90 percent success in catching precise peak action. Construction materials are (a) a block of wood approximately six inches long, three inches wide, and one inch deep; (b) two nails about two inches long; (c) a piece of tin or thin metal; (d) a five-foot length of lamp wire and a two-prong male plug; and (e) a small eyelet screw. For tools you need only a tin snip or pair of sturdy scissors, a hammer, pliers, and a soldering iron.

Dimensions are not critical. Cut the swinging "flag" out of a piece of tin (scrape off insulating materials if they are present), and allow enough metal to wrap around the nail. Cut a small V-shaped notch in one end of the flag. Next, use the pliers to gently shape the flag around one nail, allowing good contact, but freedom of movement as well. Drive the nail into the wood block and check the flag to see that it moves without binding.

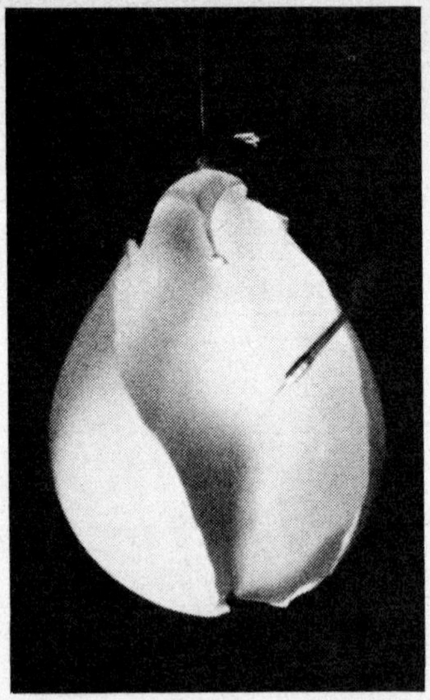

1

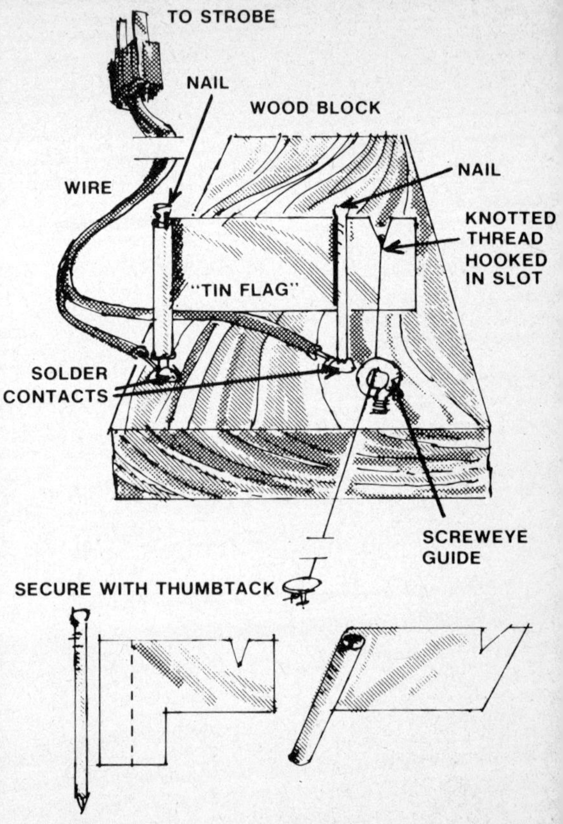

DETAIL SHOWING HOW "TIN FLAG" IS CUT AND BENT

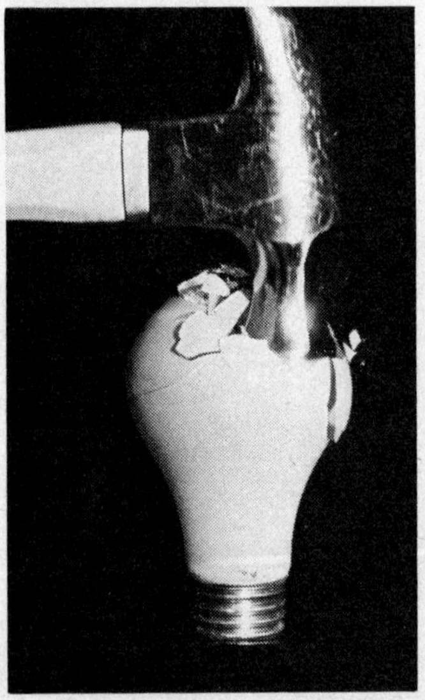

2

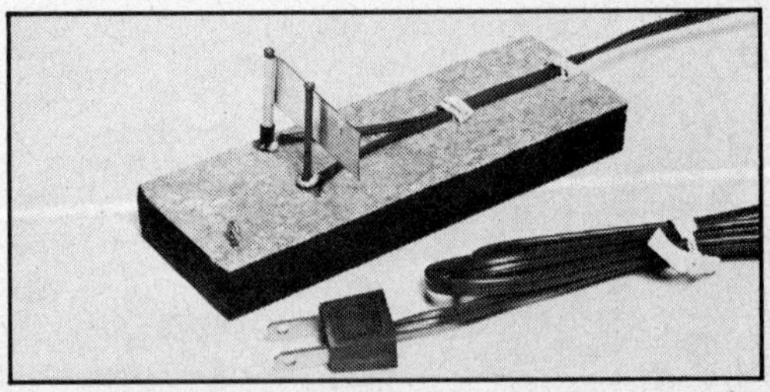

3

1. High-speed flash photograph of balloon bursting was made possible by using inexpensive gadget described in text. Balloon was balanced on table covered with piece of black velvet. A piece of string tied at top provided support to keep balloon upright. Black thread was run behind balloon, and as dart hit balloon contact was made to capture explosion. Print was made from High Speed Ektachrome original, push-processed one stop, which accounts for graininess.

2. Electric light bulb, virtually intact yet mortally wounded by hammer buried in its head, was subject. Had black thread been slightly less taut, action would have been photographed later in destruction sequence. If thread is visible in your prints, it can be easily retouched out with Kodak spotting colors.

3. Farber's unit shows simple, uncomplicated construction. When in use, black thread is run from notch in flag through eyelet. Thread is then placed over object to be photographed.

4. PC-to-H "cheater" cord (arrow) is used between flash unit and gadget. Tips of male plug may have to be filed down to permit full contact with "H" end of cheater. Such cords are available from reasonably well-stocked camera supply stores.

Drive the other nail into the wood in line with the first nail and the flag itself. Check contact against the nail, and adjust the flag so it touches completely. Split one end of the lamp wire, strip away about an inch of insulation, and wind an end around the base of each nail where you apply solder to keep the wire in place. Attach the male plug at the other end of the wire. In essence you have built a simple shorting switch.

Plug your electronic flash into the gadget's line cord, and switch on the flash unit. When the ready-lite is lit, gently push the flag against the nail-contact post, which should fire the unit if all is well. Then, to make this ingenious device work, take a length of black thread and tie a large knot in one end. Slip the knot through the eyelet guide and onto the V-shaped notch in the flag. The rest of the thread is stretched over the object to be photographed.

Here's how to use your gadget to take a classic high-speed flash photograph of a light bulb being smashed by a hammer. Place the bulb on a hard, flat surface, and anchor the gadget off to one side with some masking tape. Stretch the thread over the bulb and off to the other side where you secure it with more tape or a pushpin. Position your tripod-mounted camera so it's zeroed in on the bulb, and place your flash unit to one side, aimed at the bulb. Adjust exposure by dividing distance from flash-to-subject into the guide number, move the flag away from the contact nail about a millimeter, darken the room, open the camera shutter to "T" or "B" with a locking cable release if needed, put on some safety goggles, pick up your hammer and bring it down *hard* onto the bulb!

As the hammer makes contact and breaks the bulb, the thread will be

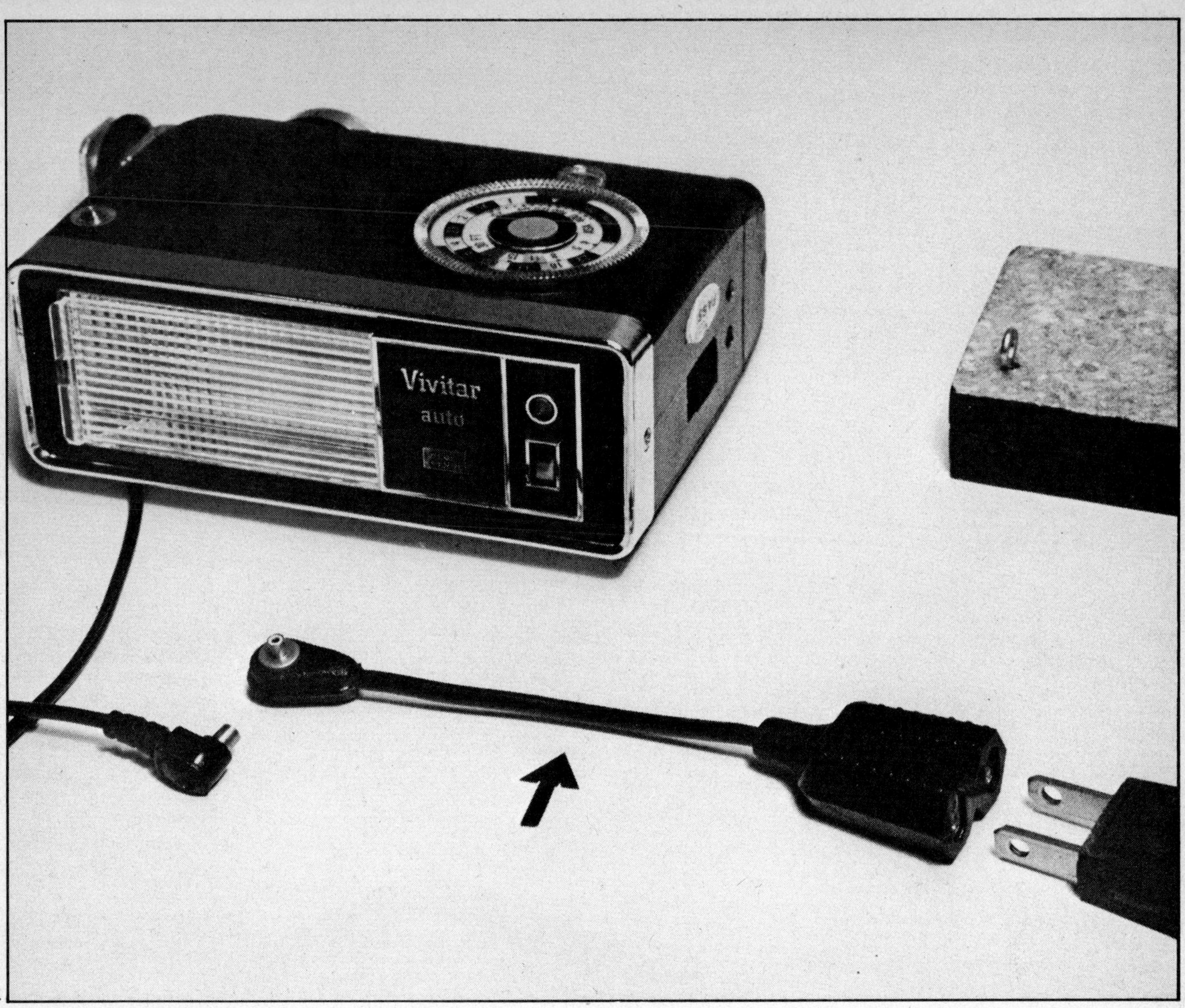

4

pulled taut, pulling the flag against the nail, thereby firing the flash unit. Close the camera shutter and turn up the room lights. If it seems worthwhile destroying another bulb, check your setup, and remember that the flash will be discharged according to the amount of slack in the thread. If the thread is taut, you'll get the "top" of the action; if it is slightly slack, then the strobe will fire in the "middle" of the action. If it's very slack, you will record the "bottom" of the action. Vary the thread and try it again if you wish.

Also, do not overlook the high-speed abilities of current automatic electronic flash units. At very close-to-subject distances, their flash duration may be as short as 1/50,000 second, which will further dramatize your super-speed stop-action gadget.

Use your imagination to create more uses for this easy-to-make device that deftly approximates results made by very expensive equipment and complex setups.

MAKING A PINHOLE CAMERA

Another interesting project is building a pinhole camera. Joe Courtland told how and explained why in the Winter 1972 *PhotoGraphic Quarterly,* and tells here why and how you should build one:

First, the idea of building your own camera is not that far-fetched. Years ago, when photography was in its infancy, many enthusiastic photographers did build their own cameras. A hardy few even made their own films, or sensitized papers which were exposed in their homemade equipment. Today, however, thanks to the easy availability of sensitized materials, you don't have to make your own film. But, the idea of making your own experimental camera is as valid as ever. The camera is called a "pinhole camera," and the cost can be measured in tenths of a dollar.

Second, you may asky why you should build your own camera. After all, you may argue, you already have an expensive piece of equipment. The answer is easy. It takes no great craftsmanship, only a few hours of your spare time, and the fun of actually making a camera that will take real pictures cannot be denied. Other members of your family may want to join in the fun, and that makes it desirable, too. But the real reason for making your own pinhole camera is this: a pinhole camera can be a great teaching aid. It can acutally help you to become a better photographer!

Consider this as the third reason: because a pinhole camera can only be loaded with one piece of film, you will become extremely choosy about the matter of making your exposure.

You won't point the camera at anything that's in front of you. You will come to realize that your *first* exposure is also your *last* exposure!

True, this type of camera is also limited. You can't take stop-action photographs. Candids are out of the question. And I don't believe that even the most patient of friends or family would sit long enough to have their portraits taken. Yet, despite these shortcomings, the camera does teach you to see—to become extremely selective and equally critical. And, when the experiments are over, hopefully you'll take your new-found abilities with you when you do pack your expensive camera. You will have learned control, constraint, and the ability to really see in a photographic sense.

Sounds good? You bet it is. So let's get to the project. You'll need the following list of easily available materials: 1/16th inch thick cardboard (this can be found in most art supply stores and is sold as mounting board). An X-acto knife or equivalent tool for cutting the cardboard. Black masking tape (also available in art supply houses, and in some camera stores). India ink (black) or black spray paint. Pencils, a ruler, and some black paper. Other incidentals will be mentioned as we proceed. Oh yes, there is one more item which you will need: a box of 2¼ x 3¼-inch sheet film. This film is available at any well-stocked camera store, or can be ordered through the camera store. Preferably you'll want a slow film, so buy Panatomic-X. You can, of course, use other size sheet films, but for our purposes the size mentioned will be sufficient.

The pinhole camera consists of an inner body, and a two-part outer case. Also, there is a pinhole aperture in front of the camera, and a place to insert the film at the other end of the camera. No shutter is used except a mechanical one that is built from scraps (which will be discussed later on). The specifications are for a camera built to accommodate the aforementioned 2¼ x 3¼ sheet film. To begin: to make the inner case you must cut four pieces of cardboard in such a way that, when they are assembled, the *inside* dimensions will be exactly the same dimensions as the film. The length of the inner body must be 3½ inches long. Using the black masking tape, bind the four pieces of cardboard along the edges, outside and inside. When finished you'll have an open ended box that has exactly the same *inside* dimensions as the film size. Paint the interior of the inner box with india ink, or carefully spray the inside with a matte black paint. Set it aside to dry thoroughly.

A film suport gate must be made to hold the sheet of film. This is made by cutting a strip of cardboard about one inch wide and twelve inches long. The cardboard is cut to size, and the pieces are carefully inserted into one end of the inner case, making certain they are recessed by a little more than 1/16th of an inch (the thickness of the cardboard). The pieces are glued into place and allowed to dry (see illustration). After they have dried into position, paint these with india ink or matte black paint.

Next, a pressure plate will have to be made. This, too, must be cut to exactly the dimensions of the film being used (2¼ x 3¼ inches). The pressure plate is attached with some of the masking tape, hinge fashion, to the bottom of the box. After taping the plate in position it must be tested. Cut a piece of paper to the size of the film being used. Place it on the film support gate. Close the pressure plate. The plate should fit flush into the end of the inner case, and hold the "film" securely. If it does not, then *this* is the time to make any needed adjustments. A look at the illustration will reveal all.

The outer case must now be constructed. This is nothing more than a box, closed at each end, and cut into two pieces. The box will form a perfect fit around the inner case. The first step is to cut four pieces of cardboard using the inner case as your guide to marking off the exact measurements—allowing for the thickness of the cardboard. Mark off each piece as you measure against the inner case so the pieces can be assembled in their proper, marked off, position. Slight inaccuracies in cutting the inner case will then be compensated for during this phase. Wrap the four cut pieces of cardboard around the inner case, and join them with the black masking tape, sealing the edges securely. Next, cut out two end pieces so they will fit flush with the ends of the outer case. Tape one end into place and *remove the inner case.* Next, tape the other end piece into place. You now have a box, sealed at both ends, that is a perfect overfit for the inner case.

Now, approximately 1½ inches from the front end of the outer shell, make a line around the box. Carefully, with a new (and sharp) X-acto blade, cut the box into two sections. Care in cutting is important! Don't crush the box. Take your time and

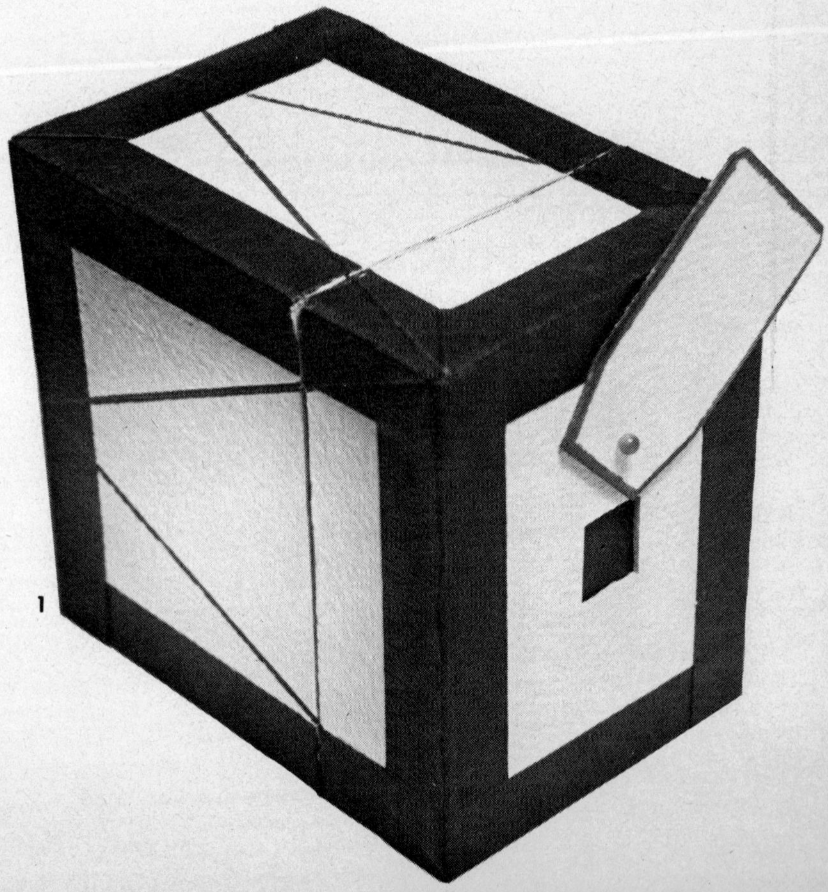

1

make repeated slices until the outer shell is cut apart. Next, take the short end of the cut apart box, and carefully cut out a square in the exact middle of the front end. Next, take this end and place a few drops of glue inside. Then slip the front end over the front end of the inner shell. Make certain the two sections are well glued. Allow the glue to dry.

The rear end of the outer shell then slips over the rear end of the inner shell, thus completing the basic camera. As you can see, the rear is removable, thus allowing entrance into the film loading area. Because the rear end of the outer shell is longer, it will form a snug pressure fit that cannot be accidentally removed unless so desired by the user.

Make certain that all joints are light tight, using more black tape as required. It pays to paint the entire interior, inner and outer shells, a flat matte black to cut down on unwanted internal reflections. Allow all paint to dry completely before proceeding.

The pinhole lens is the next step. Although we're not dealing with optical elements in the classical sense, still, the pinhole lens has been in existence for hundreds of years. The earliest "camera," the camera obscura, used such a lens. In the camera obscura (Italian: Dark room), a tiny hole was drilled into a wall. The room was completely black, and opposite the pinhole, on a far wall, an actual image was projected. Upside down, to be sure, but a recognizable picture nonetheless. The moving panorama was viewed and enjoyed by spectators in the room. Later on, when optical principles were more readily understood, the pinhole aperture was placed in a ceiling, using a mirror to deflect the image down onto a circular table thus eliminating the upside down viewing problem.

Making such a lens is not difficult. As with any lens, pinhole or optical, care must be taken to make it optically perfect. In our case we will take a small square of black paper. In the exact center of the paper puncture a hole using a #10 sewing needle. These needles are available in any notions store. Make certain you use a new needle to make as clean a puncture as possible. After you remove the needle you will find paper burrs on the exit side of the paper. These must be cleaned off and can be filed away with a fine emery board or super-fine sandpaper. Once the burrs have been removed, reinsert the needle to clean out any debris which may have accumulated in the tiny aperture during the sanding.

Before proceeding further, it's kind of fun to see what the pinhole lens can actually do. Look at some distant object such as a telephone pole. Then, while still looking at the distant object, hold up your finger a few inches before your eyes. If your eyes are anything like my eyes, then the distant object will remain sharp and the object close to your eye will be completely out of focus. Now, while still looking, interpose the pinhole between your eye and the close-up object. As you look through the tiny hole you'll notice that everything—distant object and close-up objects—appear to have the same overall sharpness. This demonstrates one of the great advantages of the pinhole lens. No focusing will ever be required because everything from infinity to the film plane itself will remain in focus! This effect can be used to another advantage which will be discussed later.

Once the pinhole lens has been made, glue it into position on the *inside* of the camera, making certain to center the tiny aperture in the center of the cut-out in the front panel. The "shutter," so-called in this case, need be nothing more elaborate than a piece of cardboard cut large enough to cover the pinhole. A straight pin can be used to connect the "shutter" to the front panel (see illustration), bending the pin to one side (inside of the camera) to hold it securely in place. A more sophisticated shutter can be made by utilizing a small cardboard pill box. Cut out the bottom of the pill box, and glue the bottom over the pinhole. Then, blacken the inside of the cover and place the cover over the lower part of the pill box. Incidentally, you should blacken the cardboard shutter described above. Some black paint or india ink on the back of the shutter is all that's needed. This completes the basic pinhole camera.

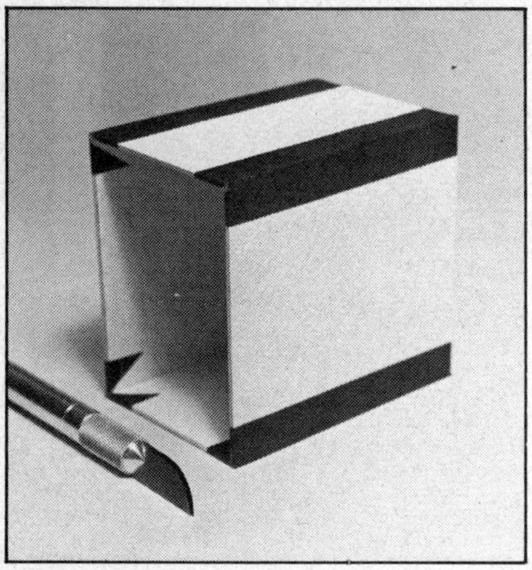
2

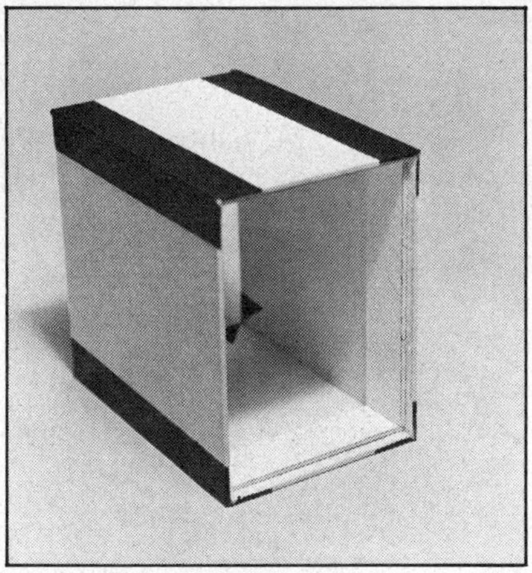
3

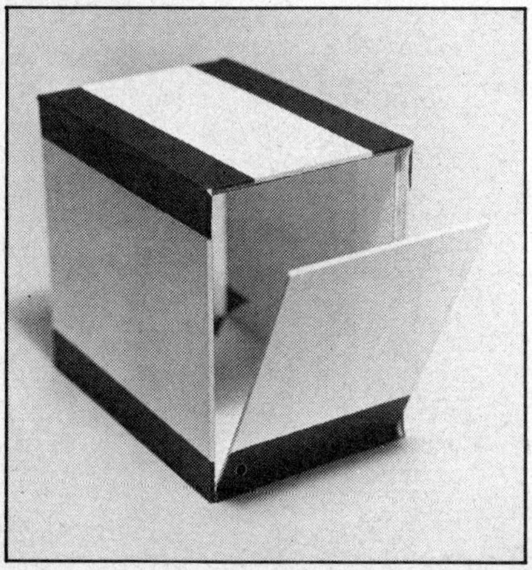
4

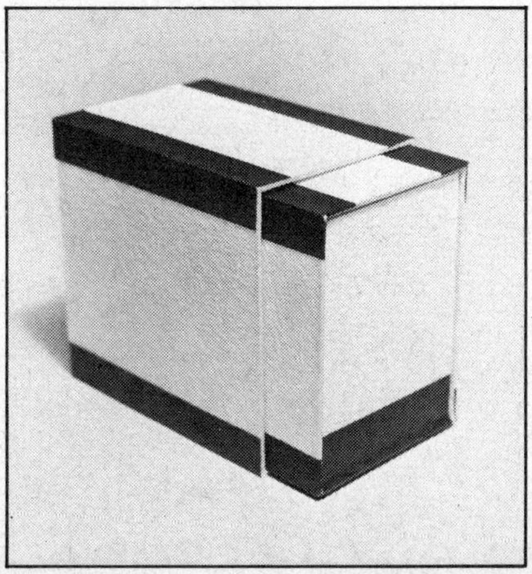
5

1. Pinhole camera is neat project you can do in spare time. Shutter is swung aside to make exposure, replaced in front of lens after exposure. Lines drawn on top and side of camera aid in aiming viewfinderless camera.

2. Inner case is made following directions given in text.

3. Film support gate is made by gluing recessed pieces of cardboard in one end of inner case.

4. Pressure plate is attached with tape hinge, fits inside inner case.

5. Outer case is made using inner case (shown partially removed for illustration purposes) as cutting guide.

Remember, you must load the camera in the dark. Take some time to practice this before putting the camera to use. Remove one sheet of film from the package, and look at it to see which is the emulsion side (this can be identified in the dark by noting the position of the film identification notches in one corner). Then, open the pressure plate, place the film in the back of the camera, emulsion side facing the front of the camera, and close the pressure plate. This will securely lock the film in position. Next, slide the back cover onto the camera to complete the procedure. The camera is now loaded to make a single exposure.

The effective aperture (f/stop) of a pinhole lens is determined by the distance of the pinhole to the film. In the case of the camera described above, the effective operating aperture is on the order of f/150! As I said, this camera does not lend itself to rapid action or candid photography. All exposures will be time exposures. There is a way to use your regular exposure meter to gain correct exposure information. Just divide your film speed by 100 (in the case of Tri-X the new rating would be 4), and set the new-found index on your exposure meter.

Take a reading as usual. Now, read the f/stops by their first two numbers only: f/150 would now be read as f/15, etc. By using this approach you can easily determine the length of exposure. In some cases, when using a fast film like Tri-X, the exposure in bright sunlight would be on the order of 1/5 second. This may be difficult to accomplish with the crude shutter we devised. So, in bright sunlit situations, you would be better off using a slower film, like Panatomic-X. In this case the adjusted film speed would be .5, and the basic exposure in bright sunlight would be two seconds.

The mechanics of making the actual exposure are easy enough. But I must stress the importance of keeping the camera rock steady. Any movement during exposure will result in blurred images (and the pinhole lens is no great shakes at sharpness itself, so you'll need all the help you can get). You can use a tripod, affixing the camera to the tripod with strong rubber bands. Or, you can use some available place such as a gate, fence, post, etc. In any event, once you've selected a subject, steady the camera. Line up the camera to in-

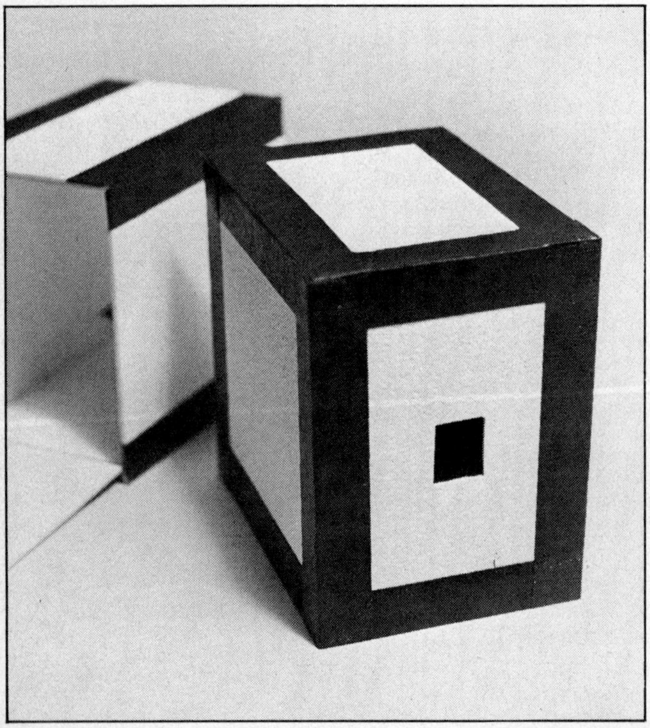
1

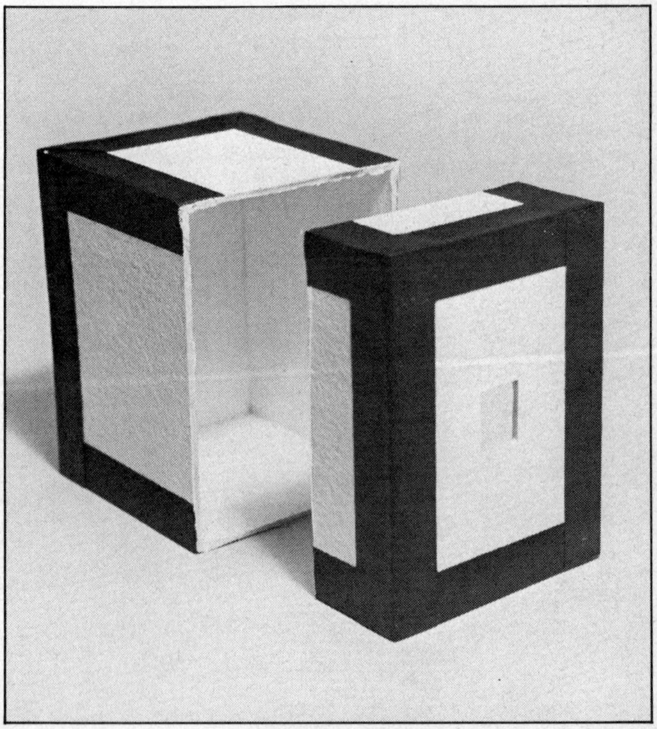
2

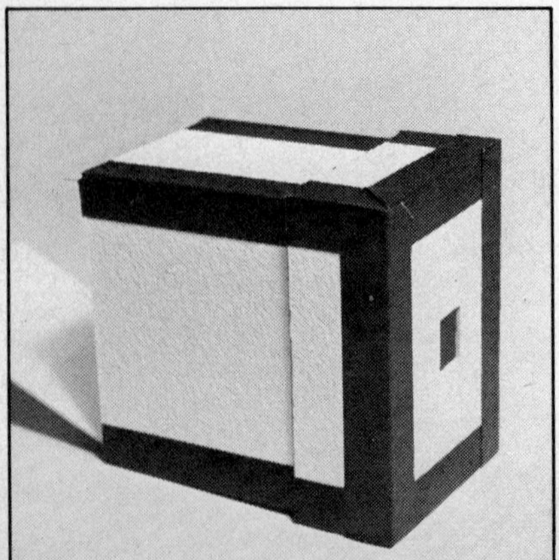
3

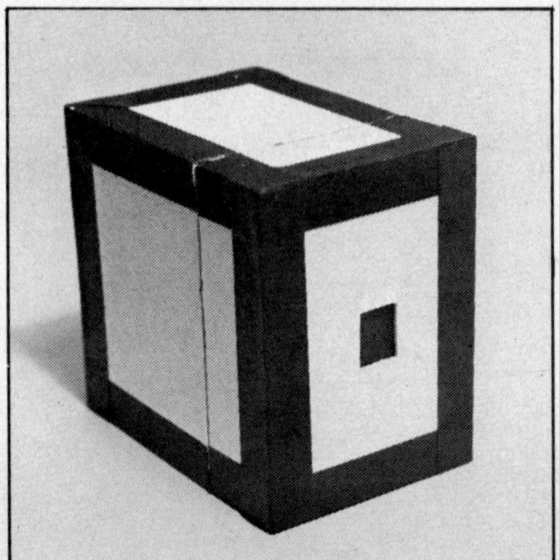
4

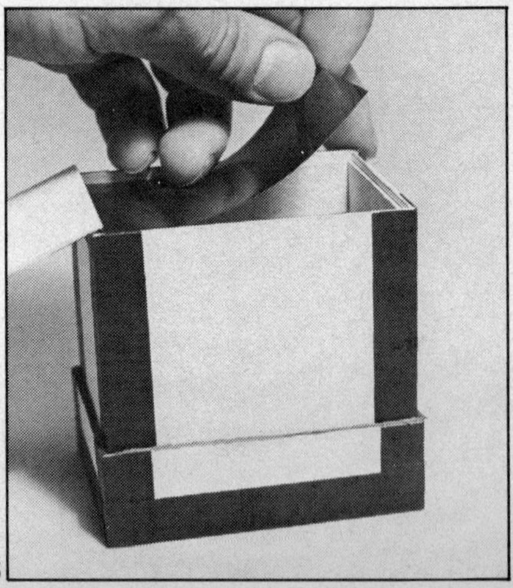
5

clude the subject as can best be determined. This takes a bit of judgment on your part as there is no kind of viewfinder to aid in composition (some lines drawn on the camera will aid in this determination—see illustration of finished camera).

In the case of the simple cardboard shutter, you would steady the camera with one hand, and then swing the shutter aside for the required exposure time. After the exposure is made the shutter is swung back over the pinhole lens, blocking the light from making any further exposure. In the case of the pill box shutter, you'd pull off the cover—holding it slightly in front of the pinhole aperture (because the inside of the cover has been blackened the pinhole will only see a black subject and no exposure will take place). Then, quickly swing the cover to one side, count off the exposure time, and reverse the process to complete the exposure.

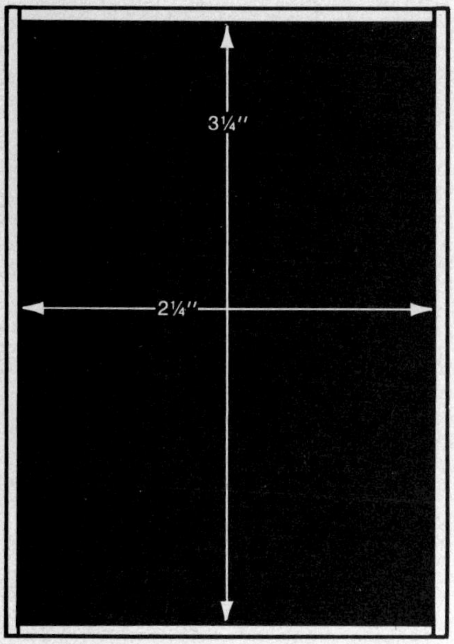

6

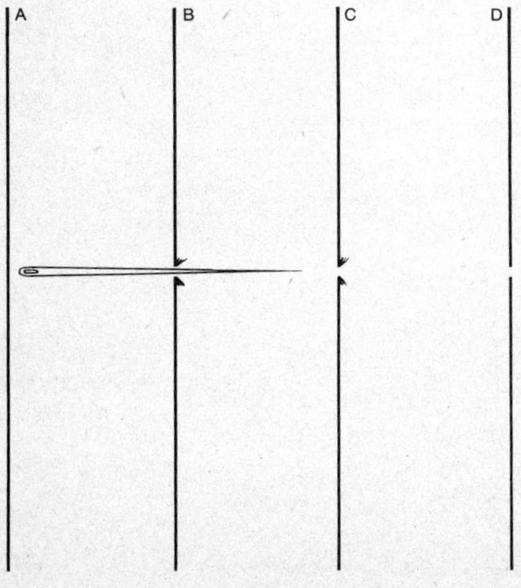

7

I said that the effective aperture of the pinhole camera was determined by the length of the camera. I should have added that the effective focal length of the camera is also determined by the length of the camera. For example, if the camera were made 10 inches long, then the focal length would be 10 inches—or, in popular camera terms, you would have the equivalent of a 250mm lens. However, because the aperture would be further from the film, the effective f/stop is reduced to f/500. On the other hand, you can get extraordinary wide angle effects by making the camera only 2 inches long. Then, the effective aperture would be increased to read f/100. So as you can see, you can make any number of cameras and get extreme wide-angle effects, to normal lens effects, to extreme telephoto effects. And all for the total investment of a little time and less than a dollar.

The following chart can be used to determine the effective aperture for the size of camera you wish to build:

CAMERA LENGTH	EFFECTIVE APERTURE
10 inches	f/500
9 inches	f/450
8 inches	f/400
7 inches	f/350
6 inches	f/300
5 inches	f/250
4 inches	f/200
3 inches	f/150

The chart can also be interpolated to gain inbetween apertures for inbetween focal lengths. Remember that all of the apertures listed above are based on the use of a #10 sewing needle to make the pinhole lens. Use of any other size needle will completely negate this information.

You may want to use a film size other than the one I suggested. If this is the case, then you can determine the proper length for the camera (for a normal lens effect) by measuring the diagonal of the film you wish to use. In the case of wanting to use 4x5 sheet film, if you measure the diagonal you'll find this to be 6¼ inches. So the camera would have to be 6¼ inches in length to obtain the normal lens effect. If the camera were made 12½ inches long you'd get a telephoto image that was twice the size of the normal effect, and if you made the camera 3⅛ inches long you'd get a wide angle effect with twice the coverage.

The quality to be expected from a pinhole negative is not on a par with the quality to be had from an optical lens. However, if you've made the pinhole with reasonable care, and if you hold your camera steady when making the exposure, then you can expect reasonably sharp negatives with slight enlarging potential. The whole idea of the project is not one of obtaining salon quality prints, but one of learning to train your perceptive eye. Remember, your *first* exposure will also be your *last* exposure!

You can process the sheet film by following the manufacturer's recommendations (which will be found on the instruction sheet that comes packed with the film). If you have a sheet film tank, then processing will be no problem. Lacking such a tank, you may have to process the negatives in open trays—which means working in the dark. Processing times are not too long to pose any serious emotional hangups about being in a dark room for several minutes. If you do your own printing so much the better. If not, then prevail upon a friend who does, or bring your negative to the processor and have a print made by him.

If you play the game, and put away your expensive equipment for a week, then, by using the pinhole camera exclusively, you will find you have materially sharpened your photographic eye. And when you do pick up your regular camera, hopefully you will carry over what you've learned.

1. End panels are taped and glued into position on outer case. Note that a cutout for lens has been left on one end panel.

2. Outer case is carefully cut apart. Cut should be made approximately 1½ inches from the front end.

3. Front end is glued to front end of inner case. Note that pressure plate is at rear of assembly.

4. Finished camera. Note pinhole lens taped to front end from inside. All that remains is to make shutter.

5. Camera is loaded in dark. Piece of film is placed against film gate. Pressure plate is then closed and back of camera is slipped on.

6. Both shells are constructed as shown. Note how 1/16-inch cardboard stock has been cut to allow for thickness of the stock. Inside dimensions of inner case (shown) must be exactly the size of film being used.

7. Making the pinhole lens. In A we see side view of piece of black paper. In B, #10 sewing needle is pushed through paper. In C, we see burrs left on exit side of paper after needle is removed. In D, finished pinhole lens is shown after burrs have been carefully filed or sanded away.

CHAPTER 13 The Care and Filing of Negatives, Prints and Slides

Take this 10-second test: Think of an outstanding picture you took some time ago. It may have been in color or black-and-white, and you may already have a print of it hanging on your wall. Suppose someone offered to buy another print from you. Would you be able to find the negative or original slide in a minute or two?

If your answer is yes, you are among those whose filing systems are efficient enough to locate pictures easily, while keeping them protected from dirt, scratches and unfriendly hands. However, if you hesitate, or know from experience that negatives and slides made months or years ago are evasively difficult to rediscover, you may be happy to hear that filing can be a cinch once you *do* have a system.

To the disorganized photographer, carefully storing negatives, prints and slides may seem like a hostile obstacle course. It takes dedication to overcome inertia and face the task of restoring order, but once you begin filing according to methods I shall recommend, you face the future with pleasure and convenience. No more odd piles of pictures, no more heckling such as, "Aren't you *ever* going to clean up that drawer full of slides?" If you start before your backlog is very large, you are in luck, for the process will take a minimum of time and effort.

Most photographers take pride in shooting with thought and care. They plan composition and lighting, they make arrangements to travel with great anticipation of picture possibilities and they may hire models and buy special equipment. The average hobbyist also shows conscientious respect for his/her cameras and lenses. When finished prints or slides are finally in hand, photographers pore over them, admiring the best and regretting the duds. Then what happens?

Too often the pictures end up in a box stored away on an obscure closet shelf, or in a drawer mixed with miscellany. Prints become bent, slides are scratched, negatives are marred, and worst of all, this year's photos are hopelessly confused with shots made months or years ago. The situation is not amusing for those who do not realize soon enough that follow-through filing is only consistent with the preparation you make and the care you take in shooting worthwhile pictures in the first place.

There are several effective ways to file negatives, prints and slides. I'll describe my own systems in detail because they have worked for me over 20 years, and I will mention briefly some alternative methods that also can be effective.

FILING NEGATIVES

By the time I left photography school I had three separate negative files, one each for 35mm, 2¼x2¼ and 4x5. The latter still exists, but is fairly inactive since I rarely shoot large negatives or transparencies

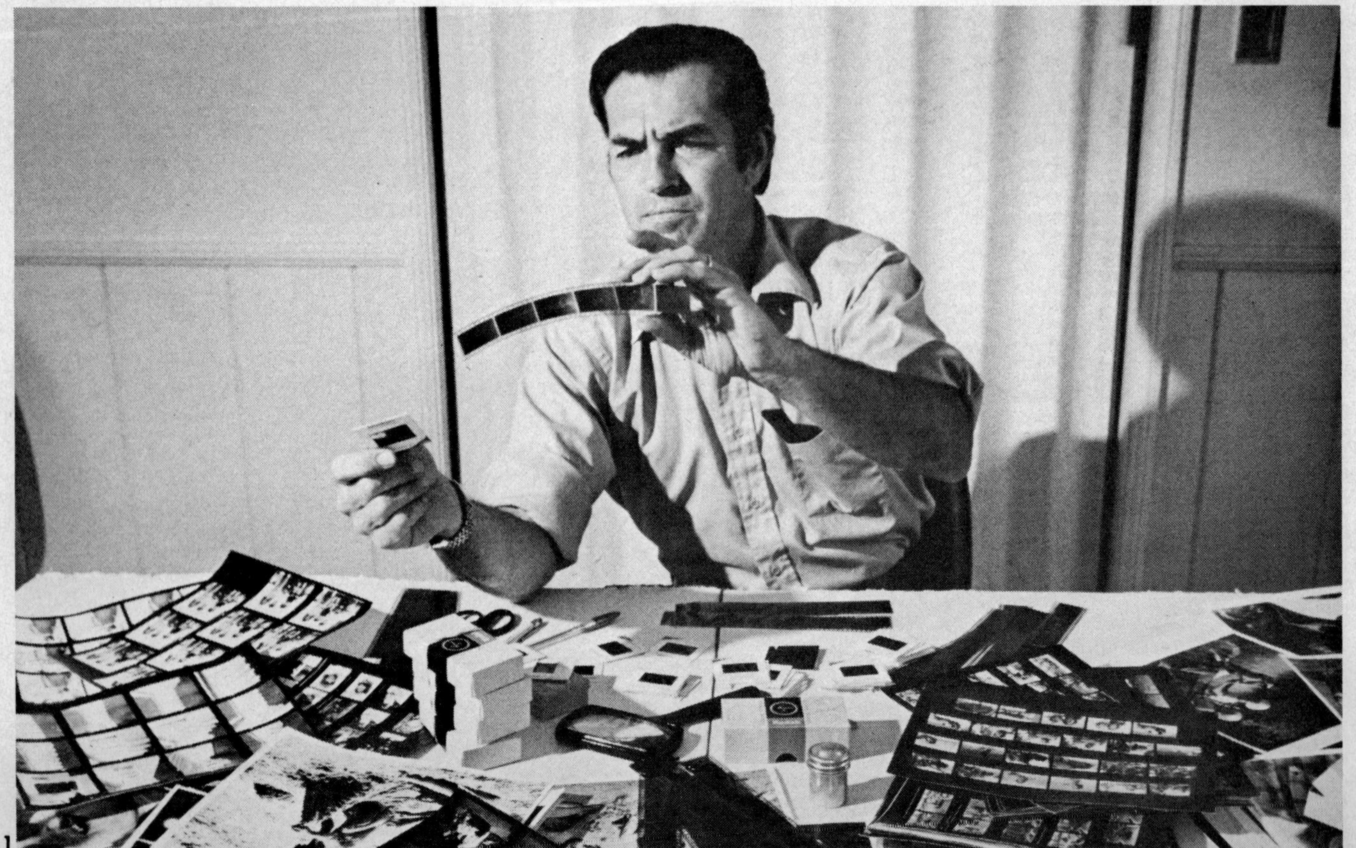

1

anymore, though I sometimes make prints from 4x5 negatives that represent some of my best work. Like most readers, however, I concentrate on smaller format materials, and it is these I will cover here.

Each roll of 35mm or 2¼x2¼ (or 126 and 127-size film if you use it) negatives is filed in its own envelope. Thirty-five millimeter negs are cut into strips of six, and each roll is stored in a standard 9½-inch white letter envelope. Glassine envelopes are also available if you want to avoid the chemical residual in ordinary stationery materials that could stain or fade negatives after a long period (more than 20 years). The larger 2¼x2¼ negatives are cut into strips of four to be contact printed, and then into twos, and stored in 6½-inch letter envelopes in a similar manner.

Each roll of film has its own number. Since I usually shoot a series of rolls, on the first envelope I note the name or description of the subject, place or event, the type of film and developer and the date(s) the pictures were shot. Knowing the day, month and year is a definite asset when you must distinguish one set of negatives (or slides) from others that may be similar. The record of film and developer may aid you when making enlargements or when including technical data on pictures submitted to publications or contests. Any other notes you wish to add about your negatives that could be useful in the unknown future takes only seconds to write.

The key to this easy filing system is a homemade index in a 4x5½-inch spiral-bound notebook. In one notebook for 35mm and another for 2¼x2¼, each roll or series of rolls is recorded by number. A typical entry might read: 2065-69—Street scenes, Las Vegas, afternoon and night. I date the top of each index page according to the first roll entered, and to keep a partial record, I add occasional dates to individual entries. This facilitates searching through the index later, for when you can pinpoint the time period when certain pictures were shot, you can concentrate on those index pages involved. Memory plays strange tricks, so if you shoot only a few rolls a month, date *each* entry for quick reference.

I have a third index for 4x5, and for 35mm and 2¼x2¼ my file probably takes about a dozen index notebooks, covering more than two decades. Each is dated on the cover and shows the file numbers of rolls indexed within. To distinguish 35mm negative numbers from 2¼x2¼, I began using an "R" in front of the latter many years ago when "R" stood for Rollei. You might choose another letter or code symbol if you file more than one size of negatives, but keep them segregated for simplified searching.

Since I shoot color negatives infrequently, I file them along with black-and-white negs in the same storage boxes, but I note color in the index in red ink, while black-and-white entries are in blue. Identifying data on the first color negative envelope is the same as described above.

Each separate group of negative envelopes is held together by a rubber band and placed in order within used 500-sheet enlarging paper boxes. If you don't have the latter, you'll find suitable discarded empty boxes with tops at stationery or variety stores. On both ends of each box I note the negative size enclosed and the index numbers of the first and last rolls. These boxes are stored on shelves in my office (behind my home). You might choose any dry closet shelf or a convenient cabinet to store your negative (and slide or print) boxes. Be sure your children (or other dependents) understand that these materials and boxes are sacred and untouchable.

Check your camera shop for negative-filing envelopes, many of which may suit you better than the plain letter envelopes I use. My main objection to many of them is you may

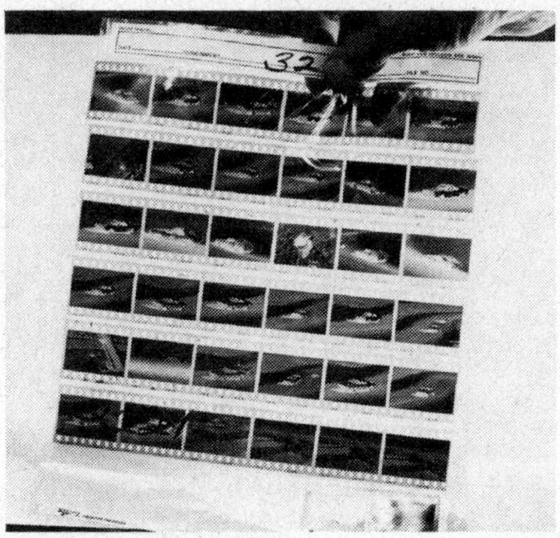

2

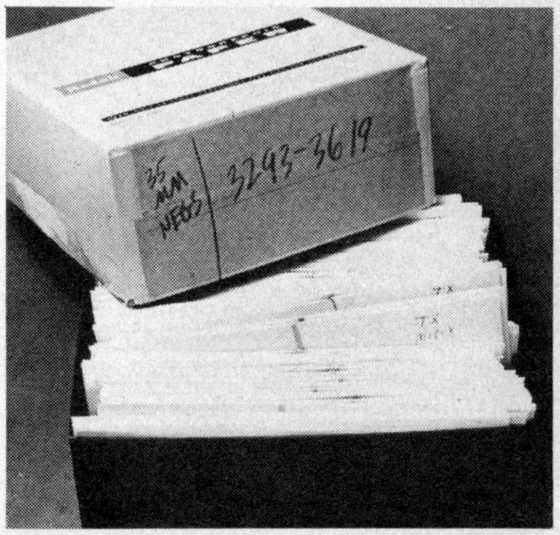

3

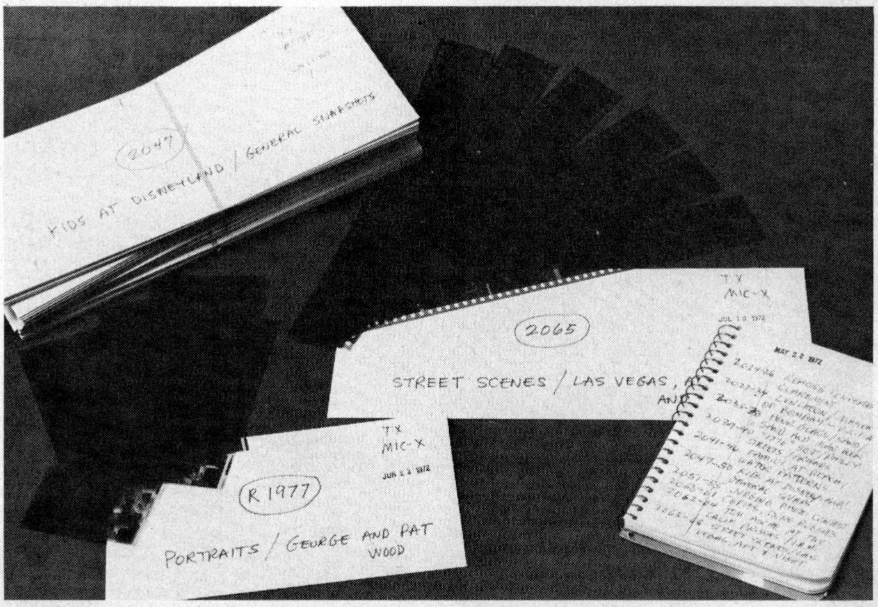

4

1. Are you one of those photographers who unfortunately has an inadequate filing system, with negatives, slides and prints somehow mixed up and hard to find? Guidelines to order are covered in this chapter.

2. Alternative negative-filing system uses clear plastic slide-in folders. Below are individual glassine envelopes with which author isolates strips of 35mm film or frames of 2¼x2¼ film that he wants to preserve more carefully.

3. Envelopes holding 35mm negatives are stored in discarded 500-sheet photo paper boxes with ends numbered to show rolls enclosed in each box.

4. Cut 35mm negatives into strips of six and place each roll in a separate envelope that is numbered, dated and that includes a brief description of the contents. Larger roll-film negatives can be filed separately. Index booklet at right is key to finding pictures quickly in author's filing system.

have to slide negatives in and out to use them, thereby subjecting them to scratches, and it takes more time to place negative strips in a fancy file-folder than it does to simply grip six strips by the edges and slip them in an envelope together. However, the type or brand of envelope is subordinate to establishing a system that creates order in which you can find negatives fast where they are preserved with care.

CONTACT-PRINT FILING

Each roll of negatives I shoot is contact printed so I can edit the pictures frame-by-frame with a magnifying glass, and decide which to enlarge. On the back of each contact print I soft-pencil (Eagle Draughting #314) the index number of that roll. Contact sheets are filed in discarded 100-sheet enlarging paper boxes, on both ends of which are noted the numbers of sheets enclosed. A series of contacts from the same shooting are paper-clipped together. At the top of the first sheet in red grease pencil I write the numbers of that series for quick reference as I flip through a file box containing many such sheets.

FILING PRINTS

Most of the black-and-white prints in my files are 8x10, and each one has a file number soft-penciled on the back in the lower-right corner. Since each roll of film has a number, and each frame is numbered by the manufacturer (I also number 2¼x2¼ negatives in sequence with India ink), there can be only one print marked 3320-18, for instance, indicating roll #3320 and frame #18. When I need to reprint, it takes only seconds to find that negative on my way to the darkroom, and when I send pictures to publications I can note their file numbers in or beside the captions for future reference.

Black-and-white prints are stored in 100-sheet paper boxes according to categories, such as "Scenics," "Children," "Action" or "Portraits." You might adapt this to your own headings such as "Vacation in Spain" or "Fun Parties." If you mount prints in

1. Contact prints are filed in sequence in discarded 100-sheet enlarging paper boxes, with ends marked for reference.

2. Author's 8x10 prints are filed in various boxes according to subjects, such as "Girls," "Children" or "Scenics." Each print has negative roll and frame number penciled on back.

3. Rows of contact print boxes stored in author's office go back more than 20 years, make pictures easy to find with help of index booklets.

4. Slides are also filed in business-size envelopes, or in the small boxes that come from processor, providing all are numbered and indexed. Slides can be shown in mount-cards or plastic sheets with pockets, or may be stored in slide trays used to project them.

5. Alternative slide compartment file has hinge-out trays that group slides, and a form in top where pictures can be indexed or described.

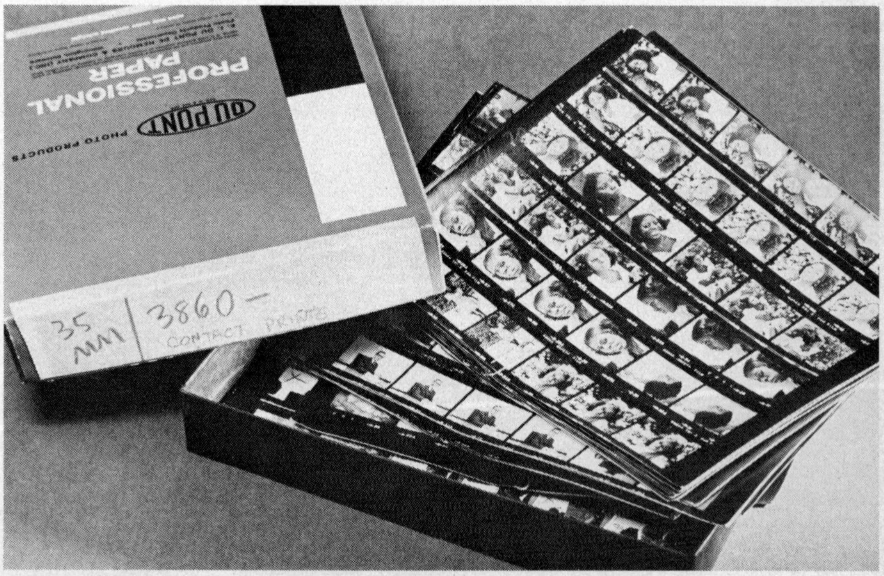

1

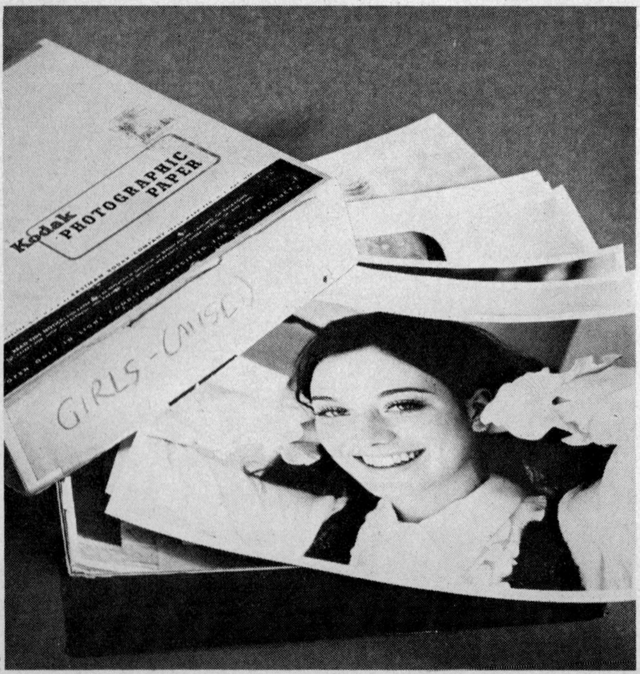

2

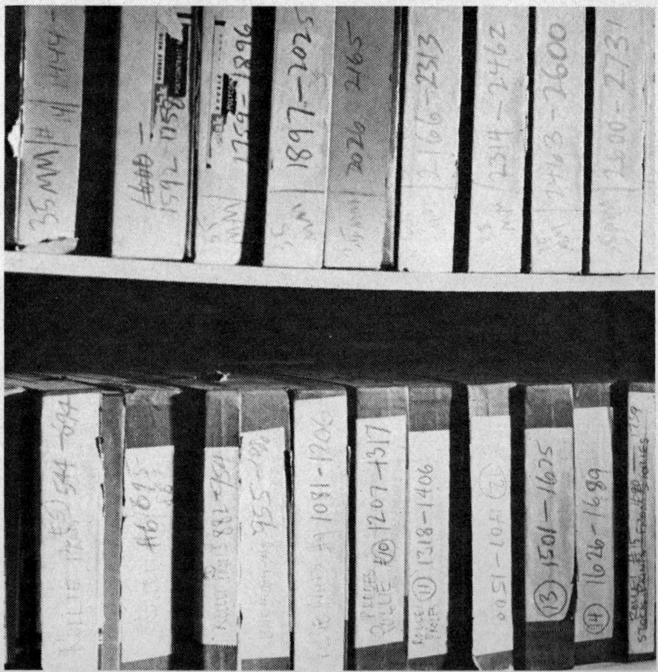

3

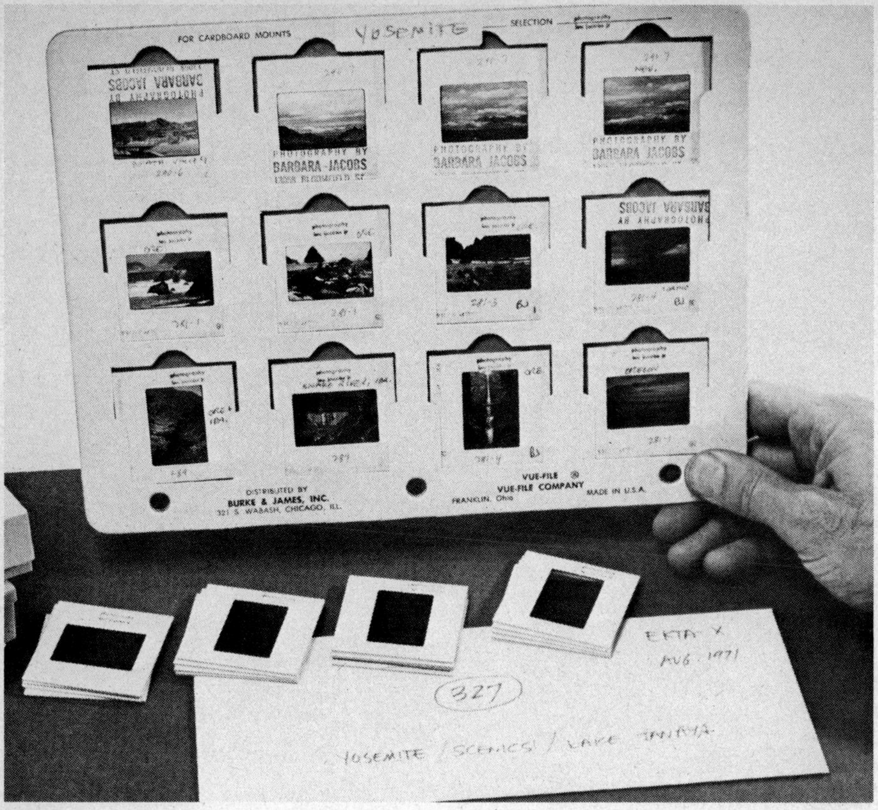

4

albums, leftovers can be stored in marked boxes for protection.

Color prints should be numbered in the same way and filed in appropriate-sized boxes, but they may present special problems. It is a bore to number stacks of 3x5 color prints we often order for albums or to give away, but for future convenience in finding the right negatives to make reprints, it's a necessity. If you don't feel like numbering small color prints, you had better curtail your shooting negatives, or simply resign yourself to a frustrated mix-up later.

FILING SLIDES

Specially made compartmented boxes or file drawers are probably the most expedient way to separate and coordinate color slides safely. Several companies make slide-file boxes and drawers which are not expensive when you think of the job they do holding and protecting irreplaceable pictures. Slides can also be filed within the projector trays you use, providing you label them and store them with covers.

My homemade system is somewhat less formal. Once I have screened my slides, or edited them with a magnifying glass (Agfa Lupe 8X) on a viewing box, I file them in the same type of 9½-inch letter envelope used for negatives. Slides taken at a specific place or event are intermixed, and

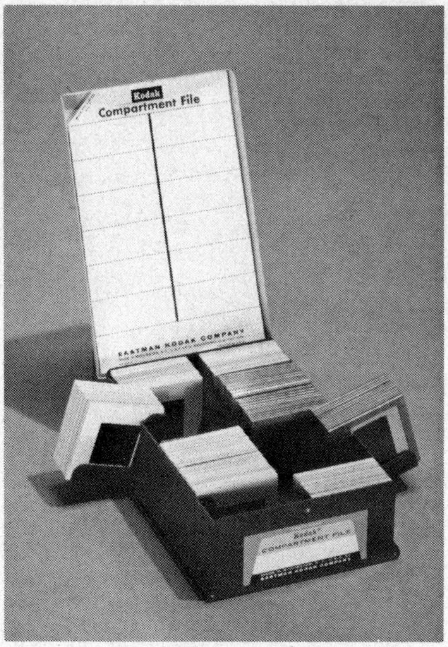

5

rather than number them by roll, I number a whole series. For instance, if I shoot six rolls of 35mm transparencies at Yosemite, I will segregate the best in display mounts that hold 16 to 20 slides each, and place the remainder in envelopes, all bearing the same Yosemite number. With approximately 16 slides to an envelope (4 stacks of 4), my Yosemite trip may fill eight or nine envelopes held together with a rubber band. On the first envelope I note the type of film, the date and the subject, and on subsequent envelopes I may use headings such as "waterfalls" or "best landscapes."

Envelopes of slides are stored in former 500-sheet paper boxes labeled accordingly. I file 2¼x2¼ transparencies with 35mm color since there seems to be no need to segregate them as there is with black-and-white negatives. All color slides are indexed in a separate notebook by number and brief description. *Each* index entry is dated for easier reference next month or next year. When I pull slides from the file to submit to publications or clients, I mark the index number of the specific set on each one. Incidentally, separate stiff transparent plastic sleeves are available for 2x2 slides to protect them during shipment, etc.

If your best slides are in files, trays or envelopes, you might store rejects worth keeping in envelopes, or in the original small containers used by processors. Labeled and stacked in larger boxes, these slides would be easy to check over if you number and index them as you do the first choice color.

If you are wondering about this system, I am probably one of the few professional photographers in the United States without a Carousel-type projector—yet. When I finally get one, I'll keep some sets of slides in trays for easy showing. At present I feed my projector by hand and intermix slides to suit my mood or the audience, packing them back in their envelopes when I am done.

There is a lot of satisfaction in orderly filing and storage of your photographs. If this chapter inspires you to dig into a collection of negatives, slides and prints now tucked away at random, take heart. The first few hours are the hardest. Once you sort things and start filing and indexing in sequence, the impetus to follow through will come naturally. After on-hand pictures are in order, keeping up to date is a matter of minutes. And the whole procedure may encourage you to toss out extraneous color slides, the blurs, washed out exposures and other rejects. It's like cleaning your garage: you wonder why you save some things in the first place.

Finally, it is a pleasure to feel that your pictures are arranged where you can lay your hands on them in moments, even years after they were shot. There is also satisfaction in realizing that your careful photography is securely tucked away from dirt and damage, ready to show or use with minimum effort. Now can you find the negative for that picture somebody wants to buy?

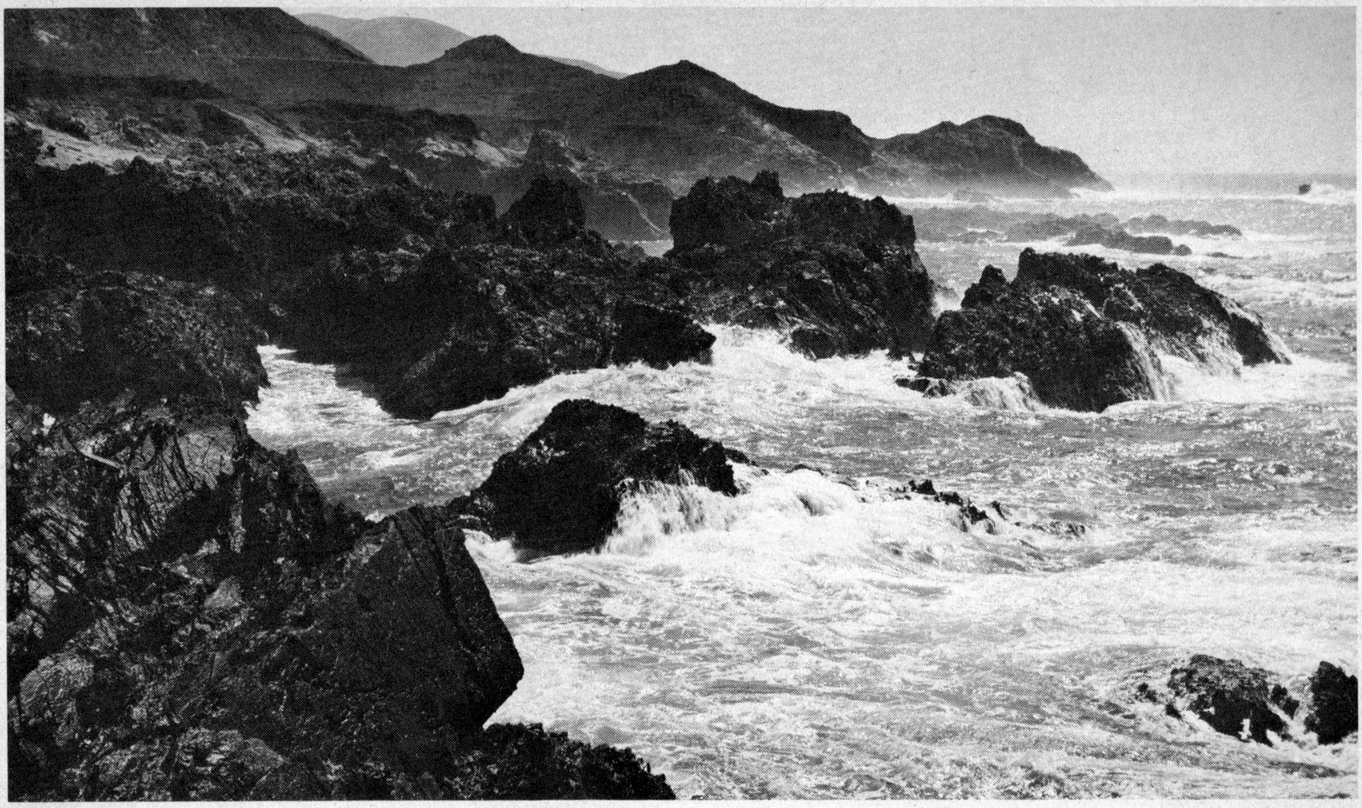

1

CHAPTER 14 On Selling Your Pictures

In addition to taking pictures as a record to remember, to send to friends and family, as a creative stimulus or to exhibit, you may also take (or hope to take) them to sell. It may sound amusing, but professional photographers sometimes mourn the loss of photography as a hobby. "It was more fun then without the pressure," they say when camera work becomes a business. But professionals gain an advantage over the part-time picture seller: they learn the markets, the prevailing rates for pictures, how to protect their rights and how to please clients with careful, painstaking photography. They also learn the art of salesmanship and how closely personality traits can be involved in success.

I have no idea how many readers may be planning to make a living with their cameras, but the opportunities to sell photographs offer a stimulating potential. Hobbyists feel it would be nice to see a few of their shots published, or sold for exhibit by someone, or awarded contest prizes. It would be nice to earn a few bucks and pay some of the expenses that photography entails, even though the money does not cover all your film and equipment. So as a mini-guide to selling prints or slides—not as a guide to professional photography in any detail—I will cover some of the possibilities in the varied marketplace.

YOUR OWN STOCK FILE

In the course of years a photographer may build up a collection of prints and/or slides that become a stock file which could be tapped for profit. Before you begin getting ideas about your whole series of slides of French *chateaux,* understand first that successful stock photographers usually work full time before their efforts really pay off. They must have literally thousands of pictures in their files, or with a stock picture agency. Even professionals who shoot occasional stock pictures of scenics, babies, farm life or whatever, find their volume is not sufficient to make more than a few hundred dollars a year. Stock agencies have several *million* photographs on file, so an individual with several hundred gorgeous slides or prints should shed any illusions of getting rich quick.

If you want to test the truth of my words, contact a good stock agency in New York (I refuse to finger one or another) and send some pictures to their files if they are willing. Then wait a year or two to discover that sales from 100 great slides and 100 great black-and-white prints have amounted to $27.50!

It is therefore preferable that you organize your stock pictures by subject, cross-index them, and let it be known around town that you have certain subjects on hand for books, magazines, record album covers, calendars, etc. Put your name in a few writers' magazine listings or ask a couple of ad agency art directors to suggest ways of promoting your stock file. In this way, you might tap local markets at first (within visiting distance), and eventually, you could approach a large stock agency or conceivably, you could even go into your own stock business.

Meanwhile, as a basic guide to pricing, rates depend on how pictures are used, plus supply and demand. Generally, a color transparency for a

1. Typical stock picture from author's files is this scenic taken on California coast. Similar photographs in color are popular with calendar publishers, a list of whom can be found in a market guide publication.

2. One of a series of photos taken for children's book, Beautiful Junk at the Watts Towers was made by author and his wife Barbara. There is no limit to subject matter used in books for children or adults, and some illustrations come from personal stock files.

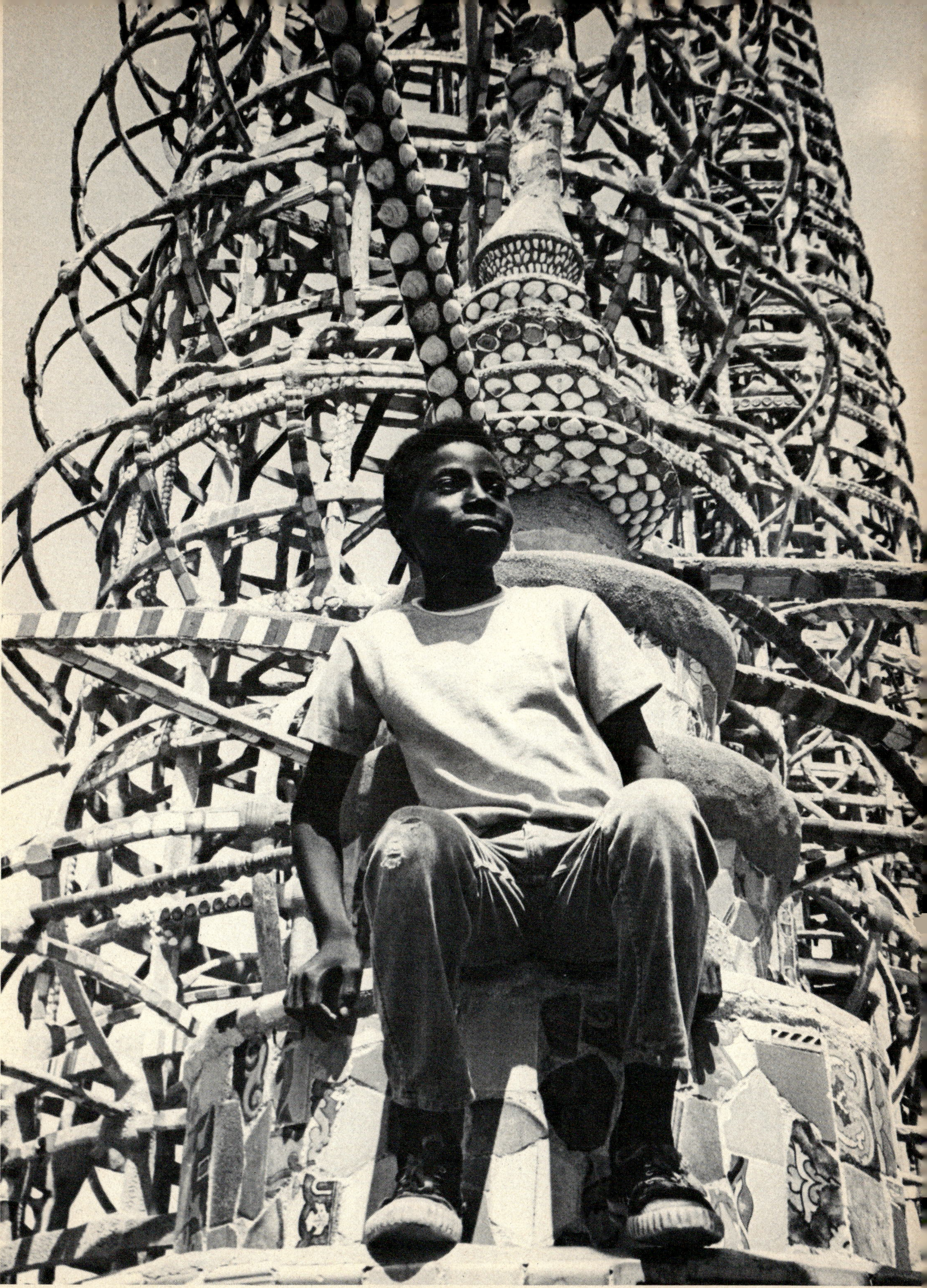

2

book or brochure or magazine starts at $150, and a black-and-white print at $50. Used in a newspaper ad, a black-and-white picture might bring $100-300, and if you are lucky enough to sell a color shot for a national magazine ad, you could ask $500 to $1000, depending on the agency and account. (These are for one-time rights, explained later.) Should you want to know stock prices more thoroughly, ask a local commercial photographer or association of photographers for a price list or guide. It is to the advantage of professionals to help amateurs in this area, because a pro doesn't want to be undercut, a non-pro wants to avoid being exploited, and both want to maintain the standards of the profession.

ALL KINDS OF MAGAZINES

Occasionally, if you read enough tips sheets (books about photo markets, writers' magazines, newsletters for free-lancers), you may hear about a magazine looking for pictures you have on hand, or even for a photographer available in your area—but don't count it. A lot of other people get the same tips, and editors are often flooded with pictures they won't return unless you send a self-addressed stamped anvelope with your submission.

On the other hand, if you visit some obscure place, or shoot some unusual pictures of a unique event, you might very well query the picture editor of *National Geographic* or a local automobile club magazine or the nearest Sunday supplement. Describe your photos by phone or letter. An editor could be turned on enough after he sees them to have an article written about the place, in order to use a few of your shots; or by amazing luck, he could have an article on hand just waiting to be illustrated. Keep in mind that weekly magazines work five to six weeks ahead, and monthly magazines plan from 3 to 12 months in advance.

Photographic magazines may also be interested in your pictures. They use single shots in "pictures-from-readers" pages, and may even do a portfolio of your pictures if the work is outstanding, beautiful, unusual or otherwise meritorious. Photo magazines may pay $25 for one photo or $60 a page for black-and-white and $100 for a color page. Covers pay better, but are much harder to sell on a random basis.

Even if your pictures are not purchased the first or second time you submit them to a magazine, you will be establishing contacts that could be valuable in terms of encouragement and inside knowledge about the publication. By all means, read and study the magazines you wish to sell to; don't send baby pictures to *Popular Mechanics* unless they're involved in a series showing how to build a better jet-powered carriage.

(For more on the subject you might read my book, *Free-Lance Magazine Photography,* AMPHOTO, New York, 1970.)

PICTURES FOR ADVERTISING

Though advertising photography pays better than almost any other type, forget it. Ad agencies rarely buy stock pictures except from agencies or photographers known to them, and the chance of selling a photo at random is even less than being hit by lightning. Ad campaigns are planned months in advance, photographers are hired or pictures gathered from familiar sources, and no art director is waiting around for the lucky break of receiving pictures from unknowns. What's more, advertising people are very stuffy about outside suggestions for either words or pictures. They seem to feel that "creative" material must originate inside the agency. Even clients who make helpful suggestions find their ideas twisted and turned (or adapted without credit) to take on the mark of the agency itself. Mixed marriage works far more often than trying to mix into the advertising business unsolicited.

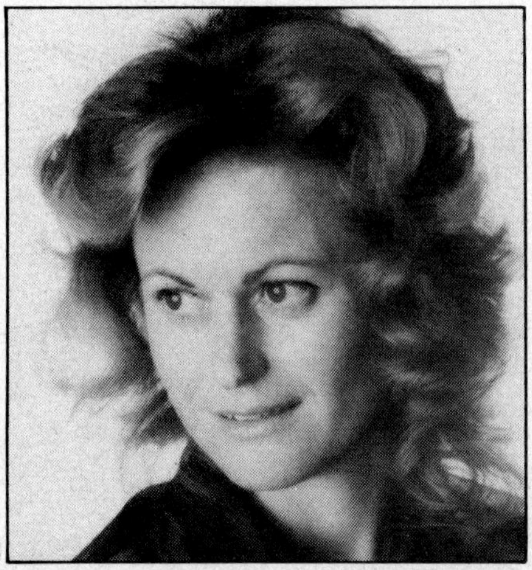

1

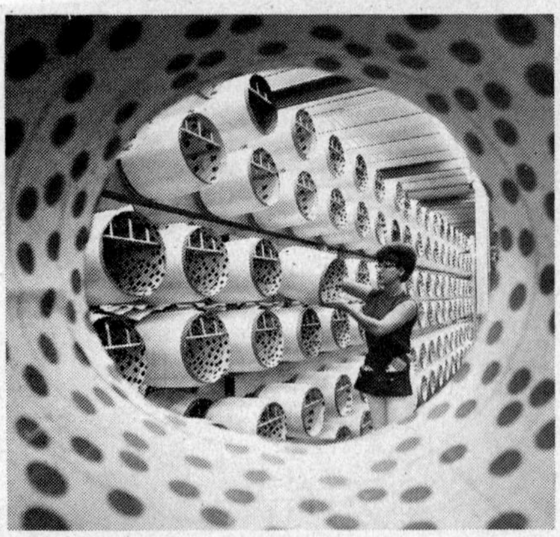

2

1. Fee of $75 was charged to subject for diffused portrait shot, including five finished prints.

2. PPG Industries, Inc., used photo of fiberglass yarn storage for promotion, and similar pictures could be included in trade magazine advertising as well.

3. Japan Air Lines sends out this stock photo of Giza Street in Tokyo to travel editors. Many airlines and travel associations use stock pictures, some of which may be bought from freelancers.

4. One of the illustrations for an unpublished book about young children and their pet chimpanzee, this is an example of the picture story, another way to sell your photos.

BOOKS AND PUBLISHING

Here the opportunities are better, but don't start counting your loot yet. There are several kinds of book publishers, and those that do textbooks and encyclopedias buy the most pictures. They need all sorts of subjects such as people, foreign lands, science, art, celebrities, sports, etc. In order to approach such markets, check the library, or find a list of publishers (from *Writer's Yearbook* or *Writer's Market)* to whom you should send the carefully prepared inventory of pictures you have for sale. Be specific in your descriptions, state whether color or black-and-white, mention sizes of transparencies, but don't quote any prices. Smart publishers will keep your photo list on hand and contact you when their needs seem to fit your subjects. They will tell you how much they are paying, or in some cases, ask you, hoping that your rates are lower than theirs. I've mentioned stock prices for books, to which I can add that if a number of pictures are bought at the same time or used several to a page, rates are reduced for quantity.

Another type of book publisher does trade books (sold in book stores), picture books or social studies books (sold largely to schools and libraries). Trade books also make it to schools and libraries, often in special bindings without jackets. These publishers are sometimes in the market for already-shot pictures to illustrate a book in preparation. The problem is to make known what you have to the right publisher (there are 50 good ones) at the right time (strictly serendipity).

Another way to break into the book field is to find and work with a writer, especially one who does factual books that lend themselves to photography. I've done this a few times (and illustrated a number of my own children's books as well), but usually with editors that knew me previously. However, if you meet a writer planning or doing a book about a subject that turns you on, there's no reason why you can't arrange with him or her to shoot a few sample pictures and submit them to the publisher with a request that you be considered to illustrate the book.

Royalty rates for picture/text books begin at 10 percent of either the retail or net (wholesale) price of the book, which the writer and photographer often split 50-50. Book contracts are complex and sometimes devious, so seek the advice of somebody who is familiar with the field before signing anything. (Avoid outright sale of your pictures with no royalty, if at all possible.) As an inspiration, Russell Munson, who shot the pictures for *Jonathan Livingston Seagull,* made an almost accidental connection with writer Richard Bach (whom he did know previously from some aviation stories). Bach had some hand-done illustrations that the publisher didn't care for, and when Munson offered his collection of seagull pictures, they were both fortuitous and welcome. This team has shared well over a million dollars in royalties so far, though I am not familiar with their particular percentage split.

If you live near enough to a book

3
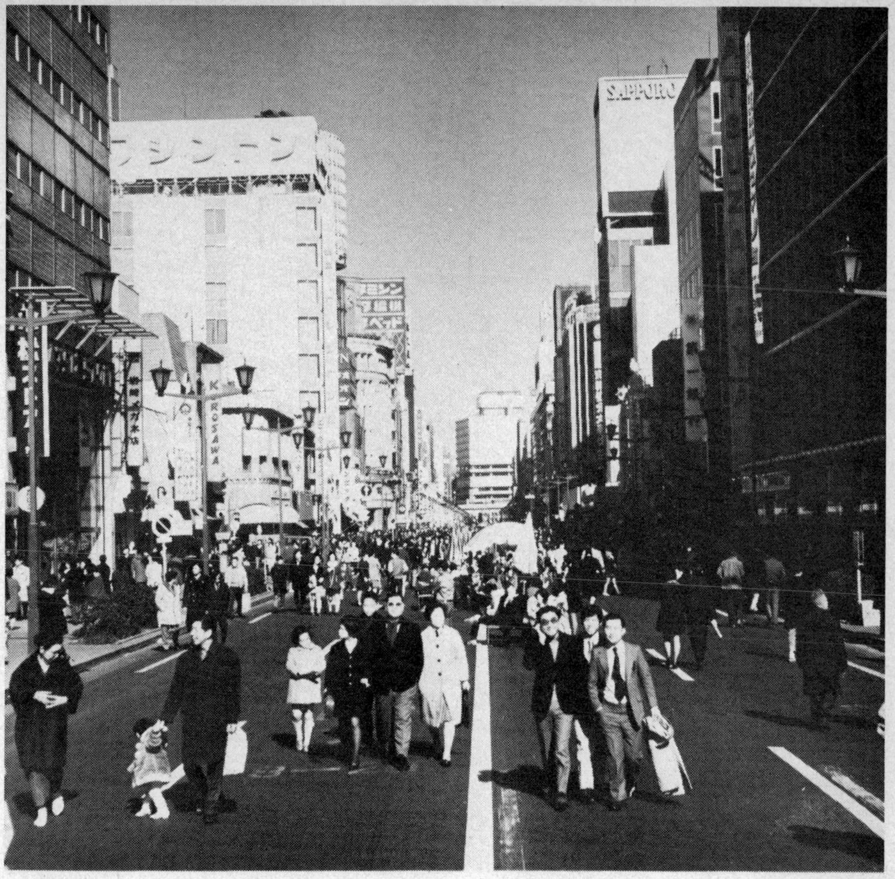

4
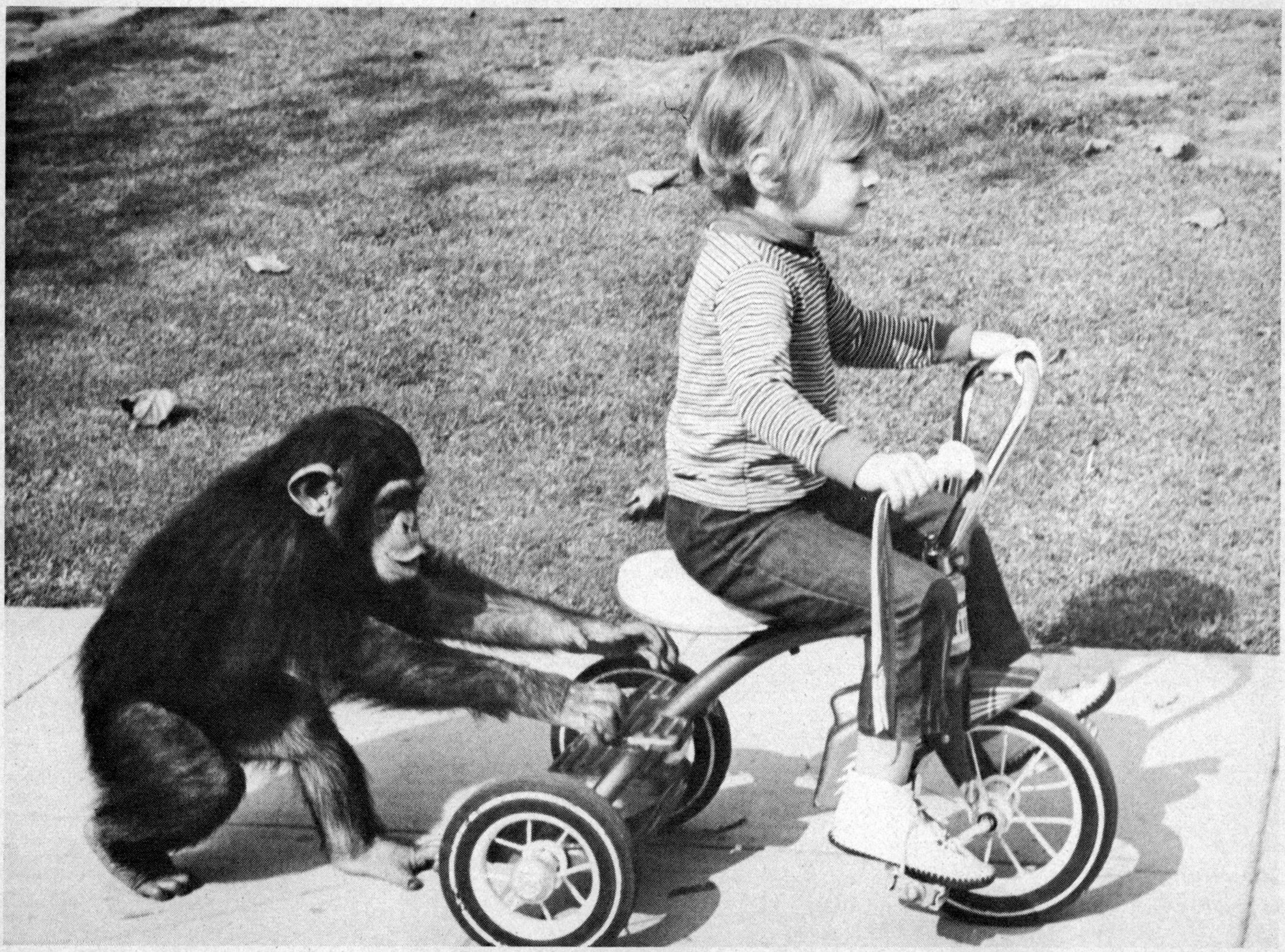

or magazine publisher to visit the editors, make the opportunity to introduce yourself and your work, and find out what the potentials are for your kind of photography.

RECORD ALBUM JACKETS

Albums are often decorated with photographs of the groups or individuals who make the music, and these pictures are almost always assigned to professionals. However, some albums use far-out imaginative color, scenics, sexy girls or other offbeat pictures to attract buyers. Study the albums around and analyze your own files to discover which companies might be solicited by mail or in person. If by mail, write first asking permission to send pictures, in order to be sure they will be welcome.

PHOTO CONTESTS

Various companies and some magazines sponsor photography contests; prizes are often valuable, sometimes nominal. Winning an award or prize in a contest is a heady way to get some personal publicity as well as loot (money or merchandise), but you should be aware of a possible trap. Read the contest rules thoroughly, not only to be certain of submitting material that is eligible, but to determine who owns the picture (slide or negative), whether you win a prize or not. It is my observation that many contest rules specify that winning pictures (occasionally *all* pictures) "become the property of the sponsor." That's fine if you win enough cash or loot, such as $500 or $1000, but it becomes potential exploitation if you win (a) a mini-value prize or (b) simply get a certificate of award.

Granted that each picture you submit may not be worth thousands of dollars, but contest-winning photos often become advertising or promotional illustrations, and very inexpensive ones at that if all you won was $100 worth of something. It seems unfair and unethical to run a contest that requires contestants to relinquish rights to a negative or slide unless the award is compatible with commercial rates for advertising or promotion, or unless additional payment is made for such use.

If you would be happy just to win something and get the recognition and publicity, without concern if your picture is used widely to benefit the sponsor, ignore my words and try your luck. However, please study contest rules to determine if an award is that much of a "prize."

SELLING TO INDIVIDUALS

How much do you charge a friend, relative or stranger who wants to buy a print (black-and-white or color) from you to hang on the wall? There is no exact answer, but there are reasonable price ranges. For one thing, the size of the finished print helps determine its price. An 8x10 mounted black-and-white print might be sold for $20-35, while an 11x14 may cost $35 and up. Color prints cost more to make, and are priced accordingly. If an 11x14 color print costs you $20 to have made and mounted, you can sell it for $40-50. As a rule of thumb, double the cost of having a print produced and ready to hang, including glass and Braquettes if you wish. If there is any question, negotiate with the buyer to reach a mutually agreeable price. A picture worth buying and hanging is worth valuing beyond its production cost, and just how much may be a matter of discussion.

RIGHTS TO PHOTOGRAPHS

In the professional creative world, writers, musicians, illustrators and photographers sell their work for reproduction in various media, but they always attempt to *retain their rights* of ownership to the work after it is used. In other words, a smart photographer sells one-time rights to pictures, meaning that negatives or transparencies are returned to him after use. In this way, a photographer can resell his work to other markets and gain residual benefits that are rightly his, just as an actor is paid for being in a movie, and paid again if the movie is shown on TV.

Photographers' rights can be a sticky area where misunderstanding and even exploitation prevail. However, if you are lucky enough to sell a picture for a commercial purpose, and you spell out that you are selling one-time rights, buyers will at least understand from the outset that they may not make additional use of the picture without further payment. Of course, you can negotiate a price for more than one use of a picture at the time you sell it, providing you stipulate in writing (a letter or a bill) that ownership of the rights to the picture remains with you.

1. Shots like this can be sold several times, so it is important to retain rights of ownership to negatives and slides so the residual value of your photographs can be realized.

2. Scenic such as this one, taken on east side of Sierras, is popular with people who buy photographs to hang on their walls at home or office.

3. One of a series of shots taken at Marineland of the Pacific for magazine story, this was also used in other publications afterward.

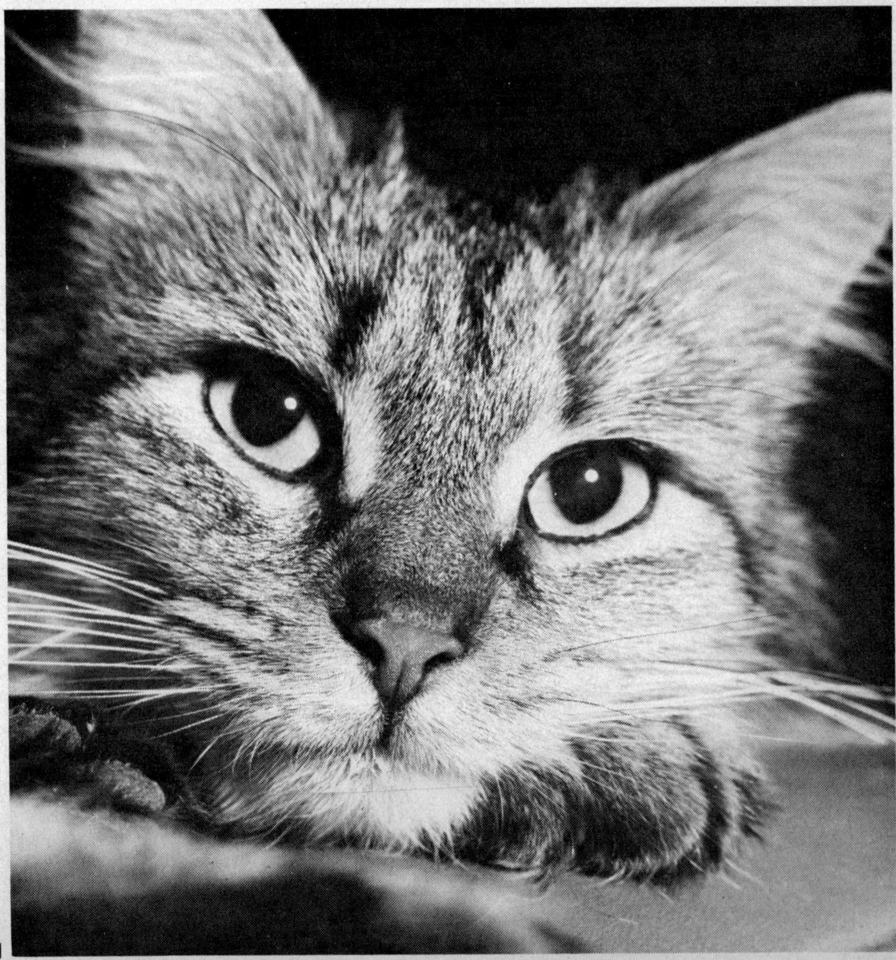

1

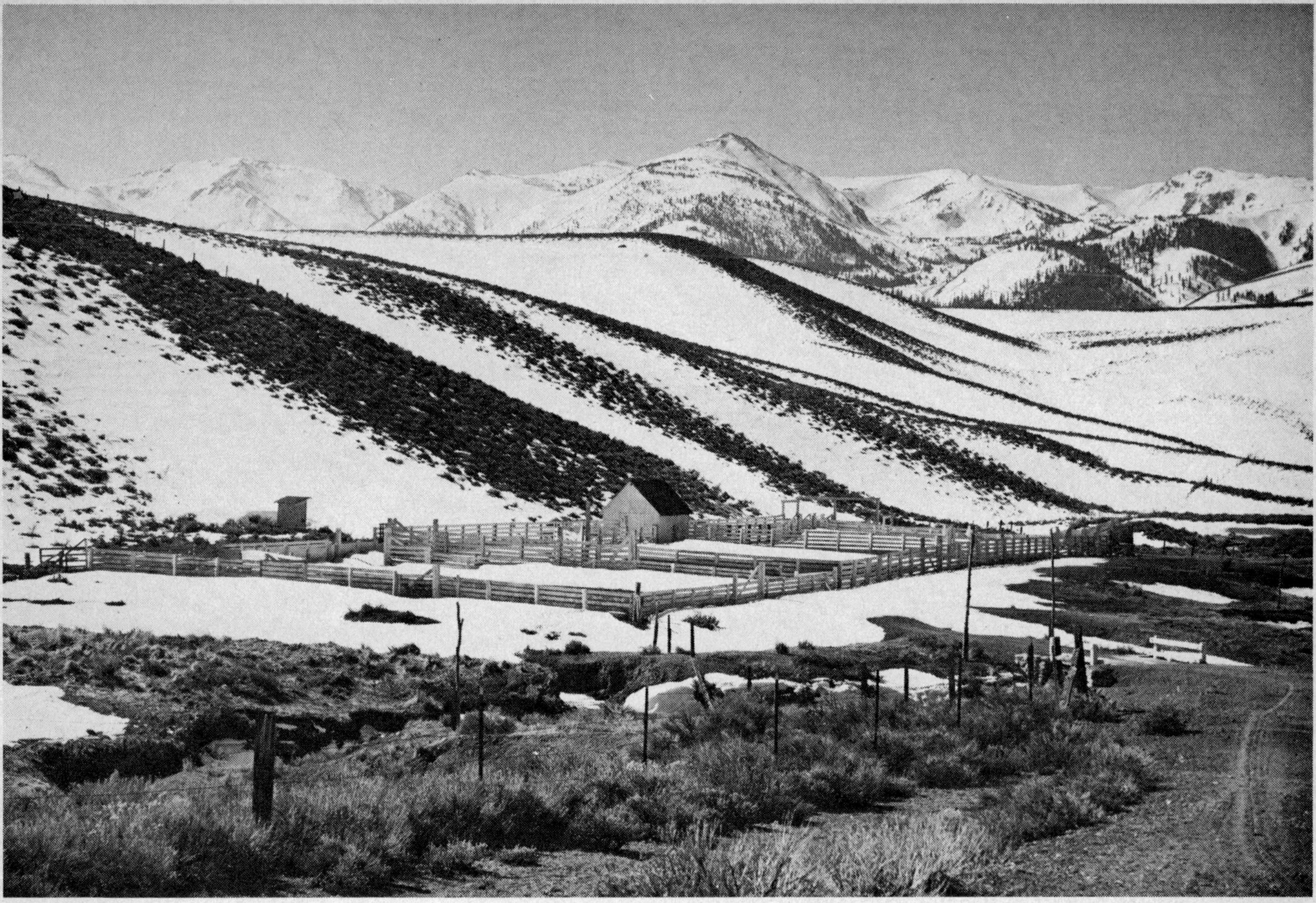

2

Should a buyer insist on exclusive rights wherein the negative or transparency are part of the purchase price, a rule of thumb is to double the one-time rate to compensate for your residual sales in the future.

This basic approach to photographers' rights pertains to any market, from magazines and books to the guy next door who owns a small public relations business. The only exception may be when you shoot color or black-and-white especially for a client, and the pictures have no potential future use to you because of the subject matter or its timeliness. In such a case, negotiate a reasonable fee, and mark on your bill the rights you are selling.

If you must sell pictures outright, that's it, but if you can restrict the use of them, be paid additionally for other uses, and maintain physical possession of the negatives or slides, that's even better. Both veteran and inexperienced photographers are up against these problems frequently, but conviction, tact and persistence make the effort worthwhile in the competitive marketplace.

HOW MUCH DO YOU CHARGE FOR TAKING PICTURES?

Before I make a token answer, if you do get involved in a photography job, contact the local commercial

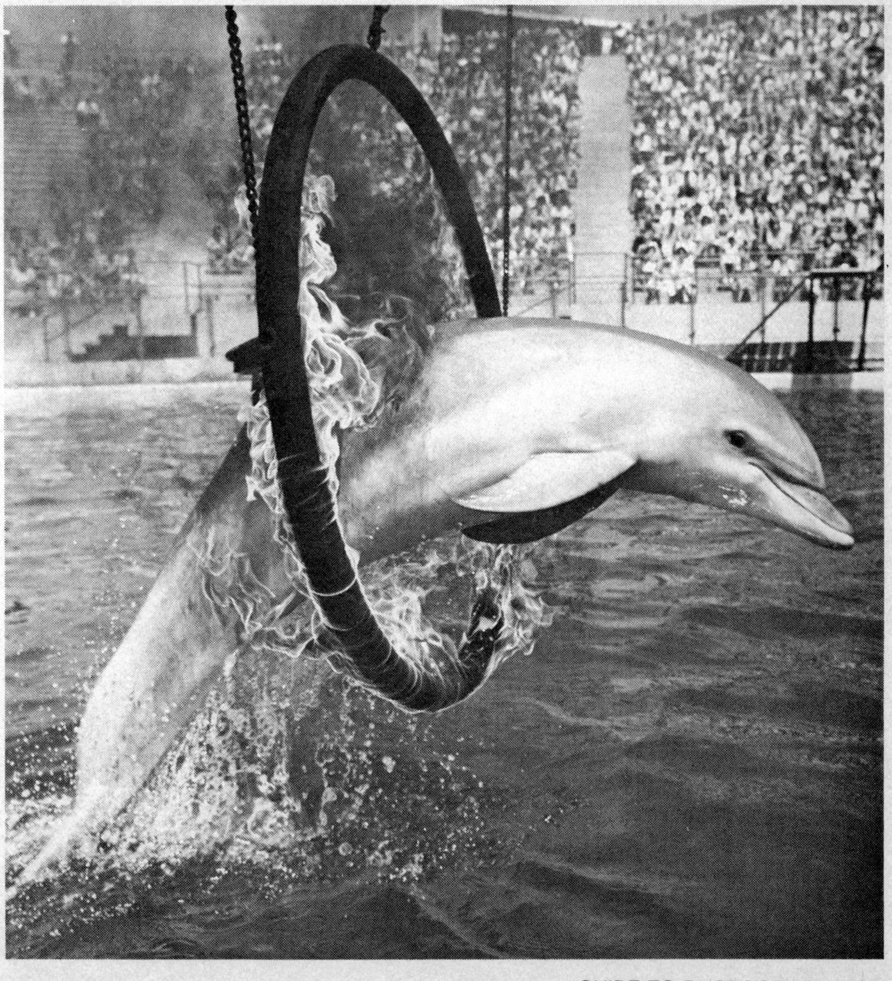

3

photographers association and ask for their rate guide. Or query a local photographer whose work you may know, for his guidance. Photographers' rates vary according to area, type of photography, use of the pictures, rights retained, time involved, experience and reputation of the photographer. I'll quote a few professional day rates which cover time, skill, imagination, good will and experience, but *not* expenses, which are charged over and above the photography fee.

The day rate set for members of the American Society of Magazine Photographers is $200 a day, and half that for travel or standing by waiting for weather, models, etc.

For a local job, taking pictures that will be reproduced in limited (local) circulation, you might begin at $150 a day, or less, depending on your experience and salesmanship. As you become more adept, you will have the confidence and validity to charge a higher rate.

Other day rates, for annual reports, advertising (sometimes priced on a day-rate basis), brochures and other media of national circulation, range from $200 a day up to $1000 a day (and more) for established pros.

If you choose to charge by the shot, establish a minimum that will cover your effort, even if only a few pictures are chosen from the set you make. For instance, with a $50 minimum, at $10 a shot and up, you will be working most reasonably, and perhaps too cheaply.

Professionals charge for the following expenses: film, processing, contact prints, prints, flash materials, mileage, telephone, food and lodging (on trips), props, special equipment, models, other professional services and gifts to people who may assist them. They may also charge for camera and equipment rental when these are out of the ordinary.

PRESENTING YOUR PICTURES

Prints should be mounted, with or without borders according to your own taste, and limited to uniform sizes such as 11x14 or 16x20. Carry prints (and color slides) in a portfolio case, and choose a comfortable number that represent you; 20 or 25 are usually sufficient for most purposes. If you want to show prints unmounted, be sure they are on double-weight paper. Make all prints as brilliant as possible with good detail and contrast, and *spot them!* Unspotted prints are a certain mark of the amateur or sloppy pro. Avoid putting titles on your prints because they are corny, but make sure your name and address are on the back of each one. A rubber stamp is an inexpensive step toward professionalism.

Color slides should be presented in acetate sheets (such as the VIS File Folios). Your name on each slide and on the display mount is essential. Some photographers carry slides in Carousel trays when they know a projector will be handy to show them. Just be sure not to carry slides in the boxes that come from the processor, because it isn't chic! Acetate sheets protect slides from fingerprints and scratches, and they can be easily viewed against a light box.

Sets of prints can be carried in separate envelopes, numbered and captioned, if they constitute a story. (Write captions on a separate sheet of paper.) Prints may also be shown in notebooks with plastic sleeves, and your selection can be changed to suit individual presentations. Don't carry negatives around—it is unnecessary, and they may be lost or damaged.

Mailing pictures/ The usual way is to enclose prints, or slides, in acetate sheets, between two pieces of sturdy corrugated cardboard held together with several rubber bands. Slip this assembly into a mailing envelope (stationery stores have various types) and stamp the outside "Photographs —Please Do Not Bend." Enclose a letter with your pictures. Send them first class or airmail, depending on weight and destination. If they weigh at least a pound, you can insure them for up to $200. Air parcel post travels with regular air mail, but heavier parcel post packages should have "special handling" to speed their journey. Black-and-white prints need not be insured, but *all color and all negatives* should be insured or registered. Enclose a self-addressed stamped envelope to publications and book publishers, and ask the Post Office for a return receipt if you want to know an insured or registered package arrived O.K.

If you do much mailing, or want an alternative way of shipping pictures, the Calumet Carton Company, 16920 State Street, South Holland, Illinois 60473, makes various sizes of self-mailing, heavy cardboard envelopes that are almost indestructible. (Write for price lists.) I use the 11x13 size (about 21 cents each with freight) to mail pictures and picture books, and enclose a check for return postage when I submit to book publishers who don't know me. They are willing to package my pictures and manuscript if I pay the postage. The Post Office has a special fourth-class rate for manuscripts with pictures, incidentally, that is very economical. I add insurance and special handling for safety and time-saving.

The more care you give your pictures in the mail, the less the chance they will be ripped or bent, and the more respect receivers will have for them, because they know *you* care.

As a last word about selling your pictures, remember that potential customers will likely put no more value on you or your work than you do yourself. If you hold your services and your photographs in reasonable esteem, this feeling is likely to be reflected by others. If you appear "cheap" or fumbling, that's the way you are probably going to find you are accepted.

Good luck!

In the early 1950's, author won photo contest with rock-and-water shot, but retained ownership of negative and rights to the picture.

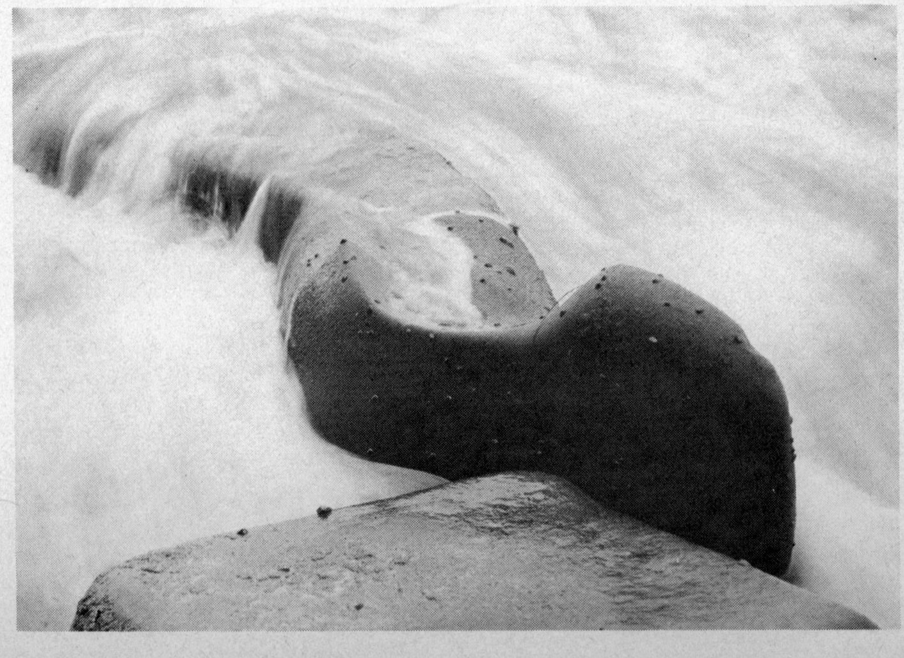

Index

Index

Credits

Bruce Aronson: 48-1. John Barringer: 80-5. Ken Biggs: 102-2; 107-4,5. Bronica: 9-5; 21-6. Robert Bush: 122-1. Celestron: 101-3. Ron Contarsy: 10-1; 20-3; 40-3; 41-5; 51-4; 57; 91; 121-4; 123-3. Jim Cornfield: 27-3; 47-3; 50; 68-2; 72-1; 95-3; 96; 104-1; 123-2. Joe Courtland: 128; 129; 130; 131. Bob D'Olivo: 8-1; 21-5. Guy Draughon: 36; 53; 54-2; 97-2,4; 98; 99; 100; 101-2; 102-1. Paul R. Farber: 34; 35; 36-4,6; 40-1,2; 102-3; 109-4,5; 110; 112-5; 113-6,7; 114-1,2; 116-2,3,4; 117-6; 126; 127. Joel Goss: 59. Martha Grose: 123-4. Sue Harris: 58. Harrison & Harrison: 33. Harvey Hill: 109-2. Honeywell: 9-4. Barbara Jacobs: 39-1; 56-1. Barry Jacobs: 83-6; 84-1. Lou Jacobs, Jr.: Cover 2; cover 3; 1; 4; 5-1; 6-2,3; 7-3; 9-3,6; 11-3,5; 13-3; 20-2,4; 22; 24; 25; 26-1; 38-1; 44-2; 45-4; 47-4; 48-2; 49-4; 51-2,3; 52-1; 54-1; 55-4; 56-2; 60; 61; 62-2; 63; 64; 68-1,3; 69; 70; 71; 72-2; 73-4; 74; 75; 76-1,4; 77-5,7; 78; 79; 80-1,3,4; 81; 82; 83-2,3,4,5; 84-3,4,5,6; 85; 86; 87; 88; 89; 90-1,2,5; 93-2,3,4; 97-5; 105-3,4,5; 106-1; 108-1; 109-3; 111-10; 112-2,4; 114-3; 115; 117-5; 118; 132; 133; 134; 135-4; 136; 137; 138-1; 139-4; 140; 141; 142. Japan Air Lines: 55-3; 139-3. Kodak: 5-2; 6-1; 37-5 (top); 113-8; 135-5. Konica: 7-4 (left). Larry Kostroski: 46-1. Dennis Krukowski: 104-2. Bill Kuniholm: 49-3. Mike Laurance: 14; 15; 16; 17; 18; 19. Philip Lee: 62-1. Robert Lewis: 76-3. Minolta: 7-4 (right); 8-2; 13-2; 20-1; 37-5; 106-2; 107-3. Darryl Norenberg: 47-2. Mark Packo: 76-2. Polaroid: 10-2; 11-4. PPG Industries: 26-2; 138-2. Debra Schuster: 52-2. Gil Smith: 41-4; 73-3; 80-2; 97-3. Mike Stensvold: 28; 29; 30; 31; 32; 38-2; 42; 43; 44-3; 65; 66; 67; 90-3,4; 93-5; 94; 95-2; 103-4,5; 111-9; 112-1,3; 116-1; 119; 120; 121-3. James Thacker: 92. United Air Lines: 44-1. Vivitar: 12. Ken Whitmore: 77-6. Parry C. Yob: 124; 125. Cover credits on page 2.